STUDY GUIDE
INCLUDING QUESTIONS, EXERCISES, AND SOLUTIONS
FOR USE WITH
FINANCIAL ACCOUNTING

STUDY GUIDE
INCLUDING QUESTIONS, EXERCISES, AND SOLUTIONS
FOR USE WITH

FINANCIAL ACCOUNTING

EIGHTH EDITION

Mary A. Meigs

San Diego State University

Robert F. Meigs

San Diego State University

Walter B. Meigs

University of Southern California

McGraw-Hill, Inc.

New York   St. Louis   San Francisco   Auckland   Bogotá   Caracas   Lisbon
London   Madrid   Mexico City   Milan   Montreal   New Delhi
San Juan   Singapore   Sydney   Tokyo   Toronto

STUDY GUIDE INCLUDING QUESTIONS, EXERCISES, AND SOLUTIONS FOR USE WITH
FINANCIAL ACCOUNTING

This book is printed on recycled paper containing 10% postconsumer waste.

1 2 3 4 5 6 7 8 9 0 SEM SEM 9 0 9 8 7 6 5 4

ISBN 0-07-043350-X

The editors were Alan Sachs, Judy Howarth, and Peggy Rehberger;
the production supervisor was Friederich W. Schulte.
Semline, Inc., was printer and binder.

CONTENTS

TO THE STUDENT

This self-study guide is designed for your use as a student taking your first course in accounting at either the undergraduate or the graduate level. It is prepared to accompany *Financial Accounting, eighth edition*, by Meigs and Meigs. However, it can be used effectively with other introductory accounting texts. The key purposes of this study guide are:

1 To help you in *mastering the material* as you initially study each chapter.

2 To *summarize the essential points* in each chapter and to *test your knowledge* with a series of objective questions and exercises, thus making it possible for you to *review the material quickly* from time to time, particularly before examinations.

3 To make the study of accounting *more enjoyable and more efficient* for you. This is accomplished by presenting an informal and concise summary of each chapter, followed by three groups of objective questions and some short exercises. The answers to these questions and exercises are provided at the end of each chapter *in order to give you immediate feedback and to point out areas that need additional attention.*

The manner in which each student uses this guide may differ. However, we recommend the following approach:

1 Study the chapter in your textbook.

2 Read the *Highlights of the Chapter* section of the study guide. If you encounter any statements that you do not understand, refer to the textbook for a more detailed discussion of the topic.

3 Work the questions and exercises in the *Test Yourself* section of the study guide, and compare your answers and solutions with those provided at the end of the chapter. This will show you how well you really understand the material contained in the related chapter of your textbook. Again, if you find something you do not understand, refer to your text for a thorough discussion of the subject.

4 Work the problems assigned as homework in your text.

Once you have mastered the material in this manner, rereading the *Highlights of the Chapter* section of the study guide will assist you in quickly reviewing the material before examinations.

Mary A. Meigs
Robert F. Meigs
Walter B. Meigs

STUDY GUIDE
INCLUDING QUESTIONS, EXERCISES, AND SOLUTIONS
FOR USE WITH
FINANCIAL ACCOUNTING

1

ACCOUNTING:
THE LANGUAGE
OF BUSINESS

HIGHLIGHTS OF THE CHAPTER

1 Accounting is the means by which we *measure* and *describe* the results of economic activities. The basic purpose of accounting is to provide financial information about a business enterprise or any other economic entity. This information is needed internally by managers and also by outsiders such as bankers, creditors, investors, and certain government agencies. In short, anyone who must make *decisions* regarding an economic activity (or about a business enterprise) has need of *accounting information*.

2 To really understand "accounting," you must understand three things:

a The nature of the economic activities described in the accounting report.

b The assumptions and measurement techniques involved in the accounting process.

c How the accounting information relates to specific decisions.

Throughout this course, you should make a concerted effort to consider every accounting measurement from each of these three perspectives.

3 For example, let us apply this "three-perspectives" approach to the discussion in Chapter 1 of the presentation of assets in a balance sheet. What should you understand about "assets"? First, know what they represent—*future economic benefits* that have been purchased by the business. Next, know that current accounting practice is to value most assets at *cost*. Thus, a balance sheet provides information about the *nature* and

dollar amount (cost) of *financial resources* owned. This information is useful in evaluating the company's ability to pay its debts, and also in determining whether its resources are being used efficiently.

4 If you look at accounting information from each of these perspectives, you should find it both interesting and meaningful. And you will acquire analytical skills that you will use throughout your career. If you concentrate only on learning technical accounting rules and procedures, you will miss much of what this course has to offer.

5 The major types of accounting reports include (a) financial statements, (b) tax returns, (c) specialized reports to management, and (d) reports to governmental regulatory agencies. In this accounting course, we shall emphasize the information contained in financial statements.

6 The process of providing financial information about a business to decision makers other than management and employees is termed *financial reporting.* These "outsiders" may include investors, creditors, financial analysts, government regulators—and in some cases, even the general public (including the company's competitors).

7 *Financial statements* are the primary means of reporting financial information about a business to persons outside of the organization. A complete "set" of financial statements for a corporation includes:

a A *balance sheet* showing the financial position of the company at a given date.

b An *income statement* indicating profitability of the business over a specific time period.

c A *statement of retained earnings* explaining changes in the amount of owners' equity in the business over a specific time period.

d A *statement of cash flows* summarizing cash receipts and cash payments over the same period covered by the income statement.

These statements are prepared by the company's accounting department; management is primarily responsible for the statements' reliability.

8 Publicly owned companies are *required by law* to provide financial statements to all owners, and also to make these statements available to the public.

Smaller businesses are not legally required to provide financial information to the public, but they often provide such information to owners, creditors, and management.

An income tax return is not a financial statement, but it is based upon many of the same accounting concepts.

For these reasons, the accounting concepts used in financial statements have become widely used throughout the business community. In fact, they often are called *generally accepted accounting principles* (GAAP).

9 Every company maintains an accounting system to meet its needs for accounting information. These needs may include financial statements, tax returns and other reports, and information used in daily business operations.

10 Regardless of whether an accounting system is operated manually or makes use of a computer, the system performs three basic functions. First, the company's economic activities are *recorded* in accounting records. Next, the recorded data are *classified* to accumulate subtotals for various types of activities. Finally, the classified data are *summarized* in accounting reports designed to meet the needs of decision makers.

11 The *transactions approach* to recording economic activities focuses upon completed transactions, that is, events that (1) cause an *immediate change* in the financial position of the business, and (2) can be *measured objectively* in monetary terms. The primary strength of this approach is that the information is reliable and can be measured objectively. A weakness is that some nonfinancial events may not be recorded.

12 If a business is to operate efficiently, the information in its accounting system *must* be reliable. All of the steps taken to ensure the reliability of a company's accounting data, to safeguard its assets, and to ensure compliance with management's policies form the company's *internal control structure.* The study of internal control and of accounting are closely related.

13 An internal control procedure relating directly to financial statements is an annual *audit.* An audit is an *investigation* of the annual financial statements performed by independent certified public accountants (CPAs). This investigation provides outsiders with reasonable assurance that the financial statements provide a fair and complete picture of the company's financial position and operations.

14 Auditors do not guarantee the accuracy of financial statements, but they do express an expert *opinion* on the statements' "fairness." Over the years, audited financial statements have developed an impressive track record of reliability. The financial statements of all publicly owned companies are audited every year.

15 Accounting information about publicly owned companies is readily available to the public. These companies issue *annual reports,* which include several years' audited financial statements and other information about the company's operations. In addition, financial analysts often make analyses and forecasts relating to these companies. A company's income tax returns, however, are *not* "public information."

16 The accounting concepts, measurement techniques, and standards of presentation used in the financial statements of publicly owned companies are called *generally accepted accounting principles (GAAP).* In addition to *comparability* (among different companies) and *reliability,* six other generally accepted accounting principles are introduced in this chapter: the *business entity concept,* the *cost principle,* the *going-concern assumption,* the *objectivity principle,* the *stable-dollar assumption,* and the *concept of adequate disclosure.*

17 In the United States, four groups which have been influential in improving accounting principles and practices are the *American Institute of Certified Public Accountants* (AICPA), the *Securities and Exchange*

Commission (SEC), the **American Accounting Association** (AAA), and the **Financial Accounting Standards Board** (FASB). The FASB conducts research and issues Statements of Financial Accounting Standards which represent authoritative expressions of generally accepted accounting principles.

18 The three most common forms of business entities are sole proprietorships, partnerships, and corporations. Accounting principles and concepts apply to all three forms of organization.

A sole proprietorship is a business owned by one individual.

A partnership is a business owned by two or more people who have agreed to act as partners.

A corporation is a business granted a charter by the state and owned by **stockholders.**

19 Ownership of a corporation is evidenced by **shares of capital stock** which may be sold by one investor to another. The stockholders elect a **board of directors** to oversee the operation of the business; the directors, in turn, appoint officers and managers of the business.

20 A corporation is legally an entity separate from its owners. Thus, the stockholders' liability for the losses incurred by an unsuccessful corporation is limited to the amount they have invested in the business. Nearly all large businesses and many small ones are organized as corporations.

21 The three most widely used financial statements are the **balance sheet,** the **income statement,** and the **statement of cash flows.** A balance sheet shows the financial position of a business at a particular date. It consists of a list of the company's assets, liabilities, and owners' equity. (The income statement will be discussed in Chapter 3; the statement of cash flows in Chapter 4.)

22 Accounting information is gathered for specific business entities. A business **entity** is any economic unit which enters into business transactions. The business entity is regarded as separate from its owners; the entity owns its own property and has its own debts. In preparing a balance sheet, the **same** definition of the "business entity" must be used in identifying the assets, liabilities, and owners' equity of the business.

23 Assets are economic resources owned by a business, such as land, buildings, and cash. Assets are valued on a balance sheet at their **cost,** rather than at current market prices, because cost is more factual and can be more **objectively determined** than current market value. Another reason for valuing assets at cost is that a business is assumed to be a **going concern** that will keep and use such assets as land and buildings rather than sell them.

24 Adhering to the cost basis of accounting implies that the dollar is a **stable** unit of measurement, as is a gallon, or an inch. The cost principle works well in periods of stable prices. Severe inflation, however, weakens the usefulness of cost as a basis for asset valuation. In recent years, the FASB has required large corporations to experiment with disclosures of "price-level adjusted" accounting data. However, the cost of developing this information was found to exceed the benefits. Thus, at present, the **cost principle** and the **stable dollar assumption** remain generally accepted accounting principles in this country.

25 Liabilities are debts. Either borrowing money or buying on credit will create a liability. Liabilities represent the claims of **creditors** to the resources of the business. Examples of liabilities are accounts payable and notes payable.

26 Owners' equity represents the owners' investment in the business; it is equal to total assets minus liabilities. Owners' equity in a corporation is called **stockholders' equity.** The equity of the owners is a residual amount. It is the claim to all resources (assets) of the business **after** the claims of the creditors have been satisfied. If a loss occurs, it is the owners' equity rather than the creditors' claims which must absorb the loss. Thus, creditors view the owners' equity as a "buffer" which protects the safety of their claims to the resources of the business.

27 Increases in stockholders' equity result from (a) the owners investing cash or other assets in the business in exchange for capital stock and (b) profitable operation of the business. Stockholders' equity is decreased by (a) the payment of **dividends** to stockholders and (b) unprofitable operation of the business.

28 In the balance sheet of a corporation, stockholders' equity is presented in two parts: capital stock and retained earnings. **Capital**

stock represents the owners' equity resulting from the owners investing assets in the business. *Retained earnings* represents the increase in owners' equity resulting from profitable operation of the business. The term retained earnings describes only those earnings which were *not* paid out as dividends to stockholders.

29 The "accounting equation" is *Assets = Liabilities + Owners' Equity*. The listing of assets shows us what things the business owns; the listing of liabilities and owners' equity tells us who supplied these resources to the business and how much each group supplied.

30 You should become familiar with the effects of various transactions upon a balance sheet.

 a Purchasing an asset for cash is merely trading one kind of asset for another. Total assets will not change.

 b Purchasing an asset on credit will cause total assets to increase because additional resources are being acquired, and none is being given up. However, total liabilities will increase by the same amount.

 c Paying a liability with cash will cause both total assets and total liabilities to decrease.

31 Financial statements are used by outsiders in making investment decisions, hence financial statements are designed to provide information useful to these decision makers. Two factors of concern to outsiders are the *solvency* and *profitability* of the business organization. Being solvent means having the liquid resources to pay debts on time. One key indicator of short-term solvency is to compare a company's liquid resources with the liabilities requiring payment in the near future. Profitable operations (discussed further in Chapter 3) increase the value of the owners' equity in the business.

32 The concept of *adequate disclosure* means that all significant facts necessary for the proper *interpretation* of the financial statements are provided to the users of the financial statements. Adequate disclosure can take place in the body of the financial statements, or in *notes* accompanying the statements.

33 In the United States, investors and creditors generally regard financial statements to be *fair and reliable* due to the following four factors: companies' systems of *internal control,* the concept of *adequate disclosure,* audits performed by independent CPAs, and *federal securities laws.*

34 Professional judgment enters into many aspects of the field of accounting. To ensure public confidence in the judgment of professional accountants, accountants must demonstrate that they possess the characteristics of *competence* and *integrity.* Professional competence is evaluated by the accounting professional and state governments through use of examinations (such as the *Uniform CPA Examination*), and imposition of "continuing education" requirements. Integrity is just as important as competence, but it is more difficult to measure and enforce. Many accounting organizations have developed *codes of professional ethics* for their members.

35 Careers in accounting may be divided into four broad areas: (a) the public accounting profession, (b) managerial accounting, (c) governmental accounting, and (d) accounting education.

36 *Public accounting* is practiced by *certified public accountants,* called CPAs. CPAs are granted a license to practice by the state, and perform professional accounting services for clients for a fee. These services include:

 a *Auditing*   An audit is an investigation of a company's accounting system by an independent CPA firm. This study enables the CPA firm to express its *professional opinion* as to the fairness and reliability of the company's financial statements.

 b *Tax services*   Taxes often play an important role in financial decisions. CPA firms offer "tax planning" services to minimize the impact of taxes on their clients and also assist in the preparation of their clients' income tax returns.

 c *Management advisory services*   CPA firms may become familiar with their clients' problems and be able to recommend corrective action. This service is actually *management consulting.*

37 *Managerial accounting* refers to the work done within an organization by the members of its accounting department. Managerial accountants develop accounting information to meet the many needs of management. There are many specialties within this field, including financial reporting, systems design, forecasting (or budgeting), cost accounting, income taxes, and internal auditing.

38 *Internal auditors* are company employees who evaluate all aspects of the internal control structure. Their basic goal is to determine that the entire business is operating efficiently. Thus, internal auditors may be called upon to investigate and evaluate any aspect of the company's operations. However, they do not perform the independent audits of the company's financial statements. As company employees, they are not viewed as "independent" of management.

39 Managerial accountants are not required to be licensed as CPAs. However, a number of them earn a *Certificate of Management Accounting (CMA)* or a *Certificate of Internal Auditing (CIA)* as evidence of their professional competence.

40 *Governmental accounting* includes many specialized areas such as monitoring regulated industries, auditing tax returns, and preparing budgets for governmental agencies. Three important governmental agencies using accounting information are:

a The *General Accounting Office (GAO)* audits many of the agencies within the federal government, and reports to Congress.

b *Internal Revenue Service*   The IRS processes the federal income tax returns filed by individuals and corporations.

c *Securities and Exchange Commission*   The SEC reviews and approves the financial disclosure by corporations that offer their securities for sale to the public.

41 *Accounting education*   The many rewarding careers available to accounting graduates have led to a shortage of accounting faculty at colleges and universities. Individuals qualified to become accounting faculty members can find positions available in virtually all parts of the country. A career as a faculty member allows an individual great freedom to pursue his or her specific professional interests.

TEST YOURSELF ON THIS INTRODUCTORY CHAPTER

True or False

For each of the following statements, circle the T or the F to indicate whether the statement is true or false.

T F   1 The basic purpose of accounting is to provide financial information to economic decision makers.

T F   2 Financial statements are confidential documents made available only to the top management of a business enterprise.

T F   3 The most useful financial statement would be a detailed list of every business transaction in which the business enterprise has been involved.

T F   4 By using the transaction approach one will be assured that all important events which happen in the firm are reflected in the financial statements of the company.

T F   5 One important element of an audit performed by a CPA firm is that users of the financial statements are guaranteed against any losses they may incur by investing in that company.

T F   6 Bookkeeping is only a small part of the field of accounting and probably the simplest part.

T F   7 A comprehensive list of all generally accepted accounting principles (GAAP) is available for accountants and users of financial statements.

T F   8 The Financial Accounting Standards Board (FASB) is an authoritative source of generally accepted accounting principles in the United States.

T F   9 One characteristic of a corporation is that its owners are personally liable for any losses incurred by the business.

T F   10 Assets are valued on the balance sheet at current liquidation values to show how much cash would be realized if the business went broke.

T F   11 The cost principle of asset valuation is no longer widely used in the U.S.

T F   12 Losses from unprofitable operations cause the owners' equity in a business enterprise to decrease.

T F   13 The purchase of a building for cash will cause total assets to increase.

T F   14 The payment of a liability will not affect total assets, but will cause total liabilities to decrease.

T F   15 In the balance sheet of a sole proprietorship, any increase in capital earned through profitable operations and retained in the business is added to the capital originally invested, and a single figure is shown for the owners' capital.

T F 16 Corporations are required to show capital stock and retained earnings separately in the balance sheet.

T F 17 A business that is unable to pay its debts is said to be *insolvent*.

T F 18 A business can become insolvent even though it is operating profitably.

T F 19 The chief accounting officer of a corporation is usually called the controller.

T F 20 A forecast for a business enterprise is always prepared by the CPA firm conducting the annual audit.

Completion Statements

Fill in the necessary words or amounts to complete the following statements:

1 A complete set of financial statements for a corporation includes:
   (a) _____ _____,
   (b) an _____ _____,
   (c) a _____ ___ _____
   _____, and (d) a _____
   _____ _____ _____.

2 The three basic steps in the accounting process are (a)_____
   transactions, (b) _____
   these events into groups, and (c) _____
   _____ the information in accounting reports.

3 The accounting concepts, measurement techniques, and standards of presentation used in the preparation of financial statements are called _____ _____
   _____ _____.

4 An investigation of the accounting system of a business to determine the fairness of the firm's financial statements is called an _____.

5 The governmental agency which reviews and approves the financial disclosure by companies which offer their securities to the public is the _____ _____
   _____ _____.

6 *Statements of Financial Accounting Standards* are authoritative expressions of generally accepted accounting principles issued by the _____ _____
   _____ _____.

7 Two primary objectives of most business concerns are (a) making a _____ and (b) remaining _____.

8 The steps taken to ensure the reliability of the accounting information and to safeguard the assets of the firm against waste, fraud, or inefficient use make up the _____ _____ structure.

9 The three common forms of business organizations are (a) _____ _____,
   (b) _____, and (c) _____.

10 The heading of a balance sheet should include (a) _____ ___ ___ _____,
   (b) _____ ___ ___ _____,
   and (c) _____.

11 Since the claims of _____ have priority over those of the _____ of a business, the owners' equity is called a _____ claim.

12 The accounting equation states that _____
   = _____ + _____.

13 Land advertised for sale at $90,000 was purchased for $80,000 cash by a development company. For property tax purposes, the property was assessed by the county at $25,000. The development firm intended to sell the property in parcels for a total of $150,000. The land would appear on the balance sheet of the development company among the _____ at a value of $_____.

14 On December 15, Shadow Mountain Golf Course had a contractor install a $90,000 sprinkler system. Since no payment to the contractor was required until the following month, the transaction was not recorded in December and was not reflected in any way in the December 31 balance sheet. Indicate for each of the following elements of the balance sheet whether the amounts were overstated, understated, or correct. Total assets _____, total liabilities, _____,
   owners' equity_____.

15 The owners' equity in a business comes from two sources: (a) _____ by owners and (b) _____ operations.

16 A transaction which causes total liabilities to increase but which has no effect on owners' equity must cause total assets to _____.

17 Retained earnings represent the total earnings (profits) of a business which have not been paid out as_____ to the _____.

18 The concept of _____ _____ requires providing with financial statements any financial facts necessary for proper interpretation of those financial statements.

Multiple Choice

Choose the best answer for each of the following questions and enter the identifying letter in the space provided.

_____ **1** The field of *accounting* may best be described as:

a Preparation of income tax returns for individuals and businesses.

b Recording of transactions in accounting records.

c Art of interpreting, measuring, and describing economic activity.

d Issuance of an independent opinion as to the fairness of a company's financial statements.

_____ **2** The principal function of *CPAs* is:

a Performing audits to lend assurance to people outside a business entity that the financial statements prepared by the company's management are reliable and complete.

b Providing managers with the accounting information needed for the daily operation of the business, as well as for long-range planning.

c Evaluating the system of internal control to ensure that accounting reports are reliable and that company policies are followed in all areas of business operations.

d Performing audits of income tax returns to determine that taxpayers are paying their fair share of income taxes.

_____ **3** The accounting staff of a large company such as IBM might perform all of the following tasks except:

a Evaluate the system of internal control throughout the business.

b Prepare financial statements.

c Issue an independent auditors' report upon the fairness of the company's financial statements.

d Develop financial forecasts.

_____ **4** The principal reason for the annual audit of a business corporation by a firm of certified public accountants (CPAs) is:

a To obtain an independent expert opinion on the fairness and dependability of the financial statements prepared by the company and distributed to stockholders, bankers, and other outsiders.

b To detect fraud on the part of company personnel.

c To assist the accounting department of the company in handling the heavy year-end work of preparing financial statements.

d To relieve management of the responsibility for financial reporting to stockholders and other outsiders.

_____ **5** *Generally accepted accounting principles:*

a Are the rules followed in preparing income tax returns.

b Are the "ground rules" followed in preparing financial statements.

c Apply to corporations, but not to businesses organized as sole proprietorships or partnerships.

d Assure management that the entire business operates according to plan.

_____ **6** The *Financial Accounting Standards Board* (FASB):

a Issues authoritative expressions of generally accepted accounting principles.

b Performs independent audits of the financial statements of large companies.

c Audits the income tax returns and accounting records of both individuals and corporations.

d Reviews the annual financial statements of all corporations which offer securities for sale to the public.

_____ **7** A strong internal control structure provides assurance that:

a The entire business operates according to management's plan.

b The business will have sufficient cash to pay its debts as they come due.

c The business will stay solvent.

d The business will operate profitably.

_____ **8** Which of the following best describes the nature of an *asset?*

a Something with a ready market value.

b An economic resource, which will provide some future benefits, owned by a business.

c Tangible property (something with physical form) owned by a business.

d The amount of the owners' investment in a business.

_____ **9** The *owners' equity* in a business may best be described as:

a An economic resource which is owned by a business and is expected to benefit future operations.

b An obligation of the business entity.

c Profits that have been retained in the business rather than being withdrawn by the owners.

d Assets minus liabilities.

_____10 The balance sheet item, **Retained Earnings:**

a Appears in the stockholders' equity section for a corporation in which earnings have exceeded dividends.

b Is always equal to the amount of cash owned.

c Appears on the balance sheet of a sole proprietorship if the earnings of the business have exceeded the withdrawals by the proprietor.

d Appears among the assets of any form of business organization in which earnings have exceeded amounts distributed to owners.

_____11 In this chapter, several accounting principles relating to the valuation of assets are discussed. Which of the following is **not** one of these principles?

a The cost principle—assets generally are recorded at cost rather than at estimated market values.

b Objectivity—accountants prefer to use values that can be objectively verified.

c Going-concern assumption—accountants assume that a business acquires assets such as land, buildings, and equipment for use and not for resale.

d The safety principle—assets are recorded in the accounting records at the lower of cost or insured value.

_____12 Which of the following equations **cannot** be derived from the basic accounting equation (Assets = Liabilities + Owners' Equity)?

a Assets – Liabilities = Owners' Equity.

b Liabilities = Assets – Owners' Equity.

c Owners' Equity = Liabilities – Assets.

d Assets – Owners' Equity = Liabilities.

_____13 Which of the following transactions causes **total assets** to **increase by $10,000?**

a Purchasing an automobile for $10,000 cash.

b Purchasing $10,000 of office furniture on account.

c Collecting a $10,000 account receivable.

d Paying a $10,000 liability.

_____14 Magic Forest Land Development Company sold a parcel of land at a profit. This will cause:

a A decrease in assets and liabilities.

b An increase in assets and owners' equity.

c An increase in assets and liabilities.

d A decrease in liabilities and owners' equity.

_____15 Lake Arrowhead Boat Shop bought a $700 electric hoist to lift engines out of boats. The boat shop paid $200 in cash for the hoist and signed a note to pay the balance in 60 days. This transaction will cause:

a The boat shop's assets to increase by $700 and liabilities to increase by $500.

b Assets to increase by $500 and owners' equity to decrease.

c No change in total assets, but a $500 increase in liabilities and a similar decrease in owners' equity

d No change in owner's equity, but a $500 increase in both assets and liabilities.

_____16 Reliability of financial statements is strengthened by:

a Audits performed by independent CPAs.

b The concept of adequate disclosure.

c The competence and integrity of the accountants involved in preparation of the financial statements.

d All of the above.

Exercises

1 Listed below are eight technical accounting terms emphasized in this chapter.

GAAP   **Capital Stock**
CPAs   **Owners' equity**
FASB   **Accounting equation**
Solvent   **Business entity**

Each of the following statements may (or may not) describe one of these technical terms. In the space provided below each statement, indicate the accounting term described, or answer "None" if the statement does not correctly describe any of the terms.

a An economic unit which enters into business transactions.

_____

b Assets minus liabilities.

_____

c The organization that issues authoritative statements as to proper methods for reporting information in financial statements.

_____

d Professional accountants who provide accounting and auditing services to clients.

_____

e Able to pay debts as they come due.

_____

f That portion of stockholders' equity resulting from retaining profits in the business, rather than distributing them as dividends to the stockholders.

_____

g The accounting standards and concepts used in the preparation of financial statements.

_____

2 In the space provided below, prepare a balance sheet for the Titan Corporation at December 31, 19__, from the following alphabetical list of accounts:

Accounts payable	$ 28,000
Accounts receivable	37,000
Automobiles	8,000
Buildings	60,000
Capital stock	100,000
Cash	14,000
Income taxes payable	12,000
Land	35,000
Office equipment	16,000
Retained earnings	30,000

TITAN CORPORATION
Balance Sheet
December 31, 19__

Assets		Liabilities & Stockholders' Equity	
	$	Liabilities:	
			$
	$		$

3 Use the following information to complete the balance sheet of the Unitrex Corporation on December 31, 19__.

a The corporation was organized on January 1, 19__, and has operated for the full year 19__.

b Earnings have amounted to $100,000, and dividends of $20,000 have been paid to stockholders.

c Cash and Accounts Receivable together amount to three times as much as Accounts Payable.

UNITREX CORPORATION
Balance Sheet
December 31, 19__

Assets		Liabilities & Stockholders' Equity		
Cash	$ 42,000	Liabilities:		
Accounts receivable		Notes payable	$	
Land	90,000	Accounts payable		
Building	260,000	Income taxes payable		40,000
Office equipment	56,000	Total liabilities		$112,000
		Stockholders' equity:		
		Capital stock	$	
		Retained earnings		
Total assets	$	Total liabilities & stockholders' equity		$592,000

4 The Billiard Den was organized by Robert Neal on July 1 of the current year. In the space below, indicate the effect of each of the following transactions on the various balance sheet items of the Billiard Den. Indicate the new balance for every item after the July 3 transaction and each subsequent transaction. The effects of the July 1 transaction are already filled in to provide you with an example.

July **1** Issued capital stock to Robert Neal in exchange for $20,000 cash invested in the business.

3 Purchased an existing pool hall at a price of $21,000 for the land and $30,000 for the building. Billiard Den paid the former owner $10,000 in cash and issued a short-term note payable for the balance of the purchase price.

10 Purchased 10 pool tables for $1,000 each, paying $6,000 cash and agreeing to pay the balance due in 30 days.

14 Sold one pool table to a friend for $1,000. The friend paid $500 cash to the Billiard Den and promised to pay the balance within 30 days.

20 Paid $2,000 of the amount owed on the pool tables.

24 Collected $200 from the friend who has bought the pool table.

30 Purchased one used pool table from another pool hall, paying $600 cash.

	Assets					=	Liabilities		+	Owners' Equity
	Cash	Accounts Receivable	Land	Building	Pool Tables		Notes Payable	Accounts Payable		Capital Stock
July 1	+$20,000									+$20,000
3										
Balances										
10										
Balances										
14										
Balances										
20										
Balances										
24										
Balances										
30										
Balances										

SOLUTIONS TO CHAPTER 1 SELF-TEST

True or False

1 T Economic decision makers include the executives and managers of the business as well as outsiders such as business owners, bankers, creditors, potential investors, labor unions, the government, etc. Information about the financial position and operating results of a business is vital in making decisions about the future.

2 F Financial statements are the main source of financial information to persons outside the business organization; they are also of great importance to management.

3 F Financial statements *summarize* information contained in the hundreds or thousands of pages comprising the detailed accounting records of a business. A detailed list of *every* business transaction would be too cumbersome to be useful to decision makers.

4 F The transactions approach records only completed transactions that cause an immediate change in the financial position of the business, and which can be measured objectively in monetary terms. Consequently, many important events are not recorded in the accounting records because they do not meet this definition of a "transaction."

5 F Although an audit performed by independent CPAs enhances reliability of the financial statements, auditors do not guarantee the accuracy of the financial statements, nor do they indemnify investors against losses.

6 T *Bookkeeping* involves only the record-making phase of accounting and tends to be mechanical and repetitive. *Accounting* also includes the design of efficient accounting systems, performance of audits, development of forecasts, income tax work, and the interpretation of accounting information.

7 F Accounting is a constantly evolving body of knowledge, and there are many problems and conflicts for which definitive answers are yet to be developed.

8 T The FASB is one of four authoritative groups influential in the improvement of financial reporting and accounting practices in the United States. The others are the American Institute of CPAs, the Securities and Exchange Commission, and the American Accounting Association.

9 F A corporation is a legal entity *separate* from its owners, unlike a sole proprietorship or partnership. In a sole proprietorship or partnership, the owner(s) are personally liable for all debts incurred by the business.

10 F An asset is shown in a balance sheet at its historical cost—the dollar amount originally paid by the business to acquire the asset.

11 F As of the current time, the cost basis is still the generally accepted method of showing assets on the balance sheet in the United States.

12 T Also, distribution of cash or other assets by the business to the owners (such as payment of dividends) causes a decrease in owners' equity.

13 F There is no change in total assets; cash was decreased by the amount paid out, but a new asset Building was acquired.

14 F Payment of a liability causes a decrease in cash (asset) and an equal decrease in liabilities.

15 T A sole proprietorship is not required to maintain a distinction between invested capital and earned capital.

16 T The state laws which govern the incorporation of businesses require that the owners' equity of a corporation be separated into categories of *earned* capital (retained earnings) and *invested* capital (such as capital stock).

17 T To be solvent is to have cash on hand sufficient to pay debts as they fall due.

18 T Many of the assets of a profitable business may consist of real estate or machinery or accounts receivable from customers. If *cash* is not available to pay debts promptly, the business is insolvent.

19 T The term *controller* recognized management's use of accounting data to "control" business operations.

20 F Financial forecasts are prepared by accountants who are employed by the business; they are *private accountants,* not the public accountants performing the audits.

Completion Statements

1(a) balance sheet, **(b)** income statement, **(c)** statement of retained earnings, **(d)** statement of cash flows. **2(a)** Recording, **(b)** classifying, **(c)** summarizing. **3** Generally accepted accounting principles. **4** Audit. **5** Securities and Exchange Commission. **6** Financial Accounting Standards

Board. **7(a)** Profit, **(b)** solvent. **8** Internal control. **9(a)** Sole proprietorships, **(b)** partnerships, **(c)** corporations. **10(a)** Name of the company, **(b)** name of the statement, **(c)** date. **11** Creditors, owners, residual. **12** Assets, liabilities, owners' equity. **13** Assets, $80,000. **14** Understated, understated, correct. **15(a)** Investments, **(b)** profitable. **16** Increase. **17** Dividends, stockholders. **18** Adequate disclosure.

Multiple Choice

1 Answer **c** is the only statement broad enough to describe the field of accounting. The other answers describe only limited parts of accounting; answer **a** describes only part of tax accounting, answer **b** describes bookkeeping, and answer **d** describes auditing.

2 Answer **a**—the principal function of CPAs is auditing. Answer **b** describes the function of management accountants; answer **c**, of internal auditors; and answer **d**, IRS auditors.

3 Answer **c**—a company's internal accounting staff cannot issue an "independent" auditors' report, because they are **not independent** of the company. The independent auditors' report is issued by a CPA firm. All the other possible answers describe legitimate functions of accountants employed by a large corporation.

4 Answer **a**—outsiders (owners, creditors, government officials, and other interested parties) rely upon audits performed by a CPA firm which is independent of the company issuing the financial statements. CPAs cannot guarantee to discover fraud in the course of the audit. Answers **c** and **d** are incorrect because the responsibility for preparation of financial statements and for reporting to stockholders belongs to management of the company, not to the independent auditors.

5 Answer **b**—generally accepted accounting principles provide the framework (or "ground rules") for financial reporting. Answer **a** describes tax law, and answer **d** describes the system of internal control. Answer **c** is incorrect because generally accepted accounting principles apply to all forms of business entities.

6 Answer **a**—the FASB is the primary source of authoritative pronouncements of generally accepted accounting principles in the United States. The other answers, respectively, describe functions performed by (**b**) CPA firms,

(**c**) IRS personnel, and (**d**) the Securities and Exchange Commission.

7 Answer **a**—internal control includes all measures to determine that the business functions according to management's plans. Answers **b**, **c**, and **d** are incorrect because a strong system of internal control cannot guarantee that a business will remain solvent or operate profitably. (Answers **b** and **c** actually say the same thing, as the term "solvent" means being able to pay debts as they come due.)

8 Answer **b**—assets are economic resources that will provide future benefits. Answers **a** and **c** are incorrect, because assets may benefit the current owner even though they have no ready market value (a special-purpose machine that cannot be moved), or are not tangible (an account receivable). Answer **d** describes owners' equity, not an asset.

9 Answer **d**—owners' equity is a residual amount, defined as total assets minus total liabilities. Answer **a** describes assets, answer **b** describes liabilities, and answer **c** describes only one component of owners' equity. (Investments by owner are also part of owners' equity.)

10 Answer **a**—retained earnings is that portion of the stockholders' equity in a corporation resulting from profits being retained rather than being distributed as dividends. Answers **b** and **d** are incorrect because retained earnings are not assets—they are part of stockholders' equity. Answer **c** is incorrect because retained earnings appear only in the balance sheets of corporations.

11 Answer **d**, the "safety principle," is not an accepted accounting principle. One obvious shortcoming of this fictitious "principle" is that all uninsured assets would be valued in the accounting records at zero. Answers **a** through **c** are basic principles of accounting affecting the valuation of assets.

12 Answer **c**—Owners' Equity = Assets − Liabilities, not Liabilities − Assets.

13 Answer **b**—purchasing a $10,000 asset on account increases both total assets and total liabilities by $10,000. Answers **a** and **c** involve the conversion of one asset into another; this type of transaction causes no change in total assets. Answer **d**, paying a liability, decreases total assets.

14 Answer **b**—one asset (land) will decrease but another asset (say, cash) will increase by a larger amount due to this transaction. The net increase in total assets is the profit on the sale, which increases owners' equity.

15 Answer **d**—one asset (hoist or equipment) increases by $700, but another asset (cash) decreases by $200 as a result of this transaction. This net increase of $500 in total assets is accompanied by a $500 increase in liabilities (a note payable due in 60 days for $500).

16 Answer **d**—items listed in answers **a**, **b**, and **c**, as well as federal securities laws, all contribute to the reliability of financial statements.

Solutions to Exercises

1

a Business entity

b Owners' equity

c FASB

d CPAs

e Solvent

f None (The statement describes retained earnings.)

g GAAP

2

TITAN CORPORATION
Balance Sheet
December 31, 19__

Assets		Liabilities & Stockholders' Equity		
Cash	$ 14,000	Liabilities:		
Accounts receivable	37,000	Accounts payable		$ 28,000
Land	35,000	Income taxes payable		12,000
Buildings	60,000	Total liabilities		40,000
Office equipment	16,000	Stockholders' equity:		
Automobiles	8,000	Capital stock	$100,000	
		Retained earnings	30,000	130,000
Total assets	$170,000	Total liabilities & stockholders' equity		$170,000

3

UNITREX CORPORATION
Balance Sheet
December 31, 19__

Assets		Liabilities & Stockholders' Equity		
Cash	$ 42,000	Liabilities:		
Accounts receivable	144,000[b]	Notes payable		$ 10,000[d]
Land	90,000	Accounts payable		62,000[c]
Building	260,000	Income taxes payable		40,000
Office equipment	56,000	Total liabilities		$112,000
		Stockholders' equity:		
		Capital stock	$400,000[g]	
		Retained earnings	80,000[f]	480,000[e]
Total assets	$592,000[a]	Total liabilities & stockholders' equity		$592,000

[a]Total assets must be $592,000 to agree with the total of liabilities and stockholders' equity.

[b]Accounts receivable must be $144,000 to achieve a total asset figure of $592,000.

[c]Cash, $42,000, plus accounts receivable, $144,000, equals $186,000. Accounts payable are stated to be one-third of the combined total of cash and accounts receivable; that is, $186,000 ÷ 3 = $62,000.

[d]Total liabilities are given as $112,000 and consist of three items. One item, income taxes payable, is given as $40,000, and we have determined a second item, accounts payable, to be $62,000 (see footnote c). Therefore, notes payable must be $10,000; that is, $112,000 – $40,000 – $62,000 = $10,000.

[e]Total liabilities and stockholders' equity is given as $592,000, and total liabilities as $112,000, therefore, the difference must be stockholders' equity of $480,000.

[f]Earnings are stated to be $100,000 and dividends $20,000; so retained earnings must be $80,000.

[g]Capital stock equals stockholders' equity of $480,000 minus retained earnings of $80,000.

4

	Assets					= Liabilities		+ Owners' Equity
	Cash	**Accounts Receivable**	**Land**	**Building**	**Pool Tables**	**Notes Payable**	**Accounts Payable**	**Capital Stock**
July 1	+$20,000							+$20,000
3	−$10,000		+$21,000	+$30,000		+$41,000		
Balances	$10,000		$21,000	$30,000		$41,000		$20,000
10	−$ 6,000				+$10,000		+$4,000	
Balances	$ 4,000		$21,000	$30,000	$10,000	$41,000	$4,000	$20,000
14	+$ 500	+$ 500			−$ 1,000			
Balances	$ 4,500	$ 500	$21,000	$30,000	$ 9,000	$41,000	$4,000	$20,000
20	−$ 2,000						−$2,000	
Balances	$ 2,500	$ 500	$21,000	$30,000	$ 9,000	$41,000	$2,000	$20,000
24	+$ 200	−$ 200						
Balances	$ 2,700	$ 300	$21,000	$30,000	$ 9,000	$41,000	$2,000	$20,000
30	−$ 600				+$ 600			
Balances	$ 2,100	$ 300	$21,000	$30,000	$ 9,600	$41,000	$2,000	$20,000

RECORDING CHANGES IN FINANCIAL POSITION

HIGHLIGHTS OF THE CHAPTER

1 Businesses do not prepare new financial statements after every transaction. Instead, the effects of individual transactions are recorded in accounting records called *journals* and *ledgers*. The recorded data then are used to prepare financial statements and other accounting reports at periodic intervals.

2 Transactions are recorded first in a journal, and the data then transferred to the ledger. But we can better illustrate the nature of these accounting records if we discuss the ledger first.

3 A ledger is a "book of accounts." A separate *ledger account* is maintained for every item in the balance sheet. Thus, we have a ledger account for each type of asset (such as Cash), each type of liability (such as Accounts Payable), and each element of owners' equity (such as Capital Stock).

4 In a manual accounting system, each ledger account is a separate page in a loose-leaf notebook, which is called "the ledger." In a computerized system, of course, the ledger is maintained using "general ledger software." But each ledger account still can be viewed separately.

5 Each ledger account lists all of the increases and decreases in a particular financial statement item, and also indicates the current "balance." For example, the Cash account shows the increases and decreases in cash resulting from individual transactions in which cash is received or paid. The account also shows the "cash balance"—that is, the amount of cash currently on hand.

6 Periodically (such as monthly or annually) a balance sheet can be prepared using the cur-rent balances of the ledger accounts for each balance sheet item. Many other types of accounting reports are prepared in a similar manner.

7 In its simplest form, a ledger account is divided into two sections by a vertical line drawn down the center of the page. The left half of the page is called the *debit* side; the right half of the page is the *credit* side.

8 An amount recorded on the left side of a ledger page is called a *debit entry;* an amount recorded on the right side is called a *credit entry.*

9 Asset accounts normally have debit balances; that is, the sum of the amounts entered on the debit (or left) side is larger than the sum of the amounts entered on the credit (or right) side. For example, Cash is an asset account and has a debit balance.

10 Liability accounts and owners' equity accounts normally have credit balances because the sum of the amounts entered on the credit (right-hand) side of such accounts is greater than the sum of the amounts entered on the debit (left-hand) side.

11 For all *asset* accounts, increases are recorded by debits, and decreases are recorded by credits.

12 For all *liability* accounts and *owners' equity* accounts, increases are recorded by credits, and decreases are recorded by debits.

13 The double-entry system of accounting (which is almost universally used) requires that *equal dollar amounts of debits and credits* be recorded for *every* transaction.

14 Most ledger accounts are actually designed in a *running balance* form. This means there is a third column, on the extreme right side of the account, which shows the

balance (the amount by which the debits exceed the credits, or vice versa) of the account.

15 Since every transaction results in recording equal dollar amounts of debits and credits (double entry), it follows that the total of the debit entries in the ledger must equal the total of the credit entries. It also follows that the total of the debit balance accounts must equal the total of the credit balance accounts. When this equality of debits and credits exists, we say the ledger is *in balance*. If not, one or more errors must have been made in recording transactions.

16 Accounts are arranged in the ledger in the same sequence as they appear on the balance sheet: asset accounts first, then liabilities, and finally owners' equity. Each account has a number, but many numbers are skipped, so that later a new account may be inserted in the ledger if the business acquires a new type of asset, liability, or owners' equity.

17 A very small business could record transactions directly in the ledger as they occurred. However, this procedure would be inefficient and it would be difficult to locate errors because you could not locate all the parts of one transaction. Therefore, virtually every business also maintains a *journal*, or *book of original entry*. A journal is a chronological record listing the transactions in the order they occur.

18 The journal shows all information about one transaction in one place. It shows (a) the date of the transaction, (b) the account(s) debited, (c) the account(s) credited, and (d) a written explanation of the transaction.

19 After a transaction has first been recorded in the journal, each debit and credit is later transferred to the proper ledger accounts. This transfer is called posting.

20 At month-end, when all entries in the journal have been posted to the ledger, the debit or credit balance of each account is computed (unless running balance form ledger accounts are maintained). These balances are listed in a *trial balance*. The trial balance is a two-column schedule listing the names and balances of all accounts in the order they appear in the ledger. Debit balances are listed in the left-hand column of the trial balance, and credit balances are listed in the right-hand column. Since the total of the debit balances should equal the total of the credit balances, the totals of the two columns of the trial bal-

ance *should be equal*, if the ledger is in balance.

21 The trial balance proves that equal dollar amounts of debits and credits were posted to the ledger and also that the arithmetic of determining the account balances was correct. However, it does not prove that all transactions were correctly recorded in the journal. For example, the trial balance would not disclose the omission of an entire transaction (both the debit and credit parts) from the journal. Also, if the *correct amount* of debits and credits was entered in the ledger but the entry was made to the *wrong account*, the trial balance would not reveal the error

22 The trial balance is not a formal financial statement but merely a preliminary step to preparing financial statements.

23 At this stage of our study, the balance sheet is prepared from the trial balance. (In the next chapter, we will see that financial statements actually are prepared from an *adjusted* trial balance.)

24 The sequence of accounting procedures used to record, classify and summarize accounting information is often termed the *accounting cycle*. The accounting cycle in preparing a balance sheet is (1) record transactions in the journal, (2) post to ledger accounts, (3) prepare a trial balance, and (4) prepare financial statements.

In a computer-based accounting system, transaction data may be initially entered into a *data base*, instead of a journal. A data base is a warehouse of information stored within the computer. The data originally entered into the computer is the same as that contained in a journal entry: the date, the accounts to be debited and credited, and an explanation of the transaction. The computer operator will only have to enter the data once; from then on the computer can arrange this information into any desired format, such as journal entries, ledger accounts, and financial statements.

TEST YOURSELF ON RECORDING CHANGES IN FINANCIAL POSITION

True or False

For each of the following statements, circle the T or the F to indicate whether the statement is true or false.

T F 1 In a prosperous and solvent business the accounts with credit balances will normally exceed in total dollar amount the accounts with debit balances.

T F 2 The term *debit* may signify either an increase or a decrease; the same is true of the term *credit*.

T F 3 All transactions are recorded in the ledger accounts by equal dollar amounts of debits and credits.

T F 4 A business transaction is always recorded in the ledger by entries to two or more different ledger accounts.

T F 5 An entry on the left side of a ledger account is called a debit entry and an entry on the right side is called a debit entry, regardless of whether the account represents an asset, a liability, or owners' equity.

T F 6 Accounts representing items which appear on the left-hand side of the balance sheet usually have credit balances.

T F 7 Decreases in a ledger account are recorded by debits and increases are recorded by credits, regardless of whether the account represents an asset, a liability, or owners' equity.

T F 8 The balance of a T account is the difference in dollars between the total debits and total credits in the account.

T F 9 A trial balance with equal debit and credit totals proves that all transactions have been correctly journalized and posted to the proper ledger accounts.

T F 10 The sequence of the account titles in a trial balance depends upon the size of the account balances.

T F 11 A journal entry may include debits to more than one account and credits to more than one account, but the total of the debits must always equal the total of the credits.

T F 12 One advantage of using a journal and a ledger rather than recording transactions directly in the ledger accounts is that the journal provides all information about a particular transaction in one place.

T F 13 The purchase of a typewriter on account would be recorded as a debit to Accounts Payable and a credit to Office Equipment.

T F 14 Of the following 10 accounts, six normally have debit balances and four have credit balances: Accounts Receivable; Accounts Payable; Buildings; Capital Stock; Cash; Land; Machinery; Mortgage Payable; Notes Payable; Notes Receivable.

T F 15 A transposition error means a posting of a journal entry to the wrong ledger account.

T F 16 The footings, or memoranda totals of the entries in a ledger account, do not relate to a specific transaction but are merely a step in determining the balance of the account.

T F 17 If a business transaction is recorded correctly, it cannot possibly upset the equality of debits and credits in the ledger.

T F 18 More knowledge of accounting is required to post amounts from the journal to the ledger than is required to record transactions in journal entry form.

T F 19 In a journal entry recording the purchase of a desk for $275.80, both the debit and credit were recorded and posted as $257.80. This *transposition error* would *not* be disclosed by the preparation of a trial balance.

T F 20 The double-entry accounting system means that transactions are recorded both in the journal and in the ledger.

T F 21 The accounting cycle begins with recording transactions in the journal and ends with the preparation of financial statements.

T F 22 A limitation of a computer-based accounting system is that computers do not know which transactions should be recorded or how to record them properly. These judgments must be made by people familiar with generally accepted accounting principles.

Completion Statements

Fill in the necessary words to complete the following statements:

1 A T account is a simplified model of a formal ledger account and consists of only three elements; an account _____, a _____ _____, and a _____ _____.

2 Increases in assets are recorded by _____, and decreases in assets are recorded by credits; increases in accounts appearing on the right side of a balance sheet are recorded by _____, while decreases in those accounts are recorded by _____.

3 In accounting, the term *debit* refers to the _____ side of a _____ _____, while the term *credit* refers to the _____ side.

4 Asset accounts appear on the _____ side of the balance sheet and normally have _____ balances. Liability and owners' equity accounts appear on the _____ side of the balance sheet and normally have _____ balances.

5 When a company borrows from a bank, two accounts immediately affected are _____ and _____ _____. The journal entry to record the transaction requires a _____ to the first account and a _____ to the second one.

6 If you charge a sweater at a clothing store where you have an account, the store will _____ your account for the amount of your purchase.

7 The journal may also be called the _____ _____ _____ _____.

8 A journal entry shows (a) the _____ of the transaction, (b) the _____ to be _____, (c) the _____ to be _____; and also (d) an _____ of the transaction.

9 A _____ _____ is prepared from the ledger accounts at the end of the month (or other accounting period) in order to prove that the total of accounts with _____ _____ is equal to the total of accounts with _____ _____.

10 When a journal entry is made, the _____ column just to the left of the debit column is left blank. When the debits and credits are later _____ to the ledger, the _____ of the ledger accounts are listed in this column to provide a convenient _____ _____ with the ledger.

11 With respect to (a) posting, (b) journalizing, (c) preparation of a balance sheet, (d) preparation of a trial balance, and (e) occurrence of a business transaction, the normal sequence of these events is denoted by the following order of letters: _____.

12 The unit of organization for a journal is the _____ and the unit of organization for the ledger is the _____.

Multiple Choice

Choose the best answer for each of the following questions and enter the identifying letter in the space provided.

_____ **1** A *ledger* contains a separate "account" for each:
a Business transaction.
b Business day.
c Asset, liability, and element of owners' equity.
d Journal entry.

_____ **2** Which of the following statements about the rules for debiting and crediting balance sheet accounts is *not true*?
a Liability accounts are reduced by debit entries.
b Accounts on the left side of the balance sheet are reduced by credit entries.
c Each transaction is recorded by equal dollar amounts of debits and credits.
d Owners' equity accounts and asset accounts are increased by debit entries.

_____ **3** The key point of *double-entry accounting* is that every transaction:
a Is recorded by equal dollar amounts of debit and credit entries.
b Is recorded in both the journal and the ledger.
c Affects both sides of the balance sheet.
d Is both recorded and posted.

_____ **4** A *journal* consists of:
a A listing of the balances of the accounts in the ledger.
b A storage center of information within a computer-based system.
c A chronological record of individual business transactions.
d A separate "account" for each asset, liability, and element of owners' equity.

_____ **5** Morris Labs acquired a computer by paying $10,000 cash and signing a note payable for $40,000. To record this purchase, Morris Labs should:
a Debit Equipment, $10,000; credit Cash, $10,000.
b Debit Cash, $10,000; debit Notes Payable, $40,000; credit Equipment, $50,000.
c Debit Equipment, $50,000; credit Cash, $10,000; credit Notes Payable, $40,000.
d Debit Notes Payable, $40,000; credit Cash, $10,000; credit Equipment, $30,000.

_____ **6** The term *posting* means:

a Entering information into a computerized data base.

b Transferring debit and credit amounts from the journal to the ledger.

c Proving the equality of debit and credits in the ledger.

d Determining the balances of the ledger accounts.

_____ **7** The purpose of a *trial balance* is:

a To determine that journal entries are in balance before posting those entries to the ledger.

b To indicate the effects of business transactions upon ledger accounts.

c To prove the equality of debits and credits in the ledger.

d To determine that the number of ledger accounts with debit balances is equal to the number with credit balances.

_____ **8** If the following steps in the *accounting* cycle were arranged in the order in which they are performed, the *third step* would be:

a Prepare financial statements.

b Post to ledger accounts.

c Record transactions in the journal.

d Prepare a trial balance.

_____ **9** In a computer-based accounting system, which of the following steps in the accounting cycle requires the most human *judgment and analysis?*

a Preparation of a trial balance.

b Preparation of financial statements.

c Recording business transactions.

d Posting to ledger accounts.

_____ **10** Red Hill Vineyards completes a transaction which causes an asset account to decrease. Which of the following *related effects* may also occur?

a An increase of equal amount in a liability account.

b An increase of an equal amount in owners' equity.

c An increase of an equal amount in another asset account.

d None of the above.

Exercises

1 Listed below are eight technical accounting terms emphasized in this chapter:

Debit entry	*Ledger*
Credit entry	*Journal*
Double-entry	*Data base*
Trial balance	*Posting*

Each of the following statements may (or may not) describe one of these technical terms. In the space provided below each statement, indicate the accounting term described, or answer "None" if the statement does not correctly describe any of the terms.

a A device that proves the equality of debit and credit balances in the ledger accounts.

_____

b An entry used to record an increase in an asset account.

_____

c The accounting record that consists of separate accounts for each asset, liability, and element of owners' equity.

_____

d A journal entry that includes more than one debit or more than one credit.

_____

e The accounting record in which transactions are first recorded in a manual accounting system.

_____

f The sequence of accounting procedures applied in recording, classifying, and summarizing accounting information.

_____

g An entry entered in the right-hand side of an account.

_____

2 Show the change in total assets, total liabilities, and total owners' equity that will be caused by posting each amount in the following journal entries. In the *effect of transaction* row, show the total change in assets, liabilities, and owners' equity that has occurred after all parts of the transaction have been posted. Hint: The effect of each transaction should be that the total change on the left side of the balance sheet (change in assets) should equal the change on the right side (change in liabilities + change in owners' equity). Explanations have been omitted from journal entries to conserve space.

Journal Entry	Dr	Cr	Assets	=	Lia-bilities	+	Owners' Equity
Example:							
Office Equipment	600		+600				
Cash		150	−150				
Accounts Payable		450			+450		
Effect of transaction			+450	=	+450	+	0
a Cash	1,230						
Accounts Receivable		1,230					
Effect of transaction				=		+	
b Cash	5,000						
Capital Stock		5,000					
Effect of transaction				=		+	
c Cash	3,800						
Notes Payable		3,800					
Effect of transaction				=		+	
d Accounts Payable	350						
Cash		350					
Effect of transaction				=		+	
e Land	9,000						
Cash		1,000					
Notes Payable		8,000					
Effect of transaction				=		+	

3 Listed below are ten accounts each identified by a number. Following this list of accounts is a series of transactions. You are to indicate for each transaction the account(s) that should be debited and credited by inserting the proper account number(s) in the space provided.

1 Cash
2 Notes Receivable
3 Accounts Receivable
4 Land
5 Buildings
6 Office Equipment
7 Delivery Equipment
8 Notes Payable
9 Accounts Payable
10 Capital Stock

Transaction	Account(s) Debited	Account(s) Credited
Example Purchased land and building for cash	4, 5	1
a Purchased office equipment on account		
b Purchased office equipment, paying part cash and signing a note payable for the balance		
c Collected an account receivable		
d Borrowed money from a bank and signed a note payable due in six months		

Transaction	Account(s) Debited	Account(s) Credited
e Paid the liability credited by transaction **a** above		
f Issued additional shares of capital stock in exchange for cash		

4 Enter the following transactions of Riviera Corporation in the T accounts provided, and then prepare a trial balance at September 30, 19__:

(1) Issued capital stock of $70,000 par value for $70,000 cash.

(2) Borrowed $12,000 cash from a bank and signed a note payable for that amount.

(3) Purchased land and building for $90,000, paying $40,000 in cash and issuing a $50,000 note payable. The land was estimated to represent one-third of the total purchase price.

(4) Purchased office equipment on credit at a cost of $6,000.

(5) Added a balcony to the building at a cost of $5,000; agreed to pay contractor in full in 30 days.

(6) Returned part of the office equipment to the supplier and received full credit of $600.

(7) Made a partial payment of $3,000 on the amount owed for office equipment.

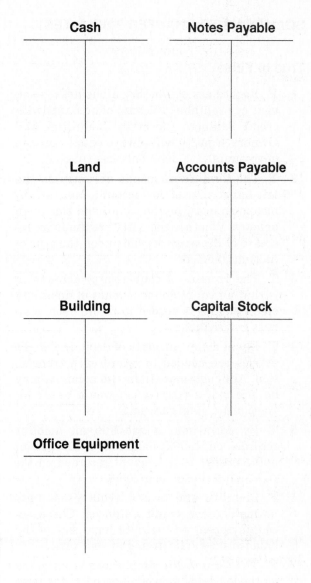

RIVIERA CORPORATION
Trial Balance
September 30, 19__

	Debit	Credit
Cash		
Land		
Building..............................		
Office equipment		
Notes payable		
Accounts payable..............		
Capital stock		
	$_____	$_____

SOLUTIONS TO CHAPTER 2 SELF-TEST

True or False

1 F Regardless of whether a business is solvent or profitable, the sum of accounts with credit balances (normally Liabilities and Owners' Equity) will always equal the sum of accounts with debit balances (Assets).

2 T The term *debit* means an entry on the left-hand side of an account, and *credit* means an entry on the right-hand side of an account. Whether the entry results in an increase or decrease depends upon the type of account affected.

3 T The premise of double-entry accounting is that an equal dollar amount of debit and credit entries is needed to record each business transaction.

4 T Equal dollar amounts of debit and credit entries are needed to record each transaction. Although more than two accounts may be affected, a transaction would never involve just a single account.

5 T By definition, a *debit* is an amount recorded on the left-hand side of an account and a *credit* is an amount recorded on the right-hand side of an account

6 F Liability and owners' equity accounts normally have credit balances. These accounts appear on the right-hand side of the balance sheets illustrated in your text.

7 F The term *debit* simply means an entry on the left-hand side of an account; the term *credit* means an entry on the right-hand side of an account. Whether an entry increases or decreases an account depends upon the nature of the account.

8 T See illustration of the Cash T account in your text.

9 F A "balancing" trial balance only gives assurance that (a) equal debits and credits have been recorded, (b) the balance of each account has been computed correctly, and (c) the addition of account balances in the trial balance has been done accurately.

10 F Accounts appear in the trial balance in the order in which they appear in the ledger, which is in financial statement order (assets, followed by liabilities, owners' equity, revenue, and expenses).

11 T An entry which includes more than one debit or more than one credit is called a *compound journal entry*.

12 T In a journal entry, the debits and credits for a given transaction are recorded together.

13 F Office Equipment is debited (asset is increased) and Accounts Payable is credited (liability is increased).

14 T The list contains six asset accounts (which normally have debit balances), three liability accounts, and one owners' equity account. (Both types of accounts normally have credit balances.)

15 F A transposition error means that the digits in an amount were mixed up or reversed when posting to the ledger from the journal, or when copying an account balance from the ledger into the trial balance.

16 T Footings are the total of all debit entries to an account, or the total of all credit entries to an account. These two amounts are subtracted in arriving at the balance of an account.

17 T Every transaction is to be recorded by an equal dollar amount of debits and credits; recording a transaction properly will maintain equality of debits and credits.

18 F *Posting* is the process of transferring (copying) the debits and credits from the general journal to the proper ledger accounts; recording transactions in the journal requires more analysis and knowledge of accounting.

19 T Since both debit and credit of the original journal entry were equal, the trial balance would still show equality of debits and credits.

20 F The premise of double-entry accounting means that equal dollar amounts of debits and credits are used to record each business transaction.

21 T The term *cycle* indicates that these procedures must be repeated to enable the business to prepare up-to-date financial statements at reasonable intervals.

22 T Computers cannot *think*; they are not able to analyze business transactions.

Completion Statements

1 Title, debit side, credit side. **2** Debits, credits, debits. **3** Left, ledger account, right. **4** Left, debit, right, credit. **5** Cash, Notes Payable, debit, credit. **6** Debit. **7** Book of original entry. **8(a)** Date, **(b)** account, debited, **(c)** account, credited, **(d)** explanation. **9** Trial balance, debit balances, credit balances. **10** L/P (ledger page), posted, numbers, cross-reference. **11** e, b, a, d, c. **12** Transaction, account.

Multiple Choice

1 Answer **c**—a separate ledger account is maintained to record the changes in each asset, liability, and element of owners' equity. Answers **a**, **b**, and **d** all relate to the journal, which consists of a chronological record of business transactions.

2 Answer **d** is false. Owners' equity accounts appear on the right-hand side of the balance sheet and are increased by credit entries.

3 Answer **a**—double-entry accounting means that equal dollar amounts of debits and credits are needed to record any business transaction.

4 Answer **c** describes a journal. Answer **a** describes a trial balance; answer **b**, a data base; and answer **d**, a ledger.

5 Answer **c**—the computer cost $50,000, which must be debited to an asset account. The cash payment and the issuance of a note payable both are recorded by credits.

6 Answer **b** describes posting. Answer **a** is a form of "journalizing," tailored to a computer-based system. Answer **c** describes the preparation of a trial balance; answer **d**, the process of footing the accounts.

7 Answer **c**—a trial balance is a listing of the balances of the accounts in the ledger. Answers **a** and **b** are incorrect because they relate to data not yet posted into the ledger.

Answer **d** is incorrect because it is the total dollar amount of debit and credit balances that must be equal, not the number of accounts with each type of balance.

8 Answer **d**—the proper sequence is (1) record transactions in the journal, (2) post to ledger accounts, (3) prepare a trial balance, and (4) prepare financial statements. (Note: The accounting cycle will be expanded in later chapters.)

9 Answer **c**—to record a transaction, the accountant must know which accounts to debit and to credit, and the appropriate dollar amounts. This requires an understanding of both the transaction and of generally accepted accounting principles.

10 Answer **c**—a decrease in one asset account must be accompanied by an increase in another asset account, or by a *decrease* in either a liability or an owners' equity account.

Solutions to Exercises

1

a Trial balance
b Debit entry
c Ledger
d None (The statement describes a *compound entry*.)
e Journal
f None (The statement describes the *accounting cycle*.)
g Credit entry

2

Journal Entry	Dr	Cr	Assets	=	Lia-bilities	+	Owners' Equity
a Cash	1,230		+1,230				
Accounts Receivable		1,230	−1,230				
Effect of transaction			0	=	0	+	0
b Cash	5,000		+5,000				
Capital Stock		5,000					+5,000
Effect of transaction			+5,000	=	0	+	+5,000
c Cash	3,800		+3,800				
Notes Payable		3,800			+3,800		
Effect of transaction			+3,800	=	+3,800	+	0
d Accounts Payable	350				− 350		
Cash		350	− 350				
Effect of transaction			− 350	=	− 350	+	0
e Land	9,000		+9,000				
Cash		1,000	−1,000				
Notes Payable		8,000			+8,000		
Effect of transaction			+8,000	=	+8,000	+	0

3

	Account(s) Debited	Account(s) Credited
a	6	9
b	6	1, 8
c	1	3
d	1	8
e	9	1
f	1	10

4

Cash

(1)	70,000	(3)	40,000
(2)	12,000	(7)	3,000

Land

(3)	30,000	

Building

(3)	60,000	
(5)	5,000	

Office Equipment

(4)	6,000	(6)	600

Notes Payable

	(2)	12,000
	(3)	50,000

Accounts Payable

(6)	600	(4)	6,000
(7)	3,000	(5)	5,000

Capital Stock

	(1)	70,000

RIVIERA CORPORATION
Trial Balance
September 30, 19__

	Debit	Credit
Cash	$ 39,000	
Land	30,000	
Building..	65,000	
Office equipment	5,400	
Notes payable		$ 62,000
Accounts payable...............................		7,400
Capital stock		70,000
	$139,400	$139,400

3

MEASURING BUSINESS INCOME AND COMPLETION OF THE ACCOUNTING CYCLE

HIGHLIGHTS OF THE CHAPTER

1 Two things can cause a change in the owners' equity in a business concern: (a) a change in the owners' investment (stockholders putting assets in or taking assets out of the business) and (b) profits or losses resulting from operation of the business.

2 The change in owners' equity resulting from profits or losses is very important to every business. Profits increase owners' equity. These profits may be either distributed to the stockholders as dividends, or retained in the business to help finance expansion and growth. Losses, however, reduce owners' equity and make the business and its owners economically worse off.

3 The increase in owners' equity resulting from operating profitably is presented in the balance sheet in the **Retained Earnings** account. Distributing profits to stockholders as **dividends** causes a decrease in total assets and owners' equity. This decrease in owners' equity decreases the Retained Earnings account. Thus, retained earnings represent only the profits **retained in the business**. Many large companies started with small investments but were able to grow by operating profitably and reinvesting their profits in the business.

4 Accountants use the term **net income** to describe the increase in owners' equity that results from profitable operations. The decrease in owners' equity resulting from **un**profitable operations is termed a **net loss**.

5 Net income (or loss) is computed by deducting the **expenses** of an accounting period from the **revenue** earned during that period.

Thus, we often say that net income is equal to **revenue minus expenses.**

6 The computation of the net income or loss for an accounting period is shown in a financial statement called an **income statement**. This statement shows the revenue, expenses, and net income (or loss) of an **accounting period**.

7 A balance sheet shows the company's financial position at **one particular date**. An income statement, however, covers a **span of time**, called the **accounting period**. Almost every business uses a one-year accounting period, but many **also** prepare income statements for shorter accounting periods, such as each month or each quarter (three-month period). The need to relate net income to a specific period of time is called the **time period principle**.

8 **Revenue** is not "money" coming in. Rather, it is the amount "earned" during the period, regardless of when payment is received. Revenue is defined as the **price of goods sold and services rendered during the accounting period**. Recognizing revenue as it is "earned" illustrates the **realization principle**—a generally accepted accounting principle.

9 To illustrate the realization principle, assume that a hospital renders services to a patient in December, bills the patient's insurance company in January, and receives payment in February. When should the hospital recognize "revenue"? The answer is in **December**—this is when the hospital rendered the services which "earned" the revenue.

10 *Expenses are the cost of goods and services used up in the effort to generate revenue.* Expenses are recorded when the good or service is *used up*, regardless of the period in which payment is made. Assume that we will not pay our employees for work done in the last two weeks of March until April 1. In which month should we recognize wages expense? The answer is **March**—that is when we used their services.

11 There is a cause and effect relationship between revenue and expenses. Revenue represents the accomplishments of the period, and expenses are the costs of goods and services used up in achieving these accomplishments. Thus, deducting the expenses of the period from the revenue earned shows us whether our activities have been profitable or unprofitable.

12 An income statement shows the revenue earned during the period and all expenses incurred in generating that revenue. This policy of offsetting revenue with the related expenses is called the *matching principle*.

13 Business often purchase assets that will be "used up" over two or more accounting periods. The matching principle requires that an effort be made to allocate an appropriate portion of the total cost as an expense in each period that the asset is "used."

14 Allocating the cost of an asset to expense often involves estimates. A building, for example, may remain in use for 20 years or more. The matching principle indicates that the total cost of this building should be allocated to expense gradually as the building is "used up." Since no one knows precisely how long the building may last, such allocations can only be estimates.

15 The debit and credit rules for recording revenue and expenses are based upon the changes caused in owners' equity. Revenue *increases* owners' equity; therefore, revenue is recorded by a *credit*. Expenses *decrease* owners' equity and are recorded by *debits*.

16 A *dividend* is a distribution of assets by a corporation to its stockholders. Dividends are similar to expenses in that they reduce owners' equity and are recorded by debits. But dividends are not listed as expenses in the income statement, because dividends are not paid in an effort to produce revenue. Thus, dividends are viewed as a change in the owners' *investment* in the business, not as a change in equity resulting from profitable operations.

17 A separate ledger account is maintained for each major category of revenue and expense. Revenue accounts have credit balances; examples are Fees Earned, Commissions Earned, and Sales. Expense accounts have debit balances; examples are Telephone Expense, Office Salaries, and Insurance Expense.

18 Whenever there is a change in owners' equity, there is a corresponding change in either total assets or total liabilities. Thus, whenever we record a revenue or expense, we must record the related change in assets or liabilities. Credits to revenue accounts usually are offset by debits to asset accounts; debits to expense accounts are offset by credits to asset accounts or to liability accounts.

19 The sequence of accounts in the ledger is as follows: (a) assets, (b) liabilities, (c) owners' equity, (d) revenue, and (e) expenses. This sequence is called *financial statement order*, because the three groups of balance sheet accounts (assets, liabilities, owners' equity) come before the income statement accounts (revenue and expenses).

20 At the end of the period a trial balance is prepared from the ledger in the same manner described in Chapter 2. But this time, we *cannot* prepare financial statements directly from the trial balance. The including of revenue and expenses in the trial balance adds an additional step to the accounting cycle before financial statements can be prepared. This additional step is the making of end-of-period *adjusting entries*.

21 Adjusting entries are needed at the end of each accounting period to record any revenue earned or expenses incurred which were *not recognized* as a result of recording routine transactions. In this chapter we illustrate only the two most common adjusting entries—those to recognize depreciation expense and income taxes expense. Other types of adjusting entries will be illustrated in Chapter 4.

22 Buildings, office equipment, and other *plant assets* have limited useful lives over which the assets are used up. A portion of the cost of the asset becomes expense (price of goods used up) during each year of its useful life. This process of allocating the cost of a plant asset over its useful life is called *depreciation*.

23 For example, if we acquire a $100,000 building with an estimated life of 25 years and no salvage value, the depreciation expense each year will be $\frac{1}{25}$ of $100,000, or $4,000. To ignore depreciation would cause expenses to be understated and therefore net income to be overstated.

24 The journal entry to record depreciation is made at the end of the period by a debit to **Depreciation Expense** and a credit to **Accumulated Depreciation**. The Accumulated Depreciation account, with a credit balance, appears on the balance sheet as a deduction from the related asset account. The net amount (asset cost minus accumulated depreciation) represents the undepreciated cost (benefits remaining) of the asset. Undepreciated cost is also called **book value** or **carrying value**.

25 Depreciation expense differs from most other expenses in two ways. First, it is **only a rough estimate**. Second, no corresponding cash outlay in or around the current period. For this reason, depreciation is often called a **"noncash expense."**

26 Profitable corporations must pay income taxes on their earnings. The exact amount of these taxes is not determined until the company prepares its annual income tax return. However, income taxes expense should be recognized in the periods in which the taxable income is earned. Normally these amounts can be estimated with reasonable accuracy.

27 Income taxes expense is determined by applying the company's **tax rate** to the amount of taxable income earned during the period. This expense is recorded by an adjusting entry debiting Income Taxes Expense and crediting the liability account, Income Taxes Payable.

28 After all end-of-period adjusting entries have been recorded and posted, the company prepares an **adjusted trial balance**. This adjusted trial balance contains the account balances that are used in the income statement, statement of retained earnings, and balance sheet.

29 The **income statement** is a formal financial statement which lists the revenue, deducts the expenses, and shows the net income of a business for a specific period of time (the accounting period.)

30 The income statement is of great interest to managers, investors, and other groups, but it has certain limitations. It is not entirely accurate, because many transactions overlap accounting periods and their effect on each period is merely an estimate. Also the economic significance of some events (such as the discovery of an oil well) cannot be objectively measured and reflected in the income statement.

31 The **statement of retained earnings** covers the same time period as the income statement. It shows the beginning balance of retained earnings, the net income or loss for the period, a deduction for any dividends, and the ending balance of retained earnings.

32 The **report form** of balance sheet contains the same information as the **account form** previously illustrated. However, in the report form the assets are listed and totaled in the upper half of the page. The liabilities and stockholders' equity constitute a separate section in the lower half of the page.

33 The stockholders' equity section of the balance sheet shows two items: Capital Stock, representing the amounts invested by stockholders, and Retained Earnings, representing the accumulated net earnings since the date of incorporation minus all dividends distributed to stockholders.

34 Stockholders' equity is increased by (a) the issuance of capital stock and (b) earning net income. It is decreased by (a) payments of dividends and (b) incurring net losses.

35 The income statement and statement of retained earnings may be viewed as "links" between two successive balance sheets. The statement of retained earnings summarizes the factors (net income and dividends) which have caused the amount of retained earnings to change between the two balance sheet dates. The income statement explains in greater detail the change in retained earnings resulting from profitable (or unprofitable) operation of the business.

36 After the financial statements have been prepared, the presence of revenue and expense accounts adds two more steps to the accounting cycle—**closing the accounts** and the preparation of an **after-closing trial balance**.

37 **Closing the accounts** means transferring the balances of the revenue and expense accounts at the end of each accounting period into an account used to measure net income, called the **Income Summary** account. If revenue (credit balances) exceeds expenses (debit balances), the Income Summary account will have a credit balance representing net income for the period. If the expenses exceed the revenue, the Income Summary account will have a debit balance, representing a net loss. In either case, the Income Summary account is then closed by transferring its balance to the Retained Earnings account.

38 Transferring a credit balance from the Income Summary account (representing net income) causes the Retained Earnings account to increase; transferring a debit balance (net loss) into Retained Earnings caused that account to decrease.

39 The Dividends account is closed by transferring its debit balance to the Retained Earnings account. *It does not go through the Income Summary account because dividends are not an expense.*

40 The principal purpose of closing the revenue and expense accounts is to reduce their balances to zero at the end of the period so that they are ready to measure the revenue and expenses of the next period.

41 Four journal entries are generally used to close the accounts: (a) close revenue accounts into the Income Summary, (b) close expense accounts into the Income Summary, (c) close the Income Summary account into the Retained Earnings account, and (d) close the Dividends account into Retained Earnings. These journal entries are called *closing entries.*

42 After closing the accounts, an *after-closing trial balance* is prepared to prove that the ledger is still in balance. The after-closing trial balance will contain *only balance sheet accounts* since all others will have zero balances.

43 The accounting procedures covered thus far may be summarized in eight steps: (a) journalize transactions, (b) post to ledger accounts, (c) prepare a trial balance, (d) make end-of-period adjustments, (e) prepare an adjusted trial balance, (f) prepare financial statements, (g) journalize and post closing entries, and (h) prepare an after-closing trial balance.

44 Procedures (a) and (d), above, involve the analysis of business transactions and judgmental decisions as to accounts to be debited and credited. Thus, they require human judgment, regardless of whether the data is processed manually or by computer. The other procedures, including the preparation of closing entries, are mechanical tasks and may be performed automatically in a computer-based accounting system.

45 The declaration and payment of dividends involve three separate dates:
a *Declaration date* The date upon which the board of directors announces (declares) that a dividend will be paid at a specified future date. The entry required at the declaration date is a debit to Dividends and a credit to Dividends Payable.
b *Date of record* The dividend will be paid to those stockholders who own the shares on the date of record.
c *Payment date* The date upon which the dividend checks actually are distributed to stockholders. At this date, an entry is made by debiting Dividends Payable and crediting Cash.

46 We have defined revenue as the price of goods and services delivered or rendered to customers during a period and we have defined expenses as the cost of goods and services used during a period, regardless of when cash payment is made. These definitions of revenue and expenses result in *accrual basis* accounting.

47 An alternative to accrual basis accounting is *cash basis* accounting. Under cash basis accounting, revenue is not recorded until received in cash; expenses are recognized in the period in which cash payment is made. The cash basis does not give a fair measure of profitability. For instance, the cash basis ignores revenue earned but not yet received and expenses incurred but not yet paid. We shall therefore use only the *accrual basis* to determine net income.

TEST YOURSELF ON MEASURING BUSINESS INCOME

True or False

For each of the following statements, circle the T or the F to indicate whether the statement is true or false.

T F **1** An income statement relates to a specified period of time whereas a balance sheet shows the financial position of a business at a particular date.

T F **2** If a real estate firm using the accrual basis of accounting sells a client's building in May but the commission is not collected until July, the revenue is earned in May and should be included in the May income statement.

T F 3 The realization principle states that a business should never record revenue until cash is collected from the customer.

T F 4 Expenses cause a decrease in owners' equity and are recorded by debits.

T F 5 If cash receipts are $10,000 greater than total expenses for a given period, the business will earn a net income of $10,000 or more.

T F 6 The journal entry to recognize a revenue or an expense usually affects an asset or liability account as well.

T F 7 Under accrual basis accounting, revenue is recognized when cash is received, and expenses are recognized when cash is paid.

T F 8 An expense may be recognized and recorded even though no cash outlay has been made.

T F 9 Buying a building for cash is just exchanging one asset for another and will not result in an expense even in future periods.

T F 10 Revenue increases owners' equity and is recorded by a credit.

T F 11 Revenue accounts are closed at the end of the period by debiting the revenue accounts and transferring their balances by crediting the Income Summary account.

T F 12 If a business is operating profitably, the entry to close the Income Summary account will consist of a debit to Income Summary and a credit to Retained Earnings.

T F 13 If expenses are larger than revenue, the Income Summary account will have a debit balance.

T F 14 Since dividends reduce assets and owners' equity, they are shown in the income statement as expenses.

T F 15 The entry to recognize depreciation is an example of an adjusting entry.

T F 16 An increase in an expense account is the equivalent of a decrease in owners' equity.

T F 17 An adjusted trial balance contains only balance sheet accounts.

T F 18 In a well-established business which had been audited annually by a CPA, it would be reasonable to expect the Depreciation Expense account and the Accumulated Depreciation account to have equal balances.

T F 19 Retained earnings represent an amount of cash available to pay dividends.

T F 20 The Retained Earnings account is closed at the end of each period, and begins the next period with a zero balance.

T F 21 The Dividends account is closed at the end of the period by transferring its balance to the Income Summary account.

T F 22 A person must be a shareholder on the date of record in order to be eligible to receive the dividend.

Completion Statements

Fill in the necessary words or amounts to complete the following statements:

1 The _____ principle of accounting states that revenue should be recognized in the period that it is earned. The _____ principle indicates that expenses should be recognized in the period in which they help produce _____.

2 The Income Summary account is used to bring together the _____ and _____ accounts.

3 The process of allocating the _____ of a plant asset to expense as that asset is used up is called _____.

4 Performance Products Company began business on July 7. The company made the following total cash sales: July, $18,000; August, $26,000. Sales on a 30-day credit were July, $31,000; August, $42,000. All the July credit sales were collected in August, and all accounts receivable originating in August were collected in September. The total revenue for July was $_____ and total revenue for August was $_____. Total cash receipts in August were $_____.

5 The principal distinction between expenses and dividends to stockholders is that expenses are incurred for the purpose of _____ _____.

A similarity between the two is that both expenses and dividends cause a _____ in _____ _____.

6 A credit balance in the Income Summary account indicates a _____ _____ for the period. This will cause owners' equity to _____.

7 If expenses exceed revenue, the Income Summary account will be closed into the _____ _____ account by an entry which _____ the Income Summary account.

8 Assets, liabilities, and owners' equity are the only accounts that will have balances after the _____ _____ have all been posted.

9 A dividend is declared by the board of directors of Sonic Corporation on July 1, and is payable on August 10 to stockholders of record on July 31. The journal entry on July 1 would consist of a debit to _____ and a credit to _____ _____. The entry on August 10 would consist of a debit to _____ _____ and a credit to _____.

Multiple Choice

Choose the best answer for each of the following questions and enter the identifying letter in the space provided.

_____ **1** Which of the following statements best describes the relationship between *revenue* and *retained earnings?*
a Revenue increases net income which, in turn, increases retained earnings.
b Revenue represents a cash receipt, whereas retained earnings is an element of stockholders' equity.
c Revenue represents the price of goods sold or services rendered, whereas retained earnings represents the cash available for paying dividends.
d Retained earnings is equal to revenue minus expenses.

_____ **2** The overall effect of declaring and distributing a dividend includes all of the following *except*:
a Reducing total assets.
b Reducing stockholders' equity.
c Reducing the balance of the Retained Earnings account.
d Reducing the net income reported for the period.

_____ **3** *The time-period principle:*
a Requires that all corporations prepare monthly, quarterly, and annual financial statements.
b Involves dividing the life of a business entity into accounting periods of equal length so that financial statement users periodically can evaluate the results of business operations.
c Requires all companies to use a fiscal year ending December 31.
d Stems from the Internal Revenue Service requirement that taxable income be reported on an annual basis.

_____ **4** *The realization principle:*
a Indicates that a business should record revenue when services are rendered or merchandise sold is delivered to customers, even if cash has not yet been received.
b Indicates that revenue should be recognized in the accounting period when cash is received, even if the business has not yet performed all the required services.
c Indicates that revenue should be recorded only after two conditions have been met: (1) the earning process is complete, and (2) the cash has been collected.
d Provides guidelines as to when expenses should be recognized.

_____ **5** A produce supplier enters into a contract with a supermarket chain on September 8 to deliver pumpkins in October. The pumpkins are delivered on October 14 at a price of $4,000, payable $2,000 on November 1 and $2,000 on December 1. When should the produce supplier record the $4,000 as revenue?
a September 8.
b October 14.
c $2,000 on November 1 and $2,000 on December 1.
d When the supermarket sells the pumpkins.

_____ **6** Which of the following is *not* an accurate statement regarding the rules of debits and credits in recording revenue and expense transactions?
a Revenue increases owners' equity; since increases in owners' equity are recorded by credits, revenue is recorded by a credit.
b Expenses decrease owners' equity; since decreases in owners' equity and recorded by debits, expenses are recorded by debits.
c In recording revenue transactions, we debit the assets received and credit the revenue account.

d Expenses use up assets; since decreases in assets are recorded by credits, expenses are recorded by credits to the expense account.

_____ **7** The *matching principle* implies that expenses:

a Should be deducted from revenue in the period in which the suppliers of the goods or services are paid.

b For a period should be equal in amount to the revenue recognized during the period.

c Should be deducted in the period in which use of the related goods or services help to produce revenue.

d Should be equal to the cash payments made during the period.

_____ **8** On April 1, Hudson Company received and paid a $700 bill for advertising done in March. In addition to this bill, the company paid $6,100 during April for expenses incurred in that month. On May 2, Hudson Company paid a $4,600 payroll to employees for work done in April. Based on these facts, total expenses for the month of April were:

a $6,100   **b** $6,800   **c** $10,700   **d** $11,400

_____ **9** If a journal entry recognizes an expense, the other part of the entry might:

a Increase an asset account.

b Decrease the Retained Earnings account.

c Decrease a liability account.

d Increase a liability account.

_____ **10** The *depreciation expense* on an automobile represents:

a The decline in the market value of the automobile during the period.

b A systematic allocation of the cost of the automobile to expense over the automobile's useful life.

c The cash payments made on the car loan during the period.

d The cost of operating the automobile during the period.

_____ **11** The *statement of retained earnings:*

a Shows the revenue and expenses of a business for a given time period.

b Indicates whether the cash position of the corporation will permit the payment of dividends.

c Provides a link between the income statement and the balance sheet.

d Has no relationship with the balance sheet.

_____ **12** Preparing *closing entries* accomplishes two basic purposes:

a (1) To update the balance of Retained Earnings, and (2) to return the balances of the revenue, expense, and dividends accounts to zero.

b (1) To determine that the ledger is in balance, and (2) to reduce the balances of the revenue, expense, and dividends accounts to zero.

c (1) To record the depreciation expense for the period, and (2) to enable the company to prepare an adjusted trial balance.

d To update the balances of (1) the Cash account, and (2) the Retained Earnings account.

_____ **13** Listed below are four steps of the *accounting cycle.* Considering *only these four steps,* which would be the *second* step to be performed?

a Prepare financial statements.

b Prepare an after-closing trial balance.

c Prepare a trial balance.

d Prepare an adjusted trial balance.

_____ **14** The *accrual* basis of accounting may be best described as:

a Recording revenue by credit entries and expenses by debit entries.

b Recording revenue when it is earned and expenses when the related goods and services are used to produce revenue.

c A series of procedures, beginning with journalizing transactions and ending with the preparation of an after-closing trial balance.

d Recording revenue when cash is collected from customers and recording expenses when cash is paid to suppliers.

Exercises

1 Listed below are eight technical accounting terms emphasized in this chapter.

Retained Earnings	*Realization*
Closing entries	*principle*
Revenue	*Accrual accounting*
Net income	*Depreciation*
Adjusting entries	*Expense*

Each of the following statements may (or may not) describe one of these technical terms. In the space provided below each statement, indicate the accounting term described, or answer "None" if the statement does not correctly describe any of the terms.

a A contra-asset account shown in the balance sheet as a deduction from the related asset account.

_____

b The price of goods sold and services rendered during the period.

_____

c Revenue earned less expenses incurred during the period.

_____

d The procedures for updating the balance of retained earnings for changes in owners' equity temporarily recorded in the revenue, expense, and dividends accounts.

_____

e The generally accepted accounting principle that expenses are to be recognized in the period that the related expenditure helps to produce revenue.

_____

f The account into which the balances of the Income Summary and Dividends accounts are closed at the end of each period.

_____

g The technique of recognizing revenue when it is earned and expenses when the related goods and services are used, without regard to when cash is received or paid.

_____

2 A list of accounts for Jones Corporation is given below followed by a series of transactions. Indicate the accounts that would be debited and credited in recording each transaction by placing the appropriate account number(s) in the space provided.
  1 Cash
  2 Accounts Receivable
  3 Office Equipment
  4 Accumulated Depreciation: Office Equipment
  5 Notes Payable
  6 Accounts Payable
  7 Dividends Payable
  8 Capital Stock
  9 Retained Earnings
  10 Dividends
  11 All Revenue Accounts
  12 All Expense Accounts
  13 Income Summary

Transactions	Account(s) Debited	Account(s) Credited
Example Purchased office equipment, paying part cash and issuing a note payable for the balance	3	1, 5
a Paid creditor amount due on open account		
b Collected from customer for services performed by Jones Corporation in previous period		
c Utility bill is received; payment will be made in 10 days		
d Performed services for a customer; $50 cash received and the balance due in 30 days		
e Office equipment purchased giving note payable		
f A dividend is declared, to be paid in the following period		
g Depreciation on office equipment is recorded		
h Entry is made to close revenue account at end of period		
i Entry is made to close expense account at end of period		
j Income Summary account is closed at end of a profitable period		
k Entry is made to close the Dividends account		

3 Using the adjusted trial balance below, prepare (a) an income statement, (b) a statement of retained earnings, and (c) a balance sheet in ***report form*** for Mission Auto Repair, Inc., for the month ended March 31, 19__.

MISSION AUTO REPAIR, INC.
Adjusted Trial Balance
March 31, 19__

	Debit	Credit
Cash	$ 18,600	
Notes receivable	4,000	
Accounts receivable	42,000	
Garage equipment	33,600	
Accumulated depreciation:		
garage equipment		$ 9,100
Notes payable		8,200
Accounts payable		12,300
Income taxes payable		10,200
Capital stock		30,000
Retained earnings, Feb. 28		28,000
Dividends	8,000	
Repair revenue		27,400
Rent expense	2,000	
Wages expense	11,350	
Advertising expense	1,400	
Utilities expense	300	
Depreciation expense:		
garage equipment	350	
Income taxes expense	3,600	
	$125,200	$125,200

a **MISSION AUTO REPAIR, INC.**
Income Statement
For the Month Ended March 31, 19__

b **MISSION AUTO REPAIR, INC.**
Statement of Retained Earnings
For the Month Ended March 31, 19__

c **MISSION AUTO REPAIR, INC.**
Balance Sheet
March 31, 19__

Assets		
Liabilities & Stockholders' Equity		

4 Bryant Engineering Co. closes its accounts at the end of each month. Among the events occurring in May were the following:
  a Paid service bill for office equipment repairs which occurred in April.
  b Created and delivered blueprints for a credit customer; payment is due June 10.
  c Prepared an adjusting entry to record depreciation of office computer and copying machine.
  d Received a bill for office supplies delivered in May. Payment due June 15.
  e Collected in full the amount due from a credit customer for services provided in April.
  f Purchased new office furniture for a new engineer in the firm, paying part cash and issuing a note payable for the balance. The new engineer is not scheduled to start until June 5.

Indicate the effects that each of these transactions will have upon the following six *total amounts* in the company's financial statements for the month of May. Use the code letters *I* for Increase, *D* for Decrease, and *NE* for No Effect. The answer to transaction **a** is provided as an example.

Trans-action	Income Statement			Balance Sheet		
	Total Revenue	– Total Expenses	= Net Income	Total Assets	= Total Liabilities	+ Owners' Equity
a	*NE*	*NE*	*NE*	*D*	*D*	*NE*
b						
c						
d						
e						
f						

5 Indicate the effect of the following errors on each of the accounting elements described in the column headings below. Use the following symbols: *O* = Overstated, *U* = Understated, *NE* = No Effect.

Error	Income Statement			Balance Sheet		
	Total Revenue	– Total Expenses	= Net Income	Total Assets	= Total Liabilities	+ Owners' Equity
Example: Rendered services to a customer and received immediate payment in cash but made no record of the transaction	*U*	*NE*	*U*	*U*	*NE*	*U*
a Payment for repairs erroneously debited to Building account						
b Recorded collection of an account receivable by debiting Cash and crediting a revenue account						
c Failed to record depreciation of the current period						
d Recorded declaration of a dividend to be paid in a later month by debiting Dividends and crediting Retained Earnings						
e Recorded the purchase of office equipment for cash as a debit to Office Equipment and a credit to Depreciation Expense						
f Recorded cash payment for advertising by debiting Repairs Expense and crediting Cash						

SOLUTIONS TO CHAPTER 3 SELF-TEST

True or False

1 **T** Net income cannot be evaluated unless it is associated with a specific time period.

2 **T** The company should recognize revenue in the month in which it renders services to the client.

3 **F** The realization principle states that revenue should be recognized when services are rendered or goods are delivered.

4 **T** Expenses offset revenue in determining net income and therefore reduce owners' equity.

5 **F** Net income equals revenue minus expenses; cash receipts and revenue are not the same.

6 **T** To record an expense, the expense account is debited and cash or a liability is credited; to record revenue, the asset received is debited and revenue is credited.

7 **F** Revenue is recognized when *earned*; expenses are recognized in the period in which the cost helps to produce revenue.

8 **T** The cash payment for an expense may occur before, after, or in the same period that an expense helps to produce revenue.

9 **F** A portion of the cost of the building will be recognized as depreciation expense each period over the building's useful life.

10 **T** Revenue is the gross increase in owners' equity resulting from business activities; all increases in owners' equity are recorded by credits.

11 **T** This entry reduces the balance in the revenue accounts to zero, so they are ready to accumulate the next period's revenue.

12 **T** If a business has been profitable, there will be a credit balance in the Income Summary account; Income Summary is debited to reduce the balance to zero.

13 **T** When revenue (credits) and expenses (debits) are closed at the end of a period, their balances are transferred to the Income Summary account.

14 **F** Although dividends reduce assets and owners' equity, they are not considered an expense because they do not serve to generate revenue. Dividends are a distribution of profits to owners of the business.

15 **T** Depreciation is a means of allocating to expense a portion of a long-lived asset; even though there may have been no cash outlay this period, the adjusting entry "adjusts" the expense amount and the carrying value of the asset.

16 **T** Expenses reduce net income, which eventually will be closed into the Retained Earnings account (part of owners' equity).

17 **F** Immediately after adjusting entries are made, the trial balance contains asset, liability, owners' equity, revenue and expense accounts.

18 **F** The Depreciation Expense account contains only the amount for the current period; the Accumulated Depreciation account contains the current period's and *all prior periods' depreciation.*

19 **F** Retained earnings represent the earnings of the corporation over the entire lifetime of the business, less all amounts distributed as dividends. The earnings have been retained in the business, but not necessarily in the form of cash.

20 **F** Revenue, expense, and dividends accounts are closed at the end of an accounting period and the balance of the Retained Earnings account is updated for the changes in these temporary accounts. The Retained Earnings account is a *permanent* or *real* account whose balance continues to exist beyond the end of the current accounting period.

21 **F** The Dividends account is closed by transferring its balance to the Retained Earnings account.

22 **T** Regardless of stock ownership at date of declaration or date of payment of a dividend, only the persons owning shares on the date of record receive a cash dividend.

Completion Statements

1 Realization, matching, revenue. **2** Revenue, expense. **3** Cost, depreciation. **4** $49,000; $68,000; $57,000. **5** Producing revenue, decrease, stockholders' equity. **6** Net income, increase. **7** Retained Earnings, credits. **8** Closing entries. **9** Dividends, Dividends Payable, Dividends Payable, Cash.

Multiple Choice

1 Answer **a**—this relationship is illustrated through the "closing process," in which the revenue accounts are closed into the Income

Summary account, which, in turn, is closed into Retained Earnings. Answers **b** and **c** are incorrect because they imply that either revenue or retained earnings represent cash. Answer **d** describes net income, not retained earnings.

2 Answer **d**—dividends are not incurred for the purpose of producing revenue and, therefore, do not enter into the determination of net income. Dividends do, however, reduce assets, stockholders' equity, and retained earnings.

3 Answer **b**—for accounting information to be useful, it must be available on a frequent periodic basis. This requires dividing the overall life of the business entity into "accounting periods." Answer **a** is incorrect because the principle does not require monthly statements. Answer **c** is incorrect because a company's fiscal year need not end on December 31. Answer **d** is incorrect because generally accepted accounting principles are not governed by income tax laws.

4 Answer **a**—under the realization principle, revenue is recognized when it is earned, regardless of when the cash is collected. Answers **b** and **c** are incorrect because they tie the recognition of revenue to the collection of cash. Answer **d** describes the matching principle, not the realization principle.

5 Answer **b**—the realization principle indicates that revenue should be recognized when it is earned—that is, when services are rendered or when goods sold are delivered to customers.

6 Answer **d**—this answer is not accurate. Although the decrease in an asset account is recorded by a credit entry, the expense is recorded by an offsetting *debit entry* to the appropriate expense account.

7 Answer **c**—expenses should be offset against the revenue produced by these expenditures. Answers **a** and **d** are incorrect because the period in which expenses are recognized may differ from the period in which the related cash payments are made. Answer **b** is incorrect because expenses may differ from revenue by the amount of any net income or net loss.

8 Answer **c**—$6,100 + $4,600. Answer **a** excludes the $4,600 in salaries expense for April. Answer **b** excludes the salaries and improperly includes $700 in advertising expense for the month of March. Answer **d** improperly includes the $700 of advertising expense applicable to March.

9 Answer **d**—the debit entry to record an expense is always accompanied by either a credit (decrease) in an asset account, or a credit (increase) in a liability account.

10 Answer **b**—depreciation represents the systematic allocation of the cost of an asset to expense. Answer **a** is incorrect because depreciation does not relate to the fluctuations in market value. Answer **c** describes a combination of interest expense and a reduction in a liability; answer **d** describes a variety of expenses, including not only depreciation, but also gasoline, insurance, and repairs.

11 Answer **c**—the statement of retained earnings show how net income (which appears in the income statement) and dividends affect the balance of retained earnings (appearing in the balance sheet). Answer **a** describes the income statement. Answer **c** is incorrect because retained earnings is an element of stockholders' equity and does not indicate the amount of cash on hand. Answer **d** is incorrect because the ending balance of retained earnings does appear in the balance sheet.

12 Answer **a** correctly describes the two purposes of closing entries. Answer **b(1)** describes the purposes of a trial balance. Answer **c** describes the purpose of adjusting entries, such as the entry to record depreciation. Answer **d** is incorrect because closing entries affect only stockholders' equity accounts, not asset accounts such as Cash.

13 Answer **d**—an adjusted trial balance is prepared after adjustments have been made to the amounts appearing in the original trial balance. Financial statements and closing entries are based upon the amounts appearing in the adjusted trial balance. An after-closing trial balance cannot be prepared until after the closing entries have been made and posted.

14 Answer **b**—under the accrual basis of accounting, revenue is recognized when it is earned and expenses when they are incurred. Answer **a** describes the debit and credit rules for revenue and expenses, answer **c** describes the accounting cycle, and answer **d** describes the cash basis of accounting.

Solutions to Exercises

1

a None (The statement describes the *Accumulated Depreciation* account.)
b Revenue
c Net income
d Closing entries
e None (The statement describes the *matching principle*.)
f Retained Earnings
g Accrual accounting

2

	Account(s) Debited	Account(s) Credited
a	6	1
b	1	2
c	12	6
d	1, 2	11
e	3	5
f	10	7
g	12	4
h	11	13
i	13	12
j	13	9
k	9	10

3a

MISSION AUTO REPAIR, INC.
Income Statement
For the Month Ended March 31,19__

Repair revenue		$27,400
Expenses:		
Rent	$ 2,000	
Wages	11,350	
Advertising	1,400	
Utilities	300	
Depreciation	350	15,400
Income before income taxes		$12,000
Less: Income taxes expense		3,600
Net income		$ 8,400

b

MISSION AUTO REPAIR, INC.
Statement of Retained Earnings
For the Month Ended March 31, 19__

Retained earnings, Feb. 30, 19__	$28,000
Net income	8,400
Subtotal	$36,400
Dividends	8,000
Retained earnings, March 31,19__	$28,400

c

MISSION AUTO REPAIR, INC.
Balance Sheet
March 31, 19__

Assets

Cash		$18,600
Notes receivable		4,000
Accounts receivable		42,000
Garage equipment	$33,600	
Less: Accumulated depreciation	9,100	24,500
Total assets		$89,100

Liabilities & Stockholders' Equity

Liabilities:		
Notes payable		$ 8,200
Accounts payable		12,300
Income taxes payable		10,200
Total liabilities		$30,700
Stockholders' equity:		
Capital stock	$30,000	
Retained earnings	28,400	58,400
Total liabilities & stockholders' equity		$89,100

4

Trans-action	Income Statement			Balance Sheet		
	Reve-nue	Ex-penses	Net Income	Assets	Lia-bilities	Owners' Equity
a	NE	NE	NE	D	D	NE
b	I	NE	I	I	NE	I
c	NE	I	D	D	NE	D
d	NE	NE	NE	I	I	NE
e	NE	NE	NE	NE	NE	NE
f	NE	NE	NE	I	I	NE

5

Error	Income Statement			Balance Sheet		
	Total Reve-nue	Total Ex-penses	Net Income	Assets	Total Lia-bilities	Total Owners' Equity
a	NE	U	O	O	NE	O
b	O	NE	O	O	NE	O
c	NE	U	O	O	NE	O
d	NE	NE	NE	NE	U	O
e	NE	U	O	O	NE	O
f	NE	NE	NE	NE	NE	NE

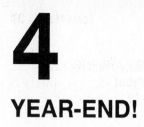

4

YEAR-END!

HIGHLIGHTS OF THE CHAPTER

1 There is much more to year-end than adjusting and closing the accounts. Accountants also prepare financial statements, income tax returns, annual reports, and budgets for the coming year. Meanwhile, CPAs may be auditing the financial statements, requiring constant access to accounting records and explanations of past transactions. That's why accountants call year-end their "busy season."

2 In this chapter, we will focus upon adjusting entries and the preparation of financial statements.

3 Annual financial statements cover the company's *fiscal year*. Most companies use the calendar year ending at December 31 as their fiscal year, but others end their fiscal year at the seasonal "low point" in their business activities. Many retailers, for example, end their fiscal year in early January.

4 Some transactions involve revenue or expenses relating to several accounting periods. In such cases, *adjusting entries* are needed at the end of each period to recognize the appropriate amount of revenue or expense. Thus, adjusting entries help accountants to achieve the goals of *accrual accounting*—recognizing revenue when it is earned, and recognizing expenses as the related goods and services are used.

5 There are four basic types of adjusting entries. Entries to: (1) apportion costs already recorded in the accounting records *(recorded costs)*, (2) apportion *unearned revenue*, (3) record expenses *not yet* recorded in the accounting records *(unrecorded expenses)*, and (4) record *unrecorded revenue*.

6 Each type of adjusting entry affects both an income statement account (revenue or expense) and a balance sheet account (asset or liability). Thus, adjusting entries serve two purposes: (1) they recognize revenue or expenses relating to the accounting period, and (2) bring various asset and liability accounts up-to-date. We will now discuss the four basic types of adjusting entries.

7 *Recorded costs* are assets that will benefit several accounting periods. As these assets are "used up," their cost is transferred to expense. Thus, "recorded cost" adjusting entries consist of transferring part (or all) of the cost of an asset to expense. This entry consists of a debit to an expense account, and a credit to the asset account (or to contra-asset account, such as Accumulated Depreciation).

8 Examples of "recorded cost" adjustments include reducing such asset accounts as Unexpired Insurance, or Office Supplies, for the portions used during the period. Of course, the most common recorded cost adjustment of them all is the entry to recognize depreciation expense.

9 *Unearned revenue* results when customers pay in advance for services (or goods) to be rendered in the future. An example is the money received in advance by a sports team for the sale of season tickets. This ticket revenue will not be "earned" until the team plays the games for which customers purchased these tickets.

10 When revenue is received in advance, a *liability* exists either to render the service or refund the customers' money. Therefore, the receipt of revenue in advance is recorded by a debit to Cash and a credit to Unearned Revenue. Unearned Revenue is a *liability* account, not a revenue account that appears in the income statement.

11 As the business renders the services for which the customers have already paid, it

earns this "unearned revenue," thereby reducing its liability to its customers. At the end of the period, an adjusting entry is made debiting (reducing) the Unearned Revenue account and crediting a revenue account for the portion of the advance payment earned during the period.

12 Adjustments to recognize **unrecorded expenses** are necessary whenever expenses have been incurred, but not yet recorded in the accounting records. These adjustments involve debiting an expense account (to record the expense), and crediting a liability account.

13 Common examples include the entries to recognize interest expense which has accrued over the period (debit Interest Expense, credit Interest Payable), and to record wages owed to employees for work performed since the last payday (debit Wages and Salaries Expense, credit Wages and Salaries Payable).

14 One special "unrecorded expense" adjustment is the one to record income taxes expense. In a profitable period, this adjusting entry consists of a debit to Income Taxes Expense and a credit to Income Taxes Payable. But an **un**profitable period may **reduce** a company's income tax expense and tax liability. Therefore, in an unprofitable period, this adjustment may consist of a **debit** to Income Taxes Payable, and a **credit** to Income Taxes Expense. In short, the entry in an unprofitable period is the **reverse** of the entry in a profitable period.

15 If at year-end, the Income Taxes Expense account has a **credit** balance, it is called "Income Tax Benefit," and, in effect, **increases** net income. (Actually, this tax benefit reduces the amount of net loss.) If the liability account Income Taxes Payable ends the year with a credit balance, it is renamed "Income Tax Refund Receivable" and is shown in the balance sheet as an **asset**. (Note: These treatments assume that the company is eligible for a refund of income taxes paid in prior years.)

16 Our final adjustment is to record revenue which has been earned, but not yet recorded. This adjustment is called an **unearned revenue** adjusting entry. Examples include interest revenue earned during the period, but

not yet received, or services which have been rendered to customers, but not yet billed. A law firm, for example, has unrecorded revenue for all of the work done for clients since the last "billing period."

17 Unearned revenue always is recorded by a debit to an account receivable and a credit to a revenue account.

18 The concept of **materiality** allows accountants to use estimated amounts and even to ignore other accounting principles if these actions will not have a "material" effect upon the financial statements. Accountants must be sure that all material items are properly reported in financial statements, but may account for **immaterial items** and events in the **easiest and most convenient manner**. The concept of materiality allows the use of estimates in end-of-period adjustments, or even ignoring adjusting entries for immaterial items.

19 An item is **material** if knowledge of the item might reasonably influence the decisions of users of financial statements. Whether or not a specific item is "material" is a matter of **professional judgment**, in which accountants consider such factors as the absolute and relative dollar amount of the item, the cumulative effect of all such items, and the nature of the item under consideration.

20 Once all adjusting entries have been journalized and posted, an adjusted trial balance is prepared to determine that the ledger is still in balance. As illustrated in Chapter 3, financial statement amounts can be drawn directly from the adjusted trial balance. After the financial statements have been prepared, the accounting cycle is completed by closing the accounts and preparing an after-closing trial balance.

21 A major step in preparing financial statements is drafting the **notes** which should accompany the statements. These notes should disclose any information that users of the statements may need to **interpret the statements properly**. Two items routinely disclosed are the useful lives used in depreciating major types of assets, and the due dates of major liabilities.

*22 A **worksheet** illustrates in one place the relationships between the unadjusted trial

---

*Supplementary Topic, "The Worksheet."

balance, and financial statements. A worksheet is simply a *spreadsheet*, which shows in columnar form the unadjusted trial balance, the effects of adjusting entries, adjusted trial balance, and the adjusted trial balance amounts arranged in the format of financial statements.

*23 Preparation of worksheet is *not* a step in the accounting cycle. Rather, it is simply a working paper (or software program) which enables accountants to "work out" the required adjusting entries. A completed worksheet is illustrated on page 172 of your textbook.

TEST YOURSELF ON YEAR-END PROCEDURES

True or False

For each of the following statements, circle the T or the F to indicate whether the statement is true or false.

T F   1 If all transactions were originally recorded in conformity with generally accepted accounting principles, there would be no need for adjusting entries at the end of the period.

T F   2 Adjusting entries contribute to accurate financial reporting by allocating revenues to the period in which they were earned and expenses to the period in which they were incurred.

T F   3 Every adjusting entry must change both an income statement account and a balance sheet account.

T F   4 An account called Unearned Commissions Revenue is a revenue account.

T F   5 Accrued revenue is a term used to describe revenue which has been received but not yet earned.

T F   6 The adjusting entry to allocate part of the cost of a one-year fire insurance policy to expense will cause total assets to increase.

T F   7 The adjusting entry to recognize that commission revenue not previously recorded (or billed to a customer) has now been earned will cause total assets to increase.

T F   8 The adjusting entry to recognize an expense which has not yet been recorded and will not be paid until some future period will cause total assets to decrease.

T F   9 The adjusting entry to recognize that a fee received in advance from a customer has now been earned will cause total liabilities to increase.

T F   10 If employees have worked eight days in a period for which they will not be paid until the first payday next period, and if no adjusting entry is made at the end of this period, total liabilities will be understated and both net income and owners' equity will be overstated.

T F   11 In a profitable period, the entry to record income taxes expense will *reduce* the amount of the company's net income and *increase* the amount of its liability for income taxes payable.

T F   12 In an unprofitable period, the entry to record income taxes expense will *reduce* the amount of the company's net loss and reduce the amount of its liability for income taxes payable.

T F   13 Income taxes normally have the effect of reducing *both* net income and net losses.

T F   14 The original cost of a building minus the accumulated depreciation is called the *book value*, or *carrying value*.

T F   15 The concept of *materiality* allows accountants to ignore transactions involving small dollar amounts.

T F   16 The dollar amounts appearing in financial statements can be taken directly from an adjusted trial balance.

T F   17 The dollar amounts appearing in financial statements cannot be determined until closing entries have been posted.

T F   18 Financial statements normally are accompanied by several pages of "notes" supplying additional information.

T F   *19 A worksheet illustrates the relationship between an unadjusted trial balance, adjusting entries, and the amounts appearing in financial statements.

T F   *20 Preparing a worksheet is a basic step in the accounting cycle.

Supplementary Topic, "The Worksheet."

T F *21 Worksheets are prepared only in manual accounting systems.

T F *22 In a worksheet, net income will appear as the balancing figure in the Income Statement debit column and the Balance Sheet credit column.

T F *23 A worksheet is better described as a tool for accountants than as a financial statement.

Completion Statements

Fill in the necessary words to complete the following statements:

1 The four types of transactions requiring adjusting entries are _____ _____, _____ _____, _____ _____, and _____ _____ transactions.

2 An adjusting entry at November 30 concerning the cost of an insurance policy serves two purposes: (a) it _____ the proper amount of _____ to November operations, and (b) it reduces the _____ account entitled _____ so that the correct amount will appear on the November 30 balance sheet.

3 Adjusting entries always recognize either a _____ or an _____.

4 The adjusting entry to record receiving some of the benefits in the current period from an expenditure made in an earlier period consists of a _____ to an _____ account and a _____ to an _____ account.

5 If a customer pays in advance for services to be rendered, the entry to record the receipt of the payment consists of a _____ to an _____ account and a _____ to a _____ account.

6 If an expense has been accumulating from day to day (such as wages) without being recorded, the proper adjusting entry would _____ an _____ account and _____ a _____ account.

7 If an expenditure will yield benefits to a business only during the period in which it is made, the entry for the expenditure consists of a _____ to an _____ account and a _____ to an _____ account and/or a _____ account.

8 If an expenditure will yield benefits to the business over several periods, the entry for the expenditure consists of a _____ to an _____ account and a credit to an _____ account and/or a _____ account.

9 The South Bay Management Company agreed to manage an apartment building beginning May 15, 19__, for one year at a management fee of $400 per month. The first $400 payment is received June 15, 19__. The adjusting entry at May 31, 19__ should consist of a debit to _____ _____ _____ and a credit to _____ _____ _____. When the first payment is received on June 15, the collection should be recorded by an entry debiting _____ for $400, and crediting _____ _____ _____ for $_____ and _____ _____ _____ for $_____.

*10 In the worksheet prepared by a business operating at a loss, the Income Statement _____ column will exceed the _____ column and the excess of the _____ over the _____ will be entered in the _____ column in order to bring the two Income Statement columns into balance.

Multiple Choice

Choose the best answer for each of the following questions and enter the identifying letter in the space provided.

_____ **1** The ***accounting period*** of a business may best be described as:
a One month.
b One year.
c The time span covered by the balance sheet.
d The time span covered by the income statement.

_____ **2** The purpose of ***adjusting entries*** is to:
a Correct errors made in the accounting records.
b Update the balance of the Retained Earnings account for changes in owners' equity temporarily recorded in revenue and expense accounts.

Supplementary Topic, "The Worksheet."

c Prepare the revenue and expense accounts for recording the transactions of the next accounting period.

d Allocate revenue and expenses among accounting periods when the related business transactions affect more than one period.

_____ 3 The entry recording the liability to employees for work done during the period for which they have not yet been paid is an example of which type of adjusting entry?

a Apportion recorded costs.

b Apportion unearned revenue.

c Record unrecorded expenses.

d Recorded unrecorded revenue.

_____ 4 A balance sheet account was debited in the amount of $1,240 for office supplies purchased during the first year of operations. At year-end, the office supplies on hand were counted and determined to represent a cost of $360. The appropriate adjusting entry would:

a Have no effect on net income.

b Consist of a debit to expense of $360 and a credit to the balance sheet account.

c Decrease assets by $1,240.

d Increase expenses $880.

_____ 5 Failure to make an adjusting entry to recognize accrued interest receivable would cause:

a An understatement of assets, net income, and owners' equity.

b An understatement of liabilities and an overstatement of net income and owners' equity.

c An overstatement of assets, net income, and owners' equity.

d No effect on assets, liabilities, net income, and owners' equity.

_____ 6 Assets would be overstated if a necessary adjusting entry were omitted for:

a Expired insurance.

b Accrued salaries.

c Accrued interest earned.

d Revenue collected in advance during the period.

_____ 7 Which of the following adjusting entries will result in a decrease in assets and owners' equity?

a The entry to record the earned portion of rent received in advance.

b The entry to record accrued wages payable.

c The entry to record revenue earned but not yet received.

d None of the above.

_____ 8 Which of the following statements concerning materiality is **not** valid?

a Generally accepted accounting principles do not provide clear-cut guidelines as to what is considered "material" in each situation.

b The concept of materiality may result in financial statements that are not completely precise.

c Strict adherence to the matching principle or the realization principle is not required for items considered "immaterial."

d The concept of materiality results in financial statements that are less useful to decision makers because many important details have been omitted or estimated.

_____ *9 The preparation of a **worksheet**:

a Constitutes creation of a formal financial statement.

b Eliminates the need for entering adjusting entries in the journal.

c Provides the information needed for journalizing adjusting and closing entries.

d Serves no purpose unless the books are to be closed.

_____ *10 When a worksheet is used, the normal sequence of accounting procedures would call for:

a Journalizing the adjusting entries before preparing the worksheet.

b Posting adjusting entries to the ledger after preparing an after-closing trial balance.

c Preparing a worksheet before journalizing adjusting and closing entries.

d Journalizing closing entries before preparing an adjusted trial balance.

_____ *11 Which of the following amounts appears in both the Income Statement credit column and the Balance Sheet debit column of a worksheet?

a Net income.

b Net loss.

c Accumulated depreciation.

d Dividends.

Exercises

1 Listed below are eight technical accounting terms emphasized in this chapter.

Accrued revenue	***Worksheet***
Unearned revenue	**Adjusting entries**
Accrued expense	**Closing entries**
Interim statements	**Notes accompanying financial statements**

Supplementary Topic, "The Worksheet."

Each of the following statements may (or may not) describe one of these technical terms. In the space provided below each statement, indicate the accounting term described, or answer "None" if the statement does not correctly describe any of the terms.

a An asset that becomes an expense as a good or service is used up.

_____

b An expense that has been incurred, but not yet paid.

_____

c A device for working out the end-of-period accounting procedures before adjusting and closing entries are entered into formal accounting records.

_____

d Corrections of errors in financial statements discovered after the annual report has been printed, but before it has been issued.

_____

e A liability that is usually settled by rendering services rather than by making cash payments.

_____

f Revenue which has been earned during the accounting period, but has not been recorded or collected.

_____

g Entries made to record revenue or expenses of the period that have not yet been recognized as a result of recording daily business transactions.

_____

2 Commuter Airlines prepares monthly financial statements. On August 31, the company's accountant made adjusting entries to record:

a Depreciation for the month of August.
b Earning ticket revenue which had been collected in advance. (When passengers buy tickets in advance, Commuter Airlines credits an account entitled Unearned Ticket Revenue.)
c The portion of the company's prepaid insurance policies which had expired in August.
d Salaries payable to employees which have accrued since the last payday in August.
e Interest revenue which had accrued on an investment in government bonds.
f A reduction in the company's income tax liability resulting from losses incurred in August.

Indicate the effect of each of these adjusting entries upon the major elements of the company's financial statements—that is, upon revenue, expenses, net income, assets, liabilities, and owners' equity. Organize your answer in tabular form, using the column headings provided and the symbols + for increase, − for decrease, and NE for no effect. The answer for adjusting entry **a** is provided as an example.

Adjusting entry	Income Statement			Balance Sheet			
	Revenue	− Expenses	= Net Income	Assets	= Liabilities	+ Owners' Equity
a	NE	+	−	−	NE	−
b						
c						
d						
e						
f						

*3 Use the following adjustments to complete the worksheet below for the month ended June 30, 19__.

a Unexpired insurance at June 30 amounted to $300.

b Office supplies on hand were determined by count to amount to $250.

c The office equipment is being depreciated on the basis of a 10-year life with no salvage value. Record one month's depreciation.

d Accrued interest on notes payable at June 30 amounted to $50.

e Commissions still unearned at June 30 amounted to $700.

f Accrued salaries payable at June 30 were $2,100.

g Income taxes applicable to taxable income earned in June are estimated at $2,400.

SOLANA CORPORATION
Worksheet
For the Month Ended June 30, 19__

	Trial Balance		Adjustments		Adjusted Trial Balance		Income Statement		Balance Sheet	
	Debit	Credit	Debit	Credit	Debit	Credit	Debit	Credit	Debit	Credit
Balance sheet accounts:										
Cash	15,960									
Accounts receivable	17,300									
Unexpired insurance	360									
Office supplies	900									
Office equipment	25,200									
Accumulated depreciation:										
office equipment		3,150								
Notes payable		10,000								
Accounts payable		1,800								
Unearned commissions		1,500								
Capital stock		15,000								
Retained earnings, June 1, 19__		17,000								
Dividends	5,000									
Interest payable										
Salaries payable										
Income taxes payable		8,000								
Income statement accounts:										
Commissions earned		21,670								
Rent expense	2,400									
Salaries expense	11,000									
	78,120	78,120								
Insurance expense										
Office supplies expense										
Depreciation expense: office equipment										
Interest expense										
Income taxes expense										
Net income										

SOLUTIONS TO CHAPTER 4 SELF-TEST

True or False

1 **F** Adjusting entries are needed whenever transactions affect the revenue or expense of more than one accounting period.

2 **T** Adjusting entries are a result of applying the realization principle and the matching principle.

3 **T** Every adjusting entry changes owners' equity by recognizing revenue or expense. Any change in owners' equity must be offset by a corresponding change in either assets or liabilities.

4 **F** Unearned Commissions Revenue represents amounts that have been received but have not been earned yet; it is a *liability* account.

5 **F** Accrued revenue describes revenue which *has been earned* but has not been recorded before the end of the period.

6 **F** As the total cost of the policy is gradually allocated to expense, total assets decrease.

7 **T** The adjusting entry consists of a debit to an asset account (a receivable) and a credit to a revenue account.

8 **F** The adjusting entry debits an expense account and credits a liability account; liabilities are increased.

9 **F** Fees received in advance are recorded as a liability; this liability is *reduced* as the fees are earned.

10 **T** The appropriate adjusting entry should have been a debit to Salaries Expense and a credit to Salaries Payable.

11 **T** In profitable periods, income taxes expense is a business expense which, like other expenses, reduces net income. Usually taxes must be paid at future dates. Therefore, the recording of income taxes expense is accompanied by an increase in the liability, Income Taxes Payable.

12 **T** In *un*profitable periods, companies often record *negative* income taxes expense, which reduces the amounts of the net loss for the period and of the company's income tax liability.

13 **T** Income taxes expense is a percentage of the income or loss before taxes. If there is income before taxes, income taxes are owed to the government, thus reducing the company's pre-tax income. But if there is a loss before taxes, income taxes from prior periods can be recovered, resulting in a tax benefit in the current period. This tax *benefit* reduces the amount of the pre-tax loss.

14 **T** Both of these terms refer to the *net* amount at which an asset is shown on the balance sheet.

15 **F** The concept of materiality allows accountants to use estimates and to account for immaterial items in the easiest and most convenient manner, but does not justify simply not recording transactions involving small dollar amounts.

16 **T** Adjusted account balances form the basis for the preparation of formal financial statements.

17 **F** Closing entries are prepared *after* the preparation of financial statements. In fact, financial statements include the balances of many accounts which are closed in the closing process.

18 **T** The notes contain information necessary for users to properly interpret the statements. These notes are part of the generally accepted accounting principle of adequate *disclosure*.

*19 **T** A worksheet begins with an unadjusted trial balance, shows the proposed adjusting entries, the adjusted account balances, and how these adjusted balances will be used in the preparation of financial statements.

*20 **F** A worksheet is really just "scratch paper" for making adjusting entries. Adjusting the accounts is a basic step in the accounting cycle, but it can be done without a worksheet.

*21 **F** Worksheets are often used in computer-based systems, though they would be called "spreadsheets."

*22 **T** In the Income Statement columns, net income is the balancing figure because it represents the difference between the totals of the revenue (credit) column and expense (debit) column. It also brings the balance sheet columns into balance because it represents an element of owners' equity (retained earnings) which previously was missing from the balance sheet columns.

---

*Supplementary Topic, "The Worksheet."

*23 T A worksheet is basically an accountant's "scratch paper." It is not a formal financial statement and seldom would be shown to anyone outside of the accounting department.

Completion Statements

1 Recorded costs, unearned revenue, unrecorded expenses, unrecorded revenue. **2 (a)** Allocates, expense, **(b)** asset, Unexpired Insurance. **3** Revenue, expense. **4** Debit, expense, credit, asset. **5** Debit, asset, credit, liability. **6** Debit, expense, credit, liability. **7** Debit, expense, credit, asset, liability. **8** Debit, asset, asset, liability. **9** Management Fees Receivable, Management Fees Earned, Cash, Management Fees Receivable, $200, Management Fees Earned, $200. **10** Debit, credit, debits, credits, credit.

Multiple Choice

1 Answer **d**—The period of time covered by the income statement. Answers **a** and **b** are incorrect because an accounting period is not limited to one specific time period. Some companies may use a month, while others use a quarter or a year. Answer **c** is incorrect because the balance sheet covers only a specific date, not an accounting period.

2 Answer **d**—when transactions affect the revenue or expenses of more than one period, adjusting entries are needed to allocate the effects of these transactions. Answer **a** is incorrect, because adjusting entries are needed even when no errors have been made in recording transactions. Answers **b** and **c** both describe the purpose of closing entries.

3 Answer **c**—record unrecorded expenses. Prior to making an adjusting entry, work done by employees since the last payroll date is an expense that has not yet been recorded in the accounting records.

4 Answer **d**—the adjusting entry would transfer the cost of supplies used ($1,240 − $360 = $880) from the asset account to an expense account.

5 Answer **a**—the entry to record accrued interest receivable increases total assets, revenue, and stockholders' equity. Therefore, failure to make this entry has the effects described in answer **a**.

6 Answer **a**—allocating expired insurance to expense reduces the asset account, Unexpired Insurance. Without this adjustment, the asset Unexpired Insurance would be overstated.

7 Answer **d**—the given answers all are incorrect. An adjustment that decreases owners' equity recognizes an expense; answers **a** and **c** relate to the recognition of revenue. Answer **b** recognizes expense, but increases a liability (wages payable) rather than decreasing an asset.

8 Answer **d**—by definition, a "material" item or event is one that might reasonably be expected to influence the decisions of financial statement users. All such material items must be reported properly; estimating or omitting immaterial details serves to make financial statements more useful in most cases, even if they are less precise. Materiality is a matter of professional judgment; GAAP do not provide definite materiality formulas to use in each situation.

*9 Answer **c**—a worksheet is a "scratch pad," from which accountants prepare formal adjusting and closing entries, as well as financial statements. It is not a formal financial statement, and does not eliminate the need to journalize and post the adjusting and closing entries. Answer **d** is incorrect, because a worksheet can be used to prepare interim financial statements even when the accounts are not being closed

*10 Answer **c**—the steps in the accounting cycle following preparation of a worksheet, listed in sequence, are: (1) prepare financial statements, (2) adjust and close the accounts, and (3) prepare an after-closing trial balance. Answer **d** is incorrect because the adjusted trial balance is part of the worksheet and is prepared before closing entries are journalized.

*11 Answer **b**—when a business incurs a net loss, the total of the debit column in the Income Statement columns of the work sheet exceeds the credit column. To bring these columns into balance, the amount of the loss is entered in the Income Statement credit column. Also, as a net loss reduces owners' equity, this amount is entered in the Balance Sheet debit column. Net income appears in the Income Statement debit column and

---

Supplementary Topic, "The Worksheet."

Balance Sheet credit column. Accumulated depreciation and dividends to not enter into the determination of net income and do not appear in the Income Statement columns.

Solutions to Exercises

1

a None (The statement describes either a *prepaid expense*, *depreciable asset*, or *recorded cost*.)

b Accrued expense

c Worksheet

d None. Notes accompanying financial statements contain additional information and are not used for correcting errors. If material errors were discovered, the annual report would be corrected and reprinted.

e Unearned revenue

f Accrued revenue

g Adjusting entries

2

Adjusting entry	Income Statement					Balance Sheet			
	Revenue	–	Net Expenses	=	Income	Assets	=	Liabilities	+ Owners' Equity
a	NE		+		–	–		NE	–
b	+		NE		+	NE		–	+
c	NE		+		–	–		NE	–
d	NE		+		–	NE		+	–
e	+		NE		+	+		NE	+
f	NE		–		+	NE		–	–

*3

SOLANA CORPORATION
Worksheet
For the Month Ended June 30, 19___

	Trial Balance Debit	Trial Balance Credit	Adjustments Debit	Adjustments Credit	Adjusted Trial Balance Debit	Adjusted Trial Balance Credit	Income Statement Debit	Income Statement Credit	Balance Sheet Debit	Balance Sheet Credit
Balance sheet accounts:										
Cash	15,960				15,960				15,960	
Accounts receivable	17,300				17,300				17,300	
Unexpired insurance	360			a 60	300				300	
Office supplies	900			b 650	250				250	
Office equipment	25,200				25,200				25,200	
Accumulated depreciation:										
office equipment		3,150		c 210		3,360				3,360
Notes payable		10,000				10,000				10,000
Accounts payable		1,800				1,800				1,800
Unearned commissions		1,500	e 800			700				700
Capital stock		15,000				15,000				15,000
Retained earnings, June 1, 19___		17,000				17,000				17,000
Dividends	5,000				5,000				5,000	
Interest payable				d 50		50				50
Salaries payable				f 2,100		2,100				2,100
Income taxes payable		8,000		g 2,400		10,400				10,400
Income statement accounts:										
Commissions earned		21,670		e 800		22,470		22,470		
Rent expense	2,400				2,400		2,400			
Salaries expense	11,000		f 2,100		13,100		13,100			
	78,120	78,120								
Insurance expense			a 60		60		60			
Office supplies expense			b 650		650		650			
Depreciation expense: office										
equipment			c 210		210		210			
Interest expense			d 50		50		50			
Income taxes expense			g 2,400		2,400		2,400			
			6,270	6,270	82,880	82,880	18,870	22,470	64,010	60,410
Net income							3,600			3,600
							22,470	22,470	64,010	64,010

ACCOUNTING FOR MERCHANDISING ACTIVITIES

HIGHLIGHTS OF THE CHAPTER

1 A *merchandising* company is one whose principal activity is buying and selling merchandise, or *inventory*. An inventory of merchandise consists of the stock of goods on hand and available for sale to customers. Inventory is a relatively liquid asset reported in the balance sheet immediately below accounts receivable. The same accounting concept and methods in use by the service-type business we studied in Chapters 1 to 4 are applicable to merchandising companies. A merchandising concern, however, requires some other accounts and techniques to control and record the purchase and sale of merchandise.

2 The *operating cycle* for a merchandising company is the period of time the business usually takes to perform its function of buying inventory, selling that inventory, and collecting the accounts receivable generated by those sales. This may be described as the period of time a business takes to convert cash into inventory, into accounts receivable, and then back into cash, as illustrated by the following diagram of the operating cycle:

(buy inventory)   (sell inventory)   (collect receivables)

Cash → Inventory → Accounts Receivable → Cash

3 Merchandising companies purchase their inventories from other business organizations in a *ready-to-sell* condition; companies that manufacture their inventories are called *manufacturers*. Merchandising companies include both *retailers*, who sell merchandise directly to the public, and *wholesalers*. Wholesalers buy large quantities of merchandise from several different manufacturers and then resell it to many retailers.

4 The principal source of revenue for a merchandising concern is from sale of goods. To succeed, it must sell its goods at prices higher than the prices paid in acquiring those goods from manufacturers or other suppliers. This cost is termed the *cost of goods sold*, and is an expense item of such importance that it is shown separately in the income statement of merchandising companies. The difference between revenue from sales and the cost of goods sold is called *gross profit*, which is not the same as net income. The company earns a net income only if the gross profit is large enough to cover the other expenses of the business.

5 A *subsidiary ledger* is an accounting record which shows separately the individual items which comprise the balance of a general ledger account. A general ledger account for which a subsidiary ledger is maintained is called a *controlling account*. Merchandising companies usually maintain the following subsidiary ledgers:

a Accounts Receivable subsidiary ledger, showing amount receivable from each customer;

b Accounts Payable subsidiary ledger, listing amount payable to each individual supplier;

c Inventory subsidiary ledger, listing separately a great many details about each product the company sells.

    In addition to the three mentioned above, subsidiary ledgers are maintained for many other general ledger accounts.

6 Portions of a journal entry that affect a subsidiary ledger account must be **double-posted**—that is, posted both to the subsidiary ledger account and to the controlling account in the general ledger. The posting to the general ledger account is indicated by entering the account number in the LP column of the journal. The posting to the subsidiary ledger account is indicated by entering a check mark ($\sqrt{}$) in the LP column.

7 Subsidiary ledgers are not used in the preparation of financial statements and are not made available to persons outside of the business organization. Periodically, a subsidiary ledger must be **reconciled** with the controlling account. That is, the sum of the subsidiary ledger account balances is determined to be equal to that of the controlling account. In a computer-based accounting system, the computer automatically reconciles the subsidiary ledgers with controlling accounts.

8 There are two alternative approaches to accounting for merchandising transactions: (a) the **perpetual inventory method**, and (b) the **periodic inventory method**. Virtually all large merchandising companies use the perpetual approach, in which the accounting records are kept perpetually up-to-date as merchandise is purchased and sold to customers.

9 In a **perpetual inventory system**, purchases of merchandise are debited to an asset account entitled Inventory. As each unit is sold, **two** entries are necessary. One recognizes the **revenue earned** by debiting Cash or Accounts Receivable and crediting the **Sales** account with the selling price of merchandise sold. The second transfers the cost of the unit from the Inventory account to an account entitled **Cost of Goods Sold**. Thus we have a perpetual or running record of the cost of goods sold during the period, as well as the cost of goods on hand (the balance in the Inventory account).

10 A perpetual inventory system usually includes an **inventory subsidiary ledger**, which contains a separate account (or "inventory card") for each type of product in the company's inventory. The Inventory controlling account balance is the aggregate cost of merchandise on hand; the inventory subsidiary ledger provides quantity and unit cost data on a product by product basis.

11 Although the Inventory account is continuously updated for all purchases and sales of merchandise in a perpetual inventory system, a complete physical count of the merchandise on hand is made at least once a year. **Taking a physical inventory** discloses discrepancies between the quantities shown in the inventory records and the quantities of merchandise actually on hand. The Inventory controlling account is adjusted to the cost of merchandise actually on hand by crediting Inventory and debiting the Cost of Goods Sold account for the dollar amount of the discrepancy, called **inventory shrinkage**. The inventory subsidiary ledger is simultaneously adjusted also.

12 The closing entries for a merchandising business with a perpetual inventory system parallel those covered previously for a service-type business. The Sales account is closed into the Income Summary along with other revenue accounts. The Cost of Goods Sold account is closed into the Income Summary in the same manner as other expense accounts.

13 Under the **periodic inventory system**, the cost of merchandise acquired is debited to an account entitled **Purchases**, instead of being debited to Inventory. As units are sold, **no entry is made to record the cost of goods sold**. Thus, the accounting records do not show from day to day the cost of the goods on hand (inventory) or the cost of goods sold during the period. Instead, the value of the inventory is determined only **periodically** at the end of each accounting period by taking a physical count of merchandise in stock.

14 In a periodic inventory system, the **cost of goods sold** is computed by the following steps:

a Add the goods on hand at the beginning of the period (the ending inventory from last period) plus any additional goods acquired during the period (purchases) to get the **cost of goods available for sale**.

b From the cost of goods available for sale, subtract the goods which were not sold (namely, the inventory on hand at the end of the current period) to get the **cost of goods sold** during the period.

15 The cost of goods sold section of the income statement of a merchandising company using the **periodic inventory method** would appear as follows for the month of May:

Inventory (Apr. 30)	$ 5,100
Purchases	6,300
Cost of goods available for sale	$11,400
Less: Inventory (May 31)	5,400
Cost of goods sold	$ 6,000

16 Once computed, the ending inventory and cost of goods sold must be recorded. (Remember, in a periodic system, the inventory account has not been adjusted for merchandise purchased or sold during the period, and no cost of goods sold has yet been recorded.) One approach is to create a Cost of Goods Sold account and adjust the Inventory account to the proper balance as part of the closing process.

17 The following two special closing entries may be used to create a Cost of Goods Sold account:

a Cost of Goods Sold XXX
  Inventory (beginning balance) XX
  Purchases XXX
  To close temporary accounts contributing to the cost of goods sold.

b Inventory (year-end balance) XXX
  Cost of Goods Sold XXX
  To reduce the balance of the Cost of Goods Sold account by the cost of merchandise still on hand at year-end.

The first brings together the costs contributing to the cost of goods sold; the second adjusts the cost of goods sold to its proper balance and records ending inventory in the Inventory account. Once the Cost of Goods Sold account and the Inventory account have the proper balances, the closing process is the same as for a company using a perpetual inventory system.

18 Although perpetual and periodic inventory systems produce the same results in annual financial statements, a perpetual system provides much useful information throughout the year that is not available in a periodic system.

a Ledger accounts for Inventory and for the Cost of Goods Sold are kept perpetually up-to-date in a perpetual system. Under the periodic system, the balance in the Inventory account does not change during the year as merchandise is purchased (remember a Purchases account is used) or sold. The cost of goods sold in a periodic system is deter-mined by a computation made at the end of the year

b A perpetual inventory system includes an inventory subsidiary ledger showing for each type of product the cost and quantities of units purchased, sold, and currently on hand. A periodic system does not include an inventory subsidiary ledger.

19 In addition to net income, two key measures used to evaluate performance of merchandising companies are trends in the company's **net sales** and **gross profit rate**. The trend in net sales from period to period is considered to be a key indicator of both past performance and future prospects. However, as some products are more profitable than others, increasing net sales alone is not enough to ensure increasing profitability. A company's **profit margin** (also called gross profit rate) is used to evaluate the profitability of sales transactions.

20 Profit margin is the dollar amount of gross profit expressed as a **percentage** of net sales revenue. Profit margins can be computed for the business as a whole, for specific departments, and for individual products. By concentrating sales efforts on the products and departments with the highest profit margins, management can increase the company's overall gross profit rate.

*21 Manufacturers and wholesalers normally sell merchandise on account and may offer a **cash discount** to encourage customers to pay invoices early. Credit terms of **2/10, n/30** would mean that customers may take a deduction of 2% of their invoice amount if they pay within 10 days. Otherwise, they have 30 days to pay the full amount of the invoice. A cash discount is called a **purchase discount** by the buyer and a **sales discount** by the seller.

*22 Most well-managed companies have a policy of taking advantage of all cash discounts available on purchases of merchandise, and therefore record purchases at the **net cost**—invoice price less any available cash discount. For example, if $1,000 of merchandise is purchased on terms of 2/10, n/30, Inventory is debited and Accounts Payable credited for $980, the net cost after discount. If the invoice is paid within 10 days, the purchaser simply records payment of a $980 account payable. If the invoice is not paid within 10 days, the purchaser must pay $1,000, rather

---

Supplemental Topic, "Additional Merchandising Transactions."

than the recorded liability of $980, and a $20 **Purchase Discounts Lost** is debited and treated as a nonoperating expense in the income statement.

*23 As an alternative to recording purchases at net cost, some companies record merchandise purchases at the gross invoice price. If payment is made within the discount period, these companies record the amount of the purchase discount **taken**. Purchase discounts taken is treated as a reduction in the cost of goods sold. Since the gross price method records only purchase discounts taken, it does not direct management's attention to discounts lost.

*24 When merchandise purchased is found to be unsatisfactory and returned to the supplier, the return is recorded by debiting Accounts Payable and crediting Inventory for the net cost of the returned items.

*25 The freight charges on goods acquired during the period are a legitimate part of the cost of the asset being acquired. Because it may be impractical to determine the portion of a shipping charge relating to specific product in inventory, many companies follow the convenient policy of debiting all transportation costs on **inbound** shipments to an account entitled **Transportation-in**. This amount is generally included in the amount reported as cost of goods sold in the income statement. Do not confuse Transportation-in with the delivery expense on **outbound** shipments. Freight on outbound shipments is a **selling expense,** not part of the cost of goods being acquired.

*26 The customers of the merchandising company may occasionally find that the goods they bought are unsatisfactory. If the customer agrees to keep the merchandise but is granted a reduction in price (a sales allowance), a **contra-revenue** account called Sales Returns and Allowances is debited and Cash (or Accounts Receivable) is credited for the amount of the price reduction. If the customer returns the merchandise, the above entry as well as an additional entry debiting Inventory and crediting Cost of Goods Sold for the cost of the returned merchandise must be made.

*27 As mentioned earlier, sellers frequently offer cash discounts to encourage their customers to pay early for purchases on account. Sellers design their accounting systems to measure the sales discounts **taken** by their customers, and consequently record the sale and account receivable at the **gross (full) invoice price**. If customers pay invoices within the discount period, a **contra-revenue** account, Sales Discounts, is debited for the amount of cash discount taken by the customer.

*28 Sales taxes are levied by most states and cities on retail sales. These taxes are imposed upon the consumer, not the seller. The seller must collect the tax at each sale, file sales tax returns, and remit the taxes collected on all taxable sales. The retailer may credit a liability account, Sales Taxes Payable, as each sale is made, **or** may wait until the end of the period and compute the tax liability as a percentage of total sales.

TEST YOURSELF ON MERCHANDISING ACTIVITIES

True or False

For each of the following statements, circle the T or the F to indicate whether the statement is true or false.

T F 1 The operating cycle of a business is the period of time between payroll dates.

T F 2 Gross profit is the profit the business would have made if all the goods available for sale had been sold during the period.

T F 3 When a cash sale is made by a merchandising business, the revenue is recorded by a debit to Cash and a credit to sales, whether or not the sales price exceeded the cost of the goods sold.

T F 4 The gross profit rate is computed by dividing net sales by gross profit.

T F 5 A subsidiary ledger is used to account for items that are immaterial or of less significance than those recorded in the general ledger controlling account.

T F 6 Although general ledger accounts are used in the preparation of financial statements, the information contained in subsidiary ledgers must be disclosed in footnotes to the financial statements.

---

*Supplemental Topic, "Additional Merchandising Transactions."

T F 7 The perpetual inventory method will reflect from day to day the cost of goods sold thus far during the period and the current balance of goods on hand.

T F 8 When a perpetual inventory system is in use, the accounting records contain an account, Cost of Goods Sold, which must be closed at the end of the accounting period.

T F 9 The perpetual inventory system is appropriate not only for businesses handling high unit cost goods, such as automobiles or fur coats, but also practical for stores with a computerized system handling a large quantity of low-priced items.

T F 10 When the periodic inventory method is used, the Inventory account is debited when merchandise is purchased and credited when goods are sold.

T F 11 In a periodic inventory system, the purchase of either merchandise or office equipment by a merchandising concern would be recorded a debit to Purchases and a credit to either Cash or Accounts Payable.

T F 12 When a periodic inventory system is in use, the cost of goods sold section contains two amounts for Inventory: a beginning inventory which is added in arriving at the cost of goods available for sale, and an ending inventory which is subtracted to determine the cost of goods sold.

T F 13 When a periodic inventory system is used, the beginning inventory figure in this period's cost of goods sold computation was the ending inventory figure in last period's computation.

T F 14 When a periodic inventory system is in use, the income statement will report the "Cost of Goods Sold" even though the accounting records do not use a Cost of Goods Sold account on an ongoing basis.

T F 15 The term "net sales" means gross sales less the cost of goods sold.

T F 16 A company with a trend of steadily increasing net sales has increasing profitability.

T F *17 The Transportation-in account contains the freight charges paid on inbound shipments of merchandise and is generally included in the amount reported in the income statement as the cost of goods sold.

T F *18 Sales Returns and Allowances and Sales Discounts accounts are contra-revenue accounts and will have debit balances.

T F *19 The income statement of a retail store usually includes a deduction for sales tax expense.

T F *20 When a customer pays an amount which includes sales tax, part of the total receipts represents a liability rather than revenue.

Completion Statements

Fill in the necessary words to complete the following statements:

1 The period of time a business usually takes to convert cash into inventory, then into receivables, and finally back into cash is called the _____ _____.

2 In a periodic inventory system, adding net purchases to the beginning inventory gives the _____ ____ _____ _____ _____. Subtracting _____ _____ from this figure leaves the _____ ____ _____ _____.

3 The excess of sales revenue over the cost of goods sold is called _____ _____.

4 The Inventory account is debited when goods are acquired and credited when they are sold according to the _____ inventory method. Inventory is determined solely by a _____ _____ when the _____ inventory method is used.

5 _____ _____ is the dollar amount of gross profit expressed as a percentage of _____ _____.

6 When merchandising companies record all purchases at **net cost**, the accounting system is set up to keep track of _____ _____ _____. If purchases are recorded at **gross invoice price**, the accounting system keeps track of _____ _____ _____.

*7 The return of merchandise to Cougar Company by a customer would be recorded on Cougar Company's books as a debit to _____ _____ _____ _____ and a credit to

either _____ or _____ _____.
An additional entry debiting _____
and crediting _____ ___ _____ _____ is
necessary in a perpetual inventory system.

*8 Glass Maker sells merchandise to Kay, Inc.,
for $2,000, at terms of 2/10, n/30. Kay, Inc.,
makes payment one week after the date of
invoice by sending a check for $_____. The
entry to be made by Glass Maker upon receipt of the check would consist of a debit to
cash for $_____, a _____ to_____
_____ for $_____, and a credit to
_____ _____ for $_____.

*9 There are two ways to account for state sales
taxes; either (a) credit a _____ account
for the amount of the tax at the time of sale
or (b) wait until the end of the period and
transfer the total tax owed out of the _____
account and into an account called _____
_____ _____.

Multiple Choice

Choose the best answer for each of the following
questions and enter the identifying letter in the
space provided.

_____ **1** Carter Stores must determine how
much it owes Hawkins Wholesale, one of Carter's
merchandise suppliers, as of December 31, 1995.
This information can be found **most directly** by
examining:
a Carter's accounts receivable subsidiary ledger.
b Carter's accounts payable subsidiary ledger.
c Carter's inventory subsidiary ledger.
d The current liability section of Carter's balance sheet as of December 31, 1995.

_____ **2** Which of the following statements is
not descriptive of the perpetual inventory
system?
a The amount of ending inventory is determined
only by physical count and the cost of goods
sold is determined by a computation made at
year-end.
b Two entries are made when merchandise is
sold.
c A ledger account keeps track of the cost of
goods sold during the period.
d The Inventory account balance is adjusted
each time merchandise is purchased or sold
during the period.

_____ **3** The inventory subsidiary ledger:
a As well as the Inventory controlling account
appears in the current asset section of the balance sheet.

b As well as the Inventory controlling account
must be adjusted each time merchandise is
purchased or sold in a perpetual inventory
system.
c Is used to keep track of inventory items not
accounted for in the Inventory controlling account.
d Is an integral part of a periodic inventory system.

_____ **4** When a perpetual inventory system is
used:
a The dollar amount of inventory shrinkage is
more difficult to determine than in a periodic
inventory system.
b Inventory shrinkage is more likely to occur
than in a periodic inventory system..
c Both the Inventory controlling account and
the inventory subsidiary ledger accounts are
adjusted to agree with the quantities determined by the physical inventory.
d Taking a physical inventory is not necessary
since up-to-date inventory and cost of goods
sold information is provided by the accounting
records.

Assume use of a *periodic* inventory system for 5 and 6.

_____ **5** By adding the purchases during the
period to the beginning inventory and deducting
the ending inventory, we obtain an amount
called the:
a Cost of goods available for sale.
b Cost of goods sold.
c Gross profit on sales.
d Operating expenses.

_____ **6** The ending inventory of Bar Marine
was $42,000. If the beginning inventory had been
$50,000 and the cost of goods available for sale
during the period totaled $104,000, the cost of
goods sold must have been:
a $196,000.
b $112,000.
c $62,000.
d None of the above.

_____ **7** The net sales of Austin Saddlery were
$200,000 for the current month. If the cost of
goods available for sale was $180,000 and the
gross profit rate was 35%, the cost of goods sold
must have been:
a $70,000.
b $130,000.
c $50,000.
d $63,000.

---

*Supplemental Topic, "Additional Merchandising Transactions."

_____ **8** The net sales of Regent Musical Supply in October were $20,000. Regent Musical Supply uses a periodic inventory system. If the cost of goods available for sale during the month was $18,000, and the gross profit was $8,000, the ending inventory must have been:
a $4,800.
b $6,000.
c $10,000.
d Some other amount.

_____ **9** Which of the following would be _least_ useful in evaluating a company's profitability?
a Profit margin for the current year.
b Trend in profit margins for the most recent 5-year period.
c Trend in earnings for the most recent 5-year period
d Net sales for the current year.

_____ ***10** Gourmet Groceries purchased canned goods at an invoice price of $1,000 and terms of 2/10, n/30. Half of the goods were mislabeled and therefore were returned immediately to the supplier. If Gourmet Groceries pays the invoice within the discount period, the amount paid will be:
a $1,000.
b $980.
c $480.
d $490.

_____ ***11** The Sales Discounts account:
a Is a credit balance account deducted from purchases on the income statement.
b Is credited at time of collection if merchandise is paid for within the discount period.
c Is a contra-revenue account deducted from gross sales on the income statement.
d Is debited at the time of each credit sale.

Exercises

1 Listed below are eight technical accounting terms emphasized in this chapter.

> _Net sales_
> _Periodic inventory system_
> _Gross profit_
> _Perpetual inventory system_
> _Cost of goods sold_
> _Inventory subsidiary ledger_
> _Gross profit rate_
> _Inventory shrinkage_

Each of the following statements may (or may not) describe one of these technical terms. In the space provided below each statement, indicate the accounting term described, or answer "None" if the statement does not correctly describe any of the terms.

a An item readily apparent upon taking a physical inventory in a perpetual inventory system, but difficult to determine in a periodic system.

_____

b Gross sales revenue less sales discounts and sales returns and allowances.

_____

c Beginning inventory, plus the delivered cost of goods purchased, minus ending inventory.

_____

d An accounting record generally not used in a periodic inventory system.

_____

e Net sales less the cost of merchandise sold.

_____

f Gross profit expressed as a percentage of net income.

_____

g System of accounting for merchandise in which a Purchases ledger account is not used.

_____

2 White Feather Corporation uses a _perpetual_ inventory system. For each of the following merchandising transactions, give the title of the account(s) that are to be debited and credited in recording each transaction. (You may ignore sales taxes.)

Transaction	Account(s) Debited	Account(s) Credited
a Purchased merchandise for cash.		
b Sold merchandise on account.		
c Collected cash from customer in **b** above.		
d Sold merchandise for cash.		
e A physical inventory at year-end disclosed a normal amount of inventory shrinkage.		

---

*Supplemental Topic, "Additional Merchandising Transactions."

3 Alcala Corporation uses a *periodic* inventory system. Each of the following four horizontal lines represents data taken from a separate multiple-step income statement. Insert the missing amount in the space provided. Indicate a net loss by placing brackets around the amount, as for example, in line **a**, (20,000).

	Net Sales	Cost of Goods Available for Sale	Ending Inventory	Cost of Goods Sold	Gross Profit	Operating and Non-Operating Expenses	Net Income or (Loss)
a	$400,000	$325,000	$ ____	$250,000	$ ____	$ ____	$(20,000)
b	700,000	____	90,000	____	290,000	235,000	____
c	250,000	210,000	____	____	72,000	105,000	____
d	____	____	82,000	$330,000	____	185,000	35,000

4 Kids' World sell children's furniture and clothing. The following information is available for sales during the month of May:

	Furniture	Clothing
Net sales	$6,400	$3,600
Cost of Goods Sold	4,160	1,440

Compute for May the profit margin (gross profit rate) for:

a Furniture sales ____%

b Clothing sales ____%

c The company as a whole ____%

SOLUTIONS TO CHAPTER 5 SELF-TEST

True or False

1 **F** The operating cycle of a business is the period of time between the purchase of merchandise and the conversion of this merchandise back into cash.

2 **F** Gross profit is the difference between revenue from sales and the cost of the goods sold.

3 **T** Sales revenue is the selling price of goods, not the cost of those goods to the seller.

4 **F** The gross profit rate is computed by dividing gross profit by net sales.

5 **F** A subsidiary ledger shows separately the *individual items* which comprise the balance of a general ledger controlling account.

6 **F** The information contained in subsidiary ledgers in not made available to persons outside the business organization and therefore would not appear in the financial statements or notes to the financial statements.

7 **T** The Cost of Goods Sold account keeps an up-to-date record of the cost of all merchandise sold; the Inventory account is continually adjusted each time merchandise is purchased from suppliers or sold to customers.

8 **T** The Cost of Goods Sold account keeps track of the cost of merchandise sold on an ongoing basis. It is a debit balance account which is closed into Income Summary at the end of the period along with other expense accounts.

9 **T** The perpetual inventory system requires recording the cost of each sale as it occurs. This approach is now feasible for stores handling large quantities of merchandise due to the use of computerized systems.

10 **F** The Inventory account is updated continually under the *perpetual* inventory system.

11 **F** The Purchases account is used only for merchandise acquired for resale.

12 **T** Beginning inventory plus net purchases equals cost of goods available for sale less ending inventory equals the cost of goods sold.

13 **T** The ending inventory of one period is the beginning inventory of the next period.

14 **T** In a periodic inventory system, the cost of goods sold reported in the income statement is determined by a computation, as illustrated in Highlight 15. The accounting records do not keep track of the cost of goods sold as merchandise is sold during the period. Some companies create a Cost of Goods Sold account and adjust the Inventory account to the proper balance during the closing process, but this account is then closed into Income Summary and is not used during the period to accumulate the cost of merchandise sold.

15 **F** Net sales is equal to the balance of the Sales revenue account (gross sales), less some minor adjustments for transactions such as refunds to customers. Net sales less the cost of goods sold is equal to gross profit.

16 **F** Net sales is a dollar amount of sales volume. The dollar amount of sales may increase by simply selling merchandise at very low prices, even at prices that may not cover the cost of merchandise. In such cases, profitability may actually be decreasing while the dollar amount of net sales increases. The trend in profit margin on sales is a better indicator of a company's profitability than is the trend in net sales dollars.

*17 **T** Transportation charges are part of the *delivered cost* of goods purchased. Although technically some of this cost applies to merchandise still in inventory, the concept of materiality justifies including the entire Transportation-in amount in cost of goods sold.

*18 **T** These items are deducted from gross sales revenue (a credit balance account) in the income statement.

*19 **F** Sales taxes are imposed upon the consumer, not upon the seller. The seller collects the tax from customers and records a liability (Sales Tax Payable) which is paid when the seller remits the tax collected to the taxing authority.

*20 **T** The sales tax portion of the receipts represents a liability (Sales Tax Payable).

Completion Statements

1 Operating cycle. **2** Cost of goods available for sale, ending inventory, cost of goods sold. **3** Gross profit. **4** Perpetual, physical count, periodic. **5** Profit margin, net sales. **6** Pur-

---

*Supplemental Topic, "Additional Merchandising Transactions."

chase discounts lost, purchase discounts taken. *7 Sales Returns and Allowances, Cash, Accounts Receivable Inventory, Cost of Goods Sold. *8 $1,960; $1,960; debit; Sales Discounts; $40; Accounts Receivable; $2,000. *9(a) Liability, (b) Sales, Sales Tax Payable.

Multiple Choice

1 Answer **b**—the accounts payable subsidiary ledger contains an account for each creditor, showing amount owed. The accounts receivable subsidiary ledger shows amounts due to Carter from each credit customer; the inventory subsidiary ledger shows for each product the quantities, per-unit costs, and total costs of all units purchased, sold, and currently on hand. Carter's balance sheet reports only aggregate accounts payable as of December 31, 1995. (Hawkins' accounts receivable subsidiary ledger would also show how much Carter owes Hawkins.)

2 Answer **a** is descriptive of the periodic inventory system. In addition to recording the sale, an entry is made to record the cost of the merchandise sold under the perpetual inventory system. A ledger account entitled Cost of Goods sold is debited and Inventory is credited **each time** a sale is made when using a perpetual inventory system.

3 Answer **b**—when merchandise is sold in a perpetual inventory system, the Inventory controlling account is credited for the cost of merchandise sold; the inventory subsidiary ledger is adjusted concurrently to reflect the specific items no longer in inventory. Since the inventory subsidiary ledger provides the detail comprising the balance in the Inventory controlling account, answer **c** is not accurate. Answer **a** would lead to a double counting of inventory in the balance sheet. Answer **d** is incorrect because periodic inventory systems do not generally use an inventory ledger

4 Answer **c**—if the quantities of merchandise determined by the physical inventory differ from the perpetual inventory records, the accounting records are adjusted to reflect actual amounts. In a periodic inventory system, inventory shrinkage is included in the amount computed to be the cost of goods sold, and is difficult to isolate. Inventory shrinkage does not depend upon the type of inventory accounting method in use, hence answer **b** is inaccurate. (It might be the case, however, that shrinkage due to employee theft is more likely in a periodic system where the dollar amount of "shrinkage" is difficult to isolate because there are no perpetual records with which to compare the physical count.) Even in a perpetual system, a physical inventory is taken at least annually.

5 Answer **b**—beginning inventory plus purchases (net of any discount and purchase returns and allowance) is the formula for cost of goods **available** (answer **a**). Answer **c** is computed by deducting cost of goods sold from net sales.

6 Answer **c**—cost of goods sold is computed by deducting ending inventory ($42,000) from the cost of goods available for sale ($104,000). Since you are given the amount of cost of goods available for sale in the problem data, you do **not** have to use the beginning inventory amount provided in solving this problem.

7 Answer **b**—since net sales were $200,000, gross profit was $70,000 (35% of $200,000) and the cost of goods sold must have been $130,000 ($200,000 net sales minus $70,000 gross profit).

8 Answer **b**—net sales ($20,000) less gross profit ($8,000) equals cost of goods sold of $12,000. If the cost of goods available for sale is $18,000 and the cost of goods sold is $12,000, the cost of goods not sold (ending inventory) must be $6,000.

9 Answer **d**—trend analysis and profit margin (on current year net sales) are more meaningful statistics than simply the dollar amount of net sales for a particular year.

*10 Answer **d** is the invoice price of half of the goods not returned, less the 2% discount on this invoice price (2% times $500 equals $10 discount; $500 less $10 discount is the amount paid of $490). Gourmet Groceries receives a 2% discount on the price of the goods they kept, not on the entire original order.

*11 Answer **c** is the only accurate statement about the Sales Discounts account. Answer **a** describes the Purchase Discounts account. Answer **b** is incorrect because the Sales Discounts account is **debited** when customers pay within the discount period. The Sales Discounts account is debited at time of collection not at time of sale as indicated in answer **d**.

Solutions to Exercises

1
a Inventory shrinkage
b Net sales
c Cost of goods sold
d Inventory subsidiary ledger
e Gross profit
f None (Gross profit rate (profit margin) is current year gross profit expressed as a percentage of current year net sales.)
g Perpetual inventory system

2

Transaction	Account(s) Debited	Account(s) Credited
a Purchased merchandise for cash.	Inventory	Cash
b Sold merchandise on account.	Accounts Receivable Cost of Goods Sold	Sales Inventory
c Collected cash from customer in **b** above.	Cash	Accounts Receivable
d Sold merchandise for cash.	Cash Cost of Goods Sold	Sales Inventory
e A physical inventory at year-end disclosed a normal amount of inventory shrinkage.	Cost of Goods Sold	Inventory

3

	Net Sales	Cost of Goods Available for Sale	Ending Inventory	Cost of Goods Sold	Gross Profit	Operating and Non-operating Expenses	Net Income or (Loss)
a	$400,000	$325,000	$75,000	$250,000	$150,000	$170,000	$(20,000)
b	700,000	500,000	90,000	410,000	290,000	235,000	55,000
c	250,000	210,000	32,000	178,000	72,000	105,000	(33,000)
d	550,000	412,000	82,000	330,000	220,000	185,000	35,000

4
a $6,400 – $4,160) ÷ $6,400 = 35%
b ($3,600 – $1,400) ÷ $3,600 = 60%
c ($6,400 + $3,600) – ($4,160 + $1,440) = $4,400;
$4,400 gross profit ÷ $10,000 total sales = 44%

6

ACCOUNTING SYSTEMS, INTERNAL CONTROL, AND AUDITS

HIGHLIGHTS OF THE CHAPTER

1 An *accounting system* consists of the personnel, procedures, devices and records used by an entity to develop accounting information and to communicate this information to decision makers. Although the structure and capabilities vary greatly from one organization to another, the basic purpose remains the same: *to meet the organization's needs for accounting information as efficiently as possible*. The two most important factors affecting the structure of an accounting system for a specific business entity are (a) the company's needs for accounting information, and (b) the resources available for operation of the system.

2 Factors such as the size of the organization and whether it is publicly owned, as well as management's philosophy, affect the type of accounting information which a company must generate. Some types of accounting information are prescribed by law, such as income and sales tax returns and SEC filings. The type, volume, and detail of other accounting information generated depends upon how *useful* management considers the information to be and the *cost* of developing the information.

3 Accounting systems should be *cost-effective*—the value of the information produced should *exceed the cost* of producing it. In many cases, the installation of a computer-based system not only increases the amount of accounting information available to management on a timely basis, but also *reduces* the cost of developing it.

4 Whether manual or computer-based, every accounting system performs the following basic functions:

a *Record* the effects of business transactions.

b *Classify* the effects of similar transactions to permit development of totals and subtotals needed for internal and external reporting purposes.

c *Summarize and communicate* the data contained in the system in a manner useful to decision makers.

5 Although small businesses usually purchase a "packaged" accounting system ready to use in their particular line of business, medium and large businesses often hire CPAs or maintain a staff of systems analysts to custom design accounting systems for their operations. The design of accounting systems is a field of specialization within the field of accounting.

6 In the preceding chapters we used the journal entry as a tool for analyzing the effects of various financial transactions and recorded each in the *general journal*. Although the general journal is flexible in that all types of transactions may be recorded, this approach is usually not cost-effective. Every general journal entry requires writing at least two account titles and an explanation of the transaction. In addition, the person maintaining a general journal must have sufficient skill to analyze and record all types of transactions. Through the use of *special journals* a business can speed up and simplify the recording process.

7 A special journal is an accounting record or device designed to record a *particular type*

of transaction quickly and efficiently. The person maintaining the special journal need not be an expert in accounting, since only one type of transaction is recorded in each special journal. Two points are basic to the design of an efficient special journal:

a The person recording the transaction should have to enter *as little data as possible*.

b The recording of transactions should be *combined with other essential business activities* to minimize time and effort involved in the accounting function.

8 Special journals may exist in several different forms, such as manual cash receipts or cash payments journals, mechanical cash registers, and electronic point-of-sale terminals. (Manual special journals are illustrated and explained in Appendix B of the textbook.)

9 In an *on-line, real-time (OLRT)* computer system, accounting records are updated instantly as business transactions are recorded through on-line input devices. An input device is "on-line" when it has direct and immediate access to the computer-based accounting records. A point-of-sale terminal is an example of an "on-line" input device. An OLRT system allows managers and other company personnel to view through computer terminals accounting information which is absolutely *current*.

10 Within an accounting system, data are usually classified and stored by one of two methods: (a) ledger accounts, or (b) computerized data bases.

11 *Ledger accounts* The phrase *chart of accounts* refers to the number and titles of the ledger accounts used by the business. The extent of detail included in the chart of accounts depends primarily upon the types of information management deems appropriate. A *responsibility accounting system* includes a chart of accounts designed along the lines of managerial responsibility to enable evaluation of the performance of individual departments and managers. The detailed composition of specific assets, liabilities, revenue, and expenses usually is accounted for in *subsidiary ledgers*, with only the related *controlling account* appearing in the general ledger.

12 *Data base systems* Transaction data stored in a data base may be sorted into many different categories according to a variety of criteria, hence a data base provides greater *flexibility* than does even a highly detailed chart of accounts. A data base consists of *unclassified* data, not yet grouped into categories. The data are accompanied by various classification *codes* which enable the computer to sort the data according to management's information needs.

13 In a ledger-based system, the effects of transactions are classified *at the time of the transaction* into specific ledger accounts; in a data base, data are stored in an *unclassified* format. A data base is not a substitute for a ledger. It is intended to provide additional information about certain types of transactions in a variety of formats.

14 The usefulness of accounting information depends upon three factors:

a The *relevance* of the information to the decisions at hand,

b The *timeliness* of the information, and

c Its *reliability*.

Recent advancements in the technologies of computers and communications have greatly enhanced the relevance and timeliness of accounting information.

15 Computers can perform routine tasks, such as posting, arithmetic computations, and the preparation of schedules, with incredible speed and accuracy. This speed creates several advantages over manual accounting systems, including the following:

a Large amounts of data can be processed quickly and efficiently.

b Account balances may be kept up-to-date.

c Additional information may be developed at virtually no additional cost.

d Instant feedback may be available as transactions are taking place.

e Additional internal control procedures may be possible in a computer-based system.

The table on page 250 in your text summarizes additional differences between a simple manual accounting system and a computer-based system.

16 A *system of internal control* consists of all steps taken to (a) safeguard resources against waste, fraud, or inefficient use; (b) ensure reliability in accounting data; (c) promote compliance with company policies; and (d) evaluate the level of performance in all divisions of the business. In short, a system of internal control consists of all measures taken by management to provide assurance that everything goes according to plan.

17 The accounting system depends upon internal control procedures to ensure the *reliability* of accounting data. Concurrently, many internal control procedures made use of accounting data in monitoring performance and keeping track of assets.

18 Internal controls may be classified into two categories:

a *Accounting controls* These are the internal controls which have a direct bearing upon the reliability of the financial statements. Accounting controls include the measures concerned with safeguarding assets, authorizing and approving transactions, and the reliability of accounting data. An example of an accounting control is the requirement that a person whose duties include handling cash shall not be responsible for maintaining accounting records.

b *Administrative controls* These are internal controls that apply primarily to operational efficiency and compliance with company policies but have *no* direct bearing upon the reliability of the financial statements. Examples of administrative controls include rules that no employees be required to work more than a specified number of consecutive hours and policies regarding refund and exchanges of merchandise by customers.

19 No "standard" system of internal control can be designed to fit all businesses; each system must be "tailor-made" to fit the needs of the organization. However, there are several basic concepts of internal control which apply to most businesses. These include:

a *A logical organization plan* This should clearly indicate the departments or persons responsible for such functions as purchasing, receiving incoming shipments, maintaining accounting records, handling cash, and approving customers' credit. A separate person (or department) should be responsible for each function. Lines of responsibility and authority can be shown by an *organization chart.*

b *Routine procedures* Each transaction should go through four steps: it should be *authorized, approved, executed,* and *recorded.*

c *Adequate subdivision of duties* No one person or department should handle all aspects of a transaction from beginning to end. When several people are involved in each transaction, the work of one employee tends to serve as a check upon the work of another.

Basic to this item is the concept that an employee who has custody of an asset (or access to an asset) should not maintain the accounting records for that asset.

d *An internal audit staff* Internal auditors have as their objective improving the operational efficiency of the business. They continuously study and evaluate both accounting and administrative controls and make recommendations to management for improving the system.

e *Preparation of financial forecasts* Internal control is strengthened by the use of financial forecasts because errors or irregularities which cause actual results to differ from planned results will be identified and investigated.

f *Personnel with competence and integrity* No system of internal control will work unless the people assigned to operate it are competent. Rotation of employees often brings to light errors or irregularities caused by employees formerly performing a given task.

g *Use of serially numbered documents* Serial numbers help keep track of all documents in a sequence. Without serial numbers, no one would know how many documents had been written or whether some had been lost or concealed.

20 While strong internal control calls for the division of duties among departments, it is necessary for these departments to know what the other departments are doing so that they may work efficiently together. Carefully designed business documents are used to coordinate the efforts of the departments and ensure that all transactions are properly authorized, approved, executed, and recorded.

21 A *purchase requisition* is issued by the sales department manager or the stores department (warehousing) when the quantity of goods on hand falls below an acceptable level. The purchase requisition (original) is sent to the purchasing department as *authorization to order goods.* A copy of the purchase requisition is sent to the accounting department.

22 A *purchase order* should always be prepared by the purchasing department when ever goods are ordered. One copy of the purchase order is sent to the supplier; this is the supplier's authorization to send the goods. Copies of the purchase order go to the department that initiated the purchase requisition and to the accounting department.

23 The seller of the goods prepares an *invoice* when a purchase order is received. The invoice describes the quantities and price of goods which will be sent to the buyer. From the viewpoint of the seller an invoice is a *sales invoice*; from the buyer's viewpoint it is a *purchase invoice*. The seller mails the invoice to the buyer at the same time the goods are shipped. At the time the invoice is issued the seller of the goods will record the sale.

24 The goods will arrive at the receiving department of the buyer. The receiving department will inspect the goods as to quality, condition, and quantities received. A *receiving report* is then prepared and sent to the accounting department.

25 The accounting department will then *verify* the invoice to see if payment should be made. Verifying an invoice consists of three basic steps:

a Comparing the invoice with the purchase order to see that the goods were actually ordered at the terms stated on the invoice.

b Comparing the receiving report with the purchase order and the invoice to see that all the goods were received in satisfactory condition.

c Verifying the arithmetic extensions and footings of the invoice.

The person who performs these steps sign an *invoice approval form* authorizing payment of the invoice by the finance department. At this time, the accounting department also records the purchase and the related liability.

26 If any discrepancy exists between the amount the buyer is willing to pay and the amount of the invoice, the buyer will send a *debit memorandum* to the seller. This is notice to the seller that the buyer is debiting (reducing) the *account payable on the buyer's books*. The seller will respond with a credit memorandum to show that the corresponding *account receivable on the selling company's books* is being credited (decreased).

27 Computers do not eliminate the need for internal control. In fact, computer-based systems enable internal control procedures such as use of *access codes* or passwords, or providing of *read-only access* to accounting information.

28 Strong internal control is more difficult to achieve in a small business than in a large one, because with only a few employees it is not possible to have extensive subdivision of duties. Even the smallest businesses, however, should follow such control procedures as using serially numbered documents and separating the responsibility for maintaining accounting records from the responsibility for handling cash. Active participation by the owner in the key control procedures also strengthens the internal control in a small business.

29 Although strong internal control is highly effective in protecting assets and increasing the reliability of accounting data, no system of internal control is foolproof. *Collusion* between two or more employees can defeat the system. Carelessness or misunderstandings can cause breakdowns in the system. Also, a system of internal control should not be so elaborate that its cost exceeds the value of the protection gained.

30 Prevention of fraud is one of the objectives of a system of internal control. *Fraud* is defined as the deliberate misrepresentation of facts with the intent of deceiving someone. Accountants use the term *errors* in reference to unintentional mistakes. *Irregularities* refer to intentional mistakes, entered into accounting records or accounting reports for some fraudulent purpose. Irregularities are further subdivided into classifications of *employee fraud* and *management fraud*.

31 *Employee fraud* refers to dishonest acts performed by the employees of a company *despite management's efforts to prevent these actions*. Embezzlement, receiving kickbacks from suppliers, and padding expense accounts are example of employee fraud. In order to protect against losses from fraud or embezzlement, many companies require that employees handling cash or other negotiable assets be *bonded*.

32 *Management fraud* refers to deliberate misrepresentations made by the *top management* of a business to persons *outside* the business organization. Top management is a willing participant in such fraudulent acts as misuse of company assets or issuance of fraudulent financial statements intended to mislead investors and creditors.

33 Internal accounting controls, due to subdivision of duties, provide limited protection against the possibility of management fraud,

but top management may be able to override these controls. *Financial audits* provide outside decision makers with more assurance as to the reliability of financial statements

34 A *financial audit* is an examination of a company's financial statements performed by independent certified public accountants (CPAs). The purpose of the audit is to provide decision makers outside the business organization with an independent expert's *opinion* as to the *fairness* of the financial statements. Auditors use the term "fair" to describe financial statements which are complete, unbiased, reliable, and presented in conformity with generally accepted accounting principles. For the auditors' opinion to have credibility the auditor must (a) be *independent* of the company issuing the statement and of its management, and (b) have a sound basis for their opinion.

35 The financial statements of a business are prepared by the company's management. The *audit* describes the *investigation* which auditors undertake to provide a basis for their opinion as to the fairness of these financial statements. An audit includes, among other procedures:

a An evaluation of the system of internal control of the business,

b Substantiation of every *material* item reported in the company's financial statements, and

c Procedures to ensure that the financial statements and accompanying notes are complete.

36 The *auditors' report* is issued upon completion of their investigation, expressing an opinion as to the fairness of the financial statements. An *unqualified opinion* is issued by the auditors when they consider the financial statement to be a fair presentation of the company's financial position and results of operations and cash flows. If the auditors *do not* consider the statements "fair," they issue a modified report—either a *qualified opinion* or an *adverse opinion*—depending upon the extent of the auditors' reservations. The auditors' report accompanies the financial statements whenever they are issued to persons outside the business.

37 The primary purpose of financial audits is to determine the overall fairness of a set of financial statements, *not* to detect any and all acts of fraud. If auditors perform an audit with *due professional care*, they are not responsible if certain errors or irregularities are not detected. If the audit is performed in a *negligent* manner, the auditors may be held financially liable for losses sustained by users of these statements.

38 Many companies not needing an audit often have their financial statements *reviewed* by a firm of CPAs. A *review* is similar to a financial audit, except that the investigation is *substantially less thorough* and therefore can be performed more quickly than an audit, and at a lower cost.

39 An *operational audit* focuses upon the *efficiency and effectiveness* of an operating unit within an organization, rather than upon the financial statements. The purpose of an operational audit is to make recommendations to management for improving the operational efficiency of a department or subunit under study. These findings are not normally communicated to decision makers outside the organization.

TEST YOURSELF ON ACCOUNTING SYSTEMS, INTERNAL CONTROL, AND AUDITS

True or False

For each of the following statements, circle the T or the F to indicate whether the statement is true or false.

T F **1** A basic characteristic of an OLRT accounting system is that it uses no journals or ledgers.

T F **2** In a data base, the effects of transactions upon ledger accounts is not relevant; ledger accounts are used only in ledger-based accounting systems.

T F **3** Sound internal control would call for the same employee to keep all the accounting records and handle all cash transactions so that responsibility for cash shortages could be attached to one person.

T F **4** When internal control is weak, the financial statements are always in error.

T F **5** Subdivision of duties to achieve strong internal control means that many employees should be authorized to make purchases or payment for purchases.

T F **6** Comparing the purchase invoice to the purchase order provides assurance that all goods ordered have been received in satisfactory condition.

T F 7 The invoice is prepared by the buyer of the goods and a copy is sent to the seller.

T F 8 Comparing the purchase order with the receiving report will show that all the goods ordered actually arrived and that all goods that arrived were actually ordered.

T F 9 The employee who authorized the purchase of merchandise should inspect the merchandise on arrival and prepare a receiving report.

T F 10 In a strong system of internal control, losses from fraud or embezzlement are impossible.

T F 11 Collusion between two or more employees can cause a breakdown in internal control.

T F 12 It is easier to achieve strong internal control in a large business than in a small one.

T F 13 Financial audits provide outsiders with more protection against management fraud than do systems of internal control.

T F 14 In a financial audit, the auditors are expressing an opinion on financial statements that they themselves have not prepared.

T F 15 Because auditors only express an opinion as to the fairness of financial statements, they are not held liable for losses suffered by users of the financial statements.

T F 16 The use of computers virtually eliminates the need to maintain a strong system of internal control.

T F 17 Separation of duties is not needed in a computer-based accounting system since the computer consolidates many job positions.

T F 18 In an *on-line, real-time processing system* the computer will process transactions instantaneously as they occur.

T F 19 *Point-of-sale terminals* often make use of magnetically coded labels and optical scanners.

Completion Statements

Fill in the necessary words to complete the following statements:

1 Every accounting system performs the following basic functions: (a) _____ effects of business transactions, (b) _____ the effects of similar transactions, and (c) _____ and _____ accounting data in a manner _____ _____ _____ _____.

2 Accounting data are most useful to decision makers when they are _____, _____, and _____.

3 Internal controls which have no direct bearing upon the reliability of the financial statements are called _____ controls and internal controls which relate to safeguarding assets and promoting the reliability of accounting data are called _____ controls.

4 Factors contributing to strong internal control include adequate _____ of duties, a logical _____ plan, use of _____ _____ documents, and an _____ _____ staff.

5 Comparison of the _____ _____ with the _____ _____ shows whether the same quantity and quality of goods were received as had been ordered.

6 The seller of goods prepares a _____ invoice and mails one copy to the buyer. The buyer refers to this document as a _____ invoice, and compares it with the _____ _____ to see that the seller is providing the same goods at the same terms the buyer has agreed to pay.

7 When the buyer returns some damaged merchandise to the seller, he or she will also send the seller a _____ _____. If the seller accepts the returned goods as partial settlement of the buyer's account, he or she will send a _____ _____ to the buyer.

8 A _____ _____ offers protection against losses from embezzlement, a type of _____ fraud. Issuing misleading financial statements and misuse of company assets are examples of _____ fraud.

9 Upon completion of a financial audit, the auditors issue the _____ _____, which expresses an opinion on the _____ of the _____ _____, and which

accompanies the financial statements when issued to outsiders.

10 When the auditors consider a company's financial statements to be a fair presentation, they issue a(n) _____ _____. If the auditors do not consider the statements "fair", a(n) _____ opinion or a(n) _____ opinion is issued, depending upon the extent of the auditors' reservations.

11 A business will usually benefit by establishing a special journal for any type of transaction that _____ _____.

Multiple Choice

Choose the best answer for each of the following questions and enter the identifying letter in the space provided.

_____ 1 Special journals are advantageous:
a Only in noncomputerized (manual) accounting systems.
b Only in computerized accounting systems.
c Only in OLRT computerized systems.
d Whenever a business must record a large number of similar transactions.

_____ 2 Contempo Corporation presently has a manual ledger-based accounting system and issues unaudited financial statements. Which of the following measures would be *most* effective in increasing the *relevance* of the accounting information that Contempo is capable of generating?
a Hiring a CPA firm to perform an annual financial audit.
b Conversion to a computerized accounting system which uses a data base.
c Conversion to a computerized ledger-based accounting system.
d Extensive use of special journals.

_____ 3 Which of the following is *not* an advantage that can be achieved by a computer-based accounting system?
a Operating data can be made available to managers faster than with a manual system.
b The accuracy of computers eliminates the need for internal control.
c Sales transactions can be recorded instantaneously in the accounting records as the salesclerk rings up the sale on an electronic cash register.
d The need for manual labor to perform the posting function can virtually be eliminated.

_____ 4 Which of the following is *not* one of the purposes of a system of internal control?

a To protect resources against waste, fraud, or inefficient use.
b To ensure the accuracy and reliability of the accounting records.
c To ensure that actual results of operations meet or exceed results anticipated in the financial forecasts.
d To evaluate the performance of individual departments.

_____ 5 Which of the following would *not* be an example of an administrative control?
a Salespersons are required to submit reports showing the names of customers called upon each day.
b An annual physical count of inventory is performed even when a perpetual inventory system is in use.
c An employee is prohibited from working more than 10 hours a day.
d A pilot is required to undergo a medical examination annually.

_____ 6 Which of the following measures would be most effective in creating a strong system of internal control in a merchandising business?
a Require two signatures of responsible officials on all purchase orders, receiving reports, and sales invoices.
b Delegate full responsibility to an appropriate employee or supervisor for all aspects of transactions with a designated group of customers or suppliers.
c Arrange for an annual audit by a firm of certified public accountants.
d Establish an organization structure that will provide separate departments for such functions as purchasing, receiving, selling, accounting, and credit and collection, so that the work of one organizational unit tends to verify that of another.

_____ 7 Internal control over purchases is strengthened when the functions of ordering and receiving merchandise are performed:
a By two separate departments.
b By the accounting department.
c By a department which has no responsibilities other than purchasing and receiving merchandise.
d By serially numbered employees.

_____ 8 If the seller ships goods to a customer but charges more than the customer had expected to pay, the discrepancies should come to light when:
a The purchase order is compared with the purchase invoice.

b The receiving report is compared with the purchase invoice.

c The receiving report is compared with the purchase order.

d The purchase invoice is compared with the sales invoice.

_____ **9** The company receiving a shipment of goods might send a debit memorandum to the supplier if:

a Some of the goods were damaged.

b The purchase invoice was understated.

c The shipment was received in good condition.

d The shipment was paid for in cash.

Use the following data to answer questions 10 and 11.

On July 1, Sea Marine Company received a purchase order dated June 28 from Bayshore Boat Sales. Sea Marine shipped the merchandise and mailed a sales invoice on July 6. The merchandise arrived and the purchase invoice was approved at Bayshore on July 8.

_____ **10** Sea Marine Company should record the sale on:

a July 1.

b July 6.

c July 8.

d June 28.

_____ **11** Bayshore Boat Sales should record the purchase and related liability on:

a July 1.

b July 6.

c July 8.

d June 28.

_____ **12** A financial audit includes each of the following *except*:

a An evaluation of the company's system of internal control.

b Verification of all transactions recorded by the company.

c Procedures designed to discover unrecorded liabilities which may exist.

d Procedures to substantiate material items reported in the company's financial statements.

_____ **13** Which of the following may be performed by a corporation's internal audit staff?

a Financial audit.

b Operational audit.

c Review of financial statements.

d Audit of the corporate income tax return.

Exercises

1 Listed below are eight technical accounting terms emphasized in this chapter.

Data base   *Debit memorandum*
Review   *Receiving report*
OLRT system   *Financial audit*
Irregularities   *Special journal*

Each of the following statements may (or may not) describe one of these technical terms. In the space provided below each statement, indicate the accounting term described, or answer "None" if the statement does not correctly describe any of the terms.

a A document used to verify unit prices in a purchase invoice.

_____

b An investigation intended to provide outsiders with a limited degree of assurance as to the reliability of the financial statements.

_____

c A system which uses terminals in direct communication with the computer to process transactions instantaneously.

_____

d A journal used in recording unusual types of transactions.

_____

e A document sent to the supplier when delivered merchandise is found to be unsatisfactory and is returned to the supplier.

_____

f Intentional misstatements within the financial statements.

_____

g An investigation conducted for the purpose of evaluating the efficiency and effectiveness of a subunit within an organization.

_____

2 Listed below are several problems that might occur in a merchandising business. Also shown is a list of internal control procedures. In the spaces provided, indicate the letter of the control procedure that would be most effective in preventing each problem from occurring. If none of the control procedures would effectively prevent a particular problem, enter an **X** in the space provided.

Problem Situations

___ Paid a supplier for goods that were never ordered.

___ Sales department makes credit sales to customers who do not meet the company's minimum credit standards.

___ Paid a supplier for goods that were never received.

___ Sales clerk makes an error in giving change to a cash customer.

___ Accounts receivable department is unaware that receivables from several customers were never recorded because copies of the sales invoices were misplaced before being sent to the accounts receivable department.

___ An inventory clerk conceals a shortage of merchandise by understating the balance of the Inventory account.

___ Prices charged by a supplier exceed the amount that the company had agreed to pay.

___ Management is unaware that the company often fails to pay its bills in time to qualify for the cash discount offered by suppliers.

Internal Control Procedures

a Use of serially numbered documents.

b Use of net cost method in recording purchases.

c Comparison of purchase invoice with receiving report.

d Separation of the accounting function from custody of assets.

e Comparison of purchase invoice with purchase order.

f Separation of responsibilities for executing and approving transactions.

X None of the above control procedures would effectively prevent this situation from occurring

3 Several steps involved in the purchase of merchandise are listed below in random order. In the column headed **Sequence**, number the steps in the order of their normal occurrence (the first step is already labeled as an example). Next, in the column headed **Department**, insert the letter designating the department in which the step is performed.

Sequence	Department	Procedure
_____	_____	File paid invoice.
1	_____	Prepare purchase requisition.
_____	_____	Send check to vendor.
_____	_____	Count and inspect goods upon arrival.
_____	_____	Perform steps to verify purchase invoice.
_____	_____	Record purchase and liability to vendor.
_____	_____	Issue purchase order.
_____	_____	Initial the invoice approval form.

Departments involved:
a. Accounting Department
b. Finance department
c. Purchasing Department
d. Receiving Department
e. Sales Department or Inventory Control Department

SOLUTIONS TO CHAPTER 6 SELF-TEST

True or False

1 F OLRT systems use input devices such as point-of-sale terminals, which are a form of special journal. Ledger accounts and subsidiary ledgers exist in an OLRT system, and are updated immediately for effects of transactions.

2 F Both types of accounting systems classify the effects of transactions in terms of ledger accounts. In a ledger-based system, this occurs when the transaction is initially recorded. In a data base system, transaction data are recorded in an unclassified format but are sorted in terms of effects upon ledger account balances in order to prepare financial statements.

3 F The employee who has custody of an asset should not maintain the accounting records for that asset.

4 F Although a weak internal control system cannot give assurance of reliable accounting data, the financial statements may be correct in spite of this deficiency due to honest and conscientious employees.

5 F Subdivision of duties means no one person or department should handle a transaction from beginning to end.

6 F A comparison of the purchase invoice and purchase order with the *receiving report* indicates that all goods ordered have been received.

7 F The invoice is initiated by the seller and sent to the accounting department of the purchasing company.

8 T The purchase order contains all details of the order and when compared with the receiving report will indicate whether all goods ordered have been received.

9 F Appropriate subdivision of duties requires that these duties be performed by separate employees (in separate departments).

10 F No system of internal control is foolproof; collusion among employees may cause a breakdown in the system.

11 T Even the most carefully planned subdivision of duties can be thwarted by collusion.

12 T A large business allows for more adequate subdivision of duties—a major premise of strong internal control.

13 T Internal accounting controls are designed to assure *management* that accounting information is reliable. Top management may override these controls when reporting to outsiders. A financial audit is an investigation of the financial statement (as well as the system of internal control) by CPAs who are *independent* of the firm and its management.

14 T Financial statements are prepared by a company's management and may be audited only by CPAs who are *independent* of the business entity. A CPA who participated in the preparation of financial statements is not independent, and could not perform an audit of those statements.

15 T If an audit is performed in a negligent manner, auditors may be held financially liable for losses sustained by those who relied upon the financial statements.

16 F The basic tenets of internal control are applicable to manual and computer-based accounting systems; additional internal control procedures may be possible in a computer-based system.

17 F Subdivision of duties remains an important internal control concept; computer output is reconciled with independent records such as physical counts of merchandise, etc.

18 T In OLRT computer systems, the employee executing the transaction is in direct communication with the computer.

19 T From the code number, the computer is able to identify the item being sold, record the amount of the sale, and transfer the cost of the item from the Inventory account to the Cost of Goods Sold account.

Completion Statements

1 (a) Record, **(b)** classify, **(c)** summarize, communicate, useful to decision makers. **2** Relevant, timely, reliable. **3** Administrative, accounting. **4** Subdivision, organization, serially numbered, internal audit. **5** Purchase order, receiving report. **6** Sales, purchase, purchase order. **7** Debit memorandum, credit memorandum. **8** Fidelity bond, employee, management. **9** Auditors' report, fairness, financial statements. **10** Unqualified opinion, qualified, adverse. **11** Occurs frequently.

Multiple Choice

1 Answer **d**—a special journal is an accounting record or **device** designed to record a specific type of transaction quickly and efficiently. Although the **form** of special journals will vary according to the type of accounting system in use, use of special journals will speed up and simplify the recording process whenever routine transactions occur frequently, regardless of the type of accounting system in use.

2 Answer **b**—answer **a** would contribute to the **reliability** of the accounting information. Answers **c** and **d** contribute primarily to the **timeliness** of accounting information. A data base allows management to arrange data in different ways at different times according to the information needs of a specific decision maker. This capability greatly enhances the **relevance** of the information to the decision maker.

3 Answer **b**—although the use of computers does have the advantages identified in answers **a**, **c**, and **d**, the need for internal control is just as great as when using a manual accounting system.

4 Answer **c**—the purposes of a system of internal control are to protect resources against waste, fraud, or inefficient use, to ensure the accuracy and reliability of accounting records, to secure compliance with management's policies, and to evaluate the performance of individual departments.

5 Answer **b**—an annual physical count of inventory even when a perpetual inventory system is in use is an example of an **accounting** control.

6 Answer **d**—separation of duties is one of the most important concepts in achieving internal control. An annual audit by CPAs my serve to identify some weaknesses in internal control but will not in and of itself **create** a strong system of internal control.

7 Answer **a**—subdivision of duties is achieved as long as two separate departments handle the function of ordering and receiving merchandise.

8 Answer **a**—both purchase order and purchase invoice have a price shown. The receiving report indicates only quantity, quality, and condition of merchandise received. The purchase invoice is the same document as the sales invoice.

9 Answer **a**—when goods are received that are unsatisfactory, the buyer may return the merchandise or request a reduction in price from the seller. In either case, the buyer usually sends the seller a debit memorandum indicating that the buyer is reducing (debiting) the liability to the seller from the amount shown on the invoice.

10 Answer **b**—Sea Marine (seller) records the sale when the goods are shipped and the sales invoice is mailed.

11 Answer **c**—Bayshore (buyer) records the liability on July 8, the date upon which the goods are received and the purchase invoice is approved by the accounting department.

12 Answer **b**—most audit procedures are based upon samples; it is simply not possible to examine and verify all transactions of an enterprise. Answers **a**, **c**, and **d** are integral parts of every financial audit.

13 Answer **b**—an operational audit involves studying, testing, and evaluating the operating procedures and system of internal control of a subunit of an organization. This type of audit may appropriately be performed by the internal audit staff of a corporation, as there is no requirement of independence. Financial audits and reviews must be performed by independent CPAs; the Internal Revenue Service (IRS) performs audits of corporate income tax returns.

Solutions to Exercises

1

a None (The statement describes a **purchase order**.)
b Review
c OLRT system
d None (The statement describes a **general journal**.)
e Debit memorandum
f Irregularities
g None (The statement describes an **operational audit**.)

2   **Problem Situations**

__e__ Paid a supplier for goods that were never ordered.

__f__ Sales department makes credit sales to customers who do not meet the company's minimum credit standards.

__c__ Paid a supplier for goods that were never received.

__x__   Salesclerk makes an error in giving change to a cash customer.

__a__   Accounts receivable department is unaware that receivables from several customers were never recorded because copies of the sales invoices were misplaced before being sent to the accounts receivable department.

__d__   An inventory clerk conceals a shortage of merchandise by understating the balance of the Inventory account.

__e__   Prices charged by a supplier exceed the amount that the company had agreed to pay.

__b__   Management is unaware that the company often fails to pay its bills in time to qualify for the cash discount offered by suppliers.

3

Sequence	Department	Procedure
8	a	File paid invoice.
1	e	Prepare purchase requisition.
7	b	Send check to vendor.
3	d	Count and inspect goods upon arrival.
4	a	Perform steps to verify purchase invoice.
6	a	Record purchase and liability to vendor.
2	c	Issue purchase order.
5	a	Initial the invoice approval form.

7

INTRODUCTION TO FINANCIAL STATEMENT ANALYSIS AND THE STATEMENT OF CASH FLOWS

HIGHLIGHTS OF THE CHAPTER

1 In keeping with the goal of accounting to provide decision-makers with useful information, most businesses prepare *classified financial statements*—statements which group related items into standard classifications. *Standard classifications* are used to develop relevant subtotals, to make the financial statements easier to read and more informative. Use of standard classifications helps decision-makers in making comparisons between companies.

2 *Comparative financial statements* are those in which the financial statement amounts for a single company for several years appear side by side in vertical columns. *Consolidated financial statements* present the financial position and operating results of the parent company and the companies it controls (its subsidiaries) as if they were a single business organization.

3 In a *classified* balance sheet, assets are usually classified into three groups: current assets, plant and equipment, and other assets. *Current assets* consist of cash and items capable of being *converted into cash* within a short period without interfering with normal business operations. Examples are marketable securities, receivables, inventories, and prepaid expenses.

4 Liabilities are divided between current liabilities and long-term debt. Those debts which must be paid within one year or the *operating cycle* (whichever is longer) are called *current liabilities*. Those maturing at more distant dates are long-term. Accounts payable and accrued wages payable are examples of current liabilities.

5 Current assets and liabilities are used to measure a firm's *solvency*, or debt-paying ability. One measure of solvency is the *current ratio*. The current ratio is computed by dividing the total of current assets by total current liabilities. A current ratio of about 2 to 1 is generally considered indicative of reasonable debt-paying ability.

6 In evaluating a financial ratio or statistic, analysts generally use two criteria. One criterion is the *trend* in the ratio over a period of years. Second, analysts often compare a company's statistics with those of *similar companies,* and also with *industry-wide averages*. The information used for trend analysis or industry-wide comparison is available to the public in annual reports and through financial publications and computer data bases.

7 Some short-term creditors prefer the quick ratio to the current ratio as a measure of short-term solvency. The *quick ratio* compares only the *most liquid* current assets—called quick assets—with current liabilities. Quick assets include cash, marketable securities, and receivables; inventory and prepaid expenses are excluded as they are the least liquid of the current assets. Quick ratios are useful in evaluating the solvency of companies that have inventories of slow-moving merchandise, or excessive amounts of inventory.

8 Another measure of solvency is the amount of *working capital*. Working capital is the *excess* of current assets over current liabili-

ties (current assets *minus* current liabilities).

9 Although the claims of creditors have priority over those of the owners, there may be insufficient assets even to make full payment to creditors if the debts of the business are great. A basic measure of the safety of creditors' claims is the *debt ratio*. A company's debt ratio is computed by dividing total liabilities by total assets; it is a measure of creditors' *long-term risk*. From the creditors' position, the *lower* the debt ratio, the safer their position.

10 The owners of *unincorporated* businesses are *personally liable* for the debts of the business. Therefore, creditors usually look at the solvency of the *owner*, rather than the business equity.

11 If the business is organized as a *corporation*, the stockholders are *not* automatically liable for the debts of the business. Unless special arrangements are made, creditors may look only to the *business entity* for payment of their claims. For this reason, creditors often require stockholders to *personally guarantee* (cosign) loans made to small corporations.

12 In a *multiple-step* income statement, costs and expenses are deducted from revenue in a series of steps. First, the *cost of goods sold* is deducted to arrive at gross profit. Next, *operating expenses* are deducted to determine the income from operations. Finally, *nonoperating revenue* is added and *nonoperating expenses* are deducted to arrive at net income. The Computer Barn income statement on page 287 in the text illustrates the multiple-step format. In a *single-step* income statement, all costs and expenses are deducted from total revenue in one single step. No subtotals are shown for gross profit or for operating income. On page 291 in the text, the income statement for Computer Barn is presented in single-step format.

13 The gross profit computed as a percentage of net sales is called the *gross profit rate.* By computing the gross profit rate of a merchandising business for several successive periods. users of financial statements gain insight into whether the business is improving or declining.

14 *Operating* expenses are incurred for the purpose of producing revenue; they are usually classified as *selling expenses* and *general and administrative expenses*.

Nonoperating items are those revenue and expenses which are not directly related to the company's primary business activity. Interest and dividends earned on investments, interest expense, and income taxes expenses are examples of nonoperating items.

15 In addition to following the dollar amount of net income (or loss), analysts often compute net income as a *percentage of net sales:* net income divided by net sales. This measurement gives an indication of management's *ability to control expenses*, and to retain a portion of net sales as profit.

16 Large corporations are required to report earnings on a per-share basis. *Earnings per share* in the simplest case is computed by dividing net income by the average number of shares of capital stock outstanding. The *trend* in earnings per share, and the *expected earnings* in future periods, are major factors affecting the market value of a company's shares.

17 The *price-earnings ratio* (or p/e ratio) reflects the relationship between a stock's market price and the underlying earnings per share. This ratio is computed by dividing the current market price per share by the annual earnings per share. The p/e ratio reflects *investors' expectations* concerning the company's *future performance.*

18 In evaluating a company's profitability, investors consider (1) the *trend* in earnings, and (2) the amount of current earnings *in relation to resources* used to produce the earnings. This second concept involves computing the *rate of return* earned on specific resources, often called *return on investment*, or *ROI.*

19 Two common applications of the ROI concept are:

 a *Return on assets* "Return" is defined as *operating income*, since interest expense and income taxes are determined by factors other than the manner in which assets are used.

$$\text{Return on assets} = \frac{\text{Operating income}}{\text{Average total assets}}$$

 b *Return on equity* "Return" to stockholders is the *net income* of the business.

$$\text{Return on equity} = \frac{\text{Net income}}{\text{Average total stockholders' equity}}$$

20 We have seen how the income statement measures the profitability of a business. But profitability alone does not assure success; a business must also have enough liquid resources to pay its maturing obligations and to take advantage of new investment opportunities.

21 In addition to an income statement, statement of retained earnings, and balance sheet, a complete set of financial statements includes a *statement of cash flows*. The term *cash flows* includes both cash receipts and cash payments. The basic purpose of a statement of cash flows is to provide information about the *cash receipts* and *cash payments* of a business during the accounting period. Cash flows are classified according to the nature of the *underlying business activity*.

22 A statement of cash flows shows separately the cash flows from (1) *operating activities*, (2) *investing activities*, and (3) *financing activities*. Each section shows the nature and amounts of cash receipts and cash payments relating to that type of activity during the period. All cash transactions that do not relate to investing or financing activities are included in the operating activities section. Thus, the statement of cash flows summarizes *all types* of cash receipts and cash payments during the period. A statement of cash flows is illustrated on page 295 in the text.

23 The *operating activities* section shows the cash effects of revenue and expense transactions. The major cash receipts from operating activities are collections from customers (including cash sales and collections on accounts receivable) and receipts of investment income, such as interest and dividends. Cash payments include cash paid to suppliers of good and services, and payments of interest and taxes.

24 *Investing activities* are the cash flows stemming from purchases and disposals of plant assets and/or investments. Cash receipts from *investing activities* include the proceeds from selling investments or plant assets, and the principal amounts collected on loans. (Receipts of interest are classified as operating activities.) Cash payments include purchases of investments and plant assets, and amounts advanced to borrowers.

25 *Financing activities* include most of the cash flows between the business and its owners (stockholders), and creditors who lend money to the business. Cash receipts from *financing activities* include proceeds from borrowing and from issuing stock. Cash pay-

ments include repayments of amounts borrowed, and distributions to owners, such as dividends or purchases of treasury stock.

26 Receipts and payments of *interest* are classified as *operating activities*, not as investing or financing activities. The reason is that the FASB wants net cash flow from operating activities to reflect the cash effects of those transactions entering into the determination of net income.

27 In the long run, a company must generate positive cash flows from *operating activities* if the business is to survive. A business with negative cash flows from operations will not be able to raise cash from other sources (investing and financing activities) indefinitely. Net cash flow from operating activities is considered a key measure of *liquidity*.

28 Investing or financing activities often result in *negative* cash flows for any given year for successful businesses. Since purchases of plant assets require cash outlays, expanding businesses usually report negative cash flows from investing activities. Major financing activities occur infrequently and may result in either positive or negative cash flows for a particular year; payment of dividends, however, is a negative cash flow from financing activities.

29 Although both the statement of cash flows and the cash budget reflect cash receipts and cash payments, a cash budget is a *forecast* of the cash flows *expected to occur in future periods*. The cash budget is *not* a financial statement; it is used primarily by management within the organization. While the statement of cash flows summarizes the overall cash flows of the entire business for a one-year period, the cash budget contains more detail and covers a much shorter time period.

30 The data used by "outsiders" in performing financial analysis is available in published annual and quarterly reports, in information filed with the SEC, from investment services that sell their investment recommendations to subscribers for a fee, or from credit-rating agencies. The financial ratios and other measurements covered in the chapter are summarized in the table on page 299 of the text.

31 Stock prices are a *measure of investors' expectations* about the future performance of the company. In the short-run, stock prices are affected by many factors, such as interest rates, current events, fads and rumors. Evaluating stock price by examining the underlying profitability of the company is termed *fundamental analysis*; this approach works better in the long run than in the short run.

TEST YOURSELF ON FINANCIAL STATEMENT ANALYSIS AND THE STATEMENT OF CASH FLOWS

True or False

For each of the following statements, circle the T or the F to indicate whether the statement is true or false.

T F 1 A current asset is one which will be used up in one year or the operating cycle of the business, whichever is longer.

T F 2 If Company A has current assets of $200,000 and Company B's current assets total $500,000, Company B is considered more solvent than Company A.

T F 3 In a multiple-step income statement, income from operations and net income are usually two different amounts.

T F 4 Income taxes expense appears only in a multiple-step income statement.

T F 5 Income taxes expense is an operating expense appearing in the income statements of corporations.

T F 6 In the computation of both *return on assets* and *return on equity*, the "return" is defined to be net income.

T F 7 Industry standards tend to place the performance of a company in a more meaningful perspective.

T F 8 Dividing the market price of a share of capital stock by the dividends per share gives the price-earnings ratio.

T F 9 A high current ratio may indicate that capital is not productively used and that inventories and receivables may be excessive.

T F 10 It is possible to improve many balance sheet ratios by completing certain transactions just before the close of the fiscal period.

T F 11 A statement of cash flows generally is organized into three major sections: cash receipts, cash payments, and non-cash investing and financing activities.

T F 12 All cash receipts and cash payments not classified as investing or financing activities are classified as operating activities.

T F 13 A statement of cash flows provides more information about the profitability of a business than does an income statement.

T F 14 In a statement of cash flows, payments of dividends are classified as operating activities.

T F 15 Cash payments to purchase merchandise are classified as investing activities.

T F 16 In a statement of cash flows, receipts and payments of interest are both classified as operating activities.

T F 17 A growing, successful company will usually show a positive net cash flow from operations.

T F 18 A growing, successful company will usually show a positive net cash flow from investing activities.

Completion Statements

Fill in the necessary words to complete the following statements:

1 In a classified balance sheet, the three groups of assets are: (a) _____ _____, (b) _____ ____ _____, and (c) _____ _____.

2 The amount by which current assets exceed current liabilities is called _____ _____. Current assets divided by current liabilities is called the _____ _____. These two computations are made to measure the _____ of a business enterprise.

3 An income statement which shows subtotals for such items as gross profit, total operating expenses, and income from operations is called a ___-_____ income statement.

4 The market price of capital stock divided by earnings per share is known as the ____ _____ _____.

5 The current ratio is 3 to 1; working capital amounts to $100,000, and the quick ratio is 1.5 to 1. Compute the following: (a) current

assets, $_____; (b) current liabilities, $_____; (c) total investment in inventories and short-term prepayments, $_____.

6 There are three major financial statements: the _____ _____ measures the profitability of a business, the _____ _____ shows the financial position of the business at the end of the period, and the _____ ___ _____ summarizes _____ transactions.

7 In a statement of cash flows, cash transactions are classified into the categories of (a)_____ activities, (b) _____ activities, and (c) _____ activities.

8 In a statement of cash flows, the payment of interest is classified as a (an) _____ activity, and the payment of a dividend is classified as a (an) _____ activity.

9 Of the three major classifications of cash flows, it is most important for a business to show a positive cash flow from _____ activities over the long run.

Multiple Choice

Choose the best answer for each of the following questions and enter the identifying letter in the space provided.

_____ 1 The Toy Castle, a retail toy store, had current assets of $72,000 and a current ratio of 2 to 1. The amount of working capital must have been:
a $144,000
b $108,000
c $72,000
d $36,000

_____ 2 In a multiple-step income statement:
a The total of all expenses is deducted from the total revenue to arrive at net income.
b Revenues and expenses are classified as current or long-term, depending upon when cash is received or paid.
c Gross profit and operating income are subtotals determined in arriving at net income.
d Income taxes and interest expense are deducted in computing income from operations.

_____ 3 Which of the following would be **least** useful in evaluating a company's profitability?
a Return on assets for the current year.
b Return on equity for the current year.
c The trend of earnings for the most recent five-year period.
d Net income for the current year.

_____ 4 An investor wants to evaluate the relative profitability of several companies of different size. In order to put the earnings into perspective, the investor would be **least** likely to compare the net income of each company with that company's:
a Stockholders' equity.
b Total assets.
c Working capital.
d Net sales.

_____ 5 Which of the following sources of financial information is **not** generally available to an individual considering investing in a large publicly held corporation?
a Data published by Standard and Poor's Corporation and other investors' services.
b The company's accounting records.
c Audited financial statements for the current and prior years.
d Financial information that has been filed with the Securities and Exchange Commission (SEC).

_____ 6 Which of the following **is not** a valuable standard of comparison in analyzing financial statements of a company engaged in the manufacture of mobile homes?
a Past performance of the company.
b Performance of another company engaged in the manufacture of mobile homes.
c Performance of all companies engaged in manufacture of mobile homes.
d Performance of companies engaged in construction of apartment buildings.

_____ 7 In projecting the future profitability of a merchandising company, **investors** will be **least** concerned with changes in:
a The gross profit rate.
b The rate earned on total assets.
c The quick ratio.
d Sales volume.

_____ 8 A statement of cash flows is **not** intended to provide readers with information about:
a The profitability of a business.
b Noncash investing and financing transactions.
c The ability of a business to continue paying dividends.
d The net cash flow from operating activities.

_____ 9 Which of the following captions should not appear in a statement of cash flows?
a Net cash provided by financing activities.
b Proceeds from sales of plant assets.
c Funds provided from operating activities.
d Net cash used by investing activities.

_____**10** A successful, growing business is *most likely* to show a negative cash flow from:
a Operating activities.
b Investing activities.
c Financing activities.
d Transactions with customers.

_____**11** Which of the following cash flows is *not* classified as a financing activity in a statement of cash flows?
a Payment of a cash dividend.
b Payment of interest.
c Short-term borrowing.
d Issuance of capital stock in exchange for plant assets.

_____**12** Which of the following would *increase* the net cash flow from operating activities?
a Sale of capital stock for cash.
b Issuance of a note payable for cash.
c Sale of goods on credit.
d Sale of goods for cash.

_____**13** A positive net cash flow from *operating activities* of $100,000:
a Represents cash flow remaining *after* payment of interest and dividends.
b Is generally viewed as sufficient by stockholders and creditors.
c Means that the company is both profitable and solvent.
d May be viewed as unsatisfactory if dividends annually are $300,000.

Exercises

1 Listed below are eight technical accounting terms introduced in this chapter.

Operating activities   *Current assets*
Financing activities   *Current ratio*
Investing activities   *Net cash flow*
Multiple-step   *Single-step*
   income statement   *income*
                                statement

Each of the following statements may (or may not) describe one of these technical terms. In the space provided below each statement, indicate the accounting term described, or answer "None" if the statement does not correctly describe any of the terms.

a A measure of the long-term safety of creditors' positions.

_____

b Cash receipts during the period, less cash payments made during the period.

_____

c The classification in a statement of cash flows that includes investments made by a business in plant assets.

_____

d Income statement which shows a subtotal for net sales minus cost of goods sold.

_____

e Cash and other assets that can be converted into cash within one year or the operating cycle, whichever is longer.

_____

f The classification of cash flows for which it is most important for cash flows to be positive over the long run.

_____

g The category within a statement of cash flows that includes investments made by owners in the capital stock of a business.

_____

2 Use the following data to compute the statistics indicated below. Dollar amounts are in thousands.

Balance sheet data:	1/1/96	12/31/96
Current assets	$540	$ 630
Total assets	960	1,040
Current liabilities	200	210
Total liabilities	260	240
Stockholders' equity	700	800

Income statement data:	
Net sales	$1,000
Gross profit	360
Operating income	250
Net income	150

a Current ratio at the *beginning* of 1996: _____ to 1
b Working capital at the *end* of 1996: $_____
c Gross profit rate for 1996: _____ %
d Return on assets for 1996: _____ %
e Return on equity for 1996: _____ %

3 The balance sheets of the Binkley Corporation at the beginning and end of 1996 and the income statement for 1996 are presented below:

BINKLEY CORPORATION
Comparative Balance Sheets

Assets	Dec. 31 1996	Jan. 1 1996
Cash	$ 60,000	$ 45,000
Marketable securities	30,000	40,000
Accounts receivable (net)	50,000	70,000
Inventory	140,000	130,000
Plant and equipment (net of accumulated depreciation)	420,000	330,000
Total assets	$700,000	$615,000

Liabilities & Stockholders' Equity

	Dec. 31 1996	Jan. 1 1996
Accounts payable	$ 95,000	$ 30,000
Accrued liabilities	10,000	15,000
Long-term debt	80,000	100,000
Capital stock (60,000 shares outstanding)	300,000	300,000
Retained earnings	215,000	170,000
Total liabilities & stockholders' equity	$700,000	$615,000

BINKLEY CORPORATION
Income Statement
For Year Ended December 31, 1996

Net sales (all on credit)	$800,000
Cost of goods sold	490,000
Gross profit on sales	$310,000
Operating expenses (includes depreciation $25,000)	160,000
Income from operations	$150,000
Other expense: Interest expense	7,000
Income before income taxes	$143,000
Income taxes	59,000
Net income	$ 84,000
Earnings per share	$ 1.40

On the basis of the information in the Binkley Corporation financial statements, fill in the blanks below with the appropriate amounts (do not compute the ratios):

a The *current ratio* at the end of 1996 would be computed by dividing $_____ by $_____.

b The *quick ratio* at the end of 1996 would be computed by dividing $_____ by $_____.

c The *rate of return earned on average investment in assets* would be determined by dividing $_____ by $_____.

d The *debt ratio* at the end of 1996 would be determined by dividing $_____ by $_____.

e The *rate of return on the average stockholders' equity* would be determined by dividing $_____ by $_____.

f The *earnings per share* of capital stock would be determined by dividing $_____ by _____ shares outstanding.

g If the capital stock had a market value at the end of the year of $42 per share, the *price-earnings ratio* would be determined by dividing $_____ by $_____.

h The *gross profit rate* (profit margin) would be computed by dividing $_____ by $_____.

4 Indicate how each of the events should be classified in a statement of cash flows for the current year. Use the following codes:

O = Operating activities
I = Investing activities
F = Financing activities

If the event does not cause a cash flow to be reported in the statement, enter an X in the space provided.

___ **a** Collected accounts receivable originating from sales in the prior year.

___ **b** Paid the interest on a note payable to First Bank.

___ **c** Paid the principal amount due on the note payable to First Bank.

___ **d** Received a dividend from an investment in AT&T common stock.

___ **e** Paid a dividend to stockholders.

___ **f** Recorded depreciation expense for the current year.

___ **g** Sold a segment of the business to another corporation; received cash.

___ **h** Paid income taxes owed for the prior year.

___ **i** Purchased machinery for use in business operations; paid cash.

___ **j** Paid invoice for merchandise to be sold to customers.

5 From the following information, complete the statement of cash flows (direct method) for Mario's Restaurant for the year ended December 31, 19__.

Purchases of plant assets	$260,000
Proceeds from sales of plant assets	25,000
Proceeds from issuing capital stock	200,000
Proceeds from short-term borrowing	50,000
Payments to settle short-term debt	35,000
Interest and dividends received	20,000
Cash received from customers	900,000
Dividends paid	100,000
Cash paid to suppliers and employees	700,000
Interest paid	30,000
Income taxes paid	60,000
Cash and cash equivalents, beginning of the year	42,000
Cash and cash equivalents, end of the year	52,000

MARIO'S RESTAURANT
Statement of Cash Flows
For the Year Ended December 31, 19__

Cash flows from operating activities:
   Cash received from customers $_____

   Cash provided by operating activities .... $_____
Cash paid to suppliers and
   employees .... $(_____)

   Cash disbursed for operating activities .... (_____)
Net cash flow from operating activities .... $_____
Cash flows from investing activities:
   $_____

Net cash used by investing activities .... (_____)

Cash flows from financing activities:
Proceeds from short-term
   borrowing .... $_____

Net cash provided by financing activities .... _____
Net increase (decrease) in cash .... $_____
Cash and cash equivalents, beginning $_____
   of the year ....
Cash and cash equivalents, end of year .... $_____

SOLUTIONS TO CHAPTER 7 SELF-TEST

True or False

1 F To qualify as a current asset, an asset must be capable of *being converted into cash* within one year or the operating cycle, whichever is longer. There is no requirement that the asset or cash be spent (used up) in a particular time period.

2 F The *relationship* between current assets and current liabilities is more important than the total dollar amount in either category in assessing solvency. In order to determine the solvency of either Company A relative to Company B, we must know the current liabilities owed by each company; then indicators such as current ratio or working capital may be used.

3 T Income from operations is increased by *nonoperating revenue* and decreased by *nonoperating expenses* to arrive at net income.

4 F Income taxes expense appear in both multiple-step and single-step corporate income statements. In a multiple-step income statement, income taxes expense is classified as a nonoperating item; in a single-step income statement, it is grouped with all other expenses.

5 F Income taxes expense does appear in the income statements of corporations, but is classified as a *nonoperating* item since it does not help produce revenue.

6 F In computing the return on assets, the "return" is usually defined to be operating income. Net income, however, is the "return" used in computing return on equity.

7 T Industry standards provide one method of comparing operating results of one company with those of its competitors.

8 F The price-earnings ratio is computed by dividing the market price of capital stock by the earnings per share.

9 T A high current ratio could indicate excessive amounts of inventory, poor collection of accounts receivable, or excessive current assets that could be invested for a greater return.

10 T Many balance sheet ratios are determined using figures in existence at balance sheet date; thus, it is possible to manipulate these amounts by strategic timing of certain transactions.

11 F The three major categories of cash flows are (1) operating activities, (2) investing activities, and (3) financing activities.

12 T If a transaction does not fall into either the financing or investing category, by default it is considered an operating activity.

13 F The income statement measures profitability, whereas the statement of cash flows provides information about cash flows from operating, investing and financing activities.

14 F Payments to owners, such as dividends, are classified as financing activities.

15 F Payments to purchase merchandise are classified as operating activities.

16 T The FASB wanted net cash flow from operating activities to reflect the cash effects of those transactions entering into the determination of net income.

17 T In the long run, a business must generate positive cash flows from operations if the business is to survive.

18 F A growing business is generally investing in plant assets and acquiring other investments; these activities could lead to a negative cash flow from investing activities.

Completion Statements

1(a) Current assets, **(b)** plant and equipment, **(c)** other assets. **2** Working capital, current ratio, solvency. **3** Multiple-step. **4** Price-earnings ratio. **5(a)** $150,000, **(b)** $50,000, **(c)** $75,000. **6** Income statement, balance sheet, statement of cash flows, cash. **7(a)** Operating, **(b)** investing, **(c)** financing. **8** Operating, financing. **9** Operating.

Multiple Choice

1 Answer **d**—if the current ratio (current assets divided by current liabilities) is 2 to 1, and current assets are $72,000, then current liabilities are $36,000. If current liabilities are $36,000, then working capital (current assets minus current liabilities is $72,000 minus $36,000.

2 Answer **c** is the only answer descriptive of a multiple-step income statement. Answer **a** refers to a single-step income statement. Income taxes and interest are nonoperating expenses that are deducted after computing the subtotal "income from operation" in a multiple-step income statement. Current and long-term are classifications for assets and liabilities on a classified balance sheet.

3 Answer **d**—trend analysis and ROI (return on investment) analysis are much more meaningful statistics than simply the dollar amount of net income in a particular year.

4 Answer **c**—to compare relative profitability of several companies, each company's earnings can be compared with its total assets and with its invested capital, as well as with sales. Total assets and invested capital are the resources utilized by management to generate earnings. Sales are the source of income generated, and the amount of profit **per dollar of sales** is a more useful indicator of profitability than the absolute dollar amount of net income. Working capital measures short-run debt-paying ability and bears no direct relationship to net income.

5 Answer **b**—answers **a**, **c**, and **d** are all available to stockholders, potential investors and creditors, and the general public. A company's internal accounting records are not made public.

6 Answer **d**—in order for a ratio or a comparison to be useful, the two amounts being compared must be logically related. Answers **a**, **b**, and **c** are all logically related in some way to the current year financial statements of a company engaged in the manufacture of mobile homes. Answer **d** refers to an unrelated industry.

7 Answer **c**—the quick ratio is a measure of the **short-term liquidity** of the firm. Changes in the statistics in answers **a**, **b**, and **d** are of more significance in projecting the future profitability of a company.

8 Answer **a**—a statement of cash flows provides information about the **solvency** of a business; the income statement provides information about **profitability**. A statement of cash flows also provides information about **noncash** investing and financing activities.

9 Answer **c**—the FASB prohibits the use of the term **"funds"** in the statement of cash flows.

10 Answer **b**—investing activities include purchases and sales of plant assets and of investments. A growing company is likely to be purchasing greater quantities of plant assets and of investments than it is selling. Thus, a growing company is likely to show a negative cash flow from investing activities.

11 Answer **b**—payment of interest is classified as an operating activity.

12 Answer **d**—the sale of goods for cash reflects a cash receipt from operating activities. Answer **c** does not result in a cash flow, while answers **a** and **b** are examples of financing activities (nonoperating activities.)

13 Answer **d**—although positive, the $100,000 cash flow from operations is insufficient to cover current year dividends. Interest payments have already been deducted in arriving at the $100,000 figure, but dividends have not, therefore answer **a** is not correct. The $100,000 net cash flow from operations must be evaluated in comparison to interest payments, net income, prior years' cash flows, dividend requirements, etc., in order to determine whether it is "sufficient." A company may operate at a loss and yet have a positive cash flow from operations. In addition, a company may generate cash flow from operations and have such substantial liabilities that it is insolvent.

Solutions to Exercises

1

a None (The **debt ratio** represents the portion of total assets financed by debt, and as such, indicates the long-term safety of creditors' claims. The lower the debt ratio, the safer the creditors' position.)

b Net cash flow

c Investing activities

d Multiple-step income statement

e Current assets

f Operating activities

g Financing activities

2 a Current ratio at the **beginning** of 1996: __2.7__ to 1
$540 current assets ÷ $200 current liabilities

b Working capital at the **end** of 1996: $ 420 (thousands)
$630 current assets − $210 current liabilities

c Gross profit rate for 1996: __36%__
$360 gross profit ÷ $1,000 net sales

d Return on assets for 1996: __25%__
$250 operating income ÷ [($960 + $1,040) ÷ 2]

e Return on equity for 1996: __20%__
$150 net income ÷ [($700 + $800) ÷ 2]

3 a $280,000 by $105,000

b $140,000 by $105,000

c $150,000 by $657,500 [($700,000 + $615,000) ÷ 2]

d $185,000 by $700,000

e $84,000 by $492,500 [($515,000 + $470,000) ÷ 2]

f $84,000 by 60,000 shares

g $42.00 by $1.40
h $310,000 by $800,000

4 a   O

   b   O

   c   F

   d   O

   e   F

   f   X   (This event does not involve receipt or payment of cash.)

   g   I

   h   O

   i   I

   j   O

5

MARIO'S RESTAURANT
Statement of Cash Flows
For the Year Ended December 31, 19___

Cash flows from operating activities:		
Cash received from customers	$ 900,000	
Interest and dividends received	20,000	
Cash provided by operating activities		$920,000
Cash paid to suppliers and employees	$(700,000)	
Interest paid	(30,000)	
Income taxes paid	(60,000)	
Cash disbursed for operating activities		(790,000)
Net cash flow from operating activities		$130,000
Cash flows from investing activities:		
Cash paid to acquire plant assets	$(260,000)	
Proceeds of sales from plant assets	25,000	
Net cash used by investing activities		(235,000)
Cash flows from financing activities:		
Proceeds from short-term borrowing	$ 50,000	
Payments to settle short-term debt	(35,000)	
Proceeds from issuing capital stock	200,000	
Dividends paid	(100,000)	
Net cash provided by financing activities		115,000
Net increase (decrease) in cash		$ 10,000
Cash and cash equivalents, beginning of the year		42,000
Cash and cash equivalents, end of year		$ 52,000

HIGHLIGHTS OF THE CHAPTER

1 The term *financial assets* includes cash and those assets easily and directly convertible into known amounts of cash. These assets include cash, short-term investments (also called marketable securities), and receivables. All of these assets represent forms of money; financial resources flow among these asset categories as businesses "store" money in these three basic forms.

2 In the balance sheet, financial assets are shown at their *current values*, meaning the amounts of cash that these assets represent. The current value of cash is simply its *face amount*. The current value of short-term investments (marketable securities) fluctuates daily; therefore, short-term investments appear in the balance sheet at their current *market values*. Receivables appear in the balance sheet at *net realizable value*—the estimated collectible amount.

3 The term *cash* includes currency, coins, checks, money orders, money on deposit with banks, and the charge slips signed by customers using bank credit cards. Cash is the most liquid of all assets and is listed first in the balance sheet. A company may have numerous bank accounts as well as cash on hand and several of the other items mentioned above, but these will be lumped together in the figure for Cash in the balance sheet. The balance of a bank account that is not available for use in paying current liabilities is *not* regarded as a current asset. Any such "restricted" cash is listed just below the current asset section of the balance sheet in the section entitled Long-Term Investments.

4 A *line of credit* is a prearranged borrowing agreement in which a bank has authorized a cash loan up to a specified credit limit. Once used, a line of credit becomes a liability. The *unused* portion of a line of credit represents the ability to borrow money quickly; it does not appear as either an asset or a liability in the balance sheet. Unused lines of credit are *disclosed* in notes accompanying the financial statements.

5 Some short-term investments are so liquid that they are termed *cash equivalents*. Examples include money market funds, U.S. Treasury bills, and commercial paper. These items are so similar to cash that they are usually combined with the amount of cash in the balance sheet. The first asset shown in the balance sheet for firms owning these types of short-term investments is *Cash and cash equivalents.*

6 Although the balance sheet reports the amount of cash and cash equivalents owned by a business at a particular date, a separate financial statement—*the statement of cash flows*—summarizes all of the cash receipts and cash disbursements during the accounting period. This required financial statement reports the cash activities that created the *change* in the cash and cash equivalents figure during an accounting period

7 The term *cash management* refers to planning, controlling, and accounting for cash transactions and cash balances. The basic objectives of cash management are:

a Provide accurate accounting for cash receipts, cash disbursements, and cash balances.

b Prevent loss from fraud or theft.

c Anticipate borrowing needs; assure adequate cash for business operations.

d Prevent excessive cash balances which produce no revenue.

To meet these objectives, management needs a strong internal control structure.

8 Cash offers the greatest temptation to theft, and this makes the problem of internal control especially important. Basic rules to

achieve strong internal control over cash include:

a Separating the handling of cash from the maintenance of accounting records.

b Preparing a **cash budget** for each department of planned cash receipts, cash payments, and cash balances for each month of the coming year.

c Preparing an immediate **control listing** of cash receipts at the time and place the money is received.

d Depositing all cash receipts in the bank daily.

e Making all significant cash disbursements by check.

f Requiring that every expenditure be verified and approved before payment is made.

g Promptly reconciling bank statements with the accounting record.

9 Cash receipts may be received over the counter from customers or through the mail. All cash received over the counter should be promptly recorded on a cash register in plain view of the customer. The participation of two or more employees in each cash receipts transaction is desirable. The person who opens the mail should prepare a **control listing** of checks received, forwarding one copy of the list to the accounting department and another copy along with the checks to the cashier who will deposit them.

10 Employees who handle cash receipts should not also have the authority to issue credit memoranda for sales returns. Issuing a credit memoranda for a fictitious sales return could conceal the theft of money collected from the customer.

11 Good internal control over cash disbursements requires that all payments (except those from petty cash) be made by prenumbered checks. The officials authorized to sign checks should not have authority to approve invoices for payment or to make entries in the accounting records. Before signing a check the official should review the documents supporting and approving the cash disbursement. These supporting documents should be stamped "Paid" and the checks should be mailed without going back to the person who prepared them.

12 One widely used means of controlling cash disbursements is the **voucher system.** A **voucher** (a serially numbered form) is prepared for each expenditure. Approval signatures are placed on the voucher to show that the expenditure was authorized, the goods or services received, the invoice prices verified, and the proper accounts debited and credited. A completed voucher must accompany every check submitted for signature. Before signing the check, the official authorized to make cash disbursements will review the voucher to determine that the expenditure has been approved.

13 Internal control is strong in a voucher system, because each expenditure must be verified and approved before a check is issued, and because the function of signing checks is separated from the functions of approving expenditures and recording cash transactions.

14 In a typical voucher system, the accounting department is responsible for approving cash payments and for recording the transaction. Once payment has been approved, the accounting department signs a voucher authorizing payment and records the transaction in the accounting records. The voucher and supporting document are then sent to the finance department, where an official reviews the voucher and supporting documents, issues and signs the check. After the check is signed, the voucher and supporting documents are perforated to prevent reuse and filed in a paid voucher file in the accounting department.

15 Each month the bank will provide the depositor with a **statement** of his or her account, showing the beginning balance, dates and amounts of deposits, deductions for checks paid, and any other charges, and the ending balance. All paid checks are returned to the depositor with the bank statement. When numerous checks are being deposited daily, it is inevitable that occasionally one will **bounce**; that is, the drawer of the check will have insufficient funds on deposit to cover it. The check will be marked **NSF** (not sufficient funds), charged back against the depositor's account, and returned to the depositor. An NSF check should be regarded as a receivable rather than cash until it is collected directly from the drawer, redeposited, or determined to be worthless.

16 The amount of **cash** included in the cash and cash equivalents figure reported in the balance sheet of a business should be the correct amount of cash owned at the close of business on that date. To determine this amount, it is necessary to **reconcile** the monthly bank statement with the balance of cash as shown by the depositor's accounting

records. The balance shown on the bank statement will usually not agree with that shown on the depositor's books because certain transactions will have been recorded by one party but not by the other. Examples are outstanding checks, deposits in transit, service charges, NSF checks, and errors by the bank or by the depositor.

17 The **bank reconciliation** will identify the items which cause the balance of cash per the books to differ from the balance of cash shown on the bank statement, and it will show the adjusted or correct amount of cash. Those reconciling items which have not yet been recorded by the depositor (or which reflect errors on the depositor's part) must be entered on the books to make the accounting records correct and up-to-date at the end of the period.

18 As previously stressed, it is desirable that all cash payments be made by check; however, in every business some small expenditures are necessary for which it is not practicable to issue checks. Postage, taxi fares, and small purchases of office supplies are common examples. To control these small payments almost every business establishes a **petty cash fund**. A check is written for perhaps $100 or $200 and is cashed, and the cash is kept on hand for making small expenditures. A receipt or **petty cash voucher** should be obtained and placed in the fund to replace each cash payment. Therefore the fund always contains a constant amount of cash and vouchers. The expenses are recorded in the accounts when the fund is replenished, perhaps every two or three weeks. The entry for the replenishment check will consist of debits to the proper expense accounts and a credit to Cash.

19 **Cash budgets** which forecast monthly cash expenditures for each department contribute to control over cash disbursements. Management or the internal auditors will investigate any expenditures in excess of budgeted amounts. Comparison of actual with budgeted levels of performance on a departmental basis requires the use of a responsibility accounting system.

20 Companies with large amounts of liquid resources often invest in **marketable securities**. Marketable securities consist of investments in bonds and in the capital stocks of publicly traded corporations. A basic characteristic of all marketable securities is that they are **readily marketable**—purchased or

sold easily at **quoted market prices.** These investments are almost as liquid as cash itself and are listed second among the current assets, immediately after cash.

21 Short-term investments in marketable securities are reported in the balance sheet at their **current market value as of the balance sheet date**. The valuation principle of **mark-to-market** requires adjusting the balance sheet valuation of these investments to market value at each balance sheet date. An offsetting entry must also be made in a special stockholders' equity account, **Unrealized Holding Gain (or Loss) on Investments.** Since the mark-to-market adjustments affects only the balance sheet (an asset account and a stockholders' equity account), it has **no effect** on the net income of the period.

22 Whether higher or lower than cost, the current market value is the amount reported in the money column in the balance sheet for short-term investments in marketable securities; the cost of the marketable securities is only disclosed in the balance sheet. The differences between cost and current market value also appears as an element of stockholder' equity, labeled Unrealized Holding Gain (or Loss) on Investments. This account may either increase stockholders' equity (in the case of a holding **gain**) or be shown as a reduction in total stockholders' equity (when market value is below cost—a holding **loss**).

23 An important factor in the growth of the American economy has been the increasing tendency to sell goods on credit. In most large businesses, the major portion of total sales is actually sales on credit. Since every credit sale creates some sort of receivable from the customer, it follows that accounts receivable and/or notes receivable will be large and important assets on the balance sheets of most businesses.

24 Accounts receivable are very liquid assets, usually being converted into cash within a period of 30 to 60 days. Some companies sell merchandise on longer-term installment plans, allowing customers to take as long as 48 months to pay. As long as the accounts receivable arise from "normal" sales transactions, accounts receivable are classified as current assets, appearing in the balance sheet after cash and cash equivalents.

25 A business can increase sales by giving its customers easy credit terms. But no business wants to sell on credit to customers who will be unable to pay their accounts. Consequently, many businesses have a credit department which investigates the credit records of new customers to see if they are acceptable credit risks.

26 Accounts receivable are shown in the balance sheet at the estimated collectible amount —the net realizable value. Even in companies with sound credit policies, a few accounts receivable will prove to be uncollectible. As long as the portion of uncollectible accounts is relatively small, it is to the advantage of the business to go ahead and incur these losses because the extension of credit to customers is also bringing in a lot of profitable business. The losses from accounts that do prove uncollectible are an *expense* resulting from the use of credit to increase sales.

27 A most fundamental accounting principle is that *revenue must be matched with the expenses incurred in securing that revenue*. Uncollectible Accounts Expense is caused by selling goods or services to customers who fail to pay their bills. The expense is therefore incurred in the *period the sale is made* even though the receivable is not determined to be uncollectible until some following period. At the end of each accounting period, we must therefore *estimate* the amount of uncollectible accounts expense. This estimate is brought on the books by an adjusting entry debiting *Uncollectible Accounts Expense* and crediting *Allowance for Doubtful Accounts*. The Allowance for Doubtful Accounts is a *contra-asset account*; it appears in the balance sheet as a deduction from Accounts Receivable and thus leads to an *estimated net realizable* value for receivables.

28 Allowance for Doubtful Accounts is sometimes called *Allowance for Bad Debts*. Uncollectible Accounts Expense is sometimes referred to as *Bad Debts Expense*.

29 Since the allowance for doubtful accounts is necessarily an estimate rather than a precise calculation, there is a fairly wide range within which the amount may be set. Accountants' *professional judgment* and the *concept of conservatism* in the valuation of assets both play considerable parts in determining the size of the allowance. Conservatism suggests that the allowance for doubtful accounts should be at least adequate. Establishing a relatively large allowance for doubtful accounts also means recording a relatively large amount of uncollectible accounts expense, thus tending to minimize net income for the current period.

30 When a customer's account is determined to be uncollectible, it should immediately be written off. The write-off consists of a debit to the Allowance for Doubtful Accounts and a credit to Accounts Receivable. The credit will be posted to the customer's account in the subsidiary ledger as well as to the controlling account in the general ledger. Since the write-off reduces both the asset Accounts Receivable and the contra-asset Allowance for Doubtful Accounts, *there is no change in the net carrying value of receivables*. Nor is there any recognition of expense at the time of the write-off. The write-off merely confirms the validity of our earlier estimate in recording uncollectible accounts expense in the period the sale was made.

31 Two methods of estimating uncollectible accounts expense are in wide use. The first method, which we call the *balance sheet approach*, relies on aging the *accounts receivable* and thereby arriving at the total amount estimated to be uncollectible. The allowance for uncollectibe accounts is then adjusted (usually increased) to this estimated uncollectible amount, after *giving consideration to the existing balance* in the allowance account.

32 An *aging schedule* for accounts receivable is a list of the balances due from all customers, with each amount placed in a column indicating its age. Thus, we might use columns with headings such as Not Yet Due, Past Due 1 to 30 Days, Past Due 31 to 60 Days, etc. Based upon past experience, the credit manager estimates the uncollectible portion for each column. The *required balance* in the Allowance for Doubtful Accounts is simply the sum of the estimated uncollectible portions for all age groups.

33 The alternative method of estimating uncollectible accounts expense stresses that the *expense* is usually a fairly constant *percentage of sales* (or of sales on credit). Therefore the amount of the adjustment is computed as a percentage of the period's sales *without regard to any existing balance* in the allowance account. This method is often called the *income statement ap-*

proach to estimating uncollectible accounts expense.

34 Some companies do not use any valuation allowance for accounts receivable. Under the **direct write-off** method of recognizing uncollectible accounts a business does not recognize any expense until a particular account receivable is determined to be uncollectible. At this point the receivable is written off with an offsetting debit to Uncollectible Accounts Expense. A shortcoming in the direct write-off method is that uncollectible account expense is not properly matched against the related revenue. However, the method is acceptable in financial statements if the distortion in net income is not material in dollar amount. Current income tax regulations **require** the use of the direct write-off method in computing taxable income.

35 For purposes of internal control, employees who maintain the accounts receivable subsidiary ledger must not have access to cash receipts. Also, they must not have authority to issue credit memoranda or to write off receivables as uncollectible.

36 Although offering credit terms is an effective means of generating sales revenue, accounts receivable are a *"nonproductive"* asset which produces no revenue prior to collection. In order to minimize the amount "tied up" in the form of accounts receivable, management may offer customers cash discounts for early payment, accept national credit cards, or factor their accounts receivable.

37 Instead of waiting until receivables are collected, management can obtain cash immediately by factoring accounts receivable. The term *factoring* means either (a) selling accounts receivable to a financial institution (factor), or (b) borrowing money by pledging accounts receivable as collateral for the loan.

38 Making credit sales to customers who use major credit cards avoids the risk of uncollectible accounts because the account receivable is paid promptly by the credit card company. Making sales through credit card companies also has the advantages of eliminating the work of credit investigations, billing, and maintaining an accounts receivable subsidiary ledger. However, credit card companies charge a fee equal to a percentage (usually 3% to 7%) of each credit sale.

39 The manner in which a credit card sale is recorded depends upon the type of credit card used by the customer. When the credit card company is a **bank** (as for Visa or MasterCard), the retailing business deposits signed credit card drafts directly into its bank account. Sales to customers using **bank** credit cards are recorded as **cash sales**. When customers use **nonbank** credit cards (such as American Express or Diners Club), the merchant records an **account receivable** from the credit card company for the full sales price. When payment is made to the merchant by the credit card company, the difference between the amount actually received and the amount of the original receivable is debited to **Credit Card Discount Expense**.

40 In analyzing financial statements it is common practice to consider the relationship between average receivables and annual credit sales. To evaluate whether the company is successful in its policies of granting credit and collecting receivables, the ratio of net sales to average receivable is computed. For example, if annual credit sales were $2,400,000 and average receivables were $600,000, the accounts receivable turnover rate is 4 times per year. This **accounts receivable turnover ratio** indicates how many times the receivables were converted into cash during the year. The higher the turnover rate, the greater the profit opportunity.

41 Another statistic useful in analyzing the liquidity of a company's accounts receivable is the average number of days required to collect these accounts. The **average number of days to collect accounts receivable** is computed by dividing the number of days in a year (365) by the accounts receivable turnover rate.

42 Companies should disclose in notes to the financial statements significant **concentrations of credit risk**. Concentrations of credit risk occur if substantial portions of a company's total accounts receivable are due from a single customer, or from a group of customers in the same industry or geographic region.

*43 There are four basic "accountable events" relating to investments in marketable securities: (1) purchase of the investment, (2) receipt of dividend revenue and interest rev-

---

*Supplemental Topic A, "Accounting for Marketable Securities."

enue, (3) sales of securities owned, and (4) the end-of-period "mark-to-market" adjustment.

*44 Investments in marketable securities originally are recorded at *cost*, which includes any brokerage commissions. In addition to the Marketable Securities ledger account (controlling), most investors also maintain a *marketable securities subsidiary ledger*, with a separate account for each type of security owned.

*45 Investments in marketable securities generate revenue in the form of interest or dividends. Most investors recognize interest and dividend revenue as it is received. (Unlike dividend revenue, interest revenue accrues from day to day. An adjusting entry to accrue interest revenue receivable could be made at the end of each accounting period, but recognition upon receipt is justified by the concept of materiality.)

*46 When an investment in marketable securities is sold, a gain or loss results whenever the sales price is different from cost. A sales price in excess of cost produces a gain, whereas a sales price below cost results in a loss.

*47 At the end of each accounting period, the balance in the Marketable Securities controlling account is adjusted to its current market value. This adjustment is termed "mark-to-market," and represents a *departure from the cost principle*. The mark-to-market adjustment involves two balance sheet accounts: (1) the Marketable Securities controlling account, and (2) a special owners' equity account, Unrealized Holding Gain (or Loss) on Investments.

*48 The adjustment to the asset account may be debit or a credit—whichever is needed to adjust the Marketable Securities controlling account to current market value. There is a corresponding change recorded in the owners' equity account, Unrealized Holding Gain (or Loss) on Investments. The Unrealized Holding Gain (or Loss) account may have either a credit or debit balance. When the current market value of the marketable securities exceeds cost, the holding gain is represented by a credit balance. When the

market value is below cost, the holding loss results in a debit balance.

*49 The gains and losses recorded in the mark-to-market adjustment process are *unrealized*, and are *not* included in the investor's income statement. At any balance sheet date, the Unrealized Holding Gain (or Loss) account represents the difference between the aggregate cost of the marketable securities owned and the aggregate current market value.

*50 Investment transactions are reflected in the financial statements in a variety of ways. Interest revenue, dividend revenue, and gains and losses from sales of investments appear in the multiple-step income statement as *nonoperating* items, after the determination of income from operations. In the statement of cash flows, receipts of dividends and interest are classified as *operating activities*; purchases and sales of marketable securities are classified as *investing activities*. Unrealized holding gains (or losses) recorded by the mark-to-market adjustment process are reported in the stockholders' equity section of the balance sheet.

**51 A promissory note is an unconditional promise in writing to pay on demand or at a future date a definite sum of money. Most notes are for periods of a year or less and are therefore classified as current assets by the payee and as current liabilities by the maker of the note. Most notes bear interest (a charge made for the use of money). Interest rates are stated on an annual basis, and a 360-day year is often assumed to simplify computations. The formula for computing interest is *Interest = principal × rate of interest × time*.

**52 The face amount of each note receivable is debited to the Notes Receivable account in the general ledger. The notes themselves when properly filed are the equivalent of a subsidiary ledger. An adjusting entry for interest accrued on notes receivable is necessary at the end of the period. The entry will debit Interest Receivable and will credit Interest Revenue. When the note is collected in the following period, the entry will be a debit to Cash offset by a credit to Notes Receivable for the face amount of the note,

---

*Supplemental Topic A, "Accounting for Marketable Securities."

**Supplemental Topic B, "Notes Receivable and Interest Revenue."

credit to Interest Receivable for the amount of the accrual, and a credit to Interest Revenue for the remainder of the interest collected.

**53 If the maker of the note defaults (fails to pay as agreed), an entry should be made to transfer the note and any interest earned to an account receivable. If both parties agree that a note should be renewed rather than paid at maturity, an entry should be made debiting and crediting the Notes Receivable account and explaining the terms of the new note.

54 In the past, some businesses **discounted their notes receivable to a bank—that is, sold the notes to a bank at a discount from the maturity value of the note. Discounting notes receivable actually is a form of factoring.

TEST YOURSELF ON FINANCIAL ASSETS

True or False

For each of the following statements, circle the T or the F to indicate whether the statement is true or false.

T F 1 The term "financial asset" has the same meaning as the term "cash equivalents."

T F 2 The balance sheet item of Cash and Cash Equivalents includes amounts on deposit with banks and also currency, money orders, and customers' checks on hand.

T F 3 For strong internal control, the employee who opens incoming mail should not also be responsible for preparing a control listing of checks received in the mail.

T F 4 Internal control over cash should include measures to prevent fraud or loss, to provide accurate records of cash transactions, and to ensure the maintenance of adequate but not excessive cash balances.

T F 5 For strong internal control, an employee who handles cash receipts should not also be responsible for issuing credit memoranda for sales returns.

T F 6 Internal control over cash receipts is most effective when one person is made solely responsible for receiving and depositing cash and making related entries in the accounting records.

T F 7 All cash receipts should be deposited intact in the bank daily, and all material cash payments should be made by check.

T F 8 The principal advantage of a **voucher system** is that it provides strong internal control over the making of expenditures and the payment of liabilities.

T F 9 A voucher is a document which shows that the necessary steps to verify the propriety of an expenditure have been performed and that a cash disbursement is justified.

T F 10 No entry is made in the accounting records at the time a small payment is made from the petty cash fund.

T F 11 The Petty Cash account should be debited when the fund runs low and a check is drawn to replenish it.

T F 12 Reconciling a bank account means determining that all deductions shown on the bank statement represent checks issued by the depositor in the current period,

T F 13 The purpose of preparing a bank reconciliation is to identify those items which cause the balance of cash per the bank statement to differ from the balance of cash per the ledger, and thereby to determine the correct cash balance.

T F 14 In preparing a bank reconciliation, outstanding checks should be deducted from the balance shown on the bank statement, and deposits in transit (or undeposited receipts) should be added to the bank balance.

T F 15 After preparing a bank reconciliation, journal entries should be made to record each of the items shown as adjustments to the balance per depositor's records.

T F 16 James Company deposited a check from a customer, Ray Prince, but the bank returned the check with the notation NSF and deducted it on James Company's bank statement. A telephone call to Prince's office indicated that he would be out of town for

---

**Supplemental Topic B, "Notes Receivable and Interest Revenue."

some weeks. James Company decided to hold the check until Prince returned. The check should be included in the figure for Cash on the balance sheet of James Company.

T F 17 Short-term investments in marketable securities are reported in the balance sheet at *cost*, but their *current market value* must be disclosed in footnotes to the financial statements..

T F 18 The practice of estimating uncollectible accounts expense at the end of each accounting period is designed to match revenue and expenses so that all expenses associated with the revenue earned in the period are recognized as expense in that same period.

T F 19 During the first year of its existence, Cross Company made most of its sales on credit but made no provision for uncollectible accounts. The result would be an overstatement of assets and owners' equity, an understatement of expense, and an overstatement of net income.

T F 20 Conservatism in the valuation of accounts receivable would call for holding the amount entered in Allowance for Doubtful Accounts to a bare minimum.

T F 21 The *balance sheet* approach to estimating uncollectible accounts expense emphasizes the aging of accounts receivable and the adjustment of the allowance account to the level of the estimated uncollectible amount.

T F 22 The *income statement* approach to estimating uncollectible accounts expense does not require the use of an allowance account.

T F 23 When the year-end provision for uncollectible accounts expense is estimated as a percentage of sales, the estimate is recorded without regard for the existing balance in the allowance account.

T F 24 The *direct write-off* method does not cause receivables to be stated in the balance sheet at their estimated realizable value.

T F 25 When a given account receivable is determined to be worthless, it should be written off the books by an entry debit-

ing Uncollectible Accounts Expense and crediting the Allowance for Doubtful Accounts.

T F 26 When a company collects an account receivable previously written off as worthless, an entry should be made debiting Accounts Receivable and crediting Allowance for Doubtful Accounts. A separate entry is then made to record collection of the account.

T F 27 The write-off of an account receivable determined to be worthless by debiting the Allowance for Doubtful Account will not affect the net carrying value of the receivables in the balance sheet.

T F 28 *Factoring accounts receivable* refers to the process of categorizing accounts receivable according to age.

T F 29 A retailer who sells to a customer using a national credit card will have an uncollectibe account if the customer never pays the credit card company.

T F 30 When a retail store sells merchandise to a customer who uses a bank card (such as Visa or MasterCard), the account to be debited is Cash rather than Accounts Receivable.

T F 31 Effective management of accounts receivable includes efforts to maximize this asset and to reduce accounts receivable turnover rate.

T F 32 A company with an accounts receivable turnover rate of 12 requires, on average, less than two weeks to collect its accounts receivable.

T F *33 When an investment in marketable securities is *sold*, gain or loss is computed by comparing sales price with the current market value of the investment reported in the most recent balance sheet.

T F *34 The balance of the Unrealized Holding Gain (or Loss) account represents the difference between the cost of securities owned and their current market values as of the balance sheet date.

T F *35 The mark-to-market adjustment for the *current period* is the same dollar amount as the *balance* of the Unrealized Holding Gain (or Loss) on Investments in Marketable Securities account.

---

*Supplemental Topic A, "Accounting for Marketable Securities."

T F **36 When a company accepts an interest-bearing note from a customer, the interest charges should be recognized as revenue at the time the note is received.

Completion Statements

Fill in the necessary words to complete the following statements:

1 The term *financial assets* includes _____, short-term investments (such as _____ _____ and _____ _____), and _____.

2 The term *cash* includes not only currency, coin, and money orders, but also _____ and the balances of _____ _____.

3 An adequate system of internal control over cash should include separating the function of handling cash from the _____ _____ _____ _____.

4 Cash frauds often begin with temporary unauthorized "borrowing" by employees of cash received from customers. One effective step in preventing such irregularities is to insist that each day's cash receipts be _____ _____ in the bank.

5 Among the most common reconciling items in a bank reconciliation are _____ _____, which should be deducted from the balance shown by the bank, and _____ _____ _____, which should be added to the balance shown by the bank statement.

6 The abbreviation *NSF* applied to a check returned by a bank means _____ _____ _____, and calls for an entry on the depositor's books debiting _____ _____.

7 In the preparation of a bank reconciliation, various reconciling items are added to or deducted from the balance per the bank statement or the balance per the depositor's records. Outstanding checks should be _____ _____ the balance per the _____ _____. Deposits in transit to the bank should be _____ _____ the balance per the _____ _____. Bank service charges should be _____ _____ the balance per the _____ _____. Collections made by the bank

on behalf of the depositor should be _____ _____ the balance per the _____ _____.

8 In a voucher system, every cash disbursement must be authorized by personnel of the _____ department but the related check must be signed by an officer of the _____ department. After a check is signed, it should be mailed directly to the _____; the related voucher should be _____ and returned to the _____ department.

9 Short-term investments in marketable securities are reported in the balance sheet at _____ _____ _____; the valuation principle applicable to marketable securities is termed _____-____-_____.

10 The accounting principle which underlies the practice of estimating uncollectible accounts expense each period is known as the _____ _____. This process is essential to the periodic determination of _____ _____.

11 If the Allowance for Doubtful Accounts is understated, the net realizable value of accounts receivable will be _____, owners' equity will be _____, and net income will be _____.

12 The income statement approach to uncollectible accounts emphasizes estimating the _____ _____ _____ for the period, while the balance sheet approach emphasizes estimating the proper level for the _____ _____ _____ _____.

13 The Inn Place made credit sales of $4,200 to customers using Global Express credit cards. Global Express charges retailers a fee of 4%. The entry to record collecting the cash from these credit sales would be a debit to Cash for $_____, a _____ to _____ _____ _____ for $_____, and a _____ to _____ _____ for $_____.

*14 When an investment in marketable securities is sold, the gain or loss recognized in the income statement is determined by comparing _____ _____ with _____ _____. The required balance in the Unrealized Holding Gain (or Loss) is determined by comparing _____ _____ with _____

---

*Supplemental Topic A, "Accounting for Marketable Securities."

**Supplemental Topic B, "Notes Receivable and Interest Revenue."

_____ of securities owned at the balance sheet date.

**15 If the interest on a 60-day note with a face value of $10,000 amounts to $250, the rate of interest is ____% per annum.

**16 The entry to record interest accrued on notes receivable at year-end consists of a debit to _____ _____ and a credit to _____ _____. Of these accounts, the one to be closed into the Income Summary is _____ _____.

Multiple Choice

Choose the best answer for each of the following questions and enter the identifying letter in the space provided.

_____ **1** Which of the following is **not** accurate with respect to financial assets?
a Financial assets include accounts receivable and notes receivable, as well as short-term investments in the stock of publicly traded corporations.
b Financial assets are reported in the financial statements at values determined in accordance with the cost principle.
c Financial assets are reported in the balance sheet at the amounts of cash these assets represent.
d All financial assets are current assets, but not all current assets are financial assets.

_____ **2** Which of the following practices is undesirable from the standpoint of maintaining adequate internal control over cash?
a Appointing as custodian of a petty cash fund an employee who has no responsibility with respect to maintenance of accounting records.
b Recording overages and shortages from errors in handling over-the-counter cash receipts in a ledger account, Cash Over and Short.
c Authorizing the cashier to make bank deposits.
d Authorizing the official who approves invoices for payment to sign checks.

_____ **3** Checks received through the mail should be:
a Transmitted to the accounts receivable department without delay.
b Deposited by the mail-room employee.
c Listed by the mail-room employee and forwarded to the cashier; a copy of the list should be sent to the accounting department.

d Handled first by the accounting department, which, after making appropriate entries in the accounts, should turn over the checks to the cashier to be made a part of the daily bank deposit.

_____ **4** Which of the following is **not** a significant element of internal control over cash disbursements?
a Perforating or stamping "Paid" on supporting invoices and vouchers.
b Using serially numbered checks and accounting for all numbers in the series.
c Use of a Cash Over and Short account.
d Establishment of a petty cash fund.

_____ **5** Which of the following is **not** a significant element of internal control over cash receipts?
a Preparing a control listing of checks received in the mail.
b Establishing a petty cash fund.
c Depositing each day's cash receipts intact in the bank.
d Prenumbering sales tickets.

_____ **6** Which of the following statements describes an advantage of use of a voucher system?
a Assures that every expenditure is reviewed and verified before payment is made.
b Provides automatically a comprehensive record of business done with particular suppliers.
c Provides a highly flexible system for handling unusual transactions.
d Reduces the number of checks that will be written during any given period.

_____ **7** In establishing and maintaining a petty cash fund:
a The Petty Cash account is debited only when the fund is first established or subsequently changed in size.
b The Petty Cash account is debited whenever the fund is replenished.
c The contents of the fund should at all times be limited to currency, coin, and checks.
d The contents of the fund should at all times be limited to currency, coin, checks, money orders, undeposited cash receipts, petty cash vouchers, and notes receivables from employees.

_____ **8** An NSF check held by the payee should be carried on its records as:
a An element of cash on hand.
b Notes receivable.
c Accounts receivable.
d Cash over and short.

***Supplemental Topic B, "Notes Receivable and Interest Revenue."*

_____ **9** When a bank reconciliation has been satisfactorily completed, the only related entries to be made on the depositor's books are:

a To record items which explain the difference between the balance per the books and the adjusted cash balance.

b To record items which explain the difference between the balance per the books and the balance per the bank statement.

c To correct errors existing in the bank statement.

d To record outstanding checks and deposit in transit.

_____ **10** Before a bank reconciliation was prepared, the accounting records of Adams Company showed a cash balance of $26,440 and the bank statement showed a balance of $32,500. The reconciling items are a deposit in transit of $2,620; outstanding checks of $8,700; and bank service charges of $20. Based upon these facts, the amount of cash that should be shown on Adams' balance sheet is:

a $35,120.

b $26,420.

c $20,360.

d Some other amount.

_____ **11** The *mark-to market* concept:

a Is the valuation method applied to all financial assets.

b Involves recognition of a current period gain or loss, as well as the adjustment of an asset account.

c Requires footnote disclosure of the current market values of marketable securities.

d Has no effect upon the net income of the period.

_____ **12** When an allowance for estimating uncollectible accounts is in use, the writing off of an individual account receivable as worthless will:

a Be recorded by a debit to Uncollectible Accounts Expense.

b Increase the balance in the allowance account.

c Decrease the debit balance in the allowance account.

d Have no effect on the working capital of the company.

_____ **13** Bryan Company, after aging its accounts receivable, estimated that $3,500 of the $125,000 of receivables on hand would probably prove uncollectible. The Allowance for Doubtful Accounts contained a credit balance of $2,300 prior to adjustments. The appropriate accounting entry is:

a A debit to Uncollectible Accounts Expense and a credit to Allowance for Doubtful Accounts for $1,200.

b A debit to Uncollectible Accounts Expense and a credit to Allowance for Doubtful Accounts for $3,500.

c A debit to Uncollectible Accounts expense and a credit to Allowance for Doubtful Accounts for $5,800.

d A debit to Allowance for Doubtful Accounts and a credit to Accounts Receivable for $3,500.

_____ **14** Pine Company uses the income statement approach in estimating uncollectible accounts expense and has found that such expense has consistently approximated 1% of net sales. At December 31 of the current year receivables total $150,000 and the Allowance for Doubtful Accounts has a credit balance of $400 prior to adjustment. Net sales for the current year were $600,000. The adjusting entry should be:

a A debit to Uncollectible Accounts Expense and a credit to Allowance for Doubtful Accounts for $5,600.

b A debit to Uncollectible Accounts Expense and a credit to Allowance for Doubtful Accounts for $6,400.

c A debit to Allowance for Doubtful Accounts and a credit to Accounts Receivable for $6,000.

d A debit to Uncollectible Accounts Expense and a credit to Allowance for Doubtful Accounts for $6,000.

_____ **15** Crawford Company uses the direct write-off method in accounting for uncollectible accounts. Crawford recognizes uncollectible accounts expense:

a As indicated by aging the accounts receivable at the end of the period.

b As a percentage of net sales during the period.

c As accounts receivable from specific customers are determined to be worthless.

d As a percentage of net credit sales during the period.

_____ **16** The entry to record a sale to a customer who uses a bank credit card (such as Visa or Mastercard) includes a debit to:

a An account receivable from the customer.

b An account receivable from the bank.

c Cash.

d Notes receivable.

_____ **17** Hayden Manufacturing's net credit sales for the current year are $5,400,000 and average accounts receivable amount to $675,000. Using 365 days to a year, which of the following is accurate?

a Hayden's accounts receivable turnover ratio is 1 to 8.

b Hayden's accounts receivable were converted into cash 46 times during the current year.

c Hayden's average days' sales uncollected is 8 days.

d Hayden's average days' sales uncollected is 46 days.

_____***18** Scott Corporation sold marketable securities costing $500,000 for $516,000 cash. This transaction is reported in Scott's income statement and statement of cash flows, respectively, as:

a A $516,000 gain and a $516,000 cash receipt.

b A $16,000 gain and a $516,000 cash receipt.

c A $16,000 gain and a $16,000 cash receipt.

d No effect on the income statement; a $516,000 cash receipt in the statement of cash flows.

_____***19** Fisher Corporation invested $400,000 cash in marketable securities in early December. On December 31, the quoted market price for these securities is $419,000. Which of the following is an accurate statement?

a If Fisher sells these investments on January 2 for $410,000, it will report a loss of $9,000 in the January income statement.

b Fisher's December 31 balance sheet reports marketable securities at $400,000 and an Unrealized Holding Gain on Investments of $19,000.

c Fisher's December 31 balance sheet reports marketable securities at $419,000 and an Unrealized Holding Gain on Investments of $19,000.

d Fisher's December income statement includes a $19,000 gain on investments.

_____****20** Which of the following statements regarding notes receivable is _false_?

a The person who signs the note and promises to pay is called the maker of the note.

b When a company lends money, the company's financial statements should report a note receivable and interest revenue.

c The maker of a note receivable records an asset by debiting Note Receivable in his or her accounting records.

d In determining the number of days used in computing interest, the note's date of origin is not included, but the note's maturity date is included.

_____****21** Mann Company accepts numerous notes receivable from its customers. When the maker of a note defaults, Mann Company should:

a Transfer the principal of the note to Accounts Receivable and write off the accrued interest as a loss.

b Make no accounting entry if the maker of the defaulted note will sign a renewal note on equally favorable terms.

c Debit Accounts Receivable for the principal of the note plus interest earned, offset by credit to Notes Receivable and Interest Revenue.

d Record a liability for the maturity value of the note.

Exercises

1 Listed below are eight technical accounting terms emphasized in this chapter.

Accounts receivable turnover	*Bank reconciliation*
Direct write-off method	*Allowance method*
Concentration of credit risk	*Cash equivalent*
	Financial asset
	Mark-to-market

Each of the following statements may (or may not) describe one of these technical terms. In the space provided below each statement, indicate the accounting term described or answer "None" if the statement does not correctly describe any of the terms.

a A large portion of receivables due from customers vulnerable to the same economic environment.

_____

b A determination of the items making up the difference between the bank balance and the balance according to the depositor's records.

_____

c Method of accounting for uncollectible receivables which fails to match revenue and related expenses.

_____

d Balance sheet valuation standard applicable to investments in marketable securities.

_____

e A ratio, computed by dividing average receivables by net sales, that indicates the liquidity of the receivables.

_____

f Contra-asset account representing the portion of receivables estimated to be uncollectible.

_____

---

*Supplemental Topic A, "Accounting for Marketable Securities."

**Supplemental Topic B, "Notes Receivable and Interest Revenue."

g Cash and assets convertible directly into known amounts of cash, such as marketable securities and receivables.

_____

2 Indicate the proper sequence of the following events in the operation of a voucher system by numbering the steps in order of their normal occurrence.

_____ Voucher reviewed by treasurer and check signed and mailed.

_____ Preparation of voucher, including verification of process, quantities, terms, and other data on vendor's invoice.

_____ Receipt of goods and preparation of receiving report.

_____ Issuance of purchase order.

_____ Purchase and related liability recorded.

_____ Voucher filed in paid voucher file.

_____ Voucher filed in unpaid voucher file by payment date.

_____ Voucher and supporting documents perforated to prevent reuse.

_____ Accounting department forwards voucher and supporting documents to finance department.

3 You are to fill in the missing portions of the bank reconciliation shown at the right for Hunter Construction at July 31, 19__, using the following additional information:

a Outstanding checks: no. 301, $2,500; no. 303, $600; no. 304, $1,800; no. 306, $1,282.

b Service charge by bank, $6.

c Deposit made after banking hours on July 31, $1,950.

d A $264 NSF check drawn by our customer Jay Kline was deducted from our account by the bank and returned to us.

e An $1,800 note receivable left by us with the bank for collection was collected and credited to our account. No interest is involved.

f Our check no. 295, issued in payment of $688 for office supplies, was written as $688 but was erroneously recorded in our accounts as $580.

HUNTER CONSTRUCTION
Bank Reconciliation
July 31, 19__

Balance per bank statement, July 31,19__ $17,018
Add:

Deduct:

Adjusted balance .... $_____

Balance per depositor's records, July 31, 19__ $11,364
Add:

Deduct:

Adjusted balance (as above) .... $_____

4 A list of account titles, each preceded by a number, appears below. In the space provided, indicate the accounts to be debited and credited in properly recording the five transactions described. In some cases more than one account may be debited or credited.

(Note that X designates any account not specified in the list.)

1 Cash
2 Notes Receivable
3 Interest Receivable
4 Accounts Receivable
5 Allowance for Doubtful Accounts
20 Interest Revenue
30 Uncollectible Accounts Expense
31 Credit Card Discount Expense
X Any account not listed

Transactions	Account(s) Debited	Account(s) Credited
Example Rendered services, receiving part cash and the balance on account.	1, 4	X
a Using an allowance method, made month-end adjusting entry to recognize current period uncollectible accounts expense.		

Transactions	Account(s) Debited	Account(s) Credited
b Wrote off the account of J. Smith as uncollectible.		
c Collected cash from a national credit card company (not a bank) for credit card sales made this week.		
d Reinstated the account of J. Smith, written off in **1** above, when Smith promised to make payment.		
e Collected the J. Smith account in full.		
**f Collected a note receivable, plus interest at maturity date. A portion of the interest collected had been accrued as of the end of the preceding month.		

5 The balance sheet of Carsoni, Inc., included the following items at November 30:

Marketable securities	$510,000
Note receivable	10,000
Interest receivable	200
Accounts receivable	100,000
Less: Allowance for doubtful accounts	2,400
Unrealized holding gain on investments in marketable securities	15,000

In the space provided, prepare general journal entries to record the following events occurring in December (explanations not required):

Dec. 4 An account receivable for $230 previously written off is unexpectedly collected. (Make two separate entries.)

Dec. 8 A $2,275 account receivable is written off as uncollectible.

**Dec. 16 A 20%, 60-day note receivable is received from a customer in settlement of a $6,000 account receivable due today.

**Dec. 30 Collected in full a 12%, 90-day $10,000 note receivable land interest due today. As of November 30, $200 interest receivable had been accrued on this note. (Remember to record interest revenue earned in December.)

Dec. 31 An aging of accounts receivable indicates the need for a balance of $3,500 in the allowance for doubtful accounts. (Consider the effects of the transactions on December 4 and December 8 before making the month-end adjusting entry.)

**Dec. 31 Prepared an adjusting entry to record accrued interest on the note received on December 16. (Assume a 360-day year in your interest computation.)

*Dec. 31 On December 31, the current market value of Carsoni's marketable securities is $518,000. This investment had originally cost Carsoni $495,000 several months ago.

	General Journal		
19__			
Dec. 4			

---

*Supplemental Topic A, "Accounting for Marketable Securities."

**Supplemental Topic B, "Notes Receivable and Interest Revenue."

		General Journal		

**6 Compute the interest on the following amounts using the assumption of a 360-day year.

a $12,000 at 14% for 60 days: $ _____

b $ 8,400 at 18% for 75 days: $ _____

c $ 4,000 at 12% for 90 days: $ _____

d $ 9,000 at 12½% for 120 days: $ _____

e $13,000 at 15% for 180 days: $ _____

**Supplemental Topic B, "Notes Receivable and Interest Revenue."

SOLUTIONS TO CHAPTER 8 SELF-TEST

True or False

1 **F** The term "financial asset" describes cash and those assets convertible into known amounts of cash (cash equivalents, marketable securities, and receivables). Cash equivalents are only **one type** of financial asset—very liquid short-term investments in money market funds, U.S. Treasury bills and high-grade commercial paper.

2 **T** All items that a bank will accept for immediate deposit, as well as certain short-term investments, are classified as Cash and Cash Equivalents.

3 **F** A copy of the control listing is sent to the cashier who makes deposits and to the accounting department. Daily comparison of the control listing with actual deposits and amounts recorded by the accounting department should reveal any errors.

4 **T** These are some of the measures essential to a good system of internal control.

5 **T** This combination of duties would enable the employee to conceal cash shortages by issuing fictitious credit memoranda.

6 **F** Subdivision of duties requires that employees who handle cash receipts should not have access to the accounting records.

7 **T** These are two of the major steps in achieving internal control over cash.

8 **T** Each transaction requiring a cash payment is verified, approved, and recorded by the accounting department before a check is issued by the finance department.

9 **T** Approval signatures are placed on the voucher as evidence that the expenditure was authorized, the goods or services received, the invoice prices verified, and the proper accounts debited and credited.

10 **T** Expenses are recorded in the accounting records only when the fund is replenished.

11 **F** The entry to replenish the fund consists of debits to various expense accounts and a credit to Cash.

12 **F** A bank reconciliation is a schedule explaining any difference between the balance shown on the bank statement and the balance shown in the depositor's records.

13 **T** The balance shown in the bank statement and that shown in the accounting records are each adjusted for any unrecorded transactions.

14 **T** These two items are the most common examples of transactions recorded by the depositor that have not been recorded by the bank.

15 **T** All reconciling items which adjust the depositor's records are entered on the books so that the accounting records reflect the correct amount of cash.

16 **F** An NSF check should be viewed as an account receivable from the maker of the check, not as cash. An entry should be made consisting of a debit to the account receivable from the customer and a credit to Cash.

17 **F** Under the mark-to-market approach, marketable securities are adjusted to market value at the balance sheet date. This current market value is used in the money columns of the balance sheet, while the cost of the investment is disclosed in notes to the financial statements.

18 **T** A fundamental principle of accounting is that revenue should be offset by the expenses incurred in generating that revenue.

19 **T** As a result of making no provision for uncollectible accounts, expense is understated and accounts receivable are overstated. Net income is therefore too big and so is owners' equity.

20 **F** Conservatism implies reporting assets at their minimum value. The Allowance for Doubtful Accounts is subtracted from Accounts Receivable to arrive at a net figure; the larger the allowance, the smaller the net amount.

21 **T** The expense is the amount of adjustment required to bring the existing balance in the allowance account to the amount determined by aging the accounts receivable.

22 **F** Uncollectible accounts expense is determined by a percentage of sales; the allowance account is credited for this amount without regard for any balance already existing.

23 **T** This approach is called the **income statement** approach to estimating uncollectible accounts.

24 **T** Accounts receivable are stated at face amount unless they are determined to be worthless, at which time they are written off (expensed).

25 **F** When the allowance method of estimating bad debts is being used, the write-off of a specific account receivable consists of a debit to the Allowance for Doubtful Accounts and a credit to Accounts Receivable.

26 T　Note that the entry to reinstate the account receivable is exactly the opposite of the entry that was made to write off the account as worthless.

27 T　The write-off reduces both the asset and the contra-asset account by the same amount; the net realizable value of accounts receivable shown in the balance sheet does not change.

28 F　The term *factoring accounts receivable* refers to the practice of obtaining cash immediately by either selling the accounts receivable, or using them as collateral for a loan. Accounts receivable are classified according to age in the preparation of an *aging schedule* (used in the balance sheet approach to estimating uncollectible accounts).

29 F　The credit card company sustains the loss.

30 T　Bank credit card drafts are deposited at the bank for immediate credit and are the equivalent of cash.

31 F　Management should strive to *minimize* amounts "tied up" in this nonproductive asset by offering cash discounts, accepting national credit cards, and factoring receivables. *Increasing* accounts receivable turnover is desirable, since this indicates that accounts receivable are being converted to cash more quickly.

32 F　The average period to collect accounts receivable is approximately 30 days (365 days ÷ 12).

***33 F**　Gain or loss on sale of an investment in marketable securities is determined by comparing sales price with *original cost* of the security.

***34 T**　This account may have either a debit or credit balance, and is reported as a component of total stockholders' equity in the balance sheet.

***35 F**　The *balance* of the Unrealized Holding Gain (or Loss) account is the difference between current market value and original cost of marketable securities owned at the balance sheet date. The current period *adjustment* is the difference between the current market value of the marketable securities and the existing balance in the marketable securities account (which may be different from cost due to previous years' mark-to-market adjustments).

****36 F**　Interest revenue is earned throughout the life of the note.

Completion Statements

1 Cash, cash equivalents, marketable securities, receivables.　**2** Checks, bank accounts.　**3** Maintenance of accounting records.　**4** Deposited intact.　**5** Outstanding checks, deposits in transit.　**6** Not Sufficient Funds, Accounts Receivable.　**7** Deducted from, bank statement, added to, bank statement, deducted from, depositor's records, added to, depositor's records.　**8** Accounting, finance, payee, perforated (or stamped paid), accounting.　**9** Current market value, mark-to-market.　**10** Matching principle, net income.　**11** Overstated, overstated, overstated.　**12** Uncollectible accounts expense, allowance for doubtful accounts.　**13** $4,032; debit; Credit Card Discount Expense, $168; credit; Accounts Receivable; $4,200.　***14** Sales price, original cost, current market value, original cost.　****15** 15%.　****16** Interest Receivable Interest Revenue, Interest Revenue.

Multiple Choice

1 Answer **b**—all financial assets are reported at current values, although current value is determined differently for each category of financial asset. The valuation of marketable securities at current market value represents an exception to the cost principle.

2 Answer **d**—a major step in achieving internal control over cash disbursements is separation of the function of approving expenditures from the function of signing checks. Answer **a** is an example of proper segregation of duties; answer **b** provides a means of identifying weakness in internal control over cash receipts. Because control listings exist for both over-the-counter sales and for cash received in the mail, there is no breakdown of internal control in having the cashier make the bank deposits.

3 Answer **c**—the control listing prepared by the mailroom employee (who then ceases to have access to the receipts) is compared to the daily bank deposits made by the cashier.

4 Answer **c**—use of a Cash Over and Short account is a means of achieving control over cash *receipts*. Cash on hand in the drawer at

---

*Supplemental Topic A, "Accounting for Marketable Securities."

**Supplemental Topic B, "Notes Receivable and Interest Revenue."

the end of the day is compared to the cash sales as shown on the register tape (control listing); any difference is debited or credited to the Cash Over and Short account.

5 Answer **b**—establishment of a petty cash fund is a mean of achieving control over small cash *disbursements* that are not normally made by check. The other answers listed are examples of internal control measures over cash receipts.

6 Answer **a**—the *accounting* department examines supporting documents for cash disbursements and signs a voucher indicating that payment is authorized. The *finance* department issues the check and marks the supporting documents in some manner to prevent them from being used again.

7 Answer **a**—when the petty cash fund is replenished, individual expense accounts are debited and Cash is credited. The petty cash box should contain cash and/or vouchers totaling the exact amount of the fund. Undeposited cash receipts should *not* be held in the petty cash fund.

8 Answer **c**—an NSF check does not constitute cash or a note receivable from the customer. (A note receivable is a *written promise to pay* at a specified time a definite sum of money.)

9 Answer **a**—the depositor wants to adjust his or her accounting records to the adjusted balance shown on the bank reconciliation—this is the amount that is to be shown on the balance sheet as "cash." Answers **c** and **d** are items that have already been recorded properly in the depositor's accounting records, so no adjusting entry is necessary.

10 Answer **b**—of the three reconciling items shown, only the bank service charges need to be subtracted from the cash balance in Adams' accounting records. We can also arrive at the adjusted cash balance an alternate way: balance on the bank statement plus the deposit in transit minus outstanding checks.

11 Answer **d**—the mark-to-market concept requires adjustment of the balance of the Marketable Securities account to current market value at the balance sheet date. This adjustment affects an asset account and a stockholders' equity account, but has no effect upon net income. Marketable securities

are reported in the balance sheet at current market value, with the *cost* of the securities disclosed in notes to the financial statements.

12 Answer **d**—working capital consists of current assets minus current liabilities. The writing off of an account receivable entails a debit to Allowance for Doubtful Accounts and a credit to Accounts Receivable. This entry decreases Accounts Receivable and also decreases the balance in the contra-asset account—Allowance for Doubtful Accounts. The *net realizable value* of accounts receivable is the same before and after the write-off; thus, there is no effect on working capital.

13 Answer **a**—the balance sheet approach of aging the accounts receivable determines the desired credit balance that should be in the Allowance for Doubtful Accounts. Since the Allowance for Doubtful Accounts already contains a credit balance of $2,300, Bryan Company must increase (credit) this account $1,200—the debit part of the entry is to Uncollectible Accounts Expense.

14 Answer **d**—under the income statement approach, the uncollectible accounts expense is estimated at some percentage of net sales (or net credit sales). The adjusting entry is made in the full amount of this estimated expense, without regard for the current balance in the Allowance for Doubtful Accounts.

15 Answer **c**—companies using the direct write-off method do not estimate uncollectible accounts expense. Instead, this expense is only recognized when specific accounts are identified as uncollectible.

16 Answer **c**—banks accept for immediate deposit the drafts signed by customers using bank credit cards. Therefore, these sales are viewed as cash sales rather than as sales on account.

17 Answer **d**—Hayden's accounts receivable turnover ratio is 8 ($5,400,000 divided by $675,000). This means that Hayden's accounts receivable turned over (were converted into cash) 8 times during the current year. The average days' sales uncollected is computed by dividing 365 days by the turnover rate—365 ÷ 8 = approximately 46 days.

*18 Answer **b**—the gain recognized in the income statement is computed by comparing the sales price of $516,000 with the cost of $500,000. In the statement of cash flows, the cash proceeds from the sale constitute a cash receipt from investing activities.

*19 Answer **c**—the mark-to-market adjustment has no effect upon the December income statement. If the marketable securities are sold in January for $410,000, Fisher recognizes a $10,000 gain in January on the sale ($410,000 sales price – $400,000 cost).

20 Answer **c—the maker of the note is the borrower of the money and records a *liability*—Note Payable.

21 Answer **c—interest earned on the note is recorded through the maturity date and is included in the account receivable from the maker. The interest receivable on a defaulted note is just as valid a claim against the maker as is the principal amount.

Solutions to Exercises

1

a Concentration of credit risk
b Bank reconciliation
c Direct write-off method
d Mark-to-market
e None (The accounts receivable turnover is net sales divided by average receivables.)
f None (The statement describes the Allowance for Doubtful Accounts.)
g Financial assets

2

<u>7</u> Voucher reviewed by treasurer and check signed and mailed.

<u>3</u> Preparation of voucher, including verification of prices, quantities, terms, and other data on vendor's invoice.

<u>2</u> Receipt of goods and preparation of receiving report.

<u>1</u> Issuance of purchase order.

<u>4</u> Purchase and related liability recorded.

<u>9</u> Voucher filed in paid voucher file.

<u>5</u> Voucher filed in unpaid voucher file by payment date.

<u>8</u> Voucher and supporting documents perforated to prevent reuse.

<u>6</u> Accounting department forwards voucher and supporting documents to finance department.

3

HUNTER CONSTRUCTION
Bank Reconciliation
July 31, 19__

Balance per bank statement, July 31,19__		$17,018
Add: Deposit on July 31		1,950
		$18,968
Deduct: Outstanding checks:		
No. 301	$2,500	
No. 303	600	
No. 304	1,800	
No. 306	1,282	6,182
Adjusted balance		$12,786
Balance per depositor's records, July 31, 19__		$11,364
Add: Note receivable collected for us by bank.		1,800
		$13,164
Deduct: Service charge.............................	$ 6	
NSF check of Jay Kline	264	
Error on check no. 295	108	378
Adjusted balance (as above)		$12,786

4

Accounts

	Debited	Credited
a	30	5
b	5	4
c	1, 31	4
d	4	5
e	1	4
**f	1	3, 20, 2

---

*Supplemental Topic A, "Accounting for Marketable Securities."

**Supplemental Topic B, "Notes Receivable and Interest Revenue."

		General Journal		
19__				
Dec. 4		Accounts Receivable	230	
		Allowance for Doubtful Accounts		230
		To reinstate as an asset an account receivable previously written off		
		as uncollectible.		
	4	Cash	230	
		Accounts Receivable		230
		To record collection of account reinstated in preceding entry.		
	8	Allowance for Doubtful Accounts	2,275	
		Accounts Receivable		2,275
		To write off an account receivable determined to be uncollectible.		
**16		Notes Receivable	6,000	
		Accounts receivable		6,000
		Received a 10%, 60-day note in settlement of an account receivable.		
**30		Cash	10,300	
		Notes Receivable		10,000
		Interest Receivable		200
		Interest Revenue		100
		To record collection of note receivable and interest due today.		
	31	Uncollectible Accounts Expense	3,145	
		Allowance for Doubtful Accounts		3,145
		To increase balance in allowance account to $3,500:		
		Required balance $3,500		
		Current balance ($2,400 + $230 − $2,275) 355		
		Required adjustment $3,145		
**31		Interest Receivable	25	
		Interest Revenue		25
		To accrue interest on note receivable for 15 days in December		
		($6,000 x 10% × $\frac{15}{360}$ = $25).		
*31		Marketable Securities	8,000	
		Unrealized Holding Gain on Investments in Marketable Securities		8,000
		To adjust Marketable Securities account to current market value of $518,000, and		
		to adjust Unrealized Holding Gain to $23,000 ($518,000 less $495,000 cost).		

**6

a $280 ($12,000 × .14 × $\frac{60}{360}$)

b $315 ($8,400 × .18 × $\frac{75}{360}$)

c $120 ($4,000 × .12 × $\frac{90}{360}$)

d $375 ($9,000 × .125 × $\frac{120}{360}$)

e $975 ($13,000 ×.15 × $\frac{180}{360}$)

*Supplemental Topic A, "Accounting for Marketable Securities."

**Supplemental Topic B," "Notes Receivable and Interest Revenue."

INVENTORIES AND THE COST OF GOODS SOLD

HIGHLIGHTS OF THE CHAPTER

1 In a retail or wholesale business, inventory consists of all goods owned and held for sale in the regular course of business. In manufacturing businesses there are three major types of inventories: finished goods, work in process, and materials. In the current asset section of the balance sheet, inventory is listed immediately after accounts receivable.

2 The primary basis of accounting for inventory is cost, which includes all expenditures necessary to place the merchandise in the proper location and condition for sale, such as transportation-in, storage, insurance while in transit, etc.

3 A *perpetual* inventory system maintains a continuously updated Inventory account. As merchandise is acquired, its cost is added to the Inventory account; as goods are sold, their cost is transferred from inventory into the cost of goods sold. A sale of merchandise requires two entries: (a) a debit to Cash (or Accounts Receivable) and credit to Sales for the sales price, and (b) a debit to Cost of Goods Sold and a credit to Inventory for the cost of the merchandise.

4 When several lots of identical merchandise are purchased at different prices during the year, which of these costs should be used as the *cost of goods sold* in recording sales transactions? In determining the *cost* of merchandise sold in a particular sales transaction, accountants may use *specific identification*, or they may adopt one of the following three *cost flow assumptions*: (a) *average cost*, (b) *first-in, first-out (FIFO)*, or (c) *last-in, first-out (LIFO)*.

5 The *specific identification* method may be used only when the actual costs of individual units can be determined from the accounting records. The actual cost of units sold is transferred from inventory into cost of goods sold.

6 If the items in inventory are similar in function, cost, and sales price, a seller may follow the convenient practice of using *cost flow assumption*, such as average cost, FIFO, or LIFO. The cost flow assumption *need not correspond to the physical movement of the company's merchandise*. Use of a flow assumption eliminates the need for separately identifying each unit sold and looking up its actual cost.

7 The *average cost* method values all merchandise—units sold and units remaining in inventory—at the *average* per-unit cost. Average cost (computed after every purchase) is computed by dividing the total cost of goods available by the number of units in inventory. Since the average cost may change following each purchase, this method also is called *moving average*. When units are sold, the average per-unit cost is transferred into cost of goods sold.

8 The *first-in, first-out (FIFO)* method is based upon the assumption that the first units purchased are the first units sold. When units are sold, the cost of the oldest units on hand is transferred into cost of goods sold. Remaining inventory, therefore, is comprised of the most recent purchases.

9 The *last-in, first-out (LIFO)* method assumes that the most recently acquired units are sold first. When units are sold, the *most recent* purchase costs are transferred from

inventory into cost of goods sold. Remaining inventory, therefore, consists of the "old" merchandise acquired in the earliest purchases.

10 During a period of changing prices, each of the four alternative inventory valuation methods will lead to different figures for cost of goods sold, gross profit on sales, net income, inventory, and owners' equity. All are acceptable, however, because they are merely alternative methods of determining *cost*.

11 During a period of rising prices, the **LIFO** method will lead to the highest figure for cost of goods sold, the smallest inventory value, the lowest net income, and the lowest income tax. This is because the most recent (and higher) costs are considered to be the cost of the units sold and the earlier (and lower) purchase prices are considered to be the cost of the unsold units comprising the ending inventory. Supporters of LIFO argue that income is most accurately measured by matching the *current* cost of merchandise against *current* sales prices, regardless of which physical units of merchandise are actually delivered to customers.

12 The **FIFO** method produces a realistic balance sheet amount for inventory close to current replacement cost, whereas the **LIFO** method produces a balance sheet value for inventory reflecting prices in the distant past.

13 Continuing inflation and high income tax rates have led to increased interest by business managers in LIFO. The LIFO method causes reported net income to reflect the increasing cost of replacing the goods sold during the year, and tends to avoid basing income tax payments on an exaggerated measurement of taxable income. Income tax regulations allow a corporation to use LIFO in its tax return only if the company also uses LIFO in its financial statements.

14 A company may use different inventory valuation methods to account for different types of inventory, or for inventories in different geographic locations. The principle of *consistency* stresses that the chosen inventory method be followed consistently from period to period. A company is permitted to change its method provided the reasons for the change are explained and the effects of the change on net income are fully disclosed.

15 When a manufacturer uses a *just-in-time (JIT)* inventory system, purchases of raw materials and component parts arrive just in time for use in the manufacturing process; in addition, the manufacturing process is completed just in time to ship finished goods to customers. A just-in-time system greatly reduces the size of raw material and finished goods inventories, but does not eliminate them entirely.

16 Taking a physical inventory is necessary at the end of each year in order to adjust the perpetual inventory records to the physical count of items actually on hand. In most cases, the year-end physical count reveals some shortages or damaged merchandise. The costs of missing or damaged units are removed from the inventory records using the same flow assumption as is used in recording the cost of goods sold. If shrinkage losses are small, the costs removed from inventory are debited directly to the Cost of Goods Sold account. If these losses are material in amount, the offsetting debit should be to a special loss account, such as Inventory Shrinkage Loss.

17 Although inventory is recorded in the accounting records at cost when purchased, the *lower-of-cost-or-market rule (LCM)* requires that inventory be reported in the balance sheet at the lower of its (a) cost, or (b) market value. In the LCM rule, "market value" means *current replacement cost*. Inventory, therefore, is valued at the lower of its cost (as determined under specific identification, average cost, FIFO, or LIFO methods) or its current replacement cost. If the current replacement cost of the ending inventory is substantially *below* the cost determined under any of the above four methods, the inventory is written down to the replacement cost; the offsetting debit is to the Cost of Gods Sold (or if material, to a special loss account).

18 Inventory includes all goods owned regardless of location. A *proper cutoff* means that purchase and sale transactions occurring near year-end are *recorded in the right accounting period*. A sale should be recorded when title to the merchandise passes to the buyer. Title passes from seller to buyer when delivery is made. For goods in transit at year-end, we must consider the terms of shipment. If the terms of shipment are *F.O.B. shipping point*, the goods in transit are the property of the buyer. If the terms are *F.O.B. destination*, the goods remain the property of the seller while in transit.

19 Although most businesses use a perpetual inventory system, some small businesses use the *periodic* system. In a periodic inventory system, the Inventory account remains unchanged until the end of the accounting period. The cost of merchandise purchased during the year is debited to a Purchases account, rather than to the Inventory account. When merchandise is sold to a customer, an entry is made recognizing the sales revenue, but no entry is made to reduce the Inventory account or to recognize the cost of goods sold. At the end of the year, a physical inventory is taken. The cost assigned to this ending inventory is used in computing the cost of goods sold according to the following formula:

Beginning inventory	XXXX
Add: Purchases during the year	XXXX
Cost of goods available for sale	XXXX
Less: Ending inventory	(XXX)
Cost of goods sold	XXXX

20 The same inventory flow assumptions used in perpetual inventory systems to determine the cost of goods sold may be used with a periodic system. In the periodic system, however, we use the flow assumption to determine the costs which are to be assigned to the *inventory* remaining at the end of the period. The cost assigned to the ending inventory (using specific identification, average cost, FIFO, or LIFO) is then subtracted from the cost of goods available for sale to arrive at the cost of goods sold.

21 Both LIFO and average cost methods result in different valuations of ending inventory (and consequently cost of gods sold) under perpetual and periodic costing procedures. Many companies that use LIFO in a perpetual inventory system *restate* their year-end inventory at the lower cost determined by the *periodic* LIFO costing procedures in order to receive the maximum tax benefit from the LIFO method. When specific identification or the FIFO method is in use, the perpetual and periodic costing procedures result in exactly the same valuation of inventory.

22 The importance of properly accounting for ending inventory derives from the *matching principle*—the accounting standard matching appropriate costs against revenue to determine net income. When we assign a value to the ending inventory, we are thereby also determining the *cost of goods sold* and the *gross profit on sales*.

23 The ending inventory of one year is the beginning inventory of the next year. Therefore an error in the valuation of ending inventory will cause the income statements of two successive years to be in error by the full amount of the error in inventory valuation.

24 a When *ending* inventory is understated, net income will be understated.
   b When *ending* inventory is overstated, net income will be overstated.
   c When *beginning* inventory is understated, net income will be overstated.
   d When *beginning* inventory is overstated, net income will be understated.

25 In other words, an inventory error is *counterbalancing* over a two-year period. If ending inventory is overstated, the income for the current year will be overstated, but income for the following year will be understated by the same amount. The reverse is also true: If ending inventory is understated, the income for the current year will be understated but income for the following year will be overstated.

26 An error in inventory valuation will cause several parts of the financial statements to be in error. On the income statement, the cost of goods sold, the gross profit on sales, and the net income will all be wrong by the full amount of the inventory error (ignoring income taxes). On the balance sheet of the year in which the inventory error occurs, the owners' equity, the total current assets, and the balance sheet totals will also be in error.

27 Since an error in inventory has a counterbalancing effect on income over a two-year period, the owners' equity and the balance sheet totals will be correct at the end of the second year.

28 The *gross profit method* of estimating inventories is useful when inventory is lost by fire or theft, or when it is desired to prepare monthly financial statements without incurring the expense of taking a physical inventory.

29 An assumption underlying the gross profit method is that the gross profit rate does not change from period to period. Thus, we may determine the current cost percentage from the income statement of the last period. The cost percentage (or cost ratio) is found by dividing the cost of goods sold by net sales.

(The cost percentage also is equal to 100% minus the gross profit rate.)

30 Once the cost ratio is known, the gross profit method is applied as follows:

a Determine the cost of goods available for sale from the general ledger records of beginning inventory and net purchases.

b Estimate the cost of goods sold by multiplying net sales for the period by the cost ratio.

c Deduct the estimated cost of goods sold from the cost of goods available for sale to find the estimated ending inventory.

31 The *retail method* may be used to estimate the cost of the ending inventory, as follows:

a Determine the retail price of goods available for sale by adding the retail value of the beginning inventory to the retail price of goods purchased during the period.

b Compute the *cost percentage* by dividing the cost of goods available for sale by the retail price of these goods.

c Estimate the *retail value* of the ending inventory by subtracting net sales from the retail value of the goods available for sale.

d Convert the ending inventory valuation to *cost* by multiplying the ending inventory at retail prices by the cost percentage determined in **b** above.

32 The retail method also may be used to simplify the pricing of the annual physical inventory taken at a retail store. The inventory would be counted and priced as follows:

a Take a physical inventory, pricing the goods at *retail prices*. This is easier than pricing the goods at cost, because the goods have price tags showing their retail price.

b Determine the cost percentage.

c Use the cost percentage to reduce the valuation of the ending inventory from retail to cost.

33 The *inventory turnover rate* (a measure of the *liquidity* of inventory) is equal to the cost of goods sold divided by the average amount of inventory. Short-term creditors are interested in this ratio because it indicates how many *times* in the course of a year the company is able to sell its average inventory. The higher this rate, the more quickly the company sells its inventory. The number of *days* required to sell inventory is computed by dividing 365 days by the inventory turnover rate.

34 The length of the *operating cycle* is the average time period between the purchase of merchandise and the conversion of this merchandise back into cash. To determine how quickly inventory converts into cash, we must combine the number of days required to *sell the inventory* (365 days divided by the inventory turnover rate) with the number of days required to *collect the accounts receivable* (365 days divided by the accounts receivable turnover rate).

35 Users of financial statements should understand that accounting methods in use by a company have an effect on financial statement amounts and analytical ratios. A company using LIFO in a period of rising prices generally reports lower net income than if FIFO were used, which affects such ratios as return on assets and return on equity. Inventory turnover rate, current ratio, current assets, and working capital are additional statistics directly affected by the choice of inventory method.

*36 The difference between the LIFO cost of an inventory and its current replacement cost is called a *LIFO reserve*. Existence of a LIFO reserve indicates that the company's inventory is *understated* in terms of its current replacement cost, and in terms of the valuation that would have resulted from the use of the FIFO method. Companies using LIFO disclose in notes to their financial statements the current replacement cost (or the FIFO cost) of inventories.

*37 *Liquidation of the LIFO reserve* occurs if inventory falls to an abnormally low level at year-end. In this case, the costs transferred to the cost of goods sold will come from older—and lower—cost layers. The inclusion of these low costs in the cost of goods sold causes a company's profits to rise dramatically. The abnormal profits which result from the liquidation of a LIFO reserve are a one-time occurrence and do not represent an improvement in financial performance. Whenever a company using LIFO ends its fiscal year with substantially less inventory than at the beginning of the year, liquidation of part of the LIFO reserve has occurred.

*38 The dollar amount of the LIFO reserve can be determined by comparing the LIFO inventory valuation shown in the balance sheet with the current replacement cost of inventories disclosed in the notes to the

---

*Supplemental Topic, "LIFO Reserves."

financial statements. A LIFO reserve represents the amount by which a company has reduced its taxable income *over a period of years* through use of the LIFO method. The aggregate tax benefit since LIFO was adopted can be computed by multiplying the LIFO reserve by the income tax rate for the company.

TEST YOURSELF ON INVENTORIES AND THE COST OF GOODS SOLD

True or False

For each of the following statements, circle the T or the F to indicate whether the statement is true or false.

T F **1** A major objective of accounting for inventories is proper measurement of net income.

T F **2** In a perpetual inventory system, ledger accounts for inventory and the cost of goods sold are continuously updated for purchases and sales of merchandise.

T F **3** The specific identification method of inventory valuation is particularly appropriate for low-priced, high-volume articles.

T F **4** Inventories are usually valued at cost, but the cost figure for an inventory can differ significantly depending upon which inventory method is used.

T F **5** The average-cost method places more weight on the prices at which large purchases were made than on the price at which small purchases were made.

T F **6** Using the first-in, first-out (FIFO) method during a period of rising prices implies that the cheaper goods have been sold and the more costly goods are still on hand.

T F **7** If we consider the "true" cost of sales to be the replacement cost of goods sold, income statements using historical costs tend to understate net income during periods of inflation.

T F **8** During a period of rapid inflation, using LIFO will maximize reported net income.

T F **9** Using the LIFO method implies that the ending inventory consists of the most recently acquired goods.

T F **10** Consistency in the valuation of inventory requires that a method once adopted cannot be changed unless the company is sold.

T F **11** It is an acceptable practice to understate inventories at year-end as long as it is done consistently from year to year.

T F **12** Taking the inventory refers to the physical count to determine the quantity of inventory on hand; pricing the inventory means determining the cost of the inventory on hand.

T F **13** The use of the lower-of-cost-or-market rule produces a conservative inventory valuation because unrealized losses are treated as actually incurred.

T F **14** If the terms of shipment are F.O.B. shipping point, the goods in transit should normally belong to the seller.

T F **15** The recording of a sale in the wrong period will have no effect on the net income for each period if the goods are excluded from inventory in the period in which the sale is recorded.

T F **16** An error in the valuation of inventory at the end of the period will cause errors in net income for two periods.

T F **17** Errors in the valuation of inventory are counterbalancing; an error which causes an overstatement of net income this period will cause an understatement next period.

T F **18** An overstatement of ending inventory will cause an understatement of net income.

T F **19** In tax audits, the IRS often investigates the taxpayer's inventory, because overstated inventory will cause the taxpayer's net income to be understated.

T F **20** The gross profit method permits a business to estimate inventory without actually taking a physical count of the goods on hand.

T F **21** The retail method of inventory valuation permits a business to take the physical inventory and price it at current retail prices rather than look up invoices to determine the cost of goods on hand.

T F **22** The operating cycle for a merchandising business is equal to 365 days divided by the inventory turnover rate.

T F *23 A LIFO reserve is the amount of money a company has saved over the years on income taxes due to the use of the LIFO inventory method.

Completion Statements

Fill in the necessary words to complete the following statements:

1 In a perpetual inventory system, purchases are recorded by a debit to _____ and a credit to Accounts Payable. Sales are recorded by two entries: (a) a debit to Accounts Receivable and a credit to _____ for the _____ price of the merchandise and (b) a debit to _____ _____ _____ _____ and a credit to _____ for the _____ of the goods.

2 The four most commonly used inventory valuation methods are: _____ _____, _____ _____, _____, and _____.

3 During a period of rising prices, using the _____ method implies that the cheaper goods are still on hand while the more expensive one were sold.

4 A _____ inventory system is designed to minimize a company's investment in inventory.

5 The lower-of-cost-or-market rule results in the recognition of a _____ in the _____ cost of inventory. However, an _____ in the _____ cost would not be recognized.

6 If goods are shipped F.O.B. destination, the _____ to the goods while in transit belongs to the _____ and the goods should be excluded from the inventory of the _____.

7 In a periodic inventory system, purchases are recorded by a debit to _____ and a credit to Accounts Payable or Cash. Sales are recorded by a single entry which debits _____ _____ and credits _____ for the _____ price of the merchandise.

8 Ending inventories are **overstated** as follows: Year 1 by $20,000; Year 2 by $8,000; and Year 3 by $15,000. Net income for each of the three years was computed at $25,000. The corrected net income figure (ignoring the effect of income taxes) for each of the three

years is: Year 1, $_____; Year 2, $_____; Year 3, $_____.

9 The method of inventory valuation frequently used by retail stores is first to value the inventory at _____ and then to convert this amount to a _____ figure by applying the _____ of cost to selling prices during the current period.

10 The inventory turnover rate is computed by dividing _____ _____ _____ _____ by _____ _____ . The accounts receivable turnover rate is computed by dividing _____ by _____ _____ _____ . The number of days required to sell inventory is computed by dividing _____ by the _____ _____ _____; the number of days required to collect receivables is computed by dividing _____ by the _____ _____ _____ _____ .

Multiple Choice

Choose the best answer for each of the following questions and enter the identifying letter in the space provided.

_____ **1** Which of the following four items would **not** be included in inventories on the balance sheet?

a Raw materials used in manufacture of chemicals.

b Building materials used in construction.

c Cars left by customers at an auto repair shop.

d Goods purchased but not yet delivered to premises (title passed).

_____ **2** A **perpetual** inventory system:

a Requires the use of the first-in, first-out (FIFO) basis of pricing inventory sold.

b Provides such strong internal control that custody of assets need not be separate from the accounting records for inventory.

c Eliminates the need for taking an annual physical inventory.

d Maintains a continuously updated Inventory account as well as a continuously updated Cost of Goods Sold account.

_____ **3** Which of the following is **not** an acceptable inventory method?

a Lower of cost or market.

b Sales value.

c Specific identification.

d First-in, first-out.

_____ **4** During a period of rising prices, which inventory pricing method might be expected to

---

*Supplemental Topic, "LIFO Reserves."

give the **lowest** valuation for inventory on the balance sheet and the **lowest** net income figure?

a Cost on a LIFO basis.

b Cost on a FIFO basis.

c Average cost.

d FIFO, lower of cost or market.

_____ **5** A physical inventory should be carefully planned in order to ensure each of the following **except**:

a Goods located in the receiving department are included.

b The correct inventory valuation method is used.

c Damaged goods are excluded.

d Merchandise for which an order has been received, but which has not been shipped, is included.

_____ **6** Goods costing $750 are sold for $1,000 at the end of Year 1, but the sale is recorded in Year 2. The goods **were** included in the ending inventory at the end of Year 1. The most likely effect of this error is:

a Net income for Year 1 was understated by $1,000.

b Net income for Year 2 was overstated by $250.

c Beginning inventory for Year 2 was understated by $750.

d Net income for Year 1 was overstated by $250.

_____ **7** Which of the following statements regarding inventory costing methods is **true**?

a Cost flow assumptions are not used in a periodic inventory system; the cost of ending inventory is determined by specific identification based upon units counted in the physical inventory.

b Perpetual and periodic inventory systems will always result in different figures for ending inventory, even if the same inventory costing method is used in each.

c Perpetual and periodic inventory systems will always result in the same figure for ending inventory, as long as the same inventory costing method is used in each.

d Applying LIFO costing procedures in a periodic system may result in a lower "cost" for ending inventory than if LIFO were applied on a perpetual basis.

_____ **8** An overstatement of $1,000 in the inventory at the end of Year 4 would:

a Understate the beginning inventory of Year 5.

b Have no effect on net income of Year 3.

c Overstate purchases for Year 5.

d Have no effect on net income of Year 4.

_____ **9** The **gross profit** method of estimating inventories:

a Is a useful means of determining the rate of gross profit without taking a physical inventory.

b Is a useful means of verifying the reasonableness of a physical inventory count.

c Provides information about the number of units in the ending inventory.

d Provides information about changes in the rate of gross profit.

_____ **10** The **retail method** of estimating inventory:

a Converts ending inventory at retail selling price to cost by multiplying the gross profit percentage.

b Computes the cost of goods sold by multiplying net sales by the cost percentage, and then deducts this amount from cost of goods available to find ending inventory.

c Requires a business to maintain records showing beginning inventory and purchases at both cost and retail prices.

d Assumes that the gross profit rate remains the same as it was in preceding years.

_____ **11** Assume Franco Company and Limerick Corporation are **identical in all respects** except that Franco uses FIFO and Limerick uses LIFO in accounting for inventory. In a period of rising prices, each of the following statements is accurate, **except**:

a Limerick reports lower net income and lower income tax expense than does Franco.

b Limerick will appear to have a higher inventory turnover rate and longer operating cycle than will Franco.

c Limerick's current ratio is lower than Franco's.

d Limerick's cost of goods sold figure more closely approximates current cost of merchandise sold than does Franco's.

_____ *****12** A **LIFO reserve**:

a Is reported as a current asset.

b Represents the amount of money a company not using LIFO could have saved if it had been using LIFO since the business was organized.

c Causes an abnormal decline in net income when it is liquidated.

d Is the amount by which the LIFO cost of inventory understates the current replacement cost of the inventory.

---

*Supplemental Topic, "LIFO Reserves."

Exercises

1 Listed below are eight technical accounting terms emphasized in this chapter.

LCM rule   *Gross profit method*
Cost ratio   *Retail inventory method*
FIFO method   *Inventory shrinkage*
LIFO method   *Consistency*

Each of the following statements may (or may not) describe one of these technical terms. In the space provided below each statement, indicate the accounting term described, or answer "None" if the statement does not correctly describe any of the terms.

a Loss due to missing or damaged units which is recorded in a separate adjusting entry in a perpetual inventory system.

_____

b A method of inventory valuation in which inventory is reported at retail prices.

_____

c A method of estimating the cost of the ending inventory based on the assumption of a constant gross profit rate.

_____

d A method of inventory valuation that assumes the ending inventory consists of goods acquired in the earliest purchases.

_____

e The ratio of cost to selling price.

_____

f A method of pricing in which inventory is valued at the lower of original cost or replacement cost.

_____

g Accounting standard that requires use of the same method of inventory pricing from year to year, with full disclosure of the effects of any change in method.

_____

2 Hom Corporation uses the FIFO method in a perpetual system and adjusts the accounting records to the physical inventory taken at year-end. In each of the situations described below, indicate the effects of the error on the various elements of financial statements prepared at the end of the *current* year, using the following code: **O** = overstated, **U** = understated, **NE** = no effect.

Situation	Revenue	Costs and/or Expenses	Net Income	Assets	Liabilities	Owners' Equity
a No record made of goods purchased on credit and received on Dec. 31; goods omitted from physical count of inventory.						
b Made sale in late December; goods were delivered on Dec. 31 but were also included in physical inventory on Dec. 31.						
c In taking the physical inventory, some goods in a warehouse were overlooked.						
d A purchase made late in year was recorded properly on the books, but the goods were not included in the physical count of inventory.						

Use the following information for Exercises 3, 4, and 5.

Widmer Corporation's accounting records disclose the following information regarding purchases of inventory item no. 329 during May:

	Units	Unit Cost	Total Cost
Beginning inventory, May 1	50	$10.10	$ 505
Purchase, May 3	40	11.00	440
Purchase, May 10	90	12.00	1,080
Purchase, May 21	20	13.75	275

On May 15, Widmer sold 150 units at a price of $16.10 each.

3 Assume Widmer uses a ***perpetual inventory system***. Compute the cost of goods sold and the cost of the ending inventory of 50 units under each of the following inventory methods:

	Cost of Goods Sold	Inventory
a FIFO cost	$_____	$_____
b LIFO cost	$_____	$_____
c Average cost	$_____	$_____

4 Assume Widmer uses a ***periodic inventory system***. Compute the cost of ending inventory of 50 units and the cost of goods sold under each of the following inventory methods:

	Inventory	Cost of Goods Sold
a FIFO cost	$_____	$_____
b LIFO cost	$_____	$_____
c Average cost	$_____	$_____

5 Assume that the replacement cost of each unit of item no. 329 on May 31 is $12.50, and that Widmer uses the FIFO cost flow assumption. Compute the cost of ending inventory and the cost of goods sold applying the ***lower-of-cost-or-market rule*** (with "cost" being defined as the FIFO cost computed in exercises 3 and 4 above).

a Cost of ending inventory using LCM rule. ... $_____
b Cost of goods sold using LCM rule. .... $_____

6 On July 20, 19__, the accountant for B Company is in the process of preparing financial statements for the year ending June 30, 19__. The physical inventory, however, was not taken until July 10, 19__, and the accountant finds it necessary to establish the approximate inventory cost at June 30, 19__, from the following data:

Physical inventory, July 10, 19__	$30,000
Transactions for period July 1–July 10:	
Sales	14,800
Purchases	16,950

The gross profit on sales of the past couple of years has averaged 22.5% of net sales. In the space below, compute the approximate inventory cost at June 30, 19__.

7 ToyMart uses the retail method to estimate its inventory at the end of each month. The following information is available at July 31:

	Cost	Retail
Inventory, June 30	$292,500	$450,000
Purchases during July	187,500	300,000
Goods available for sale during July	$480,000	$750,000

Net sales during July amounted to $350,000. Compute the following:

a The cost percentage that would be used in applying the retail method for the month of July .... _____%
b The estimated inventory at July 31, stated in retail prices .... $_____
c The estimated inventory at July 31, stated at cost .... $_____

SOLUTIONS TO CHAPTER 9 SELF-TEST

True or False

1 **T** Determining the proper valuation of inventory establishes the cost of goods sold for the period, which is used in computing net income.

2 **T** The key feature of a perpetual inventory system is that the records show continuously the amount of inventory on hand and the cost of goods sold.

3 **F** This method is best suited to inventories of high-priced, low-volume items.

4 **T** There are four inventory valuation methods discussed in the text; these methods represent alternative definitions of *cost*.

5 **T** Average cost is computed by dividing the *total* cost of goods available for sale by the total number of units available for sale.

6 **T** FIFO is based on the assumption that the first merchandise acquired (cheaper prices) is sold first.

7 **F** The use of historical costs tends to *overstate* net income because the replacement cost of the merchandise sold is really higher than the cost of goods sold deducted on the income statement.

8 **F** LIFO causes the more current (higher) costs to be included in the cost of goods sold, thus *minimizing* net income.

9 **F** Under LIFO, the ending inventory is assumed to consist of merchandise acquired in the *earliest* purchases.

10 **F** Changes are permitted; however, when a change is made, the effects of the change upon reported net income should be disclosed fully in the footnotes accompanying the financial statements.

11 **F** The validity of both the balance sheet and the income statement depend on accuracy in the valuation of inventory.

12 **T** Establishing a dollar value for inventory consists of multiplying the quantity of each inventory item by the unit cost per item.

13 **T** LCM is a method of inventory valuation in which merchandise is valued at original cost or replacement cost (market), whichever is lower.

14 **F** Title to the goods passes at point of shipment; the goods are the property of the buyer while in transit.

15 **F** The difference between sales price and cost of the inventory (the profit) will be included in net income in the wrong period.

16 **T** The ending inventory of one year is the beginning inventory of the next year.

17 **T** The ending inventory of one year is also the beginning inventory of the following year; total net income for the two-year period is correct.

18 **F** If ending inventory is overstated, the cost of goods sold figure will be understated and net income will be overstated.

19 **F** A business which wants to understate taxable income would *understate* ending inventory.

20 **T** Knowing the gross profit rate enables us to separate the net sales into the gross profit and the cost of goods sold. This cost of goods sold figure is deducted from cost of goods available for sale to estimate ending inventory.

21 **T** These retail price figures are then converted to *cost* by application of cost-to-retail percentage.

22 **F** Dividing 365 by the inventory turnover rate equals the average number of days required to sell inventory. The operating cycle consists of the average number of days required to sell inventory PLUS the average number of days required to collect accounts receivable.

*23 **F** The term "LIFO reserve" refers to the difference between current replacement cost (or FIFO cost) of a company's inventory and the LIFO cost shown in the accounting records. The cumulative tax benefit of using LIFO may be computed by multiplying the LIFO reserve by the income tax rate.

Completion Statements

1 Inventory; (a) Sales, sales; (b) Cost of Goods Sold, Inventory, cost. **2** Specific identification; average cost; first-in, first-out (FIFO); last-in, first-out (LIFO). **3** LIFO. **4** Just-in-time (JIT). **5** Decrease, replacement, increase, replacement. **6** Title, seller, buyer. **7** Purchases, Account Receivable (or Cash), Sales, sales. **8** $5,000; $37,000; $18,000. **9** Retail, cost, percentage (or ratio). **10** Cost of Goods Sold, average inventory, sales (or credit sales), average accounts receivable, 365, inventory turnover rate, 365, accounts receivable turnover rate.

Multiple Choice

1 Answer **c** is not included in the definition of inventory for either a merchandising firm or a manufacturing business. For a merchandising company, inventory consists of all goods owned and held for sale in the regular course of business (answer **d**). In a manufacturing business, there are three types of inventories: raw materials (answers **a** and **b**), goods in process of manufacture, and finished goods.

2 Answer **d**—a perpetual inventory system can be used with any acceptable inventory costing method. Although an updated Inventory account is maintained, basic internal control measures such as subdivision of duties, control of documents by serial numbers, and separation of the accounting function from custody of inventory are necessary. Even though perpetual inventory records show an up-to-date balance for inventory, an annual physical inventory still is taken to determine any "shrinkage" losses and correct any errors in the perpetual inventory records.

3 Answer **b** is not one of the acceptable inventory methods. The acceptable methods are (1) specific identification; (2) average cost; (3) first-in, first-out (FIFO); and (4) last-in, first-out (LIFO). Lower of cost or market is a method of inventory pricing in which goods are valued at original cost or replacement cost (market), whichever is lower.

4 Answer **a** (LIFO cost) yields the lowest value for ending inventory because the ending inventory is presumed to consist of units acquired in the *earliest* purchases which were the lowest costs. This smaller ending inventory figure results in a higher cost of goods sold amount than the other methods and hence a *smaller* net income.

5 Answer **b**—the selection of an inventory method is a decision made by management. The physical inventory is undertaken to establish a true count of all merchandise owned by the company and will be carried out in the same manner regardless of the inventory method selected.

6 Answer **b**—net income for Year 2 was overstated by $250, the *profit* on the sale that should have been recorded in Year 1. If the goods were sold in Year 1, the goods should not have been included in Year 1's ending inventory. Year 1's ending inventory therefore was *overstated* by the *cost* of these goods

($750); the beginning inventory of Year 2 was also *overstated* by $750.

7 Answer **d**—under a periodic system, the cost of items purchased at year-end and not yet sold are considered part of the cost of goods sold during the year; periodic LIFO *assumes* that the latest purchases are sold and that the ending inventory comes from the earliest purchases, Under a perpetual system, the cost of unsold year-end purchases is included in inventory, since the determination of the cost of goods sold is made as each sale occurs and these items were not available before year-end. Answer **a** is incorrect—all four inventory costing methods may be used in either perpetual or periodic systems. In the LIFO and average cost methods, ending inventory and cost of goods amounts would differ under perpetual and periodic systems. Under FIFO and specific identification methods, ending inventory and cost of goods amounts are the same for perpetual and periodic systems.

8 Answer **b**—Year 3 will be unaffected by an inventory error at the end of Year 4. Beginning inventory of Year 5 will be overstated because Year 4's ending inventory is Year 5's beginning inventory, but purchases for Year 5 will be unaffected. Year 4's net income will be overstated.

9 Answer **b**—the gross profit method uses the gross profit percentage to compute an estimate of the *cost* of ending inventory (not the number of *units* as in answer **c**). In using the gross profit method, it is assumed that the rate of gross profit earned in the preceding year will remain the same for the current year.

10 Answer **c**—in order to compute the cost percentage for use in the retail inventory method, a business must have amounts for the goods available at both cost and retail prices. "Goods available for sale" is the total of beginning inventory plus purchases during the current period. Answer **a** is incorrect because it mentions multiplying by the *gross profit percentage* instead of the *cost percentage*. Answer **b** is descriptive of the *gross profit method* of estimating inventory. The retail method is based upon the cost ratio of the *current year*, rather than that of the prior year.

11 Answer **b**—due solely to the use of LIFO, Limerick's inventory turnover rate will appear to be higher than Franco's, and therefore Limerick will appear to require fewer days to sell its average inventory. The operating cycle consists of the number of days required to sell inventory PLUS the number of days to collect accounts receivable. Assuming the accounts receivable turnover rate and sales are identical for both companies, Limerick would appear to have a ***shorter*** operating cycle than Franco. Answers **a**, **c**, and **d** are all accurate.

*12 Answer **d**—the amount of a LIFO reserve is computed as the difference between LIFO cost and the current replacement cost of ending inventory. This amount is ***not*** specifically reported in the financial statements, although it can be determined by comparing LIFO cost to the current replacement cost of inventory disclosed in notes to the financial statements. When inventory levels decline substantially, liquidation of part or all of the LIFO reserve occurs and results in a one-time ***increase*** in net income.

Solutions to Exercises

1

a Inventory shrinkage
b None (Only in specialized industries would inventories be valued at market prices.)
c Gross profit method
d LIFO method
e Cost ratio
f LCM rule
g Consistency

2

	Reve-nue	Costs and/or Expenses	Net Income	Assets	Liabili-ties	Owner's Equity
a	NE	NE	NE	U	U	NE
b	NE	U	O	O	NE	O
c	NE	O	U	U	NE	U
d	NE	O	U	U	NE	U

3

		Cost of Goods Sold	Inventory
a	FIFO cost:	$1,665 ($505 + $440 + $720)	$635 ($2,300 − $1,665)
b	LIFO cost:	$1,722 ($1,080 + $440 + $202)	$578 ($2,300 − $1,722)
c	Average cost:	$1,687.50 (11.25 x 150)	$612.60 ($2,300 − $1,687.50)

4

		Inventory	Cost of Goods Sold
a	FIFO cost:	$635 ($275 + $360)	$1,665 ($2,300 − $635)
b	LIFO cost:	$505	$1,795 ($2,300 − $505)
c	Average cost:	$575 ($11.50 x 50)	$1,725 ($2,300 − $575)

5

a Ending inventory (LCM rule): $625 (50 × $12.50 is lower than FIFO)
b Cost of goods sold: $1,675 ($2,300 − $625 ending inventory)

6

Physical inventory, July 10, 19__	$30,000
Less: Net purchases for period July 1–July 10	16,950
	$13,050
Add: Cost of goods sold for period July 1–July 10:	
$14,800 × 77.5% (cost percentage)	11,470
Approximate inventory, June 30, 19__	$24,520

7

a 64%   ($480,000 ÷ $750,000)
b $400,000   ($750,000 − $350,000)
c $256,000   ($400,000 × 64%)

PLANT ASSETS AND DEPRECIATION

HIGHLIGHTS OF THE CHAPTER

1 The term **plant and equipment** is used to describe long-lived assets used in the operation of the business and not held for sale to customers. A plant asset is a **stream of services** to be received by the owner over a long period of time. As the services are received, a portion of the asset is consumed and should be recognized as an expense (depreciation).

2 The major categories of plant and equipment include:

a Tangible plant assets, such as land, buildings, and machinery. Most of these assets are **subject to depreciation**, whereas land, for example, is generally **not subject to depreciation**.

b Intangible assets, such as patents, copyrights, trademarks, franchises, organization costs, leaseholds, and goodwill. The term **intangible assets** is used to describe non-current assets which have **no physical form**. The cost of intangible assets is subject to **amortization**.

c **Natural resources**, such as mining properties, oil and gas reserves, and tracts of standing timber. These assets are physically consumed and converted into inventory

3 The major "accountable events" and the accounting issues relating to plant and equipment are:

a Acquisition—determining the cost of the plant asset.

b Allocation of the acquisition cost to expense over the asset's useful life (depreciation).

c Sale or disposal—determining any gain or loss to be recognized.

4 All **reasonable** and **necessary** expenditures incurred in acquiring a plant asset and placing it in use should be recorded in an asset account. The cost may include the list price, sales or use taxes paid, freight and handling costs, installation costs, and insurance prior to the time that the asset is placed in service.

5 Cash discounts reduce the net cost of the asset. Interest paid when an asset is purchased on the installment plan should be recorded as an expense rather than as part of the cost of acquiring the asset.

6 The cost of land may include real estate commissions, escrow fees, title insurance fees, delinquent taxes (including penalties and interest), etc. Separate ledger accounts are always maintained for land and buildings. Certain land-improvement costs, such as fences, driveways, parking lots, sprinkler systems, and landscaping, have a limited life and should be recorded in a separate account and depreciated.

7 When a building is purchased, the total cost includes the price paid plus all incidental costs, such as termite inspection fees, legal fees, and major repairs necessary before the building is occupied. When a building is constructed by the owner, the total cost of the building includes all direct expenditures (labor, materials, building permit, etc.) plus interest charges during the construction period.

8 A **capital expenditure** is one that will benefit many accounting periods; a **revenue expenditure** is one that will benefit only the current accounting period. Capital expenditures are recorded in asset accounts and are deducted from revenue through the process of depreciation; revenue expenditures are recorded in expense accounts as incurred.

9 **Depreciation** is the process of **allocating the cost of plant assets** to the periods in

which services are received from the assets. A separate depreciation expense account should be maintained for each major group of depreciable assets, and the total amount of depreciation expense for the fiscal period should be disclosed in the income statement.

10 Depreciation is *not* a process of assigning a market value (or realizable value) to plant assets, nor is it a process of accumulating a fund for the replacement of assets when they become worn out or obsolete. Depreciation is an *allocation process*: The cost of an asset, less residual value, is allocated to the years that are benefited from the use of the asset.

11 The balance in the Accumulated Depreciation account represents the portion of the historical cost of plant assets which has expired to date; this account does *not* represent a fund of cash accumulated to replace plant assets.

12 The two major causes of depreciation are:
a Physical deterioration from use.
b Obsolescence due to technological changes or changing needs of the company.

13 The two most commonly used methods of computing periodic depreciation for financial statement purposes are:
a *Straight-line:*

$$\frac{\text{Depreciation}}{\text{Expense}} = \frac{\text{Cost} - \text{Residual Value}}{\text{Estimated Years of Useful Life}}$$

b *Fixed-percentage-of-declining-balance:*
An accelerated method in which the book value of the asset is multiplied by a rate which is a specified percentage of the straight-line rate.

$$\frac{\text{Depreciation}}{\text{Expense}} = \frac{\text{Remaining}}{\text{Book Value}} \times \frac{\text{Accelerated}}{\text{Depreciation Rate}}$$

(The above two methods are illustrated and explained in the chapter. Two other depreciation methods are discussed briefly in the *Supplemental Topic* at the end of the chapter.)

14 The *straight-line method* is the simplest and the most widely used method of computing depreciation. Under this method an *equal portion* of the cost of the asset (less residual value) is allocated to each period of use. This method is most appropriate when usage of an asset is fairly uniform from period to period.

15 Under *accelerated depreciation* methods, larger amounts of depreciation are recorded in the early years of use and reduced amounts in later years. Accelerated methods are particularly appropriate when obsolescence is more significant than physical deterioration in rendering the asset less useful or productive. In some cases the use of an accelerated depreciation method tends to equalize the total expense of using an asset because decreasing periodic depreciation charges are offset by increasing repair outlays as the asset gets older.

16 The most widely used accelerated depreciation method is the *fixed-percentage-of-declining-balance*, often referred to as the declining-balance method. Annual depreciation expense is computed by multiplying a depreciation rate by the current book value (undepreciated cost) of the asset. The accelerated depreciation *rate* remains *constant*; the book value of the asset declines each period. Under the *double-declining-balance* method, the depreciation rate is 200% of the straight-line rate. Another variation is *150%-declining-balance*, in which the depreciation rate is 150% of the straight-line rate.

17 When an asset is acquired in the middle of an accounting period, depreciation can be computed by rounding the calculation to the *nearest whole month*. Another approach, called the *half-year convention*, is to record six months' depreciation on all assets acquired or sold during the year.

18 A business need not use the same method of depreciation for all its assets. Also, different methods may be used for tax purposes than are being used in the accounting records and financial statements.

19 The Modified Accelerated Cost Recovery System (MACRS) is the only accelerated depreciation method allowed for federal income tax purposes for assets acquired after 1986. MACRS is used for income tax purposes only. The use of MACRS for financial reporting is *not* permitted because this system departs from generally accepted accounting principles.

20 Under MACRS, all depreciable assets are classified into one of eight "recovery periods"—the number of years over which the asset is to be depreciated. The IRS publishes tables showing the percentage of the asset's cost which can be "written off" for tax purposes each year.

21 In general, MACRS is based on the 150% declining balance method, using the half-year convention and no salvage value. The taxpayer computes the depreciation each year simply by multiplying the cost of the asset by the rate appearing in the table published by the IRS. An illustrative table appears on page 432 of your textbook.

22 Depreciation rates are based on estimates of useful life. If the estimate of useful service life is found to be in error, the estimate should be revised, and the *undepreciated cost of the asset should be allocated over the years of remaining useful life*. A change in annual depreciation expense may also result from a change in the *estimate of residual value* or from a change in the *method* of computing depreciation.

23 When units of plant and equipment wear out or become obsolete they must be discarded, sold, or traded in. To record the disposal of a depreciable asset, the cost of the asset must be removed from the asset account, *and the accumulated depreciation* (on that asset) *must be removed* from the contra-asset account.

24 When plant assets are disposed of at a date other than the end of the year, depreciation is recorded for the fractional period preceding disposal.

25 The *book value*, or carrying value, of a depreciable asset is its cost minus accumulated depreciation. If the asset is sold for a price above book value, there is a *gain* on the sale. If the asset is sold for less than book value, there is a *loss*.

26 When a depreciable asset is sold, the amount of the gain or loss is determined by comparing the book value of the asset sold with the amount received from the sale. The amount of a gain would be *credited* to a *Gain on Disposal of Plant Assets* account, and a loss would be *debited* to *Loss on Disposal of Plant Assets*.

27 As a result of using different depreciation methods, an asset's basis for income tax purposes may differ from its book value. In this event, the gain or loss on disposal of the asset computed for tax purposes will differ from that reported in the financial statements.

28 For purposes of determining taxable income, no gain or loss is recognized when a depreciable asset is *traded in* on a similar asset. The cost of the new asset is recorded as the sum of the *book value of the old asset plus any additional amount paid* (or to be paid) for the new asset.

29 A gain or loss on the trade-in of a plant asset for a similar kind of asset is recognized for financial reporting purposes whenever 25% or more of the transaction value involves cash or the creation of debt.

30 *Intangible assets* are those noncurrent assets which do not have physical substance but which contribute to the process of earning revenue. Intangibles are recorded at cost and should be *amortized* over their useful lives. It is often difficult to estimate the useful life of an intangible asset, but the maximum amortization period *may not exceed 40 years*. Intangible assets generally are amortized by the straight-line method.

31 Despite the fact that expenditures for research and development often lead to discoveries or knowledge that contribute to the earning process for many periods, the Financial Accounting Standards Board has ruled that all research and development expenditures are to be *expensed when incurred*. Hence, these types of expenditures are *not* reported in the balance sheet as intangible assets.

32 *Goodwill* is the market value of a going business *in excess of* the fair market value of the net identifiable assets of the business. It represents the *present value* of expected future earnings in excess of the normal return on the net identifiable assets of the business. The term *net identifiable assets* refers to all assets except goodwill minus liabilities.

33 Goodwill may exist in many businesses, but it should be recorded in the accounts *only when it is purchased*.

34 The following two methods are often used in *estimating* the value of goodwill owned by a business unit:

a Negotiated agreement between buyer and seller. If a business with net assets (at market value) of $80,000 is sold for $100,000, this suggests that goodwill of $20,000 is possessed by this business.

b The capitalized value of excess earning power. For example, if excess earnings amount to $5,000, and the capitalization rate agreed upon is 20%, the goodwill can be estimated at $25,000 ($5,000 ÷ .20 = $25,000).

35 Natural resources, such as mines or timber stands, are physically extracted and converted into inventory. These assets are recorded at cost and reported separately in the balance sheet.

36 *Depletion* is the process *allocating the cost* of the natural resource to the units removed. The depletion rate is computed by dividing the cost of the natural resource by the estimated number of units available to be removed. The rate is then multiplied by the number of units removed during a period to determine the total depletion charge for the period.

37 *Impairment* of an asset occurs when its economic usefulness declines, usually due to a change in economic conditions. If the book value of an asset cannot be recovered through future sale or use, the asset should be written down to its net realizable value and a loss recognized. When and if permanent impairment has occurred, as well as the dollar amount of "net realizable value," is largely a matter of professional judgment on a case by case basis.

38 The *cash effects* of plant and equipment transactions do *not* parallel the effects reported in the income statement. Depreciation expense, amortization expense, and write-downs due to impairment of assets all reduce net income, but have no immediate effects upon cash flows. These are examples of *"noncash" charges* against earnings. Cash flows occur upon purchase (cash payments) and sale (cash receipts) of plant assets. Cash flows relating to acquisitions and disposals of plant assets are reported in the *statement of cash flows*, classified as *investing activities*. (Although the income statement may report a gain or loss upon disposal, the entire cash proceeds is considered a cash flow from investing activities in the statement of cash flows.)

*39 Under the *units-of-output* method, depreciation is based upon some measure of output, other than the passage of time. When the usage of an asset fluctuates and the output can be estimated in terms of some unit (such as tons produced or miles driven), a more equitable allocation of the cost of a plant asset can be obtained by computing depreciation on the basis of output. Cost (less residual value) is divided by estimated output to obtain a depreciation rate per unit. Depreciation for a period is computed by multiplying the rate per unit by the number of units produced:

$$\frac{\text{Depreciation}}{\text{Expense}} = \frac{\text{Cost} - \text{Residual Value}}{\text{Total Estimated Units of Output}} \times \frac{\text{Units}}{\text{Produced}}$$

*40 A form of accelerated depreciation termed the sum-of-the-years'-digits, or SYD, results in depreciation expense between the double-declining-balance and the 150%-declining-balance methods. Coverage of this method, as well as of *decelerated* depreciation methods (in which *less* depreciation expense is recognized in the early years), is deferred to later accounting courses.

TEST YOURSELF ON PLANT ASSETS AND DEPRECIATION

True or False

For each of the following statements, circle the T or the F to indicate whether the statement is true or false.

T F **1** In a broad sense, the cost of a machine or a building may be viewed as a long-term prepaid expense.

T F **2** An auto owned by a glass manufacturer would be reported under Plant and Equipment, while glass owned by an auto manufacturer would be classified as Inventory.

T F **3** The cost of land that is entered in the book should not include any transaction costs, such as real estate commissions paid.

T F **4** *Capital expenditures* are those disbursements which are allocated to several accounting periods; *revenue expenditures* are charged off as current expenses.

T F **5** The cost of a plant asset should include all costs necessary to get the asset ready for use, including the cost of the units spoiled in production while the asset was being adjusted and tested.

T F **6** A small expenditure, such as $10 for a set of sparkplugs, may reasonably be charged to expense even though the expenditure may benefit several periods.

T F **7** Obsolescence may be a more significant factor than wear and tear through use in putting an end to the usefulness of many depreciable assets.

T F **8** Depreciation expense for a period should be a reasonably good estimate

---

Supplemental Topic, "Other Depreciation Methods."

of the change in the fair market value of an asset during the period.

T F 9 In practice, the residual value of an asset is often ignored in estimating annual depreciation expense.

T F 10 The Accumulated Depreciation account is a fund established for the replacement of assets, but it will not be large enough to cover the cost of replacement during a period of inflation.

T F 11 The fixed-percentage-of-declining-balance method of depreciation has a "built-in" residual value and can never allocate 100% of the original cost of an asset to expense.

T F 12 A company organized after January 1, 1986 should use the MACRS method of depreciation in its financial statements even if another method is used for income tax purposes.

T F 13 Generally accepted accounting principles require a business to use the same depreciation methods in its financial statements that it uses for income tax purposes.

T F 14 When it becomes evident that a plant asset will have a useful life longer than had been originally estimated, the depreciation rate will be revised according to the new estimate of useful life.

T F 15 For federal income tax purposes, assets acquired in recent years may be depreciated by the double-declining-balance, sum-of-the-years'-digits, or straight-line methods.

T F 16 Whenever a depreciable asset is sold, both the cost of the asset and the accumulated depreciation must be removed from the accounts.

T F 17 For both tax purposes and preparing financial statements, no gain is recognized when used plant assets are traded in on new plant assets of "like kind."

T F 18 Depletion refers to the allocation of the cost of an intangible asset over the periods that benefits are received.

T F 19 Intangible assets are assets that cannot be sold.

T F 20 The systematic write-off of intangible assets to expense is known as amortization.

T F 21 Goodwill is the present value of future earnings in excess of the normal return on net identifiable assets.

T F 22 When a business has superior earnings for many years, goodwill probably exists and should be recorded on the books.

T F 23 If a buyer of a business pays a price for the business in excess of the fair market value of the net identifiable assets, the buyer may record goodwill as one of the assets being acquired.

T F *24 The units-of-output method of depreciation yields results similar to *accelerated* methods of depreciation when the rate of output increases steadily over a period of years.

Completion Statements

Fill in the necessary words to complete the following statements:

1 The two causes of depreciation are: (a)

_____ _____

and (b) _____.

2 If a _____ expenditure is erroneously recorded as a _____ expenditure, net income will be _____ in the current period, and overstated in every future period in which depreciation should have been recognized.

3 Net income for three consecutive years was reported as follows:

Year 1	$30,000
Year 2	$39,000
Year 3	$40,000

At the beginning of Year 1 a capital expenditure of $15,000 for a new machine, which should have been depreciated over a five-year life using the 150%-declining-balance method, was erroneously charged to repair expense. The correct net income for the three years should have been as follows.

Year 1, $_____; Year 2 , $_____; Year 3, $ _____.

4 The MACRS method of depreciation may be used on assets acquired after _____. This method is allowable for _____ _____ purposes and is (widely used, not acceptable) _____ _____ for use in financial statements.

5 The entry to record the disposal of a depreciable asset will always include a credit to

---

Supplemental Topic, "Other Depreciation Methods."

the asset account for the _____ _____ of the asset, and a debit to the _____ _____ account.

6 Tax regulations provide that the cost of new equipment shall be the sum of the _____ _____ of any old equipment traded in plus any _____ _____ paid or to be paid in acquiring the new equipment.

7 The cost of intangible assets should be _____ by the _____ method over a period not to exceed _____ years.

Multiple Choice

Choose the best answer for each of the following questions and enter the identifying letter in the space provided.

_____ 1 Big Company purchased land for $80,000 subject to delinquent property taxes of $4,000. These taxes were paid immediately by Big Company along with interest of $320 on the delinquent taxes. The cost of this land should be recorded by Big Company at:
a $80,000.
b $84,000.
c $84,320.
d Some other amount.

_____ 2 If a revenue expenditure is debited to a plant asset account *in error*:
a Revenue for the current period is understated.
b Net income of the current period is overstated.
c Net income in future periods will be unaffected by this error.
d Expenses for the current period are overstated.

_____ 3 *Depreciation*, as the term is used in accounting, means:
a The systematic write-off of the cost of a natural resource over its productive life.
b The allocation of the cost of a plant asset to expense to reflect the use of asset services.
c The physical deterioration of an asset.
d The decrease in the market value of an asset.

_____ 4 The book value or carrying value of a depreciable asset is best defined as:
a The undepreciated cost of the asset.
b The price that the asset would bring if offered for sale.
c Accumulated depreciation on the asset since acquisition.
d Original cost of the asset.

_____ 5 The straight-line method of depreciation:

a Generally gives best results because it is easy to apply.
b Ignores fluctuations in the rate of asset usage.
c Should be used in a period of inflation because it accumulates, at a uniform rate, the fund for the replacement of the asset.
d Is the best method to use for income tax purposes.

_____ 6 *Accumulated depreciation*, as used in accounting, may be defined as:
a Earnings retained in the business that will be used to purchase another asset when the present asset is depreciated.
b Funds (or cash) set aside to replace the asset being depreciated.
c The portion of the cost of a plant asset recognized as expense since the asset was acquired.
d An expense of doing business.

_____ 7 A and B Companies purchase identical equipment having an estimated service of 10 years. A Company uses the straight-line method of depreciation, and B Company uses the double-declining-balance method. Assuming that the companies are identical in all other respects:
a B Company will record more depreciation on this asset over the entire 10 years than will A Company.
b At the end of the third year, the book value of the asset will be lower on A Company's books than on B Company's.
c A Company's depreciation expense will be greater in the first year than B Company's.
d A Company's net income will be lower in the ninth year than B Company's.

_____ 8 Which of the following statements about MACRS is *not* correct?
a It is the only accelerated depreciation method allowed for federal income tax purposes for assets acquired in recent years.
b All assets are assigned to specified "recovery periods."
c Depreciation rates may be taken directly from schedules published by the IRS.
d Specific salvage values are specified by law, and vary with the nature of the asset.

_____ 9 Which of the following is *not* an intangible asset?
a A patent.
b A trademark.
c An investment in marketable securities.
d Goodwill.

_____ 10 The best evidence of goodwill existing in a business is:
a The appearance of goodwill on the balance sheet.

b Numerous contributions to charitable organizations.

c A long-standing reputation for manufacturing a high-quality product.

d A long record of earnings greater than those of like-size firms in the same industry.

_____**11** Lucky Strike Mines recognizes $2 of depletion for each ton of ore mined. This year 750,000 tons of ore were mined, but only 700,000 tons were sold. The amount of depletion that should be deducted from revenue this year is:

a $2,900,000
b $1,500,000
c $1,400,000
d $100,000

_____**12** Which of the following statements regarding *impairment of long-lived assets* is not accurate?

a Impairment of an asset may involve recognition of a loss and writing the asset down to net realizable value.

b Regardless of whether or not potentially impaired assets are written down, the circumstances should be fully disclosed in footnotes accompanying the financial statements.

c The FASB has issued strict guidelines to be followed in determination of whether or not permanent impairment has occurred, as well as in computation of the dollar amount of any loss.

d At the present time, professional judgment on a case-by-case basis determines the accounting treatment to be used in cases of potentially impaired assets.

Exercises

1 Listed below are eight technical accounting terms emphasized in this chapter.

Half-year convention *Goodwill*
Revenue expenditure *Book value*
Straight-line depreciation
Accelerated depreciation
Net identifiable assets
Declining-balance method

Each of the following statements may (or may not) describe one of these technical terms. In the space provided below each statement, indicate the accounting term described, or answer "None" if the statement does not describe any of the terms.

a Depreciation methods which take less depreciation in the early years of the asset's life and more in the later years of the asset's life.

_____

b The total of all assets except goodwill, less liabilities.

_____

c The present value of future earnings in excess of the normal return on net identifiable assets.

_____

d A method of allocating the cost of an asset equally to each year of its life.

_____

e An expenditure that will benefit only the current accounting period.

_____

f The cost of an asset minus the related accumulated depreciation.

_____

g An approach to computing depreciation which records six months' depreciation on all assets acquired during a year, regardless of actual dates of purchase.

_____

2 A truck with an estimated life of four years was acquired on March 31, Year 1, for $11,000. The estimated residual value of the truck is $1,000, and the service life is estimated at 100,000 miles. Compute depreciation for Year 1 and Year 2 using the following methods (where appropriate, round depreciation to the nearest month).

	Year 1	Year 2
a Straight-line	$ _____	$_____
b Fixed-percentage-of declining-balance (twice the straight-line rate)	$ _____	$_____
c MACRS, assuming the truck is 5-year property. (Use the table on page 432 of your textbook.)	$ _____	$_____
*d Output (miles driven: Year 1, 20,000; Year 2, 40,000)	$ _____	$_____

---

*Supplemental Topic, "Other Depreciation Methods."

3 Equipment which cost $6,000 had an estimated useful life of six years and an estimated salvage value of $600. Straight-line depreciation was used. In the space provided at the top of the next page, prepare the journal entry (omitting explanation) to record the disposal of the equipment under each of the following assumptions:

a The equipment was sold for $4,000 cash after two years' use.
b After three years' use, the equipment was sold for $3,500 cash.
c After four years' use, the equipment was traded in on a similar equipment with a fair market value of $8,000. The trade-in allowance was $3,100.

General Journal		
a		
b		
c		

4 The Golden Calf, a Las Vegas gambling casino, had net identifiable assets with a fair market value of $8,000,000, and earned an average net income of $2,080,000 per year. Other Las Vegas casinos averaged a net income equal to 20% of their net identifiable assets. An investment group negotiating to buy the Golden Calf offers to pay $8,000,000 for the casino's net identifiable assets, plus an amount for goodwill.

The investment group determined the amount to be paid for goodwill by capitalizing the Golden Calf's annual earnings in excess of the industry average earnings at a rate of 25%. Compute the total price the investment group is offering to pay for the Golden Calf.

Computations:

Answer: $_____

SOLUTIONS TO CHAPTER 10 SELF-TEST

True or False

1 **T** As the stream of services from the machine is utilized, the cost of the asset is transferred to depreciation expense.

2 **T** Plant and Equipment describes long-lived assets acquired for use in the operations of the business and not intended for resale to customers.

3 **F** When land is purchased, various incidental costs (real estate commissions, escrow fees, legal fees, delinquent taxes) are added to capitalized cost in the accounting records.

4 **T** A material expenditure benefiting several accounting periods is a *capital* expenditure. An expenditure benefiting only the current period, or one that is not material in amount, is a *revenue* expenditure.

5 **T** An asset's cost equals the purchase price plus any costs necessary to make the asset ready for its intended use.

6 **T** Expenditures which are not material in dollar amount are expensed in the current period.

7 **T** Long-lived assets may become obsolete as a result of technological changes or changing needs of the company before they physically deteriorate.

8 **F** Depreciation is a process of cost allocation over an asset's useful life; it is not a process of valuation.

9 **T** Residual value is often difficult to estimate accurately; it is frequently not material in amount.

10 **F** The Accumulated Depreciation account represents the expired cost of an asset—it is *not* a fund of cash.

11 **T** Since each year's depreciation expense is computed as a percentage of the undepreciated cost of the asset, the total cost will never be written off entirely.

12 **F** For *assets* acquired after 1986, MACRS may be used for *income tax purposes*; it is *not* permitted in financial statements.

13 **F** Different methods may be used for tax purposes than are being used in the accounting records and financial statements.

14 **T** The remaining *un*depreciated cost of the asset is simply spread over the remaining useful life.

15 **F** MACRS is the only accelerated depreciation method allowed by federal income tax rules for assets acquired after 1986.

16 **T** The desired result is that the book value, or carrying value, of the asset is removed from the books.

17 **F** For tax purposes, no gain is recognized on a "like-kind" exchange. If more than 25% of the transaction value is comprised of cash or debt, however, gains *are* recognized in a company's financial statements.

18 **F** Depletion is the allocation of the cost of a *natural resource* over the periods benefited.

19 **F** Intangible assets are assets used in the operation of the business which have no physical substance and are noncurrent; they may be bought and sold.

20 **T** The usual accounting entry for amortization consists of a debit to Amortization Expense and a credit to the intangible asset account.

21 **T** Goodwill is evident when investors will pay a higher price because the business earns more than the normal rate of return on its resources.

22 **F** Although goodwill probably exists, it is recorded in the accounting records only when it is purchased.

23 **T** The fair market value of all identifiable assets is first recorded on the books of the buyer; any *excess* purchase price is then allocated to an asset account entitled Goodwill.

*24 **F** Accelerated depreciation means larger amounts of depreciation in the early years of an asset's life; units-of-output yields similar results when the rate of output *decreases* steadily.

Completion Statements

1 (a) Physical deterioration, **(b)** obsolescence. **2** Capital, revenue, understated. **3** $40,500; $35,850; $37,795. **4** 1986, income tax, not acceptable. **5** Original cost, Accumulated Depreciation. **6** Book value, additional amount. **7** Amortized, straight-line, 40.

---

*Supplemental Topic, "Other Depreciation Methods."

Multiple Choice

1 Answer **c**—the cost of land includes incidental costs such as delinquent property taxes and interest on the delinquent taxes. The taxes and interest are obligations of the former owner that were paid by Big Company as part of the acquisition cost—they are not current period expenses of Big Company, but are capitalized. Answer **a** ignores both the delinquent taxes and interest; answer **b** does not capitalize the interest.

2 Answer **b**—a revenue expenditure benefits only the current period and should be recorded by a debit to an expense account. Even though the plant asset debited in error is subject to depreciation, the depreciation expense will be smaller than the expense that should have been recorded. Since expense is understated, net income of the current period is overstated. Revenue for the current period is unaffected. Net income of future periods will be understated if the error is not corrected due to depreciation on the plant asset debited in error.

3 Answer **b**—depreciation is the allocation of the cost of a plant asset to expense in the periods in which services are received from the asset. Physical deterioration, as well as obsolescence, are justifications for this cost allocation procedure. Answer **d** is incorrect because accounting records do not purport to reflect fluctuating market values of plant assets. Answer **a** is a definition of depletion.

4 Answer **a**—book value is cost minus accumulated depreciation; that is, the undepreciated cost. Answer **b** is incorrect because accounting records contain historical cost data, not liquidation values or market values.

5 Answer **b**—straight-line depreciation allocates equal portions of an asset's cost to expense each period, regardless of actual usage. From a matching principle point of view, the straight-line method gives "best" results when usage of the asset is uniform year to year. Answer **c** is incorrect because no depreciation method accumulates a fund for the replacement of an asset. Most companies use accelerated depreciation methods in preparing income tax returns because these methods provide larger deductions for depreciation in the early years of an asset's life.

6 Answer **c**—each year the amount debited to depreciation expense is also credited to a balance sheet account called Accumulated Depreciation. The credit balance in accumulated depreciation represents the expired cost (i.e., amount expensed) since acquisition, **not** cash or earnings that could be used to purchase another asset. Answer **d** could be a description of the current period's depreciation expense, but not the balance in accumulated depreciation.

7 Answer **d**—by the ninth year of the asset's life, A Company's straight-line depreciation will be greater than B Company's double-declining-balance amount; therefore A Company's net income will be lower. A Company and B Company will record an equal amount of depreciation over the entire 10-year life of the asset. A Company's straight-line depreciation expense will be lower than double-declining-balance method in the early years of the asset's life, and A Company's book value for the asset will be higher during the early years.

8 Answer **d**—MACRS allows the taxpayer to write off 100% of the asset's cost, with no provision for salvage value.

9 Answer **c**—intangible assets are used in operation of the business, but have no physical substance and are noncurrent. Answers **a**, **b**, and **d** meet this definition. An investment in marketable securities is not used in the operation of a business.

10 Answer **d**—although answers **b** and **c** are often associated with the existence of goodwill in a **general** sense, goodwill in an **accounting** sense is the present value of future earnings in excess of a normal return on net identifiable assets. Answer **d** indicates higher than normal earnings which is evidence of the existence of goodwill, assuming the earnings continue. The appearance of goodwill on a balance sheet occurs only when one company purchases another business in its entirety; internally generated goodwill may exist, but is not recorded in the accounting records.

11 Answer **c**—total depletion is $1,500,000 (750,000 tons mined at $2 per ton). The depletion deducted from revenue is $1,400,000 (700,000 tons sold at $2 per ton). $100,000 (50,000 tons not sold at $2 per ton) should be assigned to inventory.

12 Answer **c**—the FASB currently is studying the issue of impairment of long-lived assets, but it has **not** yet taken an official position. Answers **a**, **b**, and **d** are all accurate statements.

Solutions to Exercises

1

a None (Accelerated depreciation takes **more** depreciation in the early years of the asset's life and **less** in the later years.)

b Net identifiable assets

c Goodwill

d Straight-line depreciation

e Revenue expenditure

f Book value

g Half-year convention

2

		Year 1	Year 2
a	($11,000 − $1,000) × $\frac{1}{4}$ × $\frac{9}{12}$	$1,875	
	$10,000 × $\frac{1}{4}$		$2,500
b	$11,000 × 50% × $\frac{9}{12}$	$4,125	
	($11,000 − $4,125) × 50%		$3,438
c	$11,000 × 20%	$2,200	
	$11,000 × 32%		$3,520
*d	20,000 × 10 cents	$2,000	
	40,000 × 10 cents		$4,000

3

	General Journal		
a	Cash	4,000	
	Accumulated Depreciation	1,800	
	Loss on Disposal of Equipment	200	
	Equipment		6,000
b	Cash	3,500	
	Accumulated Depreciation	2,700	
	Gain on Disposal of Equipment		200
	Equipment		6,000
c	Equipment	8,000	
	Accumulated Depreciation	3,600	
	Equipment		6,000
	Cash		4,900
	Gain on Disposal of Plant Assets		700

4 Normal earnings ($8,000,000 × .20) $1,600,000

Excess earnings ($2,080,000 − $1,600,000) $480,000

Goodwill ($480,000 ÷ .25) $1,920,000

Price offered ($8,000,000 + $1,920,000) $9,920,000

---

*Supplemental Topic, "Other Depreciation Methods."

11

LIABILITIES

HIGHLIGHTS OF THE CHAPTER

1 Liabilities are **obligations** arising from past transactions. The liability is recorded by a credit; the offsetting debit generally is either to an asset or an expense account. The dollar amount of the liability is usually clearly stated in a written or oral agreement between the debtor and the creditor. Most liabilities eventually are paid in cash. A few liabilities, such as unearned revenue, are discharged by rendering future services rather than by making a cash payment.

2 Although both creditors and owners supply financing to a business, liabilities differ from owners' equity in several respects. All liabilities eventually mature; owners' equity does not mature. The claims of creditors have **legal priority** over the claims of owners; creditors are paid in full before any distributions to owners when a business ceases operations. Creditors do not have the right to manage the business but may set restrictions on certain aspects of business operations in **indenture contracts**.

3 Many liabilities create a contractual obligation for the borrower to pay interest, as well as repaying the principal amount of the debt. Obligations to pay interest stem only from liabilities; a business does not pay interest upon its owners' equity.

4 Most liabilities are of definite dollar amounts clearly stated on an invoice or in a contract. These liabilities can be recorded promptly as the transactions occur. Sometimes, however, the amount of a liability can only be estimated at the time that it comes into existence. An example is the liability of a manufacturer to make future warranty repairs on the products it sells. **Estimated liabilities** usually are recorded by means of adjusting entries at the end of each accounting period.

5 **Current liabilities** are amounts payable to creditors within one year or the operating cycle, whichever is longer. A second requirement for classification as a current liability is the expectation that the debt will be paid from current assets (or by rendering services). A company's debt-paying ability is judged, in part, by the relationship of its current assets to its current liabilities.

6 Examples of current liabilities include accounts payable, short-term notes payable, the "current portion" of long-term debt, accrued liabilities, and unearned revenue.

7 A note payable may be issued as evidence of indebtedness to banks or to other creditors.

8 A note usually is drawn for the **principal amount borrowed**, Cash is debited, and Notes Payable is credited at the time the note is issued. No liability is recorded for the interest charges upon issuance; the liability for interest accrues daily over the life of the loan.

9 The entry to record the payment of principal and interest at maturity requires a debit to Notes Payable for the amount of principal, a debit to Interest Expense for the interest related to the current period, a debit to Interest Payable for any interest accrued (and recorded) in prior periods, and a credit to Cash for the total paid.

10 If a note is not repaid in the same period it was issued, it will be necessary to recognize the interest which has accrued (become owed) on the note during each period. The interest which has accrued during the period is recognized by a debit to Interest Expense and a credit to the liability account Interest Payable.

11 Many long-term liabilities, such as mortgages, call for monthly installment payments equal to the accrued interest charges plus a

portion of the principal amount. The portion of unpaid principal which will be repaid within one year is called the *current portion of long-term debt*, and is classified as a current liability.

12 As the maturity date of a long-term liability approaches, the obligation eventually becomes due within the current period. At this time, the obligation generally is reclassified as a current liability. An exception to this rule exists if the maturing obligation is expected to be *refinanced* (see Highlight 17).

13 *Accrued liabilities* arise from the recognition of an expense for which payment will be made in a future period. Expenses often paid *after* recognition of the expense in the accounting records include payrolls, interest, and—for corporations—income taxes.

14 Every business incurs a number of accrued liabilities relating to payrolls. The largest of these liabilities is the amount owed to employees—that is, their *net pay*. However, employers also accrue liabilities for various payroll tax expenses and for amounts withheld from employees' gross pay.

15 A liability for *unearned revenue* arises when a customer pays in advance. Often this liability is discharged by rendering services or delivering merchandise to the customer in a future period.

16 *Long-term liabilities* are those liabilities which do not mature within one year, or the operating cycle of the business, whichever is longer. In addition, some obligations maturing in the current period are classified as long-term liabilities if certain conditions are met regarding the refinancing of the liability.

17 If a liability is maturing in the current period, but management has both the *intent* and the *ability* to refinance the debt on a *long-term basis*, the liability is classified as long-term. Although "refinancing on a long-term basis" may be accomplished in several ways, the simplest examples involve extending the maturity date beyond the next year, or paying off one obligation by taking out another loan with a maturity date beyond the current point.

18 Purchases of real estate or equipment frequently are financed by *installment notes*, which call for a series of payments. Although installment notes may involve a variety of payment schemes, two commonly used approaches are the following:

a Installment payments are *equal* to the periodic interest charges with the principal amount due at a specified maturity date.

b Installment payments are *greater* than the amount of interest accruing each period. A portion of each payment represents interest expense, and the remainder reduces the principal amount of the liability.

19 If the installment payments are greater than the interest accruing each period and continue until the debt is completely repaid, the loan is said to be *fully amortizing*. A common example of a fully amortizing loan is a mortgage incurred upon purchase of real estate, payable in equal monthly installments over a period of 30 years. Over the life of a fully amortizing loan, the monthly payments include interest charges as well as repayment of the entire principal; there is no "balloon payment" at the due date for any remaining principal amount.

20 An *amortization table* is a schedule that indicates how installment payments are allocated between interest expense and repayment of principal. An amortization table begins with the original amount of the liability. If we assume equal monthly payments, interest expense is computed by applying the *monthly interest rate* to the unpaid balance at the beginning of that month. The portion of each payment that reduces the amount of the liability is simply the remainder of the payment. Although the amount of the monthly payment remains the same, the amount of interest expense *decreases* every month.

21 Up to this point, we have discussed liabilities common to most business organizations. We will now focus upon special types of liabilities found primarily in the financial statements of publicly owned corporations.

22 The issuance of bonds payable is a popular form of long-term financing in which a large loan is split into a great many units, called bonds, usually in the face amount of $1,000 each. A corporation issuing bonds to the general public must first obtain approval from the SEC, and usually utilizes the services of an *underwriter*. The underwriter guarantees the issuing corporation a specific price for the entire bond issue and makes a profit by selling the bonds to the public at a higher price. (The corporation records the issuance of bonds at the net amount received from the underwriter.)

23 Bonds of large, well-established companies are readily transferable because they are generally traded on one or more securities exchanges. The quotations for bonds are usually given in terms of a percentage of the par value. Thus, a $1,000 bond sold at 101⅞ would bring $1,018.75, before deducting commissions or taking accrued interest into account.

24 A major advantage of raising capital by issuing bonds rather than stock is that bond interest payments are *deductible* in determining taxable income, whereas dividend payments are not. Also, if a company can earn a return higher than the fixed cost of bonds, net income and earnings per share will increase. If stock were issued, the additional shares would tend to offset the increase in earnings on a per-share basis.

25 Bonds generally pay interest every six months. If bonds are issued or sold between interest dates, the buyer pays the seller for any accrued interest.

26 There usually are three accountable events in the life of a bond issue; (1) issuance, (2) interest payments, and (3) retirement of the bonds.

27 In the chapter, we assume that bonds are issued "at par"—that is, at their face amount or *maturity value*. The basic entry is a debit to Cash and a credit to Bonds Payable. If the bonds are issued *between interest dates*, the buyer is charged for the interest which has accrued since the last interest payment date. The amount of this accrued interest is included in the debit to Cash and also is credited to an account entitled Accrued Interest Payable. (The issuance of bonds at a discount or premium is discussed in the *Supplemental Topic* section of this chapter, beginning with Highlight 56.

28 Interest payments are recorded by debiting Interest Expense (and Accrued Interest Payable, if any), and crediting Cash. At the end of the accounting period, an adjusting entry is made to accrue a liability for any bond interest payable relating to the current period.

29 When bonds mature, the last interest payment is made and recorded, and the bonds are retired. If the bonds are retired at their maturity value, the entry consists of a debit to Bonds Payable and a credit to Cash.

30 While they are outstanding, bonds trade at market prices. These prices represent the

present value to investors of the future interest payments and the maturity value of the bonds.

31 The *present value* of a future cash payment is the amount that a knowledgable investor would pay *today* for the right to receive that future payment. The present value will always be less than the future amount, because money on hand today can be invested to become equivalent to a larger amount in the future. This principle is sometimes called the *time value of money*.

32 The rate of interest that will cause a given present value to increase to a given future amount is called the *discount rate*, or effective rate. At any given time, the effective interest rate required by investors is the *going market rate* of interest.

33 The price at which bonds sell is the present value to investors of the future principal and interest payments. The *higher* the going market rate of interest, the *less* investors will pay for bonds with a given contract rate of interest.

34 Thus, bond prices *vary inversely* with market interest rates. As interest rates rise, bond prices (the present value of the future cash flows) fall. As interest rates fall, bond prices rise.

35 If the market rate of interest is higher than the contractual rate stated on the bond, the bond will sell at *discount*—that is, at a price below its maturity value. If the market rate is *below* the contract rate, the bond will sell at a *premium*—a price *above* maturity value.

36 Corporate bonds are traded on organized securities exchanges at quoted market prices. After bonds are issued, their market prices vary inversely with changes in market interest rates. These fluctuations in interest rates have a far greater effect upon the market prices of long-term bonds than upon the prices of short-term bonds. In addition to the impact of current interest rates, the market prices of bonds are influenced by the length of time remaining until maturity. As a bond nears its maturity date, its market price normally moves closer to maturity value.

37 If bonds are retired before maturity at a price above their carrying value, a loss results; if bonds are retired at a price below their carrying value, a gain is realized. Gains and losses on the early retirement of bonds

should be shown in the income statement as *extraordinary items*.

38 A *lease* is a contract in which the *lessor* gives the *lessee* the right to use an asset in return for periodic rental payments. Lease contracts may be *operating leases*, in which the lessor retains the risks and returns of ownership, or *capital leases*, in which the objectives are to provide financing to the lessee for the eventual purchase of the property. Lessees should make full disclosure of the terms of all noncancelable leases in their financial statements.

39 In an operating lease, the periodic rentals are recorded as revenue by the lessor and as rental expense by the lessee. No liability is recognized by the lessee other than for any accrued monthly rentals.

40 A capital lease, which is essentially equivalent to a sale and purchase, should be recorded as a sale by the lessor and as a purchase by the lessee. The asset and related liability should be recorded by the lessee at the *present value* of the future lease payments. The lessee should depreciate the asset over its estimated useful life rather than over the life of the lease.

41 A lease which meets *any one* of the following criteria must be accounted for as a *capital* lease:

a Lease *transfers ownership* of the property to the lessee at the end of the lease.

b Lease contains a *bargain purchase option*.

c *Lease term* is *at least 75%* of the estimated useful life of the leased property.

d *Present value of the minimum lease payments* is *at least 90%* of the fair value of the leased property.

42 A pension plan is a contract between a company and its employees under which the company agrees to pay retirement benefits to eligible employees. In a *funded* pension plan, the employer makes regular payments into a pension fund managed by an independent trustee, such as an insurance company (debit Pension Expense and credit Cash). A pension plan is considered *fully funded* when the company pays to the trustee the entire amount calculated by the actuary as the current year's expense. In a fully funded pension plan, the *trustee* assumes all responsibility for paying retirement benefits to employees and *no pension liability* appears in the company's balance sheet.

43 *Nonpension retirement benefits*, such as health insurance, are accounted for in the same manner as are pension benefits, with one major difference: most companies have not fully funded their obligations for nonpension retirement benefits. That is, the amount of current year expense computed by the actuary is only partially paid in cash each year. Recognition of annual expense in this situation involves a debit to Nonpension Retirement Benefit Expense and credits to Cash (amount funded) and to Unfunded Liability for Nonpension Retirement Benefits (amount not funded).

44 Unfunded postretirement costs, like depreciation, are *noncash* expenses, meaning that no cash outlay is required in the near term. As these costs can be very large, they represent a major difference between *net income* and *net cash flow*.

45 Income taxes expense reported in a company's *income statement* is based upon the items of revenue and expense recognized during the current year according to *generally accepted accounting principles*. *Income tax regulations* govern items to be reported in the *income tax return* and often allow corporations to postpone payment of taxes to a future period. The portion of a company's income taxes expense that must be paid when the current tax return is filed is credited to Income Taxes Payable, a current liability. That portion which is deferred to future tax returns is credited to *Deferred Income Taxes*.

46 A company should *disclose* in notes to its financial statements the interest rates and maturity dates of all long-term notes, and the total amounts maturing in each of the next five years. The FASB also requires businesses to disclose the *fair value* of long-term liabilities if this value differs significantly from the amount shown in the balance sheet.

47 In evaluating debt-paying ability of a company, short-term creditors and long-term creditors have different perspectives. *Short-term creditors* (interested primarily in immediate solvency) use indicators of fluidity such as working capital, current ratio, and turnover rates for receivables and inventory. *Long-term creditors* are interested in the company's ability to pay ongoing interest obligations and to retire maturing debts.

48 Another measure of short-term liquidity is the *quick ratio*, consisting of "quick" assets divided by current liabilities. Quick assets include only cash, short-term investments, and short-term receivables. Thus, the quick ratio is a more rigid test of short-term solvency than is the current ratio.

49 The **debt ratio** and the **interest coverage ratio** are statistics examined by long-term creditors. The **debt ratio** is computed by dividing total liabilities by total assets, and indicates the percentage of total assets financed with borrowed money. Creditors prefer a low debt ratio. The **interest coverage ratio** is computed by dividing annual operating income by the annual interest expense. Creditors prefer a high interest coverage ratio.

50 Financing a business with debt is known as applying **leverage**. If the return on assets is **greater** than the costs of borrowing (interest rates paid to creditors), applying leverage will benefit stockholders by **increasing** the return on equity. But leverage can be a "double-edged sword." If the return on assets should fall **below** the cost of borrowing, large amounts of debt will dramatically **reduce** the return on equity.

51 In summary, a low debt ratio is a conservative capital structure. A high debt ratio creates the possibility of magnified returns to stockholders, but also the risk of negative returns.

*52 The term **estimated liabilities** refers to liabilities which appear in financial statements at estimated dollar amounts. Although the dolllar amounts are estimated, these liabilities are (1) known to exist, and (2) the uncertainty is not so great as to prevent making a reasonable estimate and recording the liability.

*53 **Loss contingencies** are similar to estimated liabilities, but involve much more uncertainty. A loss contingency is a **possible** loss (or expense) stemming from past events, that will be resolved by some future event. An example is a lawsuit pending against a company. Loss contingencies may relate to the possible **impairment of assets**, as well as to the possible existence of liabilities.

*54 A loss contingency (and accompanying liability) is recorded in the accounting records at an estimated amount only when:

a It is **probable** that a loss has been incurred, and

b The amount of loss can be **reasonably estimated**.

Loss contingencies which do not meet both these conditions are **disclosed in footnotes** to the financial statements whenever there is a least a **reasonable possibility** that a loss has been incurred.

*55 A **commitment** is a contract, or agreement, to carry out future transactions. Although a liability is not recorded currently in most situations, commitments should be disclosed by footnotes to the financial statements if **material**.

56 If at the date of issuance, the contract rate of interest for a bond issue were below par, the bonds could only be sold at a **discount. If the contract rate were above market levels, the bonds could be sold at a **premium**.

57 In practice, most bonds are issued **at the current market rate of interest. Thus, the bonds will sell in the marketplace very close to their face amount. But an underwriter often buys the entire bond issue from the issuing company at a slight discount, and then resells the bonds to investors at par. Thus, many bonds are issued at a very slight discount.

**58 When bonds are issued at a discount, the borrower initially records a liability equal to the issue price. Over time, this liability increases to the maturity value (face amount) of the bonds. Accounting for bonds issued at a discount is described in 59 below.

59 When bonds are issued, Cash is debited for the amount received, and Bonds Payable is credited for the **face amount of the bond issue. Any discount is debited to a contra-liability account called Discount on Bonds Payable. In the balance sheet, the discount is subtracted from the balance in the Bonds Payable account, resulting in a "net liability" equal to the amount borrowed.

**60 Over the life of the bonds, the balance in the Discount account is gradually amortized into interest expense. These entries (debit Interest Expense, credit Discount on Bonds Payable) increase the periodic interest expense and also cause the net liability to gradually increase toward the bonds' maturity value.

**61 The discount should be viewed as part of the total interest expense which is not paid to the bondholders until the bonds mature. However, the discount is recognized as expense *over the life of the bonds*.

**62 Bonds seldom are issued at a premium. If they were, the amount of the premium would be credited to an account entitled Premium on Bonds Payable. In the balance sheet, bond premium is *added* to the face amount of the bonds to determine net liability.

**63 Over the life of the bonds, the premium is amortized by entries debiting Premium on Bonds Payable and *crediting* Interest Expense. Thus, amortization of a premium *reduces* the periodic interest expense and gradually reduces the net liability toward its maturity value.

TEST YOURSELF ON LIABILITIES

True or False

For each of the following statements, circle the T or the F to indicate whether the statement is true or false.

T F 1 Existing liabilities relate to *past* transactions or events, rather than to *future* transactions or events.

T F 2 Liabilities and owners' equity are similar in that both eventually mature.

T F 3 Obligations to pay interest stem from liabilities, not from owners' equity.

T F 4 Some liabilities are recorded in accounting records at estimated amounts, rather than at the actual amount that will have to be paid.

T F 5 The balance of the account Accrued Interest Payable represents unpaid interest charges applicable to past periods.

T F 6 A company's wages and salaries expense is reduced by the amounts of income taxes and FICA taxes withheld from employees' pay.

T F 7 Unemployment taxes are levied directly upon employees.

T F 8 Social Security and Medicare taxes are levied equally upon the employee and the employer.

T F 9 The interest which must be paid on a long-term installment note payable during the next year is classified as a current liability.

T F 10 The principal amount of a long-term installment note payable that will be repaid within the next year is classified as a current liability.

T F 11 Income taxes payable do not become a liability until an income tax return is prepared and filed.

T F 12 A maturing obligation that will be refinanced on a long-term basis is classified as a long-term liability.

T F 13 The primary purpose of an amortization table is to record the gross pay, net pay, and amounts withheld for an individual employee during the year.

T F 14 An amortization table for an installment note payable probably will show increasing amounts of interest expense for each successive period.

T F 15 Unissued bonds may be reported as an asset in the balance sheet since they represent a potential source of cash.

T F 16 The time value of money concept means that the present value of a future payment is always less than the future amount.

T F 17 The lower the effective rate of interest required by investors, the lower the price at which a given bond should sell.

T F 18 If interest rates rise dramatically after bonds payable are issued, the fair market value of the bonds will rise and should be disclosed in notes to the financial statements.

T F 19 An investor who buys a bond at a premium is willing to earn a lesser rate of interest than the rate stated on the bond.

T F 20 Material gains and losses on the early retirement of bonds payable are reported in the income statement as extraordinary items.

T F 21 Leases which contain provisions indicating that they are in effect equivalent to a sale and purchase of assets are called *operating leases*.

T F 22 When lease payments are regarded as rent expense, no liability for the present value of future lease payments appears in the lessee's balance sheet.

**Supplemental Topic B, "Bonds Issued at a Discount or a Premium."

T F 23 When the lessee records an asset and a liability equal in amount to the present value of the future lease payments, part of each lease payment is regarded as interest expense.

T F 24 A company must disclose in notes to its financial statements the specific terms of every long-term liability.

T F 25 The debt ratio and quick ratio are of interest primarily to long-term creditors.

T F 26 Creditors prefer a high debt ratio and a high interest coverage ratio.

T F *27 Estimated liabilities are disclosed in footnotes to the financial statements but are not actually recorded in the accounting records.

T F *28 Loss contingencies include all types of losses which may result from future events.

T F *29 The manner in which loss contingencies are presented in financial statements depends upon the degree of certainty involved.

T F *30 A three-year contract by a baseball team to pay a player a specified salary is classified partially as a current liability and partially as a long-term liability.

T F **31 Total interest expense on a bond sold for less than its face value will be the cash paid as interest less the amortization of the discount.

T F **32 If a company issues bonds payable at a discount, the rate of interest stated on the bond is greater than the effective rate.

T F **33 Amortization of a discount on bonds payable increases interest expense and increases the carrying value of the liability.

T F **34 Amortization of a premium on bonds payable reduces interest expense and reduces the carrying value of the liability.

Completion Statements

Fill in the necessary words or amounts to complete the following statements:

1 Liabilities are _____ arising from _____ transactions.

2 When an employer withholds income tax from an employee, the amount withheld will be credited to a _____ _____ account.

3 Most corporate bonds are issued in denominations of $_____ and pay interest _____ a year.

4 For each 9%, 30-year bond issued, Red Car Transport received $925. The market quotation as shown in the newspaper for these bonds would be _____.

5 The _____ _____ of a future payment is always (more, less) _____ than the future amount because money on hand today can be invested to become a _____ amount in the future.

6 Bonds payable reacquired by the issuing company through purchase on the open market at a price (less, greater) _____ than carrying value will cause the recording of a gain, whereas bonds reacquired at a price (less, greater) _____ than carrying value will cause the recording of a loss.

7 The lessee accounts for the monthly payments on an operating lease by debiting _____ _____. The type of lease is often called _____ _____-_____ financing because the lessee records no _____ _____ for future lease payments.

8 In accounting for a capital lease used to finance the sale of merchandise, the lessor debits _____ _____ _____ and credits _____ for the _____ _____ of the future lease payments. When lease payments are received, the lessor recognizes part of each payment as _____ _____ and the remainder as a reduction in _____ _____ _____.

*9 Chrysler Corp. sells automobiles with a five-year limited warranty. At the end of each accounting period, Chrysler records a liability for the estimated cost of performing warranty repairs on cars sold during the period. The liability for warranty repairs is an example of a(n) _____ liability, and recording the related warranty repairs expense in the period in which the cars were sold is required by the _____ principle of accounting.

**10 In the accounts of the issuing company, the carrying value of bonds equals the face value plus any _____ or minus any _____.

**11 As the discount on bonds payable is amortized, the amount of the net bond liability (increases, decreases) _____; as the premium on bonds payable is amortized, the amount of the net bond liability (increases, decreases) _____.

Multiple Choice

Choose the best answer for each of the following questions and enter the identifying letter in the space provided.

_____ **1** In December, Fallbrook Lumber Co. received an invoice for legal fees rendered in November, payable by January 31. The invoice was not recorded until January 12. As a result of this delay:

a Liabilities are overstated at the end of December.

b Legal fees expense is overstated for December.

c The cost principle is violated.

d The matching principle is violated.

_____ **2** Which of the following is *not* included among the current liabilities of a manufacturing company?

a The portion of a 10-year capital lease obligation that will be paid in the next 12 months.

b The estimated liability for warranty repairs on products sold.

c The liability for income taxes withheld from employees.

d The contingent liability for an unresolved lawsuit pending against the company, to be determined within the next year.

_____ **3** The bookkeeper failed to classify a note payable as a current liability in preparing Burbank Corporation's balance sheet. As a result of this error:

a Burbank Corporation's working capital is understated.

b Burbank Corporation's current ratio is overstated.

c Burbank Corporation's liabilities are understated.

d Burbank Corporation's interest expense is understated.

_____ **4** The amounts withheld from employees' gross earnings are recorded by the employer as:

a Payroll taxes expense.

b Current assets.

c Contra-asset accounts.

d Current liabilities.

_____ **5** Which of the following would *not* be classified as a long-term liability as of December 31, 1995?

a Deferred income taxes.

b Portion of a 30-year mortgage to be paid off in the next 12 months.

c Unfunded liability for nonpension retirement benefits.

d Debt maturing in March of 1996 which has been refinanced on a long-term basis.

_____ **6** Albertson Company purchased a parcel of land for $15,000 and in exchange issued a 10-year installment note for this amount, plus interest at 12% per year. The note is *fully amortizing* and will be paid in 120 monthly installments of $215 each. With regard to this installment note, each of the following is true, *except*:

a Albertson's payments on this installment note total $25,800.

b Albertson's first payment includes $150 of interest expense.

c Over the 10-year period, Albertson will pay $10,800 interest.

d Over the 10-year period, Albertson will pay $18,000 interest.

_____ **7** Which of the following is *not* a characteristic of corporate bonds?

a Is a highly liquid, transferable investment.

b Has a specified maturity date.

c Represents ownership of the issuing corporation.

d Pays interest, usually semiannually.

_____ **8** The principal *tax advantage* of raising capital by issuing bonds instead of capital stock is that:

a More investors will be interested in purchasing bonds because they can be issued at a discount and the price will be less than the price of capital stock.

b Interest payments are deductible for income tax purposes; dividends are not.

c SEC approval is required for issuance of capital stock but not for bonds.

d The issuing corporation must pay income taxes whenever capital stock is sold, but only when bonds are sold at a premium.

***Supplemental Topic B,* "Bonds Issued at a Discount or a Premium."

_____ **9** On June 1, 1996, Eads Corporation issued $2,000,000 of 10-year, 12% bonds payable. Interest is payable semiannually, each April 1 and October 1. The bonds are issued at par *plus accrued interest* for the months since the last interest date. The journal entry to record the issuance of the bonds includes:

a A debit to Bond Interest Expense of $40,000.

b A debit to Cash of $2,040,000.

c A credit to Premium on Bonds Payable of $40,000.

d A credit to Bond Interest Payable of $80,000.

_____ **10** Refer to the data in question 9 above. How much bond interest expense should be reported in Eads Corporation's income statement for the year ended December 31, 1996, with respect to the bonds payable?

a $120,000.

b $80,000.

c $160,000.

d $140,000.

_____ **11** A corporation that wishes to retire its bonds payable:

a Must wait until the maturity date.

b Must pay bondholders a price equal to the carrying value of the bonds payable.

c Will recognize an extraordinary loss on the retirement if the price paid is greater than the *face value* of the bonds payable.

d Will recognize an extraordinary gain on the retirement if the price paid is less than the *carrying value* of the bonds.

_____ **12** Assume that a capital lease is erroneously treated as an operating lease in the accounting records of the lessee. One effect of this error will be:

a An overstatement of assets and liabilities

b An overstatement of rent expense and understatement of interest expense and depreciation expense.

c An understatement of rent expense and an overstatement of liabilities.

d None of the above.

_____ **13** Which of the following would be perceived as *most favorable* by holders of a corporation's debt maturing in seven years?

a High current ratio.

b Low debt ratio.

c Low inventory turnover ratio.

d Low interest coverage ratio.

_____ ***14** A *loss contingency* is recorded in the accounts when:

a It is reasonably possible that a loss has been incurred and the amount of loss can be estimated.

b It is probable that a loss has been incurred.

c All uncertainty surrounding the loss situation is resolved.

d It is probable that a loss has been incurred and the amount of loss can be reasonably estimated.

_____ ***15** Loss contingencies relating to pending litigation usually are:

a Disclosed in notes to the financial statements.

b Shown as current liabilities in the balance sheet.

c Shown as extraordinary items in the income statement.

d Not disclosed or recorded until the litigation has been settled.

_____ ****16** The discount on bonds payable is best described as:

a An element of interest expense on borrowed funds that will be paid by the issuing corporation at maturity.

b The payment of periodic interest at less than the rate called for in the bond contract.

c An amount below par which the bondholder may be called upon to make good.

d An asset representing interest that has been paid in advance.

_____ ****17** The account Premium on Bonds Payable is best classified in the balance sheet as:

a An addition to bonds payable.

b A restriction of retained earnings.

c A deduction from bonds payable.

d An asset.

Exercises

1 Listed below are twelve technical accounting terms introduced in this chapter.

Unfunded pension liability	*Loss contingency*
Deferred income taxes	*Commitment*
	Unemployment tax
Bond premium	*Interest coverage rate*
Bond discount	*Capital lease*
Present value of future cash flows	*Principal amount*
	Applying leverage

Each of the following statements may (or may not) describe one of these technical terms. In the space provided below each

*Supplemental Topic A, "Estimated Liabilities, Loss Contingencies, and Commitments."

**Supplemental Topic B, "Bonds Issued at a Discount or a Premium."

statement, indicate the accounting term described, or answer "None" if the statement does not correctly describe any of the terms.

a An element of interest expense included in the maturity value of bonds payable.

b The valuation concept applied to capital lease obligations.

c The portion of a loan payment representing repayment of the original amount borrowed.

d A liability that appears in the balance sheet of every company which offers its workers a pension plan.

e Financing a business with equity capital.

f A liability that results from using straight-line depreciation in financial statements and MACRS in income tax returns.

g The risk that losses future business operations may result in net losses.

h A payroll tax shared jointly by employers and employees.

i A measure of debt-paying ability used primarily by short-term creditors.

j A lease agreement in which the lessee treats the lease payments as rental expense.

2 Shown below is a summary of the annual payroll data for Carter Company:

Wages and salaries expense (gross pay)		$500,000
Amounts withheld from employees' pay:		
Income taxes	$60,000	
Social Security and Medicare	45,000	105,000
Payroll taxes expenses:		
Social Security and Medicare	$45,000	
Unemployment taxes	12,000	57,000
Workers' compensation premiums		15,000
Group health insurance premiums (paid by employer)		75,000
Contributions to employees' pension plan (paid by employer and fully funded)		30,000
Cost of other postretirement benefits:		
Funded	$16,000	
Unfunded	18,000	34,000

a Compute Carter's total payroll-related expense for the year.

$_____

b Compute the company's cash outlays during the year for payroll-related expenses (assume all short-term obligations such as insurance premiums and payroll taxes have been paid).

$_____

c Compute the annual "take home pay" of Carter's employees.

$_____

3 On October 31, 1996, Conrad Township signed a five-year installment note payable in the amount of $60,000 in exchange for two school buses. The note is fully amortizing and payable in equal monthly installments of $1,335, which include interest computed at an annual rate of 12%. The first monthly payment is made on November 30, 1996. Complete the amortization table at the bottom of the page for the first three payments, and then answer the following questions.

a Compute the amount of interest expense on this note recognized by Conrad Township in **1996** $_____.

b Conrad's balance sheet at **December 31, 1996** includes a total liability for this note payable of $_____. (Do not separate into current and long-term portions.)

c Over the five-year life of the note, how much **interest** will Conrad Township pay? $_____.

Payment Date	Monthly Payment	Interest Expense	Repayment of Principal	Unpaid Balance
Issuance	– – –	– – –	– – –	$60,000
11/30/96	$1,335	$____	$____	$____
12/31/96	$1,335	$____	$____	$____
1/31/97	$1,335	$____	$____	$____

4 On March 1, 1996 Bestek Corporation issued **at par** $8 million of 12%, 10-year bonds payable. Interest is payable semiannually each March 1 and September 1.

a The amount of **cash paid** to bondholders for interest in 1996 is $_____.

b Show adjusting entry (if any) necessary at December 31, 1996 regarding this bond issue.

c *Interest expense* on this bond issue reported in Bestek's 1996 *income statement* is $_____.

d Bestek's balance sheet at December 31, 1996 includes bonds payable of $_____ and interest payable of $_____. (Indicate $0 or "None" if the item is not reported.)

5 On July 1, 1996, Caldwell Company issued $600,000 of 10%, 10-year bonds with interest payable on March 1 and September 1. The company received cash of $614,200, including the accrued interest from March 1, 1996. Bond discount or premium is amortized at each interest payment date and at year-end using the **straight-line method. Place the correct answer to each of the following questions in the space provided. (Use the space provided below for computations.)

a What was the amount of accrued interest on July 1, 1996? $_____.

b What was the amount of bond discount or premium (state which) to be amortized over the period that the bonds will be outstanding, 116 months? $_____.

c What was the amount of cash paid to bondholders on September 1, 1996? $_____.

d What amount of accrued interest payable should appear on the balance sheet on December 31, 1996? $_____.

e What was the amount of the unamortized discount or premium on December 31, 1996? $_____.

f What was the total interest expense for 1996 relating to this bond issue? $_____.

Computations:

**6 From the data in Exercise 5, prepare journal entries required on each of the following dates:

a July 1, 1996 (issuance of bonds).

b September 1, 1996 (payment of interest and amortization for two months).

c December 31, 1996 (accrual of interest and amortization from Sept. 1 to Dec. 31).

	1996	General Journal		
a	July 1			
b	Sept. 1			

**Supplemental Topic B, "Bonds Issued at a Discount or a Premium."

		General Journal		
c	Dec. 31			

**7 Listed below are 10 transactions of Marshall-Thomas, Inc.

a On April 1, issued at a discount 20-year bonds payable dated March 1.

b On September 1, made the first semiannual interest payment on the bonds described in **a**, above, and amortized the discount for five months.

c Made a year-end adjusting entry to recognize interest expense on bonds payable issued at a premium. (These bonds are due in seven years.)

d Immediately following an interest payment date, called bonds issued at a premium at a price above the original issue price, but below current market value. (Assume that all interest expense has been recognized through the date of the call.)

e Due to an increase in interest rates, the market value of the bonds described in **a**, above, declined substantially.

f Made a monthly payment on an operating lease.

g Made a monthly payment on a capital lease. (Assume all remaining principal payments on this lease are classified as a current liability.)

h Recorded pension expense on a fully funded pension plan, including the remittance of cash to the trustee.

i Recorded expenses relating to postretirement costs other than pensions. Fifty percent of these costs are funded immediately and another 25% will be funded in each of the next two years.

j Made an adjusting entry to record income taxes expense for the current year, a portion of which is deferred. (Assume that all deferred taxes arise from the methods used in depreciating plant assets.)

Indicate the effects of these transactions upon the elements of financial statements listed below. (Assume the accounts are closed only at year-end.) Use the following code letters: *I* = Increase, *D* = Decrease, *NE* = No effect.

	Income Statement			Balance Sheet			
Trans-action	Revenue & Gains	Expenses & Losses	Net Income	Total Assets	Current Liabilities	Long-term Liabilities	Owners' Equity
a							
b							
c							
d							
e							
f							
g							
h							
i							
j							

**Includes transactions from *Supplemental Topic B*, "Bonds Issued at a Discount or a Premium."

SOLUTIONS TO CHAPTER 11 SELF-TEST

True or False

1 **T** Liabilities are *existing* obligations stemming from *past* transactions or events. Obligations relating to future transactions are called **commitments** rather than liabilities. Commitments often are disclosed in notes to financial statements, but are not yet considered liabilities.

2 **F** Liabilities mature, but owners' equity *does not*. In fact, this is perhaps the greatest *difference* between liabilities and equity.

3 **T** Interest is compensation paid to *creditors* for the use of borrowed capital, not to owners for the use of equity capital.

4 **T** Many liabilities can only be estimated at the time that they are recorded. Examples include the amount of income taxes payable and a manufacturer's liability to perform warranty work on products sold.

5 **T** Accrued interest payable is recorded by an adjusting entry recognizing the interest expense accruing over past periods.

6 **F** Amounts withheld from employees reduce the amount *paid directly to employees*, but do not reduce the employer's wages and salaries expense. The portions of wage and salaries expense withheld simply must be paid to tax authorities instead of to the employees.

7 **F** Unemployment taxes are levied upon *employers*, not directly upon employees.

8 **T** The social security and Medicare programs are funded half by amounts withheld from employees and half by payroll taxes levied upon employers.

9 **F** *No* liability exists at present for interest applicable to *future* periods.

10 **T** The principal amount of an installment note all represents a liability. That portion which is scheduled to be repaid within the next year is classified as a *current* liability.

11 **F** A liability for income taxes accrues *as profits are earned*.

12 **T** If the liability will be refinanced on a long-term basis, *it will not be paid from current assets*. Therefore, it is not classified as a current liability.

13 **F** The purpose of an amortization table is to determine how installment payments are allocated between interest and principal. It has nothing to do with payrolls.

14 **F** A portion of each installment payment usually reduces the principal amount owed. As the liability is reduced, the interest expense of each successive period usually will *decrease*.

15 **F** When bonds are *issued* (sold), the company receives an asset and records a liability for the bonds payable.

16 **T** Money received today can be invested to earn interest and grow to a larger amount in the future.

17 **F** The selling price of bonds paying a fixed rate of interest varies inversely with the investors' required rate of interest (market rate).

18 **F** Bond prices fluctuate *inversely* with interest rates. If interest rates rise after bonds are issued, the market price of the bonds should *fall*.

19 **T** The investor receives interest checks equal to the stated rate of interest, but at maturity he will get back only the face amount of the bond, not the higher price he paid for the bond.

20 **T** Regardless of whether a corporation purchases its own bonds on the open market or exercises a call provision, the FASB requires that material gains or losses on retirement of debt be reported as extraordinary items.

21 **F** *Capital* leases are regarded as essentially equivalent to a sale of property.

22 **T** For such *operating* leases, the lessee does not record any long-lived asset.

23 **T** The balance of each lease payment reduces the recorded lease payment obligation.

24 **F** It would not be feasible for a large business to disclose the terms of *every* long-term liability. Rather, the liabilities are grouped into categories of similar obligations, and the *range* of interest rates and maturity values is disclosed for each category.

25 **F** The quick ratio (quick assets divided by current liabilities) is a measure of *short-term* solvency, of interest primarily to *short-term* creditors. Long-term creditors use primarily the debt ratio and the *interest coverage ratio* in evaluating the safety of their claims.

26 **F** Creditors prefer a *low* debt ratio and a high interest coverage ratio. A low debt ratio indicates that owners have a large financial stake in the business.

*27 F The amounts of estimated items, such as future warranty repairs or income taxes, *are* entered in the accounts and appear in financial statements both as an expense and as a liability.

*28 F Loss contingencies refer to losses which already may have occurred *as a result of past events*.

*29 T If the existence of a loss is *probable* and the amount can be *reasonably estimated*, the loss contingency is recorded in the accounts at the estimated amount. If these conditions are not both met, the loss contingency is not recorded, but it must be disclosed if the existence of loss is *reasonably possible*. If the probability of a loss having been incurred is deemed remote, loss contingencies need not be recorded or disclosed.

*30 F This contract is for *future* services; therefore, it is a commitment rather than a liability.

**31 F Interest expense over the life of the bond equals cash interest payments *plus* amortization of the discount.

**32 F Bonds sell at a discount when investors require a rate of return (effective rate of interest) *greater* than that paid by the bonds (stated rate of interest).

**33 T Since the unamortized discount is subtracted from the maturity value of the bonds, the carrying value of the bonds increases as this contra liability is amortized.

**34 T Unamortized premium is added to maturity value of bonds; as this premium is amortized, the sum of maturity value plus unamortized premium (carrying value) decreases.

Completion Statements

1 Obligations, past. **2** Current liability. **3** $1,000; twice. **4** 92½. **5** Present value, less, larger. **6** Less, greater. **7** Rent Expense, off-balance-sheet, liability. **8** Lease Payments Receivable, Sales, present value, interest revenue, Lease Payments Receivable. ***9** Estimated, matching. ****10** Premium, discount. ****11** Increases, decreases.

Multiple Choice

1 Answer **d**—liabilities and legal fees expense are both *understated*. The matching principle requires that Fallbrook recognize in each period all the expenses incurred in producing the revenue of that period. By failing to record the invoice for legal fees, Fallbrook omitted the legal fees expense that is to be matched with revenue of December. The cost principle would not be violated as long as Fallbrook valued the liability for legal fees at the cost of the service received, usually the invoice amount.

2 Answer **d**—the contingent liability due to the unresolved lawsuit against the company would be disclosed in a footnote to the financial statement, unless it is known, or probable, that the manufacturing company will lose or settle the suit. At that point, the liability would be recorded in the accounts and actually appear on the balance sheet as a liability. Answers **a**, **b**, and **c** are examples of current liabilities—obligations that must be paid within one year or within the operating cycle, whichever is longer.

3 Answer **b**—by failing to classify a liability as current, current liabilities are understated. This results in a current ratio (current assets divided by current liabilities) that is overstated. Although Burbank's total liabilities are correct, working capital (current assets minus current liabilities) is overstated. Burbank's interest expense is not affected by this classification error.

4 Answer **d**—the amounts withheld must be remitted to the appropriate taxing authorities or other organizations by the employer and therefore constitute current liabilities from the employer's point of view.

5 Answer **b**—the portion of long-term debt to be paid off in the next year or operating cycle is considered a current liability. Answers **a**, **c**, and **d** are all long-term liabilities.

6 Answer **d**—total payments of $25,800 (120 months × $215) less amount toward principal of note ($15,000) equals interest paid of $10,800. Interest included in the first payment is computed as $15,000 (unpaid principal) × 1% (monthly rate), or $150.

7 Answer **c**—an investor in bonds is a *creditor* of the issuing corporation. Answers **a**, **b**, and **d** are all characteristics of corporate bonds.

8 Answer **b**—the deductibility of interest payments is a strong incentive for financing with debt rather than equity.

---

*Supplemental Topic A, "Estimated Liabilities, Loss Contingencies, and Commitments."
**Supplemental Topic B, "Bonds Issued at a Discount or a Premium."

9 Answer **b**—the amount received is $2,040,000 ($2,000,000 face amount plus *two months' accrued interest* of $40,000). The entry would consist of a debit to Cash for $2,040,000, a credit to Bonds Payable for $2,000,000 and a credit to Bond Interest Payable for $40,000. Since the bonds were issued at par, there is no discount or premium.

10 Answer **d**—Eads' 1996 income statement should report *seven months'* interest expense on the bonds (June 1 through December 31). The interest expense computation is $2,000,000 \times 12\% \times \frac{7}{12}$.

11 Answer **d**—if a corporation can eliminate a liability by paying *less* than the carrying value of that liability, the corporation recognizes a *gain* on the transaction. Answer **c** is incorrect because the price paid to retire the bonds is compared to the *face value*; it should have been compared to the *carrying value* to determine gain or loss. Corporations may retire their bonds payable by purchasing them on the open market if the bonds are not callable, or if the call price is higher than the market price.

12 Answer **b**—if the lessee records an operating lease, it recognizes rent expense and shows no asset or liability in its accounting records. Upon entering a capital lease, the lessee records both an asset and a liability; it must record interest expense relating to the liability, and depreciation expense relating to the asset. Answer **a** would be correct if worded *understatement* instead of overstatement of assets and liabilities. The error would result in the reverse of answer **c** also—an *overstatement* of rent expense and *understatement* of liabilities.

13 Answer **b**—long-term creditors evaluate the safety of their claims against a company's assets by examining statistics such as debt ratio and interest coverage ratio. Long-term creditors prefer a *low* debt ratio, and a *high* interest coverage ratio; thus, answer **b** is more favorable than answer **d**. Current ratio and inventory turnover ratio are measures of short-term liquidity, and of interest primarily to short-term creditors.

*14 Answer **d**—loss contingencies are recorded in the accounting records only when *both* of the following criteria are met: (1) it is *probable* that a loss has been incurred, and (2) the amount of loss can be *reasonably es-*

timated. If it is only reasonably possible that a loss has been incurred, footnote disclosure is appropriate. All uncertainty surrounding the situation need not be resolved.

*15 Answer **a**—contingent liabilities are disclosed in notes to the financial statements whenever there is at least a reasonable possibility that a loss has been incurred—often this is the situation before the litigation has been settled. If it is probable that a loss has been incurred and the amount can be reasonably estimated, the loss contingency and related liability can then, and only then, be recorded in the accounting records.

16 Answer **a—the issuing corporation receives less than the face amount for bonds payable issued at a discount but must repay full face amount at maturity. This "extra" amount that must be repaid for the use of the investor's money represents *interest expense* (in addition to the cash interest paid semiannually).

17 Answer **a—Premium on Bonds Payable is a credit balance account which is added to bonds payable in order to show the current carrying value of the liability on the balance sheet. Discount on Bonds Payable would be *deducted* from bonds payable.

Solutions to Exercises

1
a Bond discount
b Present value of future cash flows
c Principal amount
d None (Many companies have funded pension plans and, therefore, show no liability for pension obligations.)
e None (*Applying leverage* generally means financing the business with debt, rather than equity.)
f Deferred income taxes
g None (*Loss contingencies* are possible losses stemming from *past* events, not future operations.)
h None (Unemployment taxes are borne entirely by the employer. "Shared" payroll taxes include Social Security and Medicare.)
i None (The *interest coverage rate* is used primarily by *long-term* creditors.)
j None (This statement describes an *operating lease*, not a capital lease.)

---

*Supplemental Topic A, "Estimated Liabilities, Loss Contingencies, and Commitments."
**Supplemental Topic B, "Bonds Issued at a Discount or a Premium."

2

a $711,000 ($500,000 + $57,000 + $15,000 + $75,000 + $30,000 + $34,000)

b $693,000 (All $711,000 from **a**, less un-funded postretirement benefits of $18,000)

c $395,000 ($500,000 gross pay, less $105,000 withheld)

3

Payment Date	Monthly Payment	Interest Expense	Repayment of Principal	Unpaid Balance
Issuance	– – –	– – –	– – –	$60,000
11/30/96	$1,335	$ 600	$ 735	$59,265
12/31/96	$1,335	$ 593	$ 742	$58,523
1/31/97	$1,335	$ 585	$ 750	$57,773

a $1,193 ($600 + $593) (see amortization table)

b $58,523 (from amortization table)

c $20,100 5 yrs. × 12 × $1,335 = $80,100 total paid
$80,100 – $60,000 principal = $20,100 interest

4

a $480,000 $8,000,000 × 12% × $\frac{6}{12}$ (Sept. 1 payment)

b Bond Interest Expense 320,000
    Bond Interest Payable..   320,000
To accrue 4 months' interest.

c $800,000
$8,000,000 × 12% × $\frac{10}{12}$ (bonds outstanding 10 months)

d Bonds payable $8,000,000
Interest payable $ 320,000
(4 mos. interest accrued since payment date of September 1)

**5

a $20,000 ($600,000 × 10% × $\frac{4}{12}$)

b $5,800 *discount* ($600,000 + $20,000 – $614,200)

c $30,000 ($600,000 × 10% × $\frac{6}{12}$)

d $20,000 ($600,000 × 10% × $\frac{4}{12}$)

e $5,500 unamortized *discount* [$5,800 less amortization of $50 ($5,800 ÷ 116 months) per month for six months]

f $30,300 (interest on $600,000 at 10% for six months, $30,000, plus amortization of the discount for six months, $300)

***Supplemental Topic B*, "Bonds Issued at a Discount or a Premium."

**6

	1996	General Journal		
a	July 1	Cash	614,200	
		Discount on Bonds Payable	5,800	
		Bonds Payable		600,000
		Bond Interest Payable		20,000
		To record issuance of bonds.		
b	Sept. 1	Bond Interest Payable	20,000	
		Bond Interest Expense	10,000	
		Cash		30,000
		To record payment of interest for six months, including $20,000 which		
		was accrued on date bonds were issued.		
	1	Bond Interest Expense	100	
		Discount on Bonds Payable		100
		To amortize discount for July and August at $50 per month		
		($5,800 ÷ 116).		
c	Dec. 31	Bond Interest Expense	20,000	
		Bond Interest Payable		20,000
		To accrue interest for four months.		
	31	Bond Interest Expense	200	
		Discount on Bonds Payable		200
		To amortize discount for four months at $50 per month.		

**7

	Income Statement			Balance Sheet			
Trans-action	Revenue & Gains	Expenses & Losses	Net Income	Total Assets	Current Liabilities	Long-term Liabilities	Owners' Equity
a	NE	NE	NE	I	I	I	NE
b	NE	I	D	D	D	I	D
c	NE	I	D	NE	I	D	D
d	NE	I	D	D	NE	D	D
e	NE	NE	NE	NE	NE	NE	NE
f	NE	I	D	D	NE	NE	D
g	NE	I	D	D	D	NE	D
h	NE	I	D	D	NE	NE	D
i	NE	I	D	D	I	I	D
j	NE	I	D	NE	I	I	D

**Supplemental Topic B*, "Bonds Issued at a Discount or a Premium."

12

OWNERSHIP EQUITY: SOLE PROPRIETORSHIPS, PARTNERSHIPS, AND CORPORATIONS

HIGHLIGHTS OF THE CHAPTER

1 Three common forms of business organization found in the American economy are the *sole proprietorship*, the *partnership*, and the *corporation*. A sole proprietorship is any unincorporated business owned by one person. A partnership is an unincorporated business having two or more owners.

2 In a sole proprietorship, a *Capital account* and a *Drawing account* are maintained in the ledger to show the equity of the owner. The Capital account is credited with the amounts invested by the owner and with the net income earned by the business. The Capital account is debited when net losses are incurred. Withdrawals by the owner are debited to a Drawing account, which is closed into the Capital account at the end of the accounting period.

   The same procedures are followed for a partnership, except that separate capital and drawing accounts are maintained for each partner.

3 The income statement for a sole proprietorship does not include any salary expense for the owner or any income tax expense. The income statement for a partnership shows the amount of net income allocated to each partner but does not report an income tax expense since a partnership, like a sole proprietorship, is not a taxable entity.

4 The principal characteristics of the partnership form of organization are:
a Ease of formation.
b Limited life. (A partnership is dissolved whenever there is a change in partners.)

c Mutual agency. (Each partner has the right to bind the partnership to a contract.)
d Unlimited liability. (Each partner may be personally liable for all the debts of the partnership.)
e Co-ownership of partnership property and profits.

5 The dominant form of business organization in the United States is the *corporation*. A corporation is an "artificial being" which is regarded as a legal person, having a continuous existence apart from its owners. Literally thousands, or even millions, of individuals may be the owners of a single corporation; thus the corporation is an ideal means of amassing a great deal of investment capital.

6 Ownership in a corporation is evidenced by transferable *shares of stock*, and owners are called *stockholders*.

7 A corporation offers certain advantages not found in other forms of business organizations:
a The liability of individual stockholders for the debts of a corporation is *limited to the amount of their investment*.
b Large amounts of capital may be gathered by issuing stock to many investors.
c Shares of stock are easily transferable.
d A corporation is a separate legal entity with a perpetual existence.
e Corporations are usually run by professional management.

8 Some *disadvantages of the corporate form* of organization are:
a A corporation is a *taxable entity* and must pay a high rate of tax on its net income.

b Corporations are subject to a considerable degree of regulation and disclosure of their business and financial affairs.

c The separation of ownership and management (effective control of corporate affairs) may result in management practices which are detrimental to stockholders.

9 A corporation is organized by filing an application with the appropriate state agency. The application contains the articles of incorporation and the list of stockholders and directors. Costs of organizing a corporation are recorded in an *Organization Costs* account and generally are written off as expense over a five-year period.

10 Corporate stockholders have certain basic rights:

a To vote for directors (voting rights generally are granted only to holders of common stock).

b To share in profits by receiving dividends (distributions of earnings to the stockholders) declared by the board of directors.

c To share in the distribution of assets if the corporation is liquidated.

Stockholders *do not* have the right to intervene in the management of a corporation or to transact corporation business.

11 The primary functions of the *board of directors* are to manage the corporation and protect the interests of the stockholders. The directors formulate general policies, declare dividends, and review the actions of corporate officers. The board of directors is elected by the stockholders and often includes *outside* directors who are not officers of the corporation.

12 The corporate officers are the active, full-time professional managers of a corporation. Corporate officers usually include a president or chief executive officer (CEO), several vice-presidents, a controller, a treasurer, and a secretary.

13 Capital contributed by stockholders comes from the sale of shares of stock. In order to appeal to a large number of investors, a corporation may issue more than one class of stock. When only one class of stock is issued, it is generally referred to as *capital stock*; when two or more classes of stock are outstanding, they usually consist of *common stock* and various types of *preferred stock*.

14 The articles of incorporation specify the number of shares of capital stock which a corporation is authorized to issue and the *par value* (if any) per share. Par value (or stated value) represents *legal capital*—the amount below which stockholders' equity cannot be reduced except by losses. A dividend cannot be declared if it would reduce total stockholders' equity below the par value of the outstanding shares.

15 Capital stock is generally issued for a sum greater than the par (or stated) value; the excess is credited to *Additional Paid-in Capital*. Stock is almost never issued for less than par value. In the absence of a par or stated value, the entire proceeds are viewed as legal capital and are credited to the Capital Stock account.

16 Most *preferred stocks* have the following features: (a) full dividends to be paid before any dividends on common stock, (b) cumulative dividend rights, (c) preferred claim to assets in case of liquidation, (d) callable at the option of the corporation, and (e) no voting power.

17 The dividend preference of most preferred stocks is *cumulative*. This means if any preferred dividends are omitted, these dividends must be *made up* before any dividend can be paid to common stockholders. Omitted dividends on preferred stock are called *dividends in arrears*.

18 Dividends in arrears are not listed as liabilities because no liability to pay a dividend exists unless the dividend has been declared by the directors.

19 A share of *convertible preferred stock* can be exchanged for an agreed number of shares of common stock. A holder of convertible preferred stock has greater assurance of receiving regular dividends than does a holder of common stock, while at the same time sharing in any increase in the value of the common stock.

20 An *underwriter* may help a corporation sell a large stock issue. The underwriter guarantees the issuing company a specific price for the stock and makes a profit by selling the stock to the public at a higher price.

21 When stock is issued for assets other than cash, the *fair market value* of the noncash assets or the *market value* of the stock should be used as a basis for recording the transaction.

22 Small corporations sometimes allow investors to *subscribe* to stock by agreeing to pay for the stock in installments or at a future date. When the subscription contract is signed, the issuing corporation debits Subscriptions Receivable for the subscription price, credits Capital Stock Subscribed for the par value of subscribed shares, and credits Additional Paid-in Capital for the excess of subscription price over par value. When the subscribed shares are paid for and issued, the par value is transferred into appropriate Capital Stock accounts.

23 If assets are donated to a corporation, total assets and total stockholders' equity are increased by the fair market value of the assets received. The receipt of the gift is recorded by debiting the appropriate asset accounts and crediting **Donated Capital.** Donated Capital appears in the stockholders' equity section as an element of paid-in capital. No profit is recognized when a gift is received.

24 Ownership of stock is evidenced by a **stock certificate** showing the name of the stockholder and the number of shares owned. At the time of issue, the stock certificate is signed by the president and secretary of the issuing corporation and delivered to the stockholder. When the stockholder sells the shares, the certificate is returned to the corporation and canceled. A new certificate is issued to the new owner of the stock.

25 The balance sheet accounts relating to capital stock are actually control accounts. In order to know who the individual stockholders are, the corporation usually maintains a **stockholders subsidiary ledger.** This ledger is continually updated for changes in identity of stockholders.

26 For large corporations, a bank or trust company may serve as a **stock transfer agent** and perform the task of updating the stockholders' ledger. Another bank may act as a **stock registrar** who assumes responsibility for issuing stock certificates to stockholders.

27 Corporations may obtain funds by issuing capital stock, by borrowing money, and by retaining the resources generated from profitable operations. The stockholders' equity in a corporation consists of the capital invested by stockholders (paid-in capital), and the capital acquired through profitable operations (retained earnings). If capital contributed through operations is negative because of losses, a debit balance account called **Deficit** replaces the Retained Earnings account.

28 Cash flows from transactions with owners of a business are classified as **financing activities** in the statement of cash flows. The issuance of capital stock for cash constitutes a cash **receipt** from financing activities. Payment of cash dividends is reported as cash **used** in financing activities. Exchange of a corporation's capital stock in exchange for a noncash asset, such as a building, has **no effect** upon cash flows. However, this type of noncash transaction is included in a special schedule accompanying the statement of cash flows (to be discussed in Chapter 14).

29 When only a single class of stock is outstanding, the **book value** per share is computed by dividing the total stockholders' equity by the number of shares outstanding. When both preferred and common stock are outstanding, the book value per share of common stock is computed by dividing the number of shares of common stock into the common stockholders' equity (total stockholders' equity less the redemption value of preferred stock and any dividends in arrears.)

30 Market value of a share of stock depends on (a) the level of current and projected earnings, (b) the dividend rate per share, (c) the financial condition of the company, and (d) the mood of the stock market.

31 Investors buy **preferred** stock primarily to receive the dividends these shares pay; therefore, the dividend rate is one important factor in determining market price of a **preferred stock**. The market price of preferred stock also varies **inversely** with interest rates. As interest rates rise, preferred stock prices decline; as interest rates fall, preferred stock prices rise.

32 The dividends paid to common stockholders are not fixed in amount. Although the dividend rate and current interest rates affect the market price of a common stock, the most important factor in the market price of **common stock** is **investor's expectations** as to the profitability of future operations.

33 Once stock is issued, most further stock transactions on the open market are between investors and do not affect the corporation which issued the stock.

TEST YOURSELF ON OWNERSHIP EQUITY: SOLE PROPRIETORSHIPS, PARTNERSHIPS, AND CORPORATIONS

True or False

For each of the following statements, circle the T or the F to indicate whether the statement is true or false.

T F   1 The owner's equity for a sole proprietorship is typically reported in a single account; in a corporation the owners' equity may be reported in three accounts: Capital Stock, Additional Paid-in Capital, and Retained Earnings.

T F   2 The sole proprietorship necessarily has a limited life, whereas a partnership may have an unlimited life.

T F   3 Mutual agency means that each partner has the right to bind the partnership to contracts.

T F   4 In a traditional partnership, each partner's liability for losses is limited to his or her investment in the firm.

T F   5 Any individual stockholder in a corporation may personally be held liable for all debts incurred by the corporation.

T F   6 A corporation has continuity of existence which permits the business to continue regardless of changes in ownership or the death of a stockholder.

T F   7 A stockholder in a corporation does not have the right to transact corporate business or to intervene in the management of the business.

T F   8 Stockholders of a corporation elect the board of directors, who in turn appoint the top officers of the corporation.

T F   9 Organization costs are usually written off as expense in the period when a corporation is organized.

T F   10 Stockholders do not make withdrawals from the business as do partners or sole proprietors but receive dividends instead.

T F   11 When capital stock is sold for a price higher than par value, the Capital Stock account is credited only for the par value of the shares sold.

T F   12 In reference to question **11,** any amount received in excess of the par value of the stock sold is recorded as a credit to the Retained Earnings account.

T F   13 Dividends usually cannot be paid on common stock unless the regular dividend has been paid to preferred stockholders.

T F   14 Cash dividends are declared by the board of directors, not by the stockholders of a corporation.

T F   15 Dividends in arrears refer to bypassed preferred dividends which must be made up before any dividends may be paid on common stock.

T F   16 In case of liquidation, the claims of the preferred stockholders are given preference over the claims of creditors.

T F   17 Common stock may be issued at a price different from its par value.

T F   18 Common stock of Corporation X pays an annual $1 per share dividend and sells for $15 per share on the open market. The corporation's $1.80 convertible preferred stock is selling for $37 per share and is convertible into two shares of common stock. The holder of 100 shares of the convertible preferred stock should exchange his holdings for 200 shares of common stock because this action will increase his annual dividend revenue from $180 to $200.

T F   19 An underwriter guarantees the issuing corporation a set price for a new issue of stock and then resells the stock to the investing public at a higher price.

T F   20 Retained earnings represents cash generated from profitable operations that has been retained in the business.

T F   21 Subscriptions receivable is a current asset which results from investors subscribing to stock for which they will pay at some future date.

T F   22 The book value of a share of common stock usually approximates the market price of the stock, particularly for growth companies like Apple Computer and IBM.

Completion Statements

Fill in the necessary words or amounts to complete the following statements:

1 If the owner of a sole proprietorship withdraws merchandise for personal use, the owner's _____ account should be debited for the _____ of the merchandise withdrawn.

2 Income tax expense appears in the income statement of a _____ but does not appear in the income statement of a _____ _____ or a _____.

3 The owners of a corporation are _____ _____, and their ownership of shares of stock is evidenced by a stock _____.

4 Among the disadvantages of the corporate form of organization are _____ _____ and _____ _____.

5 The maximum possible loss of the stockholders in a corporation is limited to _____ _____ _____.

6 The two major sources of *equity* capital in a corporation are (a) the sale of _____ and (b) _____ earnings.

7 When common stock is issued at a price above par value, the _____ _____ of the shares issued is _____ to the _____ _____ account, and the excess is _____ to an account called _____ _____ ___ _____.

8 Par value represents _____ _____, which cannot be paid as dividends to stockholders.

9 Most preferred stocks are _____ at the option of the corporation at a stipulated price.

10 The conversion of preferred stock into common generally requires a debit to _____ _____ and credits to _____ _____ and _____ _____ ____ _____.

11 A corporation had total assets of $400,000 and total liabilities of $150,000 at the beginning of the current year. At the end of this year it reported total assets of $600,000 and total liabilities of $200,000. During the year it paid dividends of $48,000, representing 60% of its earnings. The total stockholders' equity at the end of the current year amounted to $_____, the earnings for the year amounted to $_____, and additional shares of capital stock were issued during the year for $_____.

Multiple Choice

Choose the best answer for each of the following questions and enter the identifying letter in the space provided.

_____ **1** Which of the following statements is applicable to *both corporations and sole proprietorships*?
a The income statement contains Income Tax Expense.
b The balance sheet shows the entire ownership equity as a single dollar amount.
c Revenue and expense accounts are closed into Income Summary, which is then closed to Retained Earnings.
d A distribution of cash to the owner(s) reduces ownership equity, but is not considered an expense of the business.

_____ **2** Which of the following is *not* a characteristic of most partnerships?
a Limited liability.
b Mutual agency.
c Limited life.
d Ease of formation.

_____ **3** One of the following is *not* a characteristic of the corporate form of organization:
a Limited liability of shareholders.
b Mutual agency.
c Centralized authority.
d Continuous existence.

_____ **4** Title to the assets of a corporation is legally held by:
a The stockholders, jointly and severally.
b The corporation, as a legal entity.
c The president of the corporation in trust for the stockholders.
d The board of directors, as trustees.

_____ **5** The *directors* of a corporation are responsible for:
a Declaring dividends.
b Maintaining stockholder records.
c The day-to-day managing of the business.
d Preparation of accounting records and financial statements.

_____ **6** One of the following is *not* an officer of a corporation:
a Stock registrar.
b Controller.
c Secretary.
d Treasurer.

_____ **7** The Aaron Corporation is authorized to issue 100,000 shares of $10 par value capital stock. It issues one-half of the stock for $25 per share, earns $20,000 during the first three months of operation, and declares a cash divi-

dend of $5,000. The total paid-in capital of the Aaron Corporation after three months of operation is:
a $1,000,000.
b $1,020,000.
c $1,250,000.
d $1,265,000.

_____ 8 Which of the following is most relevant in determining the *cost* of assets acquired in exchange for capital stock?
a Par or stated value of the stock.
b Market value of the stock.
c Issuance price of stock already outstanding.
d Estimated useful life of the assets.

_____ 9 Which of the following is *not* a characteristic of most preferred stock issues?
a Preference as to dividends.
b Participating clause.
c Preference as to assets in event of liquidation.
d No voting power.

_____ 10 Which of the following is *least* important in determining the fair market value of a share of stock?
a Dividend rate per share.
b Book value per share.
c Investors' expectations as to future profitability of the company.
d The par or stated value per share.

_____ 11 When stock is sold on a subscription basis and the entire subscription price has been collected, the *issuance of the stock* is recorded by:
a A debit to Cash and a credit to Capital Stock.
b A debit to Subscriptions Receivable: Capital Stock and a credit to Capital Stock Subscribed.
c A debit to Capital Stock Subscribed and a credit to Capital Stock.
d A debit to Capital Stock and a credit to Subscriptions Receivable: Capital Stock.

_____ 12 A *deficit* appears on the balance sheet:
a Among the assets.
b As a deduction from total paid-in capital.
c As a deduction from Income Taxes Payable.
d Among the liabilities.

_____ 13 Hayden Corporation has total stockholders' equity of $2,980,000. The company's outstanding capital stock includes 40,000 shares of $2 par value common stock and 20,000 shares of 6%, $100 par value preferred stock. The preferred stock is callable at a price of $105. (No dividends are in arrears.) The *book value per share* of common stock is:
a $24.50.   b $22.00.   c $19.00.   d $21.50.

Exercises

1 Listed below are eight technical accounting terms emphasized in this chapter:

Drawing account	*Partnership contract*
Deficit	*Organization costs*
Call price	*Uniform Partnership*
Paid-in capital	*Act*
Cumulative	
preferred stock	

Each of the following statements may (or may not) describe one of these technical terms. In the space provided below each statement, indicate the accounting term described, or answer "None" if the statement does not correctly describe any of the terms.

a Stock with a dividend preference that must be paid before dividends can be paid on common stock.

_____

b Accumulated losses incurred by a corporation.

_____

c The amount paid by a corporation for each share of preferred stock redeemed.

_____

d Account used to record withdrawal of cash or other assets by owner(s) of unincorporated businesses.

_____

e The legal capital of a corporation.

_____

f Costs incurred to form a corporation.

_____

g An agreement among partners on the formation and operation of the partnership.

_____

2 Eastern Corporation has outstanding 10,000 shares each of two classes of $100 par value stock: 5% cumulative preferred stock and common stock. The corporation reported a deficit of $20,000 at the beginning of Year 2, and preferred dividends for Year 1 were in arrears. During Year 2 the corporation earned $180,000. How large a dividend *per share* did the corporation pay on the common stock if the balance in retained earnings at the end of Year 2 amounted to $25,000? Use the space below for computations.

Dividends per share $_____

3 Complete the stockholders' equity section from the account balances shown below:

Organization costs	$ 7,000
Retained earnings...	128,000
Additional paid-in capital: preferred stock	10,000
Common stock, no-par value, 50,000 shares	200,000
$9 preferred stock, $100 par, 1,000 shares	100,000
Receivable from underwiters (from sale of stock...	40,000
Plant and equipment	315,000
Accumulated depreciation.................................	125,000
Notes payable	100,000
Donated capital	65,000

Stockholders' equity:	
$9 preferred stock, $100 par value, 1,000 shares issued and outstanding	$
Total paid-in capital	$
Total stockholders' equity	$

4 The book value of a share of capital stock is $10 per share. For each of the independent events listed below, use a check mark to indicate whether the transaction or event will increase, decrease, or have no effect on the book value per share of stock.

Transaction or Event	Increase	Decrease	No Effect
a Declaration of cash dividend			
b Net income is reported for latest year			
c Additional stock is sold at $8 per share			
d Additional stock is sold at $14 per share			

SOLUTIONS TO CHAPTER 12 SELF-TEST

True or False

1 T A sole proprietorship is not required to maintain a distinction between invested capital and earned capital, as is a corporation.

2 F *Both* sole proprietorships and partnerships are unincorporated business which have *limited lives*. Even though such businesses may operate indefinitely under a series of different owners, each change in ownership represents the creation of a new business entity.

3 T As long as a partner is acting within the apparent scope of his authority, he or she can bind the firm to contracts.

4 F Unless special legal arrangements are made, each partner has *unlimited personal liability* for partnership debts.

5 F Creditors of a corporation have a claim against the assets of the corporation only.

6 T The continuous life of a corporation despite changes in ownership is made possible by the issuance of transferable shares of stock.

7 T The stockholders own the corporation but do not manage it on a daily basis; the corporate officers appointed by the board of directors manage the business.

8 T The owners (stockholders) elect a board of directors who select the president and other corporate officers to manage the company.

9 F Although the benefit of organization costs extends over the entire life of a corporation, income tax law and general accounting practice is to write off (expense) these costs over a five-year period.

10 T A dividend refers to a distribution of cash or property by a corporation to its stockholders. The board of directors has full discretion to declare a dividend or to refrain from doing so.

11 T Regardless of the issue price, the Capital Stock account is credited with only the *par value* of the shares issued.

12 F The amount of sales proceeds received that *exceeds* par value is credited to the Additional Paid-in Capital account.

13 T Preferred stock is entitled to receive each year a specified dividend amount before any dividend is paid to the common stockholders.

14 T Dividends are distributed to stockholders only when (and if) declared by the board of directors.

15 T All dividends in arrears as well as the preferred dividend requirement for the current year must be paid before any dividend can be paid on common stock.

16 F Creditors are given preference in liquidation over all stockholders.

17 T The par value of the stock is no indication of its market value; the par value merely indicates the amount per share to be entered in the Capital Stock account.

18 F Although the annual dividend will increase as mentioned, the market values of the two types of stock do not warrant conversion. The preferred stock has a market value of $3,700 (100 shares at $37); the common stock after conversion has a market value of $3,000 (200 shares at $15). The investor could sell the preferred stock and buy *more* than 200 shares of common stock at this time instead of converting.

19 T Use of an underwriter assures the corporation that the entire stock issue will be sold promptly and that the entire amount of funds to be raised will be available on a specified date.

20 F Retained earnings is *not an asset*. Rather, it is an element of *owners' equity*, representing the accumulated profits or losses, less dividends, since incorporation.

21 T When the subscription contract is signed, a special type of receivable, Stock Subscriptions Receivable, is debited and Capital Stock Subscribed is credited.

22 F Book value is a historical concept; the market price of shares reflects the investor's expectations of the firm's profitability.

Completion Statements

1 Drawing, cost. **2** Corporation, sole proprietorship, partnership. **3** Stockholders, certificate. **4** Heavy taxation, greater regulation. **5** The amount of their investment (the amount they paid for their shares). **6** Stock, retained. **7** Par value, credited, Common Stock, credited, Additional Paid-in Capital. **8** Legal capital. **9** Callable. **10** Preferred Stock, Common Stock Additional Paid-in Capital. **11** $400,000, $80,000, $118,000.

Multiple Choice

1 Answer **d**—answers **a** and **c** are applicable to corporations only. Answer **b** applies to a sole proprietorship, but not to a corporation. A distribution of cash to stockholders (dividends) reduces stockholders' equity (the dividends account is closed into retained earnings); withdrawals of cash by the owner of a sole proprietorship are recorded in a Drawing account which is then closed into the capital account.

2 Answer **a**—for all partnerships other than limited partnerships, the partners have unlimited liability for the debts of the firm.

3 Answer **b**—the concept of mutual agency does not apply to corporations; an individual stockholder has no right to participate in the management of the business unless he has been hired as a corporate officer.

4 Answer **b**—a corporation is a legal entity having an existence separate and distinct from that of its owners or management. A corporation, as a separate legal entity, may own property in its own name. The assets of a corporation belong to the corporation itself, not to the stockholders.

5 Answer **a**—an independent fiscal agent (bank or trust company) maintains stockholder records for large corporations; the corporate secretary (one of the officers) may keep stockholder records for a small closely held corporation. The officers are responsible for the day-to-day running of the business; the controller (an officer) is responsible for accounting records and financial statements.

6 Answer **a**—the stock registrar for large publicly held corporations must be an independent fiscal agent, usually a bank or trust company. (In a small closely held corporation, the duties of maintaining stockholder records may be performed by the corporate secretary.)

7 Answer **c**—paid-in capital is the amount invested in a corporation by its stockholders. The net income and dividends mentioned in the problem increase and decrease, respectively, the retained earnings of the corporation, but have no effect on the paid-in capital.

8 Answer **b**—the cost recorded should be the current market value of the asset *received*. However, *if* an appraised value of the asset received is not available, the best evidence of market value of the asset is the market value of the shares issued in exchange. Par value and issuance price of shares already outstanding have no bearing on the current market value of shares to be issued in the transaction.

9 Answer **b**—the majority of preferred stock issues are nonvoting, and have preference over common stock issues as to dividends and assets in the event of liquidation.

10 Answer **d**—par (or stated value) represents the legal capital per share and is no indication of a stock's market value. To some extent, book value may be used in evaluating the reasonableness of the market price of a common stock; however, common stock may sell at a price well above or below book value, depending upon investors' confidence in company management. Answer **a** (and also current interest rates) are major factors affecting the market price of a preferred stock. Answer **c** is one of the most important factors in determining the market price of common stock.

11 Answer **c**—when the shares are actually issued, the Capital Stock Subscribed account is no longer necessary, and in its place we record Capital Stock. We simply exchange one type of stockholders' equity account for a different one which indicates that the shares are now outstanding.

12 Answer **b**—a deficit is a negative amount of retained earnings—the accumulated losses incurred by a corporation. It is shown in the stockholders' equity of the balance sheet as a deduction from the total of the paid-in capital accounts.

13 Answer **b**—computed as follows:

Total stockholders' equity	$2,980,000
Less: Equity of preferred stockholders:	
Call price of preferred stock	(2,100,000)
Equity of common stockholders	$ 880,000
Number of common shares outstanding	40,000
Book value per share of common stock ($880,000 ÷ 40,000 shares)	$22.00

Exercises

1

a Cumulative preferred stock
b Deficit
c Call price
d Drawing account
e None (The statement describes par value.)
f Organization costs
g Partnership contract

2

Net income for Year 2	$180,000
Less: Deficit at beginning of Year 2	20,000
Retained earnings available for dividends......	$160,000
Less: Dividends on preferred stock for	
2 years (10,000 shares × $10)	100,000
Available for common stock	$ 60,000
Less: Balance in retained earnings at	
end of Year 2	25,000
Dividends paid on common stock..................	$ 35,000
Dividends per share: $35,000 ÷ 10,000	
shares...	$3.50

3

Stockholders' equity:	
$9 preferred stock, $100 par, 1,000	
shares issued and outstanding	$100,000
Common stock, no par value, 50,000	
shares issued and outstanding	200,000
Additional paid-in capital: preferred	
stock..	10,000
Donated capital	65,000
Total paid-in capital	$375,000
Retained earnings	128,000
Total stockholders' equity......................	$503,000

4

Transaction or Event	Increase	Decrease	No Effect
a Declaration of cash dividend		✓	
b Net income is reported for latest year	✓		
c Additional stock is sold at $8 per share		✓	
d Additional stock is sold at $14 per share	✓		

13

REPORTING UNUSUAL EVENTS AND SPECIAL EQUITY TRANSACTIONS

HIGHLIGHTS OF THE CHAPTER

1 To assist users of an income statement in estimating the income likely to occur in future periods, the results of unusual and nonrecurring transactions are shown in a separate section of the income statement after the income or loss from normal business activities has been determined. Current accounting practice recognizes three categories of "unusual" transactions and accords each one a different treatment in the income statement. These categories are: (1) the operating results of a segment of the business which has been discontinued during the current year, (2) extraordinary items, and (3) the cumulative effects of changes in accounting principles.

2 A *segment* of a business is a component of a company whose activities represent a major line of business or class of customer. The assets and operating results of a segment of a business should be clearly identifiable from other assets and operating results of the company.

3 The operating results of a segment discontinued during the current period are reported separately in the income statement *after* developing the subtotal, *Income from Continuing Operations*. This subtotal presumably is a better indicator of the earning power of continuing operations than is the net income figure.

4 The revenue and expenses shown in the income statement for the year in which a segment of a business is eliminated include *only the revenue and expenses from continuing operations.* The net income or loss from discontinued operations is reported sepa-

rately; the total revenue from the discontinued segment is disclosed in the notes to the financial statements. Any gain or loss on the disposal of a segment should be reported with the results of the discontinued operations.

5 When an income statement includes sections for both continuing and discontinued operations, the company's income tax expense should be **allocated** between these sections. Only the income tax expense applicable to continuing operations should be deducted as an expense in arriving at Income from Continuing Operations. Any income tax expense (or tax savings) related to the discontinued operations should be considered along with other expenses of the discontinued segment in computing the income (or loss) from discontinued operations.

6 *Extraordinary items* are **material** transactions and events that are **both unusual in nature and occur infrequently in the operating environment of a business.** Examples of extraordinary items include:

a Effects of major casualties, such as an earthquake.

b Expropriation (seizure) of assets by foreign governments.

c Effects of prohibition of a product under a newly enacted law or regulation.

7 When a company has an extraordinary gain or loss in its income statement, *Income before Extraordinary Items* is developed as a subtotal before presentation of the extraordinary items. The extraordinary item is then subtracted from (or added to) Income before Extraordinary Items to arrive at net income.

8 Extraordinary items are shown in the income statement net of income taxes—the amount

of the extraordinary item is adjusted for any related income taxes or income tax savings.

9 Items which qualify as extraordinary losses are rare and extraordinary gains are almost nonexistent. Such things as gains and losses from disposal of plant assets and losses from strikes or lawsuits **do not qualify** as extraordinary items because they are not considered both unusual and infrequent in the environment of a business. These items may be separately identified in the income statement to focus attention on their **nonoperating** nature, but they should be included in Income from Continuing Operations.

10 One important type of "unusual" loss relates to restructuring of operations. **Restructuring charges** consist of items such as losses on write-downs or sales of productive assets, severance pay for employees, and expenses related to relocation of facilities. Restructuring charges are presented in the income statement as a single item in determining **operating** income. However, if the restructuring involves discontinuing a segment of the business, the related expenses are included in the discontinued operations section.

11 When a company makes a change in accounting principle, such as a change in the method used to compute depreciation, the new method usually is applied retroactively. The cumulative effect of the change upon the income of prior years is shown as a special item in the **income statement in the year of the change**. This "cumulative effect of an accounting change" is shown net of any related income tax effects.

12 If an income statement includes several of the special items described above, discontinued operations are shown before any extraordinary items. Thus, Income before Extraordinary Items includes the income or loss from discontinued operations. The cumulative effect of an accounting change upon the income reported in prior years always is shown last among the special items.

13 Perhaps the most widely used of all accounting statistics is **earnings per share** of common stock. To compute earnings per share, the net income **available to the common stock** is divided by the **weighted-average** number of common shares outstanding during the year. Net income available to the common stock is total net income **less the current year's dividends on preferred stock**. Earnings per share is intended to show the claim of each share of common stock to the earnings of the company.

14 Convertible preferred stock and other securities convertible into common stock pose a special problem in computing earnings per share. If these securities are converted, more common stock will be outstanding and earnings per share will be **diluted** to a smaller figure. Companies with complex capital structures show two earnings per share figures: (a) **primary earnings per share**, based upon the weighted-average number of common shares **actually** outstanding, and (b) **fully diluted earnings per share**, based on the **maximum potential** number of shares outstanding.

15 Earnings per share based upon reported net income is shown at the bottom of the income statement. If the income statement includes Income from Continuing Operations and/or Income before Extraordinary Items, these subtotals also are shown on a per-share basis.

16 A **dividend** is generally understood to mean a pro rata cash distribution by a corporation to its stockholders. Dividends are declared by the board of directors after giving careful consideration to such factors as the balance in retained earnings and the company's cash position. Four dates are usually involved in the distribution of a dividend:

a Date of declaration.
b Date of record.
c Ex-dividend date.
d Date of payment.

17 Dividends paid in a form other than cash, such as securities of other corporations or merchandise, are called **property** dividends. A **liquidating dividend** usually takes place when a corporation pays a dividend that exceeds the balance in the Retained Earnings account. A **stock dividend** is a distribution to stockholders of additional shares of the corporation's own stock.

18 A **stock dividend** causes no change in assets or in the total amount of the stockholders' equity. The only effect of a stock dividend is the transfer of a portion of the retained earnings into the Capital Stock and the Additional Paid-in Capital: Stock Dividends accounts. A stock dividend increases the number of common shares outstanding and decreases the book value per share. Each stockholder owns a larger number of shares

after the stock dividend, but his or her total equity in the corporation remains unchanged.

19 A "small" stock dividend may range from 1% of the outstanding stock to a maximum of 20 to 25%. Stock dividends of this size are recorded by a debit to Retained Earnings equal to the total *market value* of the additional shares being distributed, a credit to Stock Dividend to Be Distributed equal to the par or stated value of the additional shares, and a credit to Additional Paid-in Capital: Stock Dividends equal to the excess of market value over par (or stated) value of the "dividend" shares. When the shares are distributed, Stock Dividend to Be Distributed is debited and Capital Stock is credited.

20 Stock dividends in excess of, say, 20 to 25% are not considered small and are subject to different accounting treatment. They should be recorded by transferring only the *par or stated value* of the dividend shares from Retained Earnings to the Capital Stock account.

21 A *stock split* is effected by reducing the par or stated value of the capital stock and issuing a larger number of shares to each stockholder. In a 5 for 1 split, for example, the par value is reduced from $10 to $2, and a shareholder owning 100 shares before the split would own 500 shares after the split.

22 Assume that a company discovers that a material error was made in the measurement of the net income of a prior year. How should this error be corrected? Since the net income of the prior year has been closed into Retained Earnings, the error is corrected by adjusting the balance of the Retained Earnings account. Such adjustments are called *prior period adjustments.* A prior period adjustment has no effect upon the net income of the current period and does not appear in the income statement; it is shown in the statement of retained earnings.

23 The *statement of retained earnings* is a vehicle for reconciling the beginning balance in retained earnings with the ending balance. The usual format of the statement is to combine any prior period adjustments with the beginning balance as originally reported. The restated beginning balance is then increased by the net income for the current year and reduced by the amount of dividends declared in arriving at the ending balance.

24 Retained earnings of a corporation are either unrestricted and available for dividends or restricted (earmarked) for some specific purpose, such as to finance an expansion of plant facilities. Most companies disclose restrictions upon the availability of retained earnings for dividends in a note to their financial statements.

25 If a corporation acquires its own stock from stockholders, the reacquired stock is referred to as *treasury stock*. Treasury stock may be held indefinitely or may be reissued; it is not entitled to receive dividends or to vote.

26 Treasury stock is generally recorded at cost and is deducted from the total of the paid-in capital and retained earnings in the balance sheet. *Treasury stock is not an asset.* If the treasury stock is reissued, the Treasury Stock account is credited for the cost of the shares sold, and Additional Paid-in Capital: Treasury Stock Transactions is debited or credited for the difference between the cost and the resale price. Regardless of resale price, *no gain or loss is recognized on treasury stock transactions*.

27 The purchase of treasury stock is similar to a dividend in that the distribution of cash is made to stockholders. If a corporation is to keep its paid-in capital intact, it must not pay out to its stockholders any more than it earns. Thus retained earnings equal to the cost of treasury stock purchased is restricted and is not available for cash dividends.

28 Cash transactions between the corporation and its owners are reported in the statement of cash flows as *financing activities*. Cash flow from financing activities is *decreased* by payment of cash dividends, and by the purchase of treasury stock. Cash flow from financing activities is *increased* by the sale of stock for cash as well as by reissuance of treasury stock for cash. Stock dividends, property dividends, and stock splits have no effect upon cash flow.

29 Many companies prepare an expanded version of the statement of retained earnings, called a *statement of stockholders' equity*. This financial statement contains all of the information found in a statement of retained earnings and also includes additional columns showing the changes in all other stockholders' equity accounts. While widely used, a statement of stockholders' equity is not a required financial statement.

TEST YOURSELF ON UNUSUAL EVENTS AND SPECIAL EQUITY TRANSACTIONS

True or False

For each of the following statements, circle the T or the F to indicate whether the statement is true or false.

T F 1 A basic purpose of developing income statement subtotals such as Income from Continuing Operations is to assist the users of financial statements in predicting future earnings.

T F 2 Assume Rite-Price owns nine grocery stores and two restaurants. The disposal of two grocery stores during the current year should be reported in the income statement as "discontinued operations."

T F 3 Assume Rite-Price owns nine grocery stores and two restaurants. The disposal of the two restaurants during the current year should be reported in the income statement as "discontinued operations."

T F 4 Assume that Pepisco, the soft drink company, sells its Taco Bell chain of fast-food restaurants. The resulting gain or loss is an example of an extraordinary item.

T F 5 Assume that a new federal law outlaws use of one ingredient in Weight Begone's product, "Slim-Lunch." The company therefore destroys a $12 million inventory of this product. This loss is an example of an extraordinary item.

T F 6 There is no such thing as an extraordinary gain.

T F 7 If a company discontinues a segment of its operations during the current year, the amount of Income from Continuing Operations will always be greater than the amount of net income.

T F 8 Discontinued operations appear in the published financial statements of large corporations more frequently than do extraordinary items.

T F 9 The "cumulative effect of a change in accounting principle" is actually computed by recalculating the net income of *prior* years.

T F 10 The income statement of a corporation should always include the subtotal Income from Continuing Operations.

T F 11 Income tax effects should be ignored in reporting the income or loss from a discontinued segment of the business.

T F 12 The statistic "earnings per share" relates to a corporation's common stock.

T F 13 Fully diluted earnings per share usually is a smaller figure than primary earnings per share.

T F 14 When a company reports discontinued operations, the earnings per share figure appearing in the income statement is based upon Income from Continuing Operations, rather than net income.

T F 15 The investor who purchases shares of the X Co. on the ex-dividend date will not receive the next dividend paid by X Co.

T F 16 A 10% stock dividend decreases the total stockholders' equity of the issuing corporation by 10%.

T F 17 A 10% stock dividend increases the market value of each stockholders' investment by 10%.

T F 18 A 10% stock dividend increases the number of shares outstanding by 10% but does not cause any change in total stockholders' equity.

T F 19 A 100% stock dividend has the same effect upon the number of shares outstanding as does a 2 for 1 stock split.

T F 20 The purpose of a stock split is to decrease the market price per share.

T F 21 A corporation's stockholders' equity accounts will be the same whether it declares a 100% stock dividend or splits its stock 2 for 1.

T F 22 Prior period adjustments are shown net of income taxes in a special section of the income statement.

T F 23 The purchase of treasury stock reduces both total assets and stockholders' equity.

T F 24 The reissuance of treasury stock at a price above cost results in a gain to be reported in the income statement.

T F 25 A statement of stockholders' equity contains all of the information shown in a statement of retained earnings and also explains the changes in the other stockholders' equity accounts.

Completion Statements

Fill in the necessary words to complete the following statements:

1 Large unexpected losses from liability to collect accounts receivable or from the shrinkage in the value of inventories should be taken into account in computing _____ before _____ _____.

2 Companies with convertible preferred stock outstanding generally report both _____ earnings per share based upon the _____ _____ number of common shares outstanding, and _____ _____ earnings per share, based upon the potential number of outstanding shares.

3 The correction of an error in the measurement of the net income of a prior year is called a _____ _____ _____ and is reported in the _____ ____ _____ _____ as an adjustment to the balance of _____ _____ at the _____ of the current period.

4 On January 1, the Avery Corporation had 100,000 shares of capital stock with a par value of $10, additional paid-in capital of $300,000, and retained earnings of $700,000. During the year the company split its stock 2 for 1 (reducing the par value of $5 per share) and subsequently declared a 2% stock dividend (its first) when the market value of the stock was $40. It earned $200,000 during the year and paid no cash dividends. (a) At the end of the year the balance in the Capital Stock account will be $_____; (b) the balance in Additional Paid-in Capital will be $_____; and (c) the balance in Retained Earnings will be $_____.

5 A _____ ____ _____ _____ includes all of the information found in a statement of _____ _____ and also explains the changes in the balances of all other stockholders' equity accounts.

6 If IBM were to purchase shares of its own stock, the cost would be debited to the _____ _____ account. In the balance sheet, this latter account is classified as a _____ in the amount of _____ _____.

7 Cash dividends, purchases, and sales of treasury stock are reported in the statement of cash flows as _____ _____.
Cash dividends, purchases, and sales of treasury stock have **no effect** upon _____ _____. Stock dividends and stock splits have **no effect** upon _____ _____, as well as **no effect** upon _____ _____.

Multiple Choice

Choose the best answer for each of the following questions and enter the identifying letter in the space provided.

_____ 1 Which of the following would **not** be shown in a separate section of the income statement, after the determination of the income from normal, ongoing activities?
a The operating results of a segment of the business discontinued during the year.
b The cumulative effect of a change in accounting principles upon the income reported in prior years.
c An extraordinary item.
d A prior period adjustment.

_____ 2 Revenue and expenses relating to a segment of business discontinued during the year are:
a Netted and reported as an extraordinary item.
b Included in total revenue and expenses as reported in the income statement.
c Netted and reported as a separate item following income from continuing operations.
d Netted and reported as a prior period adjustment.

_____ 3 Which of the following qualifies as an extraordinary item?
a Gain on sale of unprofitable consumer goods division.
b A large loss due to restructuring of the corporation's operations.
c A write-off and abandonment of goods in process inventory because of a new government regulation prohibiting the use of one of the ingredients.
d Additional depreciation recorded because of reduction in useful life of assets.

_____ 4 The financial statements of Fields Corporation reported earnings of $4,000,000 from continuing operations, a $700,000 loss (net of income tax benefit) from a segment of the business discontinued during the year, a $300,000 decrease (net of related tax effects) in retained earnings as a result of a prior period adjustment, and a $500,000 extraordinary loss (net of income tax benefit). The amount appearing in the income statement as Income before Extraordinary Items was:

a $4,000,000.
b $3,300,000.
c $3,000,000.
d Some other amount.

_____ 5 The *cumulative effect of a change in accounting principle* may best be described as:

a A correction of an error in the measurement of the income of prior periods.
b A material and unusual event that is not expected to recur in the foreseeable future.
c The adjustment to the amount of income reported in prior accounting periods as a result of retroactively applying a different accounting method; this effect is reported in the *current year* income statement.
d The income or loss associated with the disposal of a segment of the business.

_____ 6 Boston Office Supplies reported net income of $2,000,000. The company had outstanding 100,000 shares of $5 preferred stock and 100,000 shares of common stock. Earnings per share amount to:

a $15.
b $20.
c $25.
d None of the above.

_____ 7 *Fully diluted earnings* per share may best be described as:

a A hypothetical case showing the impact that conversion of convertible securities could have upon primary earnings per share.
b Earnings per share of common stock, after giving consideration to preferred stock dividends.
c Earnings per share for a company that has issued a stock dividend or a stock split during the current year.
d The earnings per share of a corporation that has incurred a net loss for the year.

_____ 8 The distribution of a 20% stock dividend on common stock:

a Reduces the market price per share of common stock outstanding.
b Does not change the number of shares of common stock outstanding.
c Decreases total stockholders' equity.
d Increases the net assets of the corporation.

_____ 9 In recording a large stock dividend, say 50 or 100%, the amount of retained earnings transferred to paid-in capital is generally measured by:

a The market value of the stock on the date of declaration.

b The book value of the stock on the date of declaration.
c The par (or stated) value of the additional shares issued.
d The amount authorized by the board of directors to be transferred from the Retained Earnings account.

_____ 10 Which of the following is most likely to increase the market price per share of common stock?

a A large stock dividend.
b A 2 for 1 stock split.
c Higher than expected earnings per share.
d The arrival of the "ex-dividend" date.

_____ 11 The James Corporation had 100,000 shares of common stock and 5,000 shares of preferred stock outstanding at the beginning of Year 1. On April 1, 10,000 shares of common stock were sold for cash and on November 3, the common stock was split 2 for 1. The weighted-average number of shares outstanding for Year 1 in computing primary earnings per share is:

a 255,000.
b 220,000.
c 205,000.
d 215,000.

_____ 12 *A prior period adjustment:*

a Is shown in a separate section of the income statement.
b Results in a change in the amount of paid-in capital.
c Shows the retroactive effect upon the income of the prior periods of switching to a different account period.
d Is shown in the statement of retained earnings as a correction to retained earnings at the beginning of the period.

_____ 13 A statement of retained earnings could properly disclose each of the following *except*:

a The declaration of a 10% stock dividend.
b The cumulative effect of a change in accounting principle.
c Net loss incurred by the corporation in the current year.
d A prior period adjustment.

_____ 14 Treasury stock is best described as:

a Unissued stock.
b Reacquired stock which was previously outstanding.
c An asset acquired by making a cash disbursement.
d Retirement of a portion of outstanding stock which increases total stockholders' equity.

_____**15** Reissuing treasury stock at a price above cost results in a(n):

a Gain to be reported as a separate item in the income statement.

b Prior period adjustment to be reported in the statement of retained earnings.

c Increase in paid-in capital.

d Restriction of retained earnings.

_____**16** Which of the following would **not** affect McGill Corporation's cash flows from financing activities?

a Payment of a cash dividend.

b Purchase of shares of Xerox Corporation stock for cash.

c Purchase of shares of McGill Corporation stock for cash.

d Issuance of new shares of McGill Corporation stock for cash.

_____**17** Which of the following events is **not** disclosed in a statement of stockholders' equity?

a A correction of an error in the amount of income reported in a prior year.

b The purchase of treasury stock.

c Cash dividends declared during the period.

d The cumulative effect of a change in accounting principle upon the income of prior years.

Exercises

1 Listed below are eight technical accounting terms emphasized in this chapter:

Stock split	*Marketable*
Date of record	*equity*
Stock dividend	*securities*
Extraordinary item	*Prior period*
Earnings per share	*adjustment*
Ex-dividend date	

Each of the following statements may (or may not) describe one of these technical terms. In the space provided below each statement, indicate the term described, or answer "None" if the statement does not correctly describe any of the terms.

a An increase in the number of shares outstanding with a corresponding decrease in the par value per share.

_____

b The date before which you must purchase stock if you want to receive the most recently declared dividend.

_____

c Net income applicable to common stock, divided by the weighted-average number of shares outstanding during the year.

_____

d The effect upon the income of prior periods of retroactively applying a different accounting method.

_____

e Shares of a corporation's own capital stock that have been reacquired by the issuing company.

_____

f A distribution of cash to stockholders in proportion to the number of shares owned.

_____

g An event that is shown separately in the income statement because it is unusual, material in amount, and not expected to recur in the foreseeable future.

_____

2 The Axel Company had issued 105,000 shares of capital stock, of which 5,000 shares were reacquired and held in the treasury throughout the year. During the year, the company reported income from continuing operations of 5% of sales, and a loss from a segment of the business discontinued during the year of $300,000 (net of the income tax benefit). Sales from continuing operations were $4,200,000, gross profit rate on sales amounted to 30%, and income taxes were 40% of income before taxes. In the space below prepare the income statement for Axel Company, including the earnings per share figures.

AXEL COMPANY
Income Statement
for the Current Year

Sales	$4,200,000
Cost of goods sold	_____
Gross profit on sales (30%)	$
Operating expenses	_____
Operating income (before taxes)	$
Income taxes (40% of operating income) ...	_____
Income from continuing operations	$
Loss from discontinued operations, net of income tax benefit	(300,000)
Net loss	$ _____
Per share of capital stock:	
Income from continuing operations	$
Loss from discontinued operations	_____
Net loss	$ _____

3 The income statement of Windjammer Company shows income from continuing operations of $490,000 and income from a segment of the business discontinued near year-end of $182,000 (net of income taxes). The company had 100,000 shares of common stock and 10,000 shares of $6 preferred stock outstanding throughout the year. Compute the following earnings per share figures for Windjammer Company:

Earnings from continuing operations:

$_____

Net earnings:

$_____

4 At the beginning of the year, Bender Mfg. Company had 250,000 shares of $5 par value common stock outstanding. In the space provided below, prepare journal entries to record the following selected transactions during the year:

Mar. 1	Declared a cash dividend of 80 cents per share, payable on Mar. 21.
Mar. 21	Paid cash dividend declared on Mar. 1.
Aug. 10	Declared 5% stock dividend. The market price of the stock on this date was $40 per share.
Sept. 2	Issued 12,500 shares pursuant to 5% stock dividend declared on Aug. 10.
Dec. 21	Declared and issued a 100% stock dividend. The market price of the stock on this date was $60 per share.
Dec. 30	Acquired 1,000 shares of its own common stock on the open market at $30 per share.

General Journal			
19__			
Mar. 1	Dividends		
	Declared cash dividend of $0.80 per share on 250,000 shares.		
21			
Aug. 10			
Sept. 2			
Dec. 21			
30			

SOLUTIONS TO CHAPTER 13 SELF-TEST

True or False

1 T Unusual and nonrecurring activities are shown in a separate section of the income statement after a subtotal for results of normal business activities.

2 F Rite-Price is not disposing of the entire segment of its grocery business.

3 T Since the restaurants service a distinct category of customers and the entire segment has been disposed of, this situation should be reported as "discontinued operations."

4 F The sale of Taco Bell by Pepsico is shown separately in the income statement as "discontinued operations."

5 T This loss is material in amount, unusual in nature, and not expected to recur.

6 F Gains *and losses* that meet the three criteria are classified as extraordinary items.

7 F In cases where the disposal of a segment produces a gain, the net income will be greater than Income from Continuing Operations.

8 T Corporate restructuring, often accompanied by the disposal of segments, has become commonplace.

9 T Although the cumulative effect is reported in the *current year* income statement, the amount is determined as the difference between restated net income and originally reported net income for all prior years.

10 F The subtotal Income from Continuing Operations is reported only when a segment of the business has been discontinued during the year. In this situation, the income statement includes sections for both continuing and discontinued operations.

11 F The income or loss from operating the segment prior to its disposal and the gain or loss on disposal are each shown net of income tax effect in the "discontinued operations" section of the income statement.

12 T Preferred stockholders have no claim to earnings beyond the stipulated preferred stock dividends.

13 T Fully diluted earnings per share shows the impact that hypothetical conversion of any convertible preferred stock would have upon primary earnings per share.

14 F In this situation, earnings per share figures are required for both the subtotal Income from Continuing Operations and Net Income.

15 T An investor who purchases the stock *before* the ex-dividend date is entitled to receive the dividends.

16 F In a stock dividend, no assets are distributed; there is no change in total stockholders' equity.

17 F Since assets, liabilities, and stockholders' equity of the issuing corporation are the same amounts as before, the market value per share *should* fall in proportion to the number of shares issued. (For small stock dividends, the decrease in market value per share might not be proportional to the percentage increase in shares.)

18 T The market value of the shares is transferred from retained earnings to paid-in capital accounts, but total stockholders' equity is not changed.

19 T Both double the number of shares outstanding.

20 T The intent is to make the stock more attractive to investors by lowering the market price.

21 F A 100% stock dividend causes a transfer from the Retained Earnings account to the Common Stock account equal to the par or stated value of the dividend shares, whereas the stock split does not change the dollar balance of any account. Both double the number of outstanding shares without changing the total amount of stockholders' equity.

22 F Prior period adjustments are shown net of taxes in the statement of retained earnings as an adjustment to beginning retained earnings.

23 T A Treasury Stock account is debited for the cost of the shares purchased; it appears as a deduction in the stockholders' equity section of the balance sheet.

24 F The excess of reissue price above cost is credited to a stockholders' equity account called Additional Paid-in Capital: Treasury Stock Transactions.

25 T A statement of stockholders' equity is often substituted for a statement of retained earnings because it presents a more complete description of transactions affecting stockholders' equity.

Completion Statements

1 Income, extraordinary items. **2** Primary, weighted-average, fully diluted. **3** Prior period adjustment, statement of retained earnings, retained earnings, beginning. **4(a)** $1,020,000; **(b)** $440,000; **(c)** $740,000. **5** Statement of stockholders' equity, retained earnings. **6** Treasury Stock, reduction, stockholders' equity. **7** Financing activities, net income, net income, cash flows.

Multiple Choice

1 Answer **d**—prior period adjustments are shown in the statement of retained earnings as adjustments to the balance of retained earnings at the beginning of the period.

2 Answer **c**—revenue and expenses relating to a segment of business discontinued during the year are shown separately in the "discontinued operations" section of the income statement.

3 Answer **c**—an extraordinary item must be material in amount, unusual in nature, and not expected to recur in the foreseeable future. Answers **a**, **b**, and **d** describe items classified as discontinued operations, continuing operations, and a change in accounting estimate, respectively.

4 Answer **b**—the subtotal Income before Extraordinary Items would reflect Fields Corporation's earnings of $4,000,000 from continuing operations and its $700,000 loss from discontinued operations.

5 Answer **c**—the "cumulative effect" of an account change is the effect upon the income of prior periods of retroactively applying the new accounting method. Answers, **a**, **b**, and **d**, respectively, describe a prior period adjustment, an extraordinary item, and discontinued operations.

6 Answer **a**—[$2,000,000 − (100,000 preferred shares × $5)] ÷ 100,000 shares common shares = $15 per share.

7 Answer **a**—the purpose of disclosing fully diluted earnings per share is to warn stockholders of the possible dilution of earnings that could occur from conversion of various securities into additional shares of common stock.

8 Answer **a**—the market value of stock *should* fall in proportion to the number of new shares issued; however, many factors besides number of shares outstanding influence market prices of stock.

9 Answer **c**—large stock dividends are recorded by transferring only the par value of the dividend shares from the Retained Earnings account to the Common Stock account.

10 Answer **c**—stock price is closely related to stockholders' expectations of future earnings. Answers **a**, **b**, and **d** should all cause the market price of the stock to decline.

11 Answer **d**—computed as follows:

100,000 shares × $\frac{3}{12}$ of a year	25,000
110,000 shares × $\frac{9}{12}$ of a year	82,500
	107,500
Adjustment for effect of 2 for 1 stock split	107,500
Weighted-average number of common shares outstanding	215,000

12 Answer **d**—a prior period adjustment is a correction of an error in the amount of net income reported in a prior period. As the Income Summary account for the prior period was closed into the Retained Earnings account, the error is corrected by adjusting the balance of retained earnings at the beginning of the period when the error is discovered. This adjustment is reported in the statement of retained earnings, not in the income statement. The adjustment affects retained earnings, not paid-in capital. Answer **c** describes the cumulative effect of a change in accounting principle.

13 Answer **b**—a cumulative effect of an accounting change upon the income of prior years is shown in the *income statement* of the year of the change.

14 Answer **b**—treasury stock refers to shares of a corporation's own capital stock which have been issued and later reacquired by the issuing company but which have not been canceled or retired.

15 Answer **c**—purchases and sales of treasury stock are investment transactions between the corporation and its stockholders. Therefore, these transactions affect paid-in capital and do not give rise to gains or losses.

16 Answer **b**—purchase of stock in another company is considered an investing activity. Answers **a**, **c**, and **d** are all transactions of McGill with its owners and, as such, constitute financing activities.

17 Answer **d**—a statement of stockholders' equity explains the changes in each stockholders' equity account. The cumulative effect of an accounting change is shown as a separate item in the ***income statement***. Although net income causes a change in the Retained Earnings account and is shown in the statement of stockholders' equity, this statement does not disclose the individual components of net income.

Solutions to Exercises

1
a Stock split
b Ex-dividend date
c Earnings per share
d None (The statement describes the cumulative effect of a change in accounting principle.)
e None (The statement describes treasury stock.)
f None (The statement describes a cash dividend, not a stock dividend.)
g Extraordinary item

2

AXEL COMPANY
Income Statement
For the Current Year

Sales	$4,200,000
Cost of goods sold (70%)	2,940,000
Gross profit on sales (30%)	$1,260,000
Operating expenses [$1,260,000 − ($210,000 ÷ .6)]	910,000
Operating income before taxes ($210,000 ÷ .6)	$ 350,000
Income taxes ($350,000 × .4)	140,000
Income from continuing operations ($4,200,000 × .05)	$ 210,000
Loss from discontinued operations, net of income tax benefit	(300,000)
Net loss	$ (90,000)
Per share of capital stock:	
Income from continuing operations	$ 2.10
Loss from discontinued operations	(3.00)
Net loss	$ (.90)

3 Earnings from continuing operations:

($490,000 − $60,000) ÷ 100,000 shares $4.30

Net earnings:

($672,000 − $60,000) ÷ 100,000 shares $6.12

4

		General Journal		
19__				
Mar.	1	Dividends	200,000	
		Dividends Payable		200,000
		Declared cash dividend of $0.80 per share on 250,000 shares.		
	21	Dividends Payable	200,000	
		Cash		200,000
		Paid dividend declared Mar. 1.		
Aug.	10	Retained Earnings	500,000	
		Stock Dividend to Be Distributed		62,500
		Additional Paid-in Capital: Stock Dividends		437,500
		Declared 5% stock dividend on 250,000 shares of $5 par value stock.		
Sept.	2	Stock Dividend to Be Distributed	62,500	
		Common Stock		62,500
		Distributed 12,500-share stock dividend.		
Dec.	21	Retained Earnings	1,312,500	
		Common Stock		1,312,500
		Declared and issued 100% stock dividend on 262,500 shares		
		of $5 par stock.		
	30	Treasury Stock	30,000	
		Cash		30,000
		Purchased 1,000 common shares for treasury.		

HIGHLIGHTS OF THE CHAPTER

1 We have seen how the income statement measures the profitability of a business. But profitability alone does not assure success; a business must also have enough liquid resources to pay its maturing obligations and to take advantage of new investment opportunities. To some extent, a balance sheet shows whether or not a business is solvent at a particular date. To assist investors in assessing a company's ability to remain solvent, companies prepare a third major financial statement called the *statement of cash flows*.

2 The basic purpose of a statement of cash flows is to provide information about the *cash receipts* and *cash payments* of a business during the accounting period. A second purpose is to provide information about all *investing* and *financing* activities of the business. The statement helps assist investors, creditors, and others in assessing such factors as:

a The ability of the company to generate positive cash flows.

b The ability of the company to meet its obligations and to pay dividends.

c The company's need for external financing.

d The reasons for differences between reported profits and the related cash flows.

e The cash and noncash aspects of the company's investing and financing activities during the period.

f The causes of the change during the period in the company's cash balance.

3 A statement of cash flows shows separately the cash flows from (a) *operating activities*, (b) *investing activities*, and (c) *financing activities*. Each section shows the nature and amounts of cash receipts and cash pay-

ments relating to that type of activity during the period. All cash transactions that do not relate to investing or financing activities are included in the operating activities section. Thus, the statement of cash flows summarizes *all types* of cash receipts and cash payments during the period. A statement of cash flows is illustrated on page 606 in your textbook.

4 The major cash receipts from *operating activities* are collections from customers (including cash sales and collections on accounts receivable) and receipts of investment income, such as interest and dividends. Cash payments include cash paid to suppliers of goods and services, and payments of interest and taxes.

5 Cash receipts from *investing activities* include the proceeds from selling investments or plant assets, and the principal amounts collected on loans. (Receipts of interest are classified as operating activities.) Cash payments include purchases of investments and plant assets, and amounts advanced to borrowers.

6 Cash receipts from *financing activities* include proceeds from borrowing and from issuing stock. Cash payments include repayment of amounts borrowed, and distributions to owners, such as dividends or purchases of treasury stock.

7 Some investing and financing activities *do not involve cash flows*. For example, land might be purchased by issuing a long-term note payable. One purpose of the statement of cash flows is to disclose all investing and financing activities during the period. Therefore, the noncash aspects of these transactions should be *disclosed in a sup-*

plementary schedule to the statement of cash flows. (See paragraph **17**.)

8 Receipts and payments of *interest* are classified as *operating activities*, not as investing or financing activities. The reason is that the FASB wants net cash flow from operating activities to reflect the cash effects of those transactions entering into the determination of net income.

9 In the long run, a company must generate positive cash flows from operating activities if the business is to survive. A business with negative cash flows from operations will not be able to raise cash from other sources (investing and financing activities) indefinitely.

10 In a statement of cash flows, "cash" is defined as including not only currency and bank accounts, but also all cash equivalents. *Cash equivalents* are short-term, highly liquid investments, such as money market accounts, Treasury bills, and commercial paper. Transfers of cash between bank accounts and cash equivalent are *not* viewed as cash receipts or cash payments. However, any interest earned from a cash equivalent is considered a cash receipt from operating activities.

11 Captions and amounts appearing in a statement of cash flows are not the titles and balances of specific ledger accounts. This financial statement summarizes cash transactions, but accounting records usually are maintained on the *accrual basis* of accounting, not the cash basis.

12 In most situations, it usually is more practical to prepare a statement of cash flows by analyzing an income statement and the changes during the period in all of the balance sheet accounts *except for Cash*. To illustrate, consider the changes during the period in the Marketable Securities account. Debits to this account indicate purchases of securities, while credits indicate sales. Both types of transactions involve cash flows which should appear in the investing activities section of a statement of cash flows. Of course the credit entries to the Marketable Securities account represent only the cost of the securities sold. This dollar amount must be *adjusted for any gain or loss* appearing in the income statement to determine the cash proceeds from the sale.

13 To determine cash flow from operations, we convert the company's accrual-basis measurements of revenue and expenses to the cash basis.

a *Net sales* can be converted to cash received from customers by adding any decrease (or subtracting any increase) in accounts receivable. A similar approach may be used to convert interest revenue from the accrual basis to the amount of cash received.

b The *cost of goods sold* can be converted to cash payments to suppliers by adding any increase (or subtracting any decrease) in inventory, and then adding any decrease (or subtracting any increase) in accounts payable to suppliers.

c *Expenses* are converted to the cash basis as follows: first, deduct any noncash expenses, such as depreciation; next, add any increase (or subtract any decrease) in short-term prepayments. Finally, add any decrease (or subtract any increase) in related accrued liabilities.

14 The computations described above may be used to compute the major operating cash flows, such as "Cash received from customers." This approach is called the *direct method* of determining the cash flow from operations. An acceptable alternative is the *indirect method*. Instead of listing cash outflows and cash inflows, the indirect method shows a reconciliation of net income to the net cash flow from operating activities.

15 Differences between net income and cash flow from operations are caused by:

a *Depreciation and other noncash expenses* Depreciation and amortization reduce net income, but do not affect cash flows of the period.

b *Short-term timing differences* Under the accrual basis of accounting, revenue is recognized when it is earned and expenses are recognized when the goods and services are used. In either case, this may differ from the period in which cash is received or paid.

c *Nonoperating gains and losses* Nonoperating gains or losses do affect cash flows, but, by definition, they do not affect cash flows from operating activities. Most nonoperating gains and losses affect the amount of cash received from investing activities.

16 The direct and indirect methods result in exactly the same net cash flow from operations. The FASB has stated its preference for the direct method. However, either method is acceptable. The indirect method is covered in the Supplemental Topic in this chapter and in later accounting courses.

17 Two supplementary schedules accompany a statement of cash flows. The first reconciles the **net income** for the period to the **net cash flow reported from operating activities**. The second supplementary schedule reports **noncash investing and financing activities**, such as the issuance of capital stock in exchange for land.

18 Of the three categories in the statement of cash flows, the net cash flow from **operating activities** is of most interest to users of financial statements. Even more important than the dollar amount of net cash flow from operating activities in any one year is the **trend** of this cash flow, and **consistency** of the trend, over a period of years.

19 **Free cash flow** is a statistic used by some analysts to put a company's cash flows into perspective. Free cash flow represents the cash flow available to management for discretionary purposes, **after** the company has met all of its basic business obligations. As there is disagreement as to what constitutes "basic business obligations," different analysts compute free cash flow different ways. One common method of computing free cash flow is to start with net cash flow from operating activities and subtract any net cash used for investing activities as well as any dividends paid.

*20 Net cash flows from **operating activities** may be reported using either the **direct** or the **indirect** method. Although the FASB encourages use of the direct method, the indirect method is a permissible alternative and remains in widespread use.

*21 The two methods of computing net cash flow from operating activities are based upon the same accounting data and result in the **same amount of net cash flow**. Both methods convert accrual-based income statement amounts into cash flows by adjusting for changes in related balance sheet accounts.

*22 The differences between the two methods lie only in **format**. The **direct method** describes the nature and dollar amounts of the specific cash inflows and outflows comprising the operating activities of the business. The **indirect method** reconciles net income (as shown in the income statement) with net cash flow from operating activities.

*23 Net cash flow from operating activities differs from net income for three major reasons:

a **"Noncash" expenses** Some expenses, such as depreciation, reduce net income but require no cash outlay during the current period.

b **Timing differences** Net cash flow reflects the effects of current period **cash** transactions. Revenue and expenses are measured using the concepts of **accrual** accounting and may be recognized in an accounting period other than that in which a related cash flow occurs.

c **"Nonoperating" gains and losses** By definition, net cash flow from operating activities shows only the effects of those cash transactions classified as **"operating activities."** Net income, however, includes gains and losses relating to investing and financing activities as well.

*24 The adjustments involved in reconciling net income with net cash flow from operating activities are determined using a working paper or computer program and do **not** appear in the company's accounting records.

*25 **Adjusting for noncash expenses** To reconcile net income with net cash flow, we add back the amount of depreciation and any other "noncash" expenses, such as amortization, depletion, etc.

*26 **Adjusting for timing differences** Timing differences between net income and net cash flow arise whenever revenue or expense is recognized by debiting or crediting either an asset account (**other than cash**) or a liability account. Accounts giving rise to these timing differences include accounts receivable, inventories, prepaid expenses, accounts payable, and accrued expenses payable.

a **Changes in accounts receivable** A net **increase** in accounts receivable indicates that revenue from credit sales exceeds collections from customers. Thus, this increase is **deducted** from net income in order to arrive at net cash flow from operations. A net **decrease** in receivables is **added** to net income.

b **Changes in inventory** A net **increase** in inventory indicates that purchases during the period **exceed** the cost of goods sold. To reconcile net income with net cash flow from operations, we **deduct the net increase** from net income. A net **decrease** in inventory is **added** to net income.

c **Changes in prepaid expenses** A net **increase** indicates that cash payments made

---
*Supplemental Topic A, "The Indirect Method."

for items such as insurance or rent *exceed* the amounts recognized as expense; this increase is *deducted* from net income in order to arrive at net cash flow from operations. A net *decrease* in prepaid expenses is *added* to net income.

d *Changes in accounts payable* A net *increase* indicates that the accrual-based figure for purchases (included in the cost of goods sold) is *greater* than the cash payments made to suppliers. The increase is *added* to net income to arrive at net cash flow from operations. A net *decrease* is *subtracted* from net income.

e *Changes in accrued expenses payable* A net *increase* indicates that expenses recognized in the current period *exceed* the related cash payments. The increase is *added* to net income to arrive at net cash flow from operations. A net *decrease* is *subtracted* from net income.

*27 A *helpful hint* for all related asset and liability accounts that explains timing differences—a net *credit change* in the account's balance is always added to net income; a net *debit change* is always subtracted from net income to arrive at net cash flow from operating activities.

*28 *Adjusting for nonoperating gains and losses* "Nonoperating" gains and losses do not affect *operating* activities but do enter into the determination of net income. In converting net income to net cash flow from operating activities, we add back any nonoperating losses and deduct any nonoperating gains included in net income.

*29 Nonoperating gains and losses include gains and losses from sales of investments or plant assets, gains and losses on discontinued operations, and gains and losses on the early retirement of debt.

*30 *The indirect method appears in all statements of cash flows.* If the *indirect* method is used to compute cash flows from operating activities, it will appear either in the body of the statement of cash flows or in a supplementary schedule. However, companies using the *direct* method to compute cash flows from operating activities are required to provide as well a *supplementary schedule* showing a reconciliation of net income with net cash flows from operating activities (that is, the indirect presentation.)

*Supplemental Topic A, "The Indirect Method."

TEST YOURSELF ON CASH FLOWS

True or False

For each of the following statements, circle the T or the F to indicate whether the statement is true or false.

T F **1** A statement of cash flows generally is organized into three major sections: cash receipts, cash payments, and noncash investing and financing activities.

T F **2** All cash receipts and cash payments not classified as investing or financing activities are classified as operating activities.

T F **3** One purpose of a statement of cash flows is to provide information about financing and investing activities, even if these activities do not involve cash receipts or cash payments.

T F **4** Accounts receivable from large corporations are considered cash equivalents.

T F **5** A statement of cash flows provides more information about the profitability of a business than does an income statement.

T F **6** In a statement of cash flows, the transfer of cash from a bank account to a money market fund is shown among the investing activities.

T F **7** In a statement of cash flows, payments of dividends are classified as operating activities.

T F **8** Cash payments to purchase merchandise are classified as investing activities.

T F **9** In a statement of cash flows, receipts and payments of interest are both classified as operating activities.

T F **10** A growing, successful company will usually show a positive net cash flow from operations.

T F **11** A growing, successful company will usually show a positive net cash flow from investing activities.

T F **12** The easiest way to prepare a statement of cash flows is by analyzing the debit and credit entries in the Cash account.

T F 13 Credits to the Notes Receivable account normally represent cash receipts from investing activities.

T F 14 Debits to the Notes Payable account normally represent cash payment relating to financing activities.

T F 15 If accounts receivable are increasing over the period, cash received from customers probably exceeds net sales.

T F 16 Large increases in inventory tend to cause cash payments to suppliers to exceed the cost of goods sold.

T F 17 Depreciation expense increases the net cash flow resulting from operating activities.

T F 18 Depreciation expense decreases the net cash flow resulting from operating activities.

T F 19 The amount of net cash flow from operating activities will be the same, regardless of whether this amount is computed by the direct method or the indirect method.

T F 20 Depreciation expense reduces net income but has no effect on net cash flow from operating activities.

T F 21 If unexpired insurance decreases over the period, the cash paid to the insurance agency probably exceeds the amount recognized as insurance expense.

T F 22 A loss on the sale of a plant asset is an example of a noncash expense.

T F *23 Although the FASB requires that net cash flows from operating activities be reported using the direct method, the indirect method is widely used.

T F *24 Both the indirect and the direct method result in the same net dollar amount of cash flow from operating activities.

T F *25 The indirect method describes the nature and dollar amounts of the specific cash inflows and outflows comprising the operating activities of the business.

Completion Statements

Fill in the necessary words to complete the following statements:

1 There are three major financial statements: The _____ _____ measures the profitability of a business, the _____ _____ shows the financial position of the business at the end of the period, and the _____ ____ _____ _____ summarizes _____ transactions.

2 In a statement of cash flows, cash transactions are classified into the categories of (a) _____ activities, (b) _____ activities, and (c) _____ activities.

3 In a statement of cash flows, the payment of interest is classified as a (an) _____ activity, and the payment of a dividend is classified as a (an) _____ activity.

4 Of the three major classifications of cash flows, it is most important for a business to show a positive cash flow from _____ activities over the long run.

5 For purposes of preparing a statement of cash flows, "cash" includes currency, bank deposits, and _____ _____, such as money market funds, Treasury bills, and commercial paper.

6 The proceeds from short-term borrowing are equal to the sum of the (debit, credit) _____ entries in the Notes Payable account.

7 The amount of cash received from customers is equal to the amount of net sales, plus any (increase, decrease) _____ in _____ _____ over the period.

8 Net cash flow from operating activities may be computed in either of two ways: the _____ method identifies the major operating cash flows, whereas the _____ method reconciles the reported amount of _____ _____ with the net cash flow from operating activities.

9 The cash flow available to management after basic business obligations have been met is termed _____ _____ _____.

*10 Net cash flow from operating activities differs from net income as a result of (a) _____ _____, (b) _____ _____, or (c) _____ _____ _____ _____.

---

*Supplemental Topic A, "The Indirect Method."

*11 Depreciation is an example of a _____ _____. Depreciation expense reduces _____ _____ with no corresponding cash _____. Under the indirect method, in reconciling net income with _____ _____ _____ _____ _____ _____, the amount of depreciation is _____ _____ net income.

*12 _____ _____ may arise as the result of revenue and/or expense recognition in an accounting period different from that in which a related _____ _____ occurs.

*13 To reconcile net income with net cash flow from operating activities, the ____ _____ in accounts receivable is deducted from net income, and a _____ _____ in inventory is added to net income.

*14 By definition, nonoperating gains and losses do not affect operating activities. In converting net income to net cash flow from operating activities, we add back any _____ _____ _____ and deduct any _____ _____ included in net income.

*15 A company which computes the cash flow from operating activities by the direct method must still show a reconciliation of net income to net cash flow from operating activities in a _____ _____.

Multiple Choice

Choose the best answer to the following questions and enter the identifying letter in the space provided.

_____ 1 A statement of cash flows is **not** intended to provide readers with information about:
a The profitability of a business.
b Noncash investing and financing transactions.
c The ability of a business to continue paying dividends.
d The net cash flow from operating activities.

_____ 2 Which of the following captions should **not** appear in a statement of cash flows?
a Net cash provided by financing activities.
b Proceeds from sales of plant assets.
c Funds provided from operating activities.
d Net cash used by investing activities.

_____ 3 A successful, growing business is **most likely** to show a negative cash flow from:
a Operating activities.
b Investing activities.
c Financing activities.

d Transactions with customers.

_____ 4 Which of the following cash flows is **not** classified as a financing activity in a statement of cash flows?
a Payment of a cash dividend.
b Payment of interest.
c Short-term borrowing.
d Issuance of capital stock in exchange for plant assets.

_____ 5 Which of the following indicates a cash **receipt**?
a A decrease in accounts receivable.
b An increase in accumulated depreciation.
c An increase in prepaid rent.
d A decrease in accounts payable.

_____ 6 Which of the following indicates a **cash payment**?
a A credit change in the Capital Stock account.
b A debit change in the Notes Payable account.
c A credit change in the Accounts Receivable account.
d A debit change in the Cash account.

_____ 7 Which of the following will cause cash payments to suppliers of goods and services to **exceed** the amount of expense recorded on the accrual basis?
a Depreciation expense.
b An increase in accrued expenses payable.
c An increase in prepaid insurance.
d Payment of a cash dividend declared in a prior period.

_____ 8 Dexter Corporation reported net income in excess of its net cash flow from operating activities. A possible explanation for this is:
a Depreciation expense.
b Nonoperating gains.
c Nonoperating losses.
d An increase in accounts payable over the period.

_____ 9 The accounting records of Tiger Corp. include a $200,000 debit to the Land account. This transaction should appear in a statement of cash flows as a:
a Cash inflow from investing activities.
b Cash outflow from financing activities.
c Cash inflow from financing activities.
d Cash outflow from investing activities.

_____ 10 During the current year, the Marketable Securities account of Trend Co. was debited for $150,000 and credited for $200,000. The income statement includes a gain on sales of marketable securities of $45,000. Based upon this information, the investing activities section

*Supplemental Topic A, "The Indirect Method."

of the company's statement of cash flows should include a cash receipt of:

a $245,000.

b $155,000.

c $195,000.

d None of the above.

_____**11** MedVac, Inc., purchased land by issuing a long-term note payable. No cash down payment was made. In the company's statement of cash flows, this transaction should appear:

a Among the cash flows from financing activities.

b Among the cash flows from investing activities.

c In a supplementary schedule.

d Nowhere, as no cash was received or paid.

_____**12** Which of the following would *increase* the net cash flow from operating activities?

a Sale of capital stock for cash.

b Issuance of a note payable for cash.

c Sale of goods on credit.

d Sale of goods for cash.

_____***13** In a comparison of the direct and indirect methods of computing net cash flow from operating activities, which of the following is *not* correct?

a Both methods begin with items reported in an accrual-based income statement.

b Both methods provide readers of the cash flow statement with amounts of specific cash inflows and outflows comprising operating activities.

c Both methods result in the same amount of net cash flow from operating activities.

d Both methods focus upon net changes during the period in related balance sheet accounts.

_____***14** Navarro Corporation uses the indirect method in preparing its statement of cash flows. Under this approach, depreciation expense is added to net income because depreciation expense:

a Represents amounts deposited in a reserve fund maintained for the replacement of plant assets.

b Reduces net income, but results in an inflow of cash.

c Reduces net income, but does not involve an outflow of cash.

d Is a source of cash.

_____***15** The debit and credit entries to record several common transactions are shown in answers **a** through **d**. Which situation would *not* give rise to a timing difference in preparing the

statement of cash flows using the *indirect method*?

a A debit to Accounts Receivable accompanied by a credit to Sales Revenue.

b A debit to Interest Expense accompanied by a credit to Interest Payable.

c A debit to Inventory accompanied by a credit to Cash.

d A debit to Rent Expense accompanied by a credit to Prepaid Rent.

_____***16** The balance sheet of Pickering, Inc., shows a net increase in receivables of $520 and a net decrease in inventory of $280. To arrive at net cash flow from operating activities, net income should be:

a Reduced by $240.

b Increased by $240.

c Reduced by $800.

d Increased by $800.

_____***17** At the beginning of the year, NTA Corporation bought equipment for $1,500 by issuing a note payable. The equipment was assumed to have a 10-year life and was depreciated using the straight-line method. To arrive at net cash flow from *operating activities*, net income should be:

a Increased by $150.

b Increased by $1,350.

c Reduced by $1,350.

d No adjustment is necessary as no cash was received or paid.

_____***18** At the end of the *first year* of operation, Wilbur Showers, Inc., had the following account balances: Accounts Receivable, $200; Accounts Payable, $300; Inventory, $500. The corporation reported net income of $650 for the year. Net cash flow from *operating activities* should be reported as:

a $1,050,

b $850.

c $1,650.

d $250.

_____***19** The Jayne Corporation is preparing its statement of cash flows using the indirect method. The following information has been gathered for the current period:

Loss on sale of equipment	$ 7,500
Common stock issued for cash	200,000
Net income	76,000
Depreciation expense	32,000
Cash received from sale of equipment	60,000
Increase in inventory	4,500

Supplemental Topic A, "The Indirect Method."

Based only upon the above information, Jayne's net cash flow from operating activities is:

a $120,000.
b $111,000.
c $371,000.
d $171,000.

Exercises

1 Listed below are eight technical accounting terms introduced or emphasized in this chapter:

Operating activities   *Solvent*
Financing activities   *Cash equivalent*
Investing activities   *Net cash flow*
Statement of cash   *Balance sheet*
*   flows*

Each of the following statements may (or may not) describe one of these technical terms. In the space provided below each statement, indicate the accounting term described, or answer "None" if the statement does not correctly describe any of the terms.

a The financial statement that best describes the profitability of a business.

_____

b Cash receipts during the period, less cash payments made during the period.

_____

c The classification in a statement of cash flows that includes investments made by a business in plant assets.

_____

d The condition of consistently earning revenue in excess of expenses.

_____

e A short-term, highly liquid investment, such as a money market fund.

_____

f The classification of cash flows for which it is most important for cash flows to be positive over the long run.

_____

g The category within a statement of cash flows that includes investments made by owners in the capital stock of a business.

_____

2 Indicate how each of the events should be classified in a statement of cash flows for the current year. Use the following code: **O** = Operating activities, **I** = Investment activities, **F** = Financing activities.

If the event does not cause a cash flow to be reported in the statement, enter an X in the space provided.

____ a Collected accounts receivable originating from sales in the prior year.

____ b Paid the interest on a note payable to First Bank.

____ c Paid the principal amount due on the note payable to First Bank.

____ d Received a dividend from an investment in AT&T common stock.

____ e Paid a dividend to stockholders.

____ f Recorded depreciation expense for the current year.

____ g Sold a segment of the business to another corporation.

____ h Transferred cash from a money market fund into a checking account.

____ i Purchased marketable securities.

____ j Made a year-end adjusting entry to record accrued interest payable on bonds payable.

3 The financial statements of Canyon Street Galleries provide the following information:

	End of Year	Beginning of Year
Accounts receivable	$ 29,000	$25,000
Inventory	35,000	28,000
Prepaid expenses	500	1,500
Accounts payable (for merchandise)	17,000	14,000
Accrued liabilities	2,000	750
Net sales	320,000	
Cost of goods sold	200,000	
Operating expenses (including depreciation of $8,000)	90,000	
Net income	30,000	

Using these data, compute:

a Cash received from customers.

b Cash payments for purchases of merchandise.

c Cash paid for operating expenses.

4 From the following information, complete the statement of cash flows (direct method) for

Tycor Distributors for the year ended December 31, 19__.

Purchases of plant assets	$ 520,000
Proceeds from sales of plant assets	50,000
Proceeds from issuing capital stock	400,000
Proceeds from short-term borrowing	100,000
Payments to settle short-term debt	70,000
Interest and dividends received	40,000
Cash received from customers	1,800,000
Dividends paid	200,000
Cash paid to suppliers and employees	1,400,000
Interest paid	60,000
Income taxes paid	120,000
Cash and cash equivalents, beginning of the year	84,000
Cash and cash equivalents, end of the year	?

TYCOR DISTRIBUTORS
Statement of Cash Flows
For the Year Ended December 31, 19__

Cash flows from operating activities:
  Cash received from customers .... $

  _____

  Cash provided by operating activities .... $
  Cash paid to suppliers and
  employees .... $(   )

  _____

  Cash disbursed for operating activities .... (_____)
Net cash flow from operating activities .... $
Cash flow from investing activities:
  $

  _____

Net cash used by investing activities .... (   )

Cash flows from financing activities:
  Proceeds from short-term
  borrowing .... $

  _____

Net cash provided by financing activities ....
Net increase (decrease) in cash .... $
Cash and cash equivalents, beginning of
  the year ....
  _____
Cash and cash equivalents, end of the year .... $

Supplemental Topic A, "The Indirect Method."

*5 Listed below are eight technical accounting terms emphasized in Supplemental Topic A.

Noncash expense	*Operating activities*
Indirect method	*Direct method*
Net cash flow	*Timing difference*
Nonoperating gains and losses	*Net cash flow from operating activities*

Each of the following statements may (or may not) describe one of these technical terms. In the space provided below each statement, indicate the accounting term described, or answer "None" if the statement does not correctly describe any of the terms.

a Amounts reported in the income statement that relate to investing and/or financing activities.

_____

b A method of reporting net cash flow from operations by listing specific types of cash inflows and outflows.

_____

c The category of expense which reduces net income, yet requires no cash outflow.

_____

d Amount determined by application of either the direct method or the indirect method.

_____

e Cash receipts during the period, less cash payments made during the period.

_____

f The result of recognizing either a revenue or an expense with no corresponding cash flow during the same accounting period.

_____

g A measurement of a company's performance reflecting both operating and nonoperating transactions on an accrual basis.

_____

*6 In the computation of net cash flow from operating activities by the *indirect method*, determine whether each of the following items would be added to net income, deducted from net income, or omitted from the computation. Indicate your answer in the space provided by using the following symbols: **+** (added to net income), **–** (deducted from net income), or O (omitted from computation).

____ **a** Depreciation for the year amounted to $500.

____ **b** Dividends were declared in December, to be paid early next year.

____ **c** Accounts receivable increased by $400 during the year.

____ **d** Dividends, declared at the end of last year, were paid to shareholders during the current year.

____ **e** Gain was recognized when equipment was sold in exchange for a note receivable.

____ **f** Accounts payable decreased during the year.

____ **g** Prepaid expenses increased during the year.

*7 The data below was taken from the financial statements of the Stilwell Company:

Income statement:		**1996**
Net income		$65,000
Depreciation expense		23,000
Amortizaton of patents		7,000
Loss on sale of investments		15,000
Gain on sale of land		6,000

Balance sheet:	**12/31/96**	**12/31/95**
Accounts receivable	$55,000	$62,000
Inventory	78,000	82,000
Prepaid advertising	4,000	2,000
Accounts payable (to supplier)	58,000	61,000
Accrued expenses payable	27,000	21,000

Compute the partial statement of cash flows for the year ended December 31, 1996, showing the computation of *net cash flow from operating activities* by the *indirect method*:

STILWELL COMPANY
Partial Statement of Cash Flows
For the Year Ended December 31, 1996

Cash flow from operating activities:

  Net income .... $

  Add:

  Subtotal .... $

  Less:

  Net cash flow from operating activities .... $

Supplemental Topic A, "The Indirect Method."

SOLUTIONS TO CHAPTER 14 SELF-TEST

True or False

1 F The three major categories of cash flows are (a) operating activities, (b) investing activities, and (c) financing activities.

2 T If a transaction does not fall into either the financing or investing category, by default it is considered an operating activity.

3 T The FASB requires that a supplementary schedule disclosing any "noncash" investing and financing activities accompany the statement of cash flows.

4 F Cash equivalents are short-term, highly liquid investments, such as money market funds, commercial paper, and Treasury bills.

5 F The income statement measures profitability, whereas the statement of cash flows provides information about cash flows from operating, investing, and financing activities.

6 F Cash in a money market account is considered a cash equivalent.

7 F Payments to owners, such as dividends, are classified as financing activities.

8 F Payments to purchase merchandise are classified as operating activities.

9 T The FASB wanted net cash flow from operating activities to reflect the cash effects of those transactions entering into the determination of net income.

10 T In the long run, a business must generate positive cash flows from operations if the business is to survive.

11 F A growing business is generally investing in plant assets and acquiring other investments; these activities could lead to a negative cash flow from investing activities.

12 F It is easier to prepare the statement of cash flows by examining the income statement and the *changes* in all balance sheet accounts except Cash.

13 T A credit to Notes Receivable usually represents cash received. Investing activities can include cash receipts as well as cash disbursements.

14 T Debit entries to long-term debt accounts usually indicate cash payments. Borrowing and repayment of borrowing constitute financing activities.

15 F If accounts receivable are increasing, some of the credit sales have *not* been collected from customers.

16 T If the company is increasing its inventory, it is buying more merchandise than it is selling. If accounts payable are not increasing by the same amount as the inventory increase, the payments to suppliers are greater than the cost of goods sold.

17 F Depreciation is a noncash expense that does not affect cash flows from operation activities.

18 F Depreciation is a noncash expense; it has no effect on cash flows from operating activities.

19 T The indirect method is simply an alternative approach to determine net cash flow from operations.

20 T Depreciation is a noncash expense, requiring no cash outlay during the current period.

21 F A net decrease in unexpired insurance indicates that the company exhausted a portion of the insurance it had paid for *previously*. In this case, the amount recognized as insurance expense would exceed the current period cash outlay.

22 F A loss on the sale of a plant asset is an example of a nonoperating loss.

*23 F While the FASB encourages the use of the direct method, it *does not require* use of this method and permits use of the indirect method.

*24 T The direct method and the indirect method of computing net cash flow from operating activities differ only in format—both methods result in the same amount of net cash flow from operating activities.

*25 F The indirect method begins with reported net income and reconciles this figure to the net cash flow from operating activities.

Completion Statements

1 Income statement, balance sheet, statement of cash flows, cash. **2(a)** Operating, **(b)** investing, **(c)** financing. **3** Operating, financing. **4** Operating. **5** Cash equivalents. **6** Credit. **7** Decrease, accounts receivable. **8** Direct, indirect, net income. **9** Free cash flow. ***10(a)** Noncash expenses, **(b)** timing differences, **(c)** nonoperating gains and losses. ***11** Noncash expense, net income, outlay, net cash flow from operating activities, added to. ***12** Timing differences, cash flow. ***13** Net increase, net decrease. ***14** Nonoperating losses, nonoperating gains. ***15** Supplementary schedule.

Multiple Choice

1 Answer **a**—A statement of cash flows provides information about the *solvency* of a business; the income statement provides information about *profitability*. A statement of cash flows also provides information about *noncash* investing and financing activities.

2 Answer **c**—the FASB prohibits the use of the term *"funds"* in the statement of cash flows.

3 Answer **b**—investing activities include purchases and sales of plant assets and of investments. A growing company is likely to be purchasing greater quantities of plant assets and of investments than it is selling. Thus, a growing company is likely to show a negative cash flow from investing activities.

4 Answer **b**—payment of interest is classified as an operating activity.

5 Answer **a**—accounts receivable decrease when cash is collected from customers. Answers **c** and **d** indicate cash payments. Answer **b** occurs when depreciation expense is recorded and involves no cash receipt or payment.

6 Answer **b**—a debit change in the Notes Payable account indicates that payment has been made on a note payable. Answer **a** indicates the issuance of capital stock, answer **c** indicates collection of an account receivable, and answer **d** indicates an increase in the Cash account. Thus, answers **a**, **c**, and **d** all indicate receipts of cash.

7 Answer **c**—an increase in a prepaid expense requires a cash outlay that is not recognized as expense in the current period. Answers **a** and **b** cause expenses recorded in the period to exceed the amount of cash payments. Answer **d** does not involve a cash payment to suppliers of goods or services.

8 Answer **b**—nonoperating gains increase net income and *total* net cash flow they do not, however, increase the net cash flow from *operating* activities.

9 Answer **d**—a debit to the Land account indicates a purchase of land, which is an investing activity requiring a cash outflow.

10 Answer **a**—the credits to the Marketable Securities account indicate that marketable securities costing $200,000 were sold during the period. The $45,000 gain in the income statement means that the sales price must have been $45,000 above cost, or $245,000.

11 Answer **c**—the FASB requires that *noncash* investing and financing activities be disclosed in a supplementary schedule accompanying the statement of cash flows. As the transaction does not involve a cash receipt or a cash payment, it would not appear among the cash flows from financing or investing activities.

12 Answer **d**—the sale of goods for cash reflects a cash receipt from operating activities. Answer **c** does not result in a cash flow, while answers **a** and **b** are examples of financing activities (nonoperating activities).

*13 Answer **b**—the *direct* method discloses amounts of specific cash inflows and outflows comprising operating activities. The *indirect* method reconciles reported net income with net cash flow from operating activities.

*14 Answer **c**—because the computation of net cash flow from operating activities begins with reported net income under the indirect method, noncash expenses such as depreciation are added back to net income in order to arrive at the net cash flow from operations. Depreciation expense does not generate an inflow of cash, nor is there a fund of cash set aside as a result of recording depreciation expense.

*15 Answer **c**—a timing difference arises when a revenue or expense is recognized by debiting or crediting either an asset account (*other than cash*), or a liability account.

*16 Answer **a**—both a net increase in accounts receivable and a net decrease in inventory represent timing differences. The $520 net increase in accounts receivable is deducted from net income, while the $280 net decrease in inventory is added to net income—a net $240 reduction of net income to arrive at net cash flow from operating activities.

*17 Answer **a**—depreciation of $150 ($1,500 ÷ 10 years) is an example of a noncash expense which reduces net income yet does not entail a current period cash outlay.

*18 Answer **d**—since this is Wilbur Showers, Inc.'s first year of operations, the account balances reflect net increases. An increase in

---

*Supplemental Topic A, "The Indirect Method."

accounts payable is added to net income; the increases in accounts receivable and in inventory are deducted from net income to arrive at net cash flow from operating activities. ($650 + $300 − $200 − $500 = $250 net cash flow from operating activities.)

*19 Answer **b**—

	$ 76,000	net income
	32,000	depreciation expense
	(4,500)	increase in inventory
	7,500	nonoperating loss
	$111,000	net cash flow from
		operating activities

The issuance of common stock is classified as a financing activity; the sale of equipment is classified as an investing activity.

Solutions to Exercises

1

a None (The statement describes the *income statement*.)
b Net cash flow
c Investing activities
d None (Statement describes *profitable*, not *solvent*.)
e Cash equivalent
f Operating activities
g Financing activities

2

a	O
b	O
c	F
d	O
e	F
f	X
g	I
h	X
i	I
j	X

3 **a** $316,000 ($320,000 − $4,000)
b $204,000 ($200,000 + $7,000 − $3,000)
c $79,750 ($90,000 − $8,000 − $1,000 − $1,250)

4

TYCOR DISTRIBUTORS
Statement of Cash Flows
For the Year Ended December 31, 19__

Cash flows from operating activities:			
Cash received from customers ...	$ 1,800,000		
Interest and dividends received ..	40,000		
Cash provided by operating activities		$1,840,000	
Cash paid to suppliers and			
employees	$(1,400,000)		
Interest paid	(60,000)		
Income taxes paid	(120,000)		
Cash disbursed for operating activities		(1,580,000)	
Net cash flow from operating activities		$ 260,000	
Cash flows from investing activities:			
Cash paid to acquire plant			
assets	$(520,000)		
Proceeds of sales from plant			
assets	50,000		
Net cash used by investing activities		(470,000)	
Cash flows from financing activities:			
Proceeds from short-term			
borrowing...................................	$ 100,000		
Payments to settle short-term			
debt	(70,000)		
Proceeds from issuing capital			
stock	400,000		
Dividends paid	(200,000)		
Net cash provided by financing activities		230,000	
Net increase (decrease) in cash		$ 20,000	
Cash and cash equivalents, beginning			
of the year		84,000	
Cash and cash equivalents, end of the year		$ 104,000	

*5

a Nonoperating gains and losses
b Direct method
c Noncash expense
d Net cash flow from operating activities
e Net cash flow
f Timing difference
g None (The statement describes *net income*.)

---

*Supplemental Topic A, "The Indirect Method."

*6

a +

b O (Cash payment of a dividend is classified as a *financing* activity; in addition, no cash was paid in this transaction.)

c –

d O (Cash payment of a dividend is classified as a *financing* activity.)

e –

f –

g –

*7

STILWELL COMPANY
Partial Statement of Cash Flows
For the Year Ended December 31, 1996

Cash flow from operating activities:		
Net income		$ 65,000
Add: Depreciation expense	$23,000	
Amortization of patents	7,000	
Decrease in accounts receivable	7,000	
Decrease in inventory	4,000	
Increase in accrued expenses payable	6,000	
Nonoperating loss on sale of investments	15,000	62,000
Subtotal		$127,000
Less: Increase in prepaid advertising	$ 2,000	
Decrease in accounts payable	3,000	
Nonoperating gain on sale of land	6,000	(11,000)
Net cash flow from operating activities		$116,000

Supplemental Topic A, "The Indirect Method."

15

ACCOUNTING CONCEPTS, PROFESSIONAL JUDGMENT, AND ETHICAL CONDUCT

HIGHLIGHTS OF THE CHAPTER

1 *Generally accepted accounting principles* are the ground rules for financial reporting. The financial statements of all publicly owned corporations are prepared in conformity with these principles.

2 Accounting principles are not natural laws—rather, they are developed by humans. In some ways, accounting principles are like the rules for a game such as baseball or basketball. For example, accounting principles, like sports rules:

a Originate from a combination of tradition, experience, and official decree.

b Must be understood and observed by all participants in the process.

c Are sometimes arbitrary.

d May change over time as shortcomings in existing rules come to light, in response to technological change, or to reflect a widespread belief that a rule change would "improve the game."

3 In order to qualify as "generally accepted," an accounting principle should be widely used and should be supported by one or more of the following groups:

a The *AICPA* (the professional association of licensed CPAs), through its research efforts and the pronouncements of the *Accounting Principles Board* (APB). (The APB has been replaced by the Financial Accounting Standards Board.)

b The *Financial Accounting Standards Board* (an organization with representatives from public accounting, industry, government and accounting education), through publication of *Statements of Financial Accounting Standards*.

c The *Securities and Exchange Commission* (an agency of the federal government), through its legal power to establish and enforce financial reporting and disclosure requirements for all large, publicly owned corporations. In the past, the SEC has usually adopted the *Statements* issued by the FASB, giving these *Statements* the force of law.

4 Not all generally accepted accounting principles can be found in the "official pronouncements" of the standard-setting organizations. When the method of accounting for a particular situation is not explained in any official literature, generally accepted accounting principles are based upon such considerations as (a) accounting practices in widespread use, (b) practices recommended in authoritative but "unofficial" accounting literature, and (c) broad theoretical concepts that underlie most accounting practices.

5 One basic accounting concept is that the information in an accounting report is compiled for a carefully defined *accounting entity*. An accounting entity is any economic unit which controls resources and engages in economic activities. An individual, a division of a corporation, or a whole business enterprise are all examples of possible accounting entities. The important thing is that the entity is clearly defined before the reports are prepared, and then only the activities of that entity are reported.

6 Another important principle is the *going-concern assumption*. This means that we assume that a business will continue in operation for an indefinite period of time sufficient to carry out all its commitments. The going-concern principle is the reason why all

assets are not valued at their liquidation value.

7 The preparation of periodic financial reports reflects the *time period principle*. To be useful, financial statements must be timely and available at frequent intervals so that decision makers may observe trends and changes in the economic condition of an accounting entity. However, when the life of a business is divided into relatively short accounting periods, many amounts can only be *estimated*. For instance, the portion of the cost of a building to be deducted from the revenue of the current month is based upon an estimate of how long the building will be used.

8 Whenever accountants add or subtract dollar amounts originating in different accounting periods, they are assuming that the "dollar" is a *stable unit* for measuring value, just as the mile is a stable unit for measuring distance. Unfortunately, the dollar is not an entirely stable measure of value—the "value" of the dollar tends to decrease over time as a result of inflation. In periods of low inflation, the *stable-dollar assumption* does not cause serious problems. In periods of high inflation, however, this assumption causes distortions that lessen the usefulness of accounting information.

9 *Objectivity* is one of the most basic accounting principles. This means that the valuation of assets and liabilities is based on *objective evidence*, such as actual *exchange prices*. An objective value is one that is free from *bias* and can be verified by an independent party. Objectivity is one reason why assets are valued at historical cost (an actual exchange price) rather than at estimated current market value.

10 Even though objectivity is a major goal of accounting, some measurements must still be estimates based on judgment. Depreciation, for example, is not completely objective because it depends upon an estimate of useful life.

11 Both the balance sheet and the income statement are affected by the *cost principle*. Assets are valued at their *cost*, rather than at their current market values. Expenses represent the *cost* of goods and services used up in the effort to generate revenue. The major argument supporting the cost principle is that cost can be determined *more objectively* than can current market value.

12 The timing of revenue recognition is determined by the *realization principle*. Accountants usually do not recognize revenue until it is realized. Revenue is realized when (a) the earning process is essentially complete, and (b) objective evidence exists as to the amount of revenue earned.

13 In theory it is possible to recognize revenue:
a As production takes place.
b When production is completed.
c When sale or delivery of the product is made or the services are rendered.
d As cash is collected from customers.
In most cases, the accountant recognizes revenue at the time of sale of goods or the rendering of services.

14 Companies selling goods on the installment plan sometimes use the *installment method* of reporting for income tax purposes. Under the installment method, the seller recognizes the gross profit on sales gradually over an extended period of time as the cash is actually collected from customers. The installment method is used primarily for tax purposes; it is seldom used in financial statements.

15 Under special circumstances, accountants deviate from the realization principle. For example, the *percentage-of-completion* method of accounting for long-term construction projects recognizes revenue during production.

16 The timing of expense recognition is governed by the *matching principle*. In short, this principle requires that the expenses be offset against the revenue that these expenses help to produce. The matching principle may be applied in either of two major ways: (a) direct association of costs with specific revenue transactions, or (b) systematic allocation of costs over the useful life of the expenditure.

17 In some cases, accountants do not have sufficient objective evidence to apply the matching principle using either of the approaches described above. In these cases, accountants do not attempt to apply the matching principle; rather they charge the expenditure *immediately to expense*. Examples of expenditures usually charged directly to expense include advertising, research and development, and the cost of employee-training programs.

18 *Consistency* is the principle which means that once an accounting method is selected, it will be consistently used and not changed from period to period. For example, if we used straight-line depreciation on our building last month, we should not switch to double declining balance this month. If we did, there would be a change in net income caused by the change in an accounting method rather than any real economic changes.

19 The principle of *disclosure* means that all *material* (significant) and *relevant* facts concerning financial position and the results of operations must be communicated to the users of financial statements. This disclosure may be made either in the financial statements or in *footnotes* to the financial statements.

20 Another basic concept of accounting is *materiality*. An item is "material" if knowledge of it might reasonably influence the decisions of users of financial statements. As *immaterial* items are of little or no interest to decision makers, they may be treated in the easiest and most convenient manner. Thus, the concept of materiality allows accountants to ignore other accounting principles with respect to items that are *not material.*

21 The concept of *conservatism* often is not viewed as an accounting principle, but it plays an important role in financial reporting. Conservatism means that when estimates must be made, the accountant will lean toward *understatement* of asset values and net income rather than toward overstatement.

22 Today, the most influential organization in setting new accounting standards is the FASB. In setting new standards, the FASB issues *Discussion Memoranda and Exposure Drafts*, encouraging interested parties to respond and to express their views. The FASB also tries to make each new accounting standard consistent with the *conceptual framework project*.

23 The conceptual framework project is a general framework of accounting theory developed by the FASB and set forth in a series of *Statements of Financial Accounting Concepts*. These "concepts statements" address such broad issues as the objectives of financial reporting, the desired characteristics of accounting information, the elements of financial statements, and the criteria for deciding what information to include in financial statements. The primary purpose of these statements is to guide the FASB in developing future accounting standards that are logical and consistent. The concepts statements themselves *do not* represent "official" accounting principles.

24 Accountants' *professional judgment* plays a major role in financial reporting. Examples of the need for professional judgment include:

a Determining the appropriate accounting treatment for events not specifically covered by a professional pronouncement.

b Deciding what is material.

c Selecting appropriate accounting methods.

d Making estimates, including estimating the useful lives of depreciable assets, the allowance for doubtful accounts, and evaluating loss contingencies.

25 In general terms, *ethics* are the moral principles that govern individual behavior. Although some ethical concepts apply to almost all situations, others apply specifically to a particular type of activity. To understand and appreciate the ethics applicable to a specialized type of activity, such as the practice of accounting, one must first understand the *nature of the profession*.

26 All recognized professions have developed *codes of professional ethics*, whose basic purpose is to provide members with guidelines for conducting themselves in a manner consistent with the responsibilities of the profession. Codes of ethics developed by professional associations generally hold the practicing professional to *higher* standards of conduct than do statutes regulating that profession. The term *self-regulating* means that a profession has established its own rules of "professional conduct" for practicing members, and adopted measures to enforce those rules.

27 The practice of accounting includes such diverse activities as public accounting, consulting, management accounting, income tax accounting, internal auditing, and education, among others. Your text examines the ethical codes developed by two of the largest professional association of accountants—the *American Institute of Certified Public Accountants (AICPA) and the Institute of Management Accountants (IMA)*.

28 The AICPA's *Code of Professional Conduct* focuses upon ethical concepts specifically relating to the practice of *public accounting*. Most CPAs are members of the AICPA and are engaged in some aspect of public accounting, such as performing audits, income tax work, and accounting services for a variety of different clients.

29 The AICPA *Code* consists of two sections. The first section, *Principles*, discusses in broad terms the professional's responsibilities to the public, to clients, and to fellow practitioners. The principles provide the framework for the second section, entitled *Rules*. Two of the eleven specific rules are discussed in your text: Rule 102, regarding *integrity* and *objectivity*, and Rule 301, which addresses *confidentiality*.

30 The AICPA *Code of Professional Conduct* is binding upon all CPAs who are members of the AICPA. Most large CPA firms require all their partners to be members of this organization, and therefore to adhere to the Code. Most of the principles and rules in the Code apply to all aspects of a CPA's professional practice, and may extend to the CPA's personal life as well. To assist CPAs in applying ethical concepts contained in the Code, the AICPA publishes *interpretations* and *ethics rulings*.

31 CPAs performing audits of a company's financial statements are expressing their professional opinion as to the fairness of those financial statements. If the auditor's report is to lend credibility to the audited financial statements, the auditors must be fair and impartial—*independent* of the company issuing the financial statements. "Independent" means that the auditor must not be perceived as being under the company's influence or control, or as having any vested interest in the results reported in the financial statements. The concept of independence applies primarily to the CPA's role as an *auditor*. CPAs are not required to be independent of their clients in rendering income tax services, consulting services, and many types of accounting services.

32 *Integrity* and *objectivity*, two of the most important concepts in the AICPA Code, specify that in the performance of any professional engagement, a member shall *not knowingly misrepresent facts*. In this context, facts are considered to be misrepresented if the accounting document does not contain *adequate disclosure* of information relevant to *interpretation* of the facts. A CPA may not be associated with misleading financial statements, income tax returns, or other accounting reports. If a client insists upon preparing an accounting document in a misleading manner, the CPA must *resign from the engagement*.

33 The ethical standard of *confidentiality* is embodied in Rule 301 of the AICPA *Code*: "A member in public practice shall not disclose any confidential client information without the specific consent of the client." This rule does not relieve a CPA from his or her professional obligation to correctly and fully disclose facts in accounting documents. If a client refuses to make appropriate disclosures as required by applicable reporting standards, the CPA should resign from the engagement. Even after withdrawal from an engagement, a CPA must view information obtained during the engagement as confidential, unless the CPA has a *legal obligation* to disclose it.

34 *Management accountants* are those accountants working for one particular employer, such as a private company, nonprofit organization, or government agency. The members of the IMA have adopted a code of professional ethics designed to assist management accountants in performing their duties in an ethical and professional manner. The IMA Code addresses the following standards as applicable to management accountants: *competence*, *confidentiality*, *integrity*, and objectivity. The IMA's Code applies to all members of the organization in their role as managerial accountants; and to all Certified Management Accountants (CMAs).

35 The concept of *confidentiality* for *management accountants* is similar to that for public accountants. Confidentiality does not justify withholding disclosures from an accounting document. As in the case of public accountants, the legal obligation for the accountant to make disclosures takes precedence over confidentiality.

36 The concept of *independence* is absent from the IMA's Code. Independence is an ethical concept applicable *only to public accountants* engaged in *auditing* activities. Management accountants, however, are bound by an *objectivity standard* which is similar to that applicable to public accountants. Management accountants must be not associated with any financial statement, tax return, or other accounting report that the accountant believes to be misleading.

37 In resolving ethical conflicts involving management accountants, the IMA advocates first following established policies within the

d The production of manufactured goods is complete.

_____ **6** Which of the following does **not** represent a generally accepted accounting principle?

a Accounting information is compiled for an accounting entity.

b Consistency in the application of particular accounting methods enables the user of accounting data to interpret changes in income or in financial position from period to period.

c The going-concern assumption justifies ignoring liquidation values in presenting assets in the balance sheet.

d Constant-dollar financial statements are the primary means of financial reporting by large corporations.

_____ **7** Parker Construction Company enters into a contract to build an apartment complex at a price of $12,000,000. Parker estimates that its costs will total $8,000,000 and that the complex will be completed over a four-year period. Actual costs incurred during the first year were $2,400,000. Using the percentage-of-completion method, Parker should recognize a profit of

a $3,600,000.

b $4,000,000.

c $1,200,000.

d No profit should be recognized until the contract is completed.

_____ **8** Which of the following requires the **least** professional judgment on the part of the accountant?

a Preparing a year-end adjusting entry to record accrued interest payable.

b Estimating the useful life of a newly acquired computer system.

c Recording an appropriate amount of uncollectible accounts expense.

d Selecting the method to be used in the valuation of inventory.

_____ **9** Making a personal profit on "insider information" obtained while performing an audit of a client's financial statements **violates** the ethical concepts of:

a Integrity.

b Confidentiality.

c Materiality.

d Independence.

_____ **10** The ethical concept of **independence** applies:

a To all certified public accountants, regardless of the type of accounting services they are performing.

b To management accountants as well as public accountants.

c Only to management accountants.

d Only to public accountants engaged in auditing activities.

_____ **11** The ethical concepts of **integrity** and **objectivity**:

a Apply to both public accountants and management accountants in performing any type of professional accounting services.

b Apply only to CPAs who are members of the AICPA.

c Apply only to accountants involved in the preparation or auditing of financial statements issued to the public.

d Prohibit an accountant from owning stock in a company for which he or she performs accounting services.

Exercises

1 Listed below are eight technical accounting terms emphasized in this chapter:

Consistency	*Entity concept*
Matching principle	*Materiality*
Realization principle	*Conservatism*
Disclosure principle	*Objectivity*

Each of the following statements may (or may not) describe one of these technical terms. In the space provided below each statement, indicate the accounting term described, or answer "None" if the statement does not correctly describe any of the terms.

a An assumption that increases the comparability of financial statements from period to period.

_____

b The principle of recognizing revenue only when the earning process is complete.

_____

c The comparison of revenue to expenses incurred in generating this revenue.

_____

d The principle of preparing financial statements for relatively short accounting periods of equal length.

_____

e The relative importance of an item or an event.

_____

f The principle that requires all material and relevant information about the financial position and operating results of the business to be included in the financial statements.

_____

g An assumption that a business entity will continue in operation indefinitely.

---

2 Within the current framework of generally accepted accounting principles, show the immediate effect upon total assets, liabilities, and owners' equity that would be recorded for each of the following situations. Revenue and expenses are to be considered changes in owners' equity. Use the following code: **I** = Increase, **D** = Decrease, **NE** = No effect.

Situation	Assets	Liabilities	Owners' Equity
a An item with a long life and a material cost (a machine) is purchased for cash.			
b An item with a long life and an immaterial cost (a pencil sharpener) is purchased for cash.			
c An item of merchandise is acquired for cash at a price far below the price it will be sold for.			
d The item in **c** is sold for cash at a price above cost.			
e Cash is collected from a customer for a sale made last period.			
f A contractor using the percentage-of-completion method of accounting for long-term contracts finds 10% of the costs have been incurred and they total less than 10% of the contract price.			
g The contractor in **f** finds 40% of the costs have been incurred and they exceed 40% of the contract price.			

3 For each of the situations described below, indicate the accounting principle or concept that is being **violated**. You may choose from the following list of accounting principles; a given answer may be used more than once. If the described practice does not violate any of the listed principles, answer "None."

Realization　　*Matching*
Objectivity　　*Materiality*
Consistency　　*Disclosure*
Stable dollar　　*Entity*

a As a matter of convenience, Hi-Tech Mfg. Co. uses the direct write-off method to recognize uncollectible accounts receivable.

b Stacy's Department Store uses the LIFO method in valuing its inventories, while Nichol's Discount Stores uses the FIFO method.

c Morris Construction Co. charged the cost of the Morris family's summer vacation to travel expense.

d ADP Corporation paid $2 million to acquire special-purpose equipment for use in manufacturing its products. As this equipment has virtually no resale value, the entire $2 million was immediately charged to expense.

e Reliable Television sells appliances on 12- or 24-month payment plans. The company uses the installment method of recognizing income in its income tax returns and in its financial statements. Uncollectible accounts consistently range between 2% and 2½% of net sales.

f Innovative Toy Co. has been sued for $20 million as a result of injuries sustained by children from one of its toys. As this lawsuit has not yet been settled, no mention is made of the matter in the company's current financial statements.

g Channel 100 has signed up advertisers willing to pay $4 million for advertising time on an upcoming miniseries. This amount was recorded as revenue at the time that the contracts were signed by the advertisers.

4 Magnum Stereo Co. makes most of its sales on installment plans, allowing customers to make payments over a period from 12 to 48 months. During June of the current year, the company sold for $400,000 merchandise that had cost $220,000. Of the $400,000 in June sales, $52,000 was collected in cash during the month, and the remainder is due on account. In addition, the company collected $300,000 in amounts due on account from installment sales made in prior months. The average gross profit rate on these prior months' installment sales was 48%. Compute the gross profit from installment sales to be recognized in June of the current year. (Ignore interest revenue.)

Computations

$_____

5 Marshall Construction uses the percentage-of-completion method to recognize profit on long-term construction projects. In 1994, the company began work on a three-year project at a contract price of $15,000,000. Throughout 1994 and 1995, the company estimated that the total cost of completing the project would be $9,000,000. From the data below, compute the gross profit to be recognized on this project each year. Also show the total gross profit for the three-year period.

Year	Cost Incurred during the Year	Gross Profit Recognized during the Year
1994	$1,800,000	$_____
1995	6,300,000	_____
1996	980,000	_____
Total	$9,080,000	$_____

SOLUTIONS TO CHAPTER 15 SELF-TEST

True or False

1   T   Making a company's financial statements comparable to those of prior years assists users of the statements in evaluating trends. Making the statements comparable to those of other companies assists users in making efficient resource allocation decisions.

2   T   It is *not possible* for the official literature to address every issue; therefore, many accounting concepts simply evolve from experience and widespread use.

3   F   The most influential source of generally accepted accounting principles today is the Financial Accounting Standards Board (FASB).

4   F   The statement describes the *SEC*, not the FASB. The FASB is a private institution, not a government agency.

5   T   In order for the balance sheet to "balance," that is, for assets to equal liabilities plus owners' equity, the same definition of the accounting entity must be used in defining all three terms.

6   F   The going-concern assumption suggests that a business will continue in operation long enough to use its assets for their intended purposes, thus indicating that immediate liquidation values are not the relevant basis for asset valuation.

7   F   The use of relatively short accounting periods increases the need for estimates and for judgment in, for example, estimating useful lives of assets and evaluating the possible outcomes of pending loss contingencies.

8   T   Assuming a stable dollar means assuming that inflation does not exist. (The FASB recommends disclosing the effects of inflation in notes to the financial statements, but such disclosures are voluntary and are supplementary to the statements themselves.)

9   F   The objectivity principle does favor the use of cost as a basis for valuing plant assets, but it does not eliminate the need for professional judgment in this area. Accountants still exercise professional judgment in estimating the useful lives over which these assets should be depreciated, in selecting depreciation methods, and in determining which expenditures are sufficiently material to be classified as assets rather than being charged to expense.

10   T   Cost provides a more reliable basis for asset valuation than does the estimated market value, because the cost figure can be verified, while market value is largely a matter of opinion. On the other hand, the market value of an asset is often more relevant than its historical cost for making decisions in the current accounting period.

11   F   The realization principle indicates that revenue should not be recognized until (a) the earning process is essentially complete, and (b) objective evidence exists as to the amount of revenue earned.

12   F   Under the installment method, the recognition of profit is delayed until cash is collected from the customer. Also, the method exists primarily for income tax purposes; it is not widely used for financial reporting purposes.

13   T   The percentage-of-completion method of accounting for long-term construction projects is an exception to the realization principle in that profit is recognized during the earning (production) process.

14   F   The matching principle suggests that expenditures should be charged to expense in those periods that the expenditures *help to produce revenue*. Charging R&D expenditures immediately to expense recognizes the expense *before* any related revenue. Thus, the treatment accorded to R&D is an exception to the matching principle, based upon the conclusion that accountants do not have sufficient objective evidence to apply the matching principle to R&D expenditures.

15   F   The consistency principle relates to the accounting methods used by a given company from one accounting period to the next, not to the methods used by different companies within an industry.

16   T   Adequate disclosure means that all material and relevant facts concerning financial position and operating results be communicated to users of the financial statements, even if the relevant events occur after the balance sheet date (but before the financial statements are issued).

17   T   Transactions that are not material are not considered to be of importance to decision makers. Thus, when a transaction is not material, it may be accounted for in the easiest and most convenient manner. (However, accountants must also consider the cumulative effect of all transactions classified as immaterial—this cumulative effect may be a material amount.)

18 F The concept of conservatism suggests that accountants should resolve doubt by selecting those values that lead to the lower financial position and net income for the current. As the Allowance for Doubtful Accounts is a contra-asset account, conservatism would suggest that the controller establish a larger, rather than a smaller, allowance.

19 T The conceptual framework project has produced a broad framework of accounting theory which should provide guidelines to the FASB in developing future accounting standards that are logical and internally consistent.

20 F Materiality is a matter of professional judgment, to be decided on a case-by-case basis. Materiality is based upon the nature of the item as well as upon its dollar amount. Thus, there is no "officially recognized" dollar amount that serves as a "cutoff" for materiality.

21 T The concept of independence is only applicable to ***public accountants*** engaged in ***auditing*** services, not to management accounts working in the internal audit department of their employer.

22 F Although the concept of confidentiality continues to apply even after a client relationship is terminated, the legal obligation to disclose information (for example, in the case of illegal activities harmful to the public) may take precedence over confidentiality either during or after the engagement.

23 F The AICPA and the IMA, two of the largest professional associations of accountants, have adopted and enforce codes of professional conduct for their members. The accounting profession in this regard is ***self-regulated***.

Completion Statements

1 American Institute of Certified Public Accountants, Financial Accounting Standards Board, American Accounting Association, Securities and Exchange Commission.   **2** Going-concern.   **3** Objective, consistency, disclosure.   **4** Cost, market.   **5** During production, when production is complete, when the sale is made, when cash is collected from customers.   **6** Public accounting, management accountants.

Multiple Choice

1 Answer **b**—due to the need for estimates in accounting, financial statements are always somewhat tentative in nature. Because the statements are based upon selected accounting concepts, such as the use of cost as the basis for asset valuation, they cannot be relevant to all possible types of business decisions.

2 Answer **b**—the Internal Revenue Service concerns itself with methods of accounting suitable for income tax purposes, and not generally accepted accounting principles.

3 Answer **b**—in the case of an enterprise that is about to liquidate, the going-concern assumption is dropped, and assets are reported at their current liquidation values.

4 Answer **c**—the stable-dollar assumption disregards the purchasing power of money. In periods of inflation, a sale of an item at a price greater than its original cost will result in an accounting "gain," even though the amount received may represent less "buying power" than the amount originally paid.

5 Answer **c**—revenue is recognized when the earning process is essentially complete and objective evidence exists as to the amount of revenue earned. At the time a sale is made, the business has essentially completed the earning process and the sales value of the goods can be measured objectively.

6 Answer **d**—the cost principle requires that assets be initially recorded in the account at cost, and that no adjustment be made to this valuation in later periods, except to allocate a portion of the original cost to expense as the assets expire.

7 Answer **c**—since 30% of the work was completed during the first year ($2,400,000 cost incurred ÷ $8,000,000 estimated total cost = 30%), 30% of the estimated total profit of $4,000,000 is considered earned ($4,000,000 × 30% = $1,200,000).

8 Answer **a**—preparing a year-end adjusting entry to record accrued interest payable is a highly objective and mechanical computation, requiring little professional judgment. The other decisions all involve selecting from a number of acceptable alternatives and, therefore, do require professional judgment.

9 Answer **b**—the concept of confidentiality prohibits disclosing sensitive information about a client company to the company's competitors or to other outsiders, as well as using that information for the CPA's personal gain.

10 Answer **d**—independence is an ethical concept pertaining only to public accountants engaged in auditing activities; it does not apply to public accountants performing income tax work or other accounting services, nor does it apply to management accountants.

11 Answer **a**—both the AICPA and the IMA have incorporated these two concepts into their codes of ethics applicable to all aspects of accounting services performed. The concept of independence prohibits only public accountants engaged in auditing a company from owning stock in that company.

Solutions to Exercises

1
a Consistency
b Realization principle
c Matching principle
d None (The statement refers to the time-period principle.)
e Materiality
f Disclosure principle
g None (The statement refers to the going-concern assumption.)

2

	Assets	Liabilities	Owners' Equity
a	NE	NE	NE
b	D	NE	D
c	NE	NE	NE
d	I	NE	I
e	NE	NE	NE
f	I	NE	I
g	D	NE	D

3
a Matching
b None (Consistency refers to successive years, not to different companies.)
c Entity
d Matching (also the going-concern assumption, which is not listed as an answer)
e Realization (The revenue was realized at the date of sale.)
f Disclosure
g Realization (The revenue will not be realized until the ads are aired.)

4

Gross profit rate on June installment sales [($400,000 – $220,000) ÷ 400,000]	45%
Gross profit realized in June on June installment sales ($52,000 × 45%)	$23,400
Gross profit realized in June on installment sales from prior months ($300,000 collected × 48% gross profit rate)	144,000
Total gross profit recognized in June under the installment method	$167,400

5

Year		Profit Consideration Earned
1994	$1,200,000	[($15,000,000 – $9.000,000) × $1,800,000/$9,000,000]
1995	4,200,000	($6,000,000 × $6,3000,000/$9,000,000)
1996	520,000	($15,000,000 – $9,080,000 – $1,200,000 – $4,200,000)
Total	$5,920,000	($15,000,000 – $9,080,000)

HIGHLIGHTS OF THE APPENDIX

1 In Appendix A, we present the 1993 annual report of Toys "R" Us, a publicly owned corporation. Throughout the text—and notably in Comprehensive Problem 3—we refer to elements of this report. You should view this annual report as *reference material*; do not memorize it, learn how to *locate information* within it.

   The coverage of Appendix A in this *Study Guide* includes "Highlights," but no "Test Yourself" section.

2 There are numerous elements to an annual report. The major ones are described briefly in the following paragraphs. These paragraphs follow the sequence in which these items appear in the Toys "R" Us report.

3 **Financial Highlights** (A–1) This section provides a ten-year summary of key financial statistics. It is useful in quickly identifying important trends.

4 **To Our Stockholders** (A–2 through A–5) This is a letter to the stockholders from the Company's chief executive officer. It tells you much about the Company, but primarily the information that management *wants* to make known. **Management's Discussion**, discussed below, contains similar information, but in more objective terms.

5 **Management's Discussion—Results of Operations and Financial Condition.** In this section, management discusses in objective and quantitative terms the issues affecting the Company's operations and liquidity.

6 **Consolidated Financial Statements** (A–7 through A–10) Toys "R" Us presents the four basic financial statements discussed in this text. They show balance sheets as of the beginning and end of the current year. The statements of earnings (income statements),

cash flow, and stockholders' equity cover the last three years. (Like most companies, Toys "R" Us uses as Statement of Stockholders' Equity in lieu of a statement of retained earnings.) All of these financial statements have been audited by the firm of Ernst & Young.

7 The word "Consolidated" appearing at the top of each financial statement indicates that the statements include the operating results and financial position of the Company's subsidiaries—that is, other companies owned by Toys "R" Us. The largest of these subsidiaries is Kids "R" Us, a chain of children's clothing stores.

8 **Notes to Consolidated Financial Statements** (A–11 through A–14) These "notes" disclose information necessary to the proper *interpretation* of the financial statements. They should be viewed as an *integral part* of the statements. They too have been audited.

9 **Report of Management** (A–15) This short report describes management's responsibility for the financial information contained in the annual report. Management is *primarily* responsible for the reliability and completeness of this information.

10 **Report of Independent Auditors** (A–15) In this section of the annual report, an independent firm of Certified Public Accountants (CPAs) express their professional opinion as to the *fairness* of the financial statements contained in the annual report. The CPAs also have reviewed the other elements of the annual report, and consider them to be consistent with the information contained in the financial statements.

11 As stated earlier, we do not provide a "Test-Yourself" section for Appendix A.

APPENDIX B
MANUAL SPECIAL JOURNALS

HIGHLIGHTS OF THE APPENDIX

1 The accounting record in which transactions first are recorded is called a *journal*. In illustrations throughout this text, we illustrate transactions in the form of *general journal entries*. These entries are well suited to textbook illustrations because they may be used to illustrate the effects of any kind of transaction. The general journal, however, would be a very *inefficient* way of recording transactions in an actual accounting system.

2 Devices designed for recording transactions efficiently are called *special journals*. The term is derived from the phrase "special-purpose journals," because a special journal is designed to efficiently record *only one type* of transaction.

3 Special journals increase efficiency by reducing the amount of writing involved in the recording of transactions and also by reducing the amount of posting required. Only one person can use a journal at one time. By using many special journals, a business can divide the task of recording transactions among many employees.

4 Many special journals are machines, such as cash registers, point-of-sale terminals, and computers. However, all businesses also have various *manual* special journals—that is, accounting records specifically designed for efficiently recording transactions by hand. Often manual special journals serve as a backup for use whenever the computer-based system is "down."

5 The most common form of manual special journal is the *check register* found inside

every checkbook. This check register enables the person writing the check to efficiently record cash transactions affecting that checking account.

6 Special journals should be used in recording any type of transaction which *occurs frequently*. These journals also are designed to fit the needs of a *particular business entity*. In the remainder of this appendix, we will consider four manual special journals which might be used by a small merchandising company. Many of the concepts illustrated in the use of these manual special journals also are applicable to computer-based systems.

7 The four special journals discussed in the appendix, and the types of transactions recorded in each of these journals, are summarized below:

Special Journal	Transactions Recorded
Sales journal	Sales of merchandise on account
Purchases journal	Purchases of merchandise on account
Cash receipts journal	All transactions involving the receipt of cash
Cash payments journal	All transactions involving the payment of cash

Our illustration assumes that a *periodic* inventory system is in use.

8 These four special journals may be used for recording, say, 90% or more of a small company's transactions. The business also must maintain a *general journal*, however, for recording transactions which do not "fit" any of the special journals. For example, none of the special journals described above could be used for recording adjusting entries or closing entries.

9 The *sales journal* is used for recording *all sales on account*. This journal requires only one "money column," that is, only one column for recording dollar amounts. It also has columns for recording such additional data as the transaction date, customer account name (or number), invoice number, and discount terms.

10 The dollar amount entered in the single money column represents *both* a debit to Accounts Receivable *and* a credit to Sales. This amount is posted promptly to the customer's account in the accounts receivable *subsidiary ledger*. At month-end, only the *column total* is posted to the general ledger as a debit to Accounts Receivable and a credit to Sales.

11 A business may use many sales journals—one at each location where credit sales occur. Thus, the work of recording routine sales transactions is spread over many people (salesclerks) and does not require specialized accounting skills.

12 A *purchases journal* is used to record all *purchases of merchandise on account*. Again, only one money column is required. At month-end, this column is totaled and the total is posted to the general ledger as a debit to Purchases and a credit to Accounts Payable. During the month, the individual transaction amounts are posted promptly as credits to the individual supplier's accounts in the accounts payable *subsidiary ledger*.

13 A *cash receipts journal* is used for recording any transaction which involves the *receipt of cash*. In these transactions, the Cash account always is debited, but many other accounts also may be debited or credited. Therefore, a cash receipts journal has *several money columns*. Separate columns are maintained for Cash and for any other accounts *frequently* debited or credited, such as Sales, Sales Discounts, and Accounts Receivable. In addition, columns must be provided for writing in the titles of any other accounts involved in a cash transaction and entering the amounts debited or credited to these "other accounts."

14 Every entry in the Accounts Receivable credit column is posted to the Accounts Receivable subsidiary ledger. Debits and credits in the Other Accounts columns are posted to the general ledger either daily or at convenient intervals. The totals of every column relating to a specific general ledger account are posted to the general ledger at the end of the month.

15 A *cash payments journal* is used for recording transactions involving *cash payments*. Separate money columns are established for Cash and for any account debited or credited frequently, such as Accounts Payable. Debit and credit columns also are provided for "other accounts," so that any account title involved in the transaction may be written in. The posting process is similar to that described for the cash receipts journal in Highlight **14** above.

16 Before column totals are posted at month-end, both the cash receipts journal and the cash payments journal should be *cross-footed*. That is, the sum of the debit column totals in the journal should be agreed to the sum of the credit column totals.

17 As stated earlier, a general journal must be maintained for recording those transactions which do not fit the format of any of the special journals.

18 *Posting references* provide a cross reference between entries in ledgers and journals. In the ledger, we use the following symbols to indicate the journal from which an entry was posted: *S*, sales journal; *P*, purchase journal; *CR*, cash receipts journal; *CP*, cash payments journal; and *J*, general journal. This reference is followed by the journal page number on which the entry appears.

19 Remember, special journals are designed to *suit the needs of a particular business*. Therefore, many variations occur in the design of these journals and in types of special journals in use.

TEST YOURSELF ON MANUAL SPECIAL JOURNALS

True or False

For each of the following statements, circle the T or the F to indicate whether the statement is true or false.

T F   1 Special journals are used for recording special types of transactions which occur infrequently.

T F   2 A business with a computer-based accounting system is not likely to have manual special journals.

T F 3 The number of special journals in use and the design of these journals varies from one business to the next.

T F 4 A check register is a special journal suited to recording both cash disbursements and cash receipts.

T F 5 Special journals reduce the amount of posting required, as well as the time involved in recording transactions.

Questions 6 through 13 are based upon the formats of the four special journals discussed in this appendix.

T F 6 The amount entered in a "one-column" sales journal represents both a debit to Cost of Goods Sold and a credit to Sales.

T F 7 A "one-column" purchases journal is used to record credit purchases of merchandise, supplies, and plant assets.

T F 8 Special journal entries affecting the balances of subsidiary ledger accounts generally are posted promptly to those subsidiary ledger accounts.

T F 9 Special journal entries affecting the balances of general ledger controlling accounts generally are posted promptly to those controlling accounts.

T F 10 The cash payments journal and cash receipts journal require columns for debiting or crediting "other accounts."

T F 11 The sale of merchandise for a 10% cash down payment, with the balance due in 30 days, would be recorded in the sales journal.

T F 12 At month-end, the total of the Cash column in a cash receipts journal is posted as a credit to the Cash account in the general ledger.

T F 13 The total of the Other Accounts column in a cash payments journal is posted at month-end to a general ledger account.

T F 14 When manual special journals are in use, a subsidiary ledger should be in agreement with the related controlling account throughout the month.

T F 15 If a company uses a perpetual inventory system, an additional money column should be added to the sales journal.

Completion Statements

Fill in the necessary words to complete the following statements:

1 Special journals have the advantage of saving much time in journalizing and _____.

2 When merchandise is purchased on credit, the transaction is recorded in the _____ journal. If a portion of the merchandise is returned for credit to the supplier, the return is recorded in the _____ journal and the _____ side of the entry is double-posted.

3 The column total of the sales journal is posted at the end of the month as a _____ to _____ _____ and as a _____ to _____.

4 The symbol (X) placed below a column total in the cash receipts journal or cash payments journal means the column total should _____ _____ _____.

5 A business will usually benefit by establishing a special journal for any type of transaction that _____ _____.

Multiple Choice

Choose the best answer for each of the following questions and enter the identifying letter in the space provided.

_____ **1** The total of a single-column purchases journal is posted at the end of the month:
a As a debit to Accounts Payable and a credit to Purchases.
b To the Purchases account, Cash account, and Sales account.
c To the Purchases account only.
d As a debit to Purchases and a credit to Accounts Payable.

_____ **2** The Rex Company records all transactions in a two-column general journal but is considering the installation of special journals. The number of sales on credit during January was 325 and the number of sales for cash was 275. Therefore:
a The use of a sales journal in January would have saved 324 postings to the Sales account.
b The use of a cash receipts journal would have reduced the number of postings to the Cash account but would not have affected the number of postings to the Sales account.
c The total number of transactions recorded in the sales journal (if one had been used in January) would have been 600, but only two postings would have been necessary from that journal.

d If special journals were installed, the entry to close the Sales and Purchases accounts at the end of the period would be made in the sales journal and the purchases journal, respectively.

_____ **3** The purchases journal is a book of original entry used to record:
a Purchase of any asset on credit.
b Purchase of merchandise for cash or on credit.
c Purchase of merchandise on credit only.
d Purchases and purchase returns and allowances.

_____ **4** When a general journal and four special journals are in use, the entries in the Cash account will come:
a From all of the book of original entry.
b From the four special journals.
c From only two of the four special journals.
d Principally at month-end from adjusting and closing entries.

_____ **5** The cash receipts journal is used:
a For transactions involving a debit to Cash and credits to other balance sheets accounts.
b For all transactions involving the receipt of cash, regardless of the number of other accounts involved.
c For transactions involving not more than two accounts.
d For transactions involving the receipt of cash but not affecting subsidiary ledgers.

Exercises

1 For each of the following transactions, indicate the journal which should be used by placing the appropriate symbol in the space provided. *S* = sales journal; *P* = purchases journal; *CR* = cash receipts journal; *CP* = cash payments journal; *J* = general journal.

a Sold merchandise on credit ....
b Purchased merchandise for cash ....
c Purchased truck for cash for use in business ......
d Collected account receivable and allowed a cash discount ....
e Recorded depreciation for the period ....
f Made entry to close the expense accounts at end of period ....
g Accepted note receivable from customer in settlement of account receivable ....
h Paid employee salaries ....
i Made entry to accrue salaries at end of year ......
j Sold merchandise for cash ....
k Purchased merchandise on credit ....
l Returned merchandise to supplier for credit ....
m Purchased office equipment on credit ....
n Allowed customer to return merchandise for credit ....

2 For each of the following general ledger accounts indicate the source of debit and credit posting by entering a symbol representing the proper journal. Use the same code as in Exercise 1.

	Debit	Credit
a Purchases		
b Purchase Returns and Allowances		
c Purchase Discounts		
d Sales		
e Sales Returns and Allowances		
f Sales Discounts		
g Accounts Payable		
h Accounts Receivable		
i Cash		
j Depreciation Expense		

3 Collins Company uses a sales journal to record all sales of merchandise on account. During July the following transactions were recorded in this journal:

Sales Journal

Date		Account Debited	Invoice No.	√	Amount
July	6	Robert Baker	923		3,600
	15	Minden Company	924		8,610
	17	Pell & Warden	925		1,029
	26	Stonewall Corporation	926		17,500
	27	Robert Baker	927		3,000
					33,739

Entries in the general journal during July include one for the return of merchandise by a customer, as follows:

General Journal

Date			LP	Debit	Credit
July	18	Sales Return and Allowances		500	
		Accounts Receivable (Minden Company)			500
		Allowed credit to customer for return of			
		merchandise from sale of July 15.			

a Post to the following subsidiary ledger accounts (in T-account form) the appropriate entries from the sales journal and general journal. Make appropriate references in the journals to indicate completion of the posting process.

SUBSIDIARY LEDGER FOR ACCOUNTS RECEIVABLE

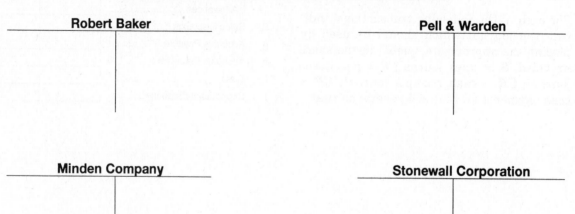

Robert Baker	Pell & Warden

Minden Company	Stonewall Corporation

b Post to the following general ledger accounts (in T-account form) the appropriate entries from the sales journal and the general journal. Insert appropriate posting references in the journals.

GENERAL LEDGER

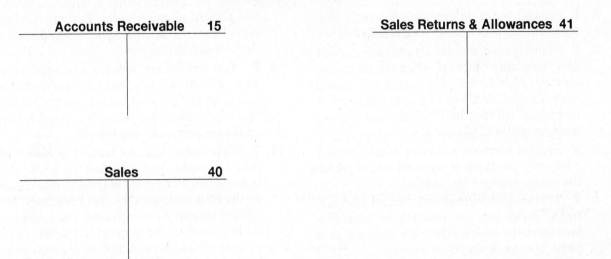

Accounts Receivable 15		Sales Returns & Allowances 41

Sales   40

c Prepare a schedule of accounts receivable at July 31 to prove that the subsidiary ledger is in agreement with the controlling account.

COLLINS COMPANY
Schedule of Accounts Receivable
July 31, 19__

Robert Baker	$
Minden Company	
Pell & Warden	
Stonewall Corporation	
Total (per balance of controlling account)	$

SOLUTIONS TO APPENDIX B SELF-TEST

True or False

1 F Special journals are used for recording transactions which occur *frequently*.

2 F Manual special journals still are needed as a temporary "backup" when the computer system "goes down." Some manual special journals such as check registers are used in recording transactions which occur away from computer input devices.

3 T Special journals are designed to record efficiently the types of transactions in which the entity engages frequently.

4 T This special journal includes all transactions—whether cash receipts or cash disbursements—which affect the balance in a particular bank checking account.

5 T Often many transactions can be posted as a single-column total.

6 F In a one-column sales journal, the amount entered represents a debit to *Accounts Receivable* and a credit to Sales.

7 F In a "one-column" journal, the amount entered is always a debit to one specific ledger account and a credit to another specific account. In the case of a one-column purchases journal, the amount is a debit to the Purchases account (assuming a periodic inventory system) and a credit to Accounts Payable. Thus, the journal records only purchases of *merchandise* on account. The journal could be designed to also record credit purchases of supplies and plant assets, but this would require the use of additional money columns.

8 T Subsidiary ledgers are kept continuously up-to-date, as these account balances often are needed in daily business operations.

9 F Posting to general ledger controlling accounts often are performed at monthly (or other convenient) intervals, as these balances are used primarily in financial statements and other periodic reports. Posting many transactions to the general ledger account in the form of a single-column total is one of the efficiencies of special journals.

10 T These journals are used in recording transactions which may involve debits or credits to almost any ledger account.

11 F Any transaction involving the receipt of cash is recorded in the *cash receipts journal*.

12 F The total of the Cash column in the cash receipts journal represents *receipts* of cash and is posted as a *debit* to the Cash account.

13 F The total of the Other Accounts column is *not posted* at month-end. Rather, the individual entries in this column are posted as the transactions occur.

14 F The subsidiary ledgers are kept up-to-date on a daily basis, but the controlling accounts in the general ledger are not brought up-to-date until the special journal column totals are posted at month-end.

15 T This money column is used to record the cost of goods sold relating to each sales transaction. Individual entries in this column are posted promptly to the inventory subsidiary ledger. At month-end, the column total is posted to the general ledger as a debit to Cost of Goods Sold and as a credit to the Inventory controlling account.

Completion Statements

1 Posting. **2** Purchases, general, debit. **3** Debit, Accounts Receivable, credit, Sales. **4** Not be posted. **5** Occurs frequently.

Multiple Choice

1 Answer **d**—the purchases journal is used to record purchases of merchandise on credit. At the end of the month a single debit to Purchases and a single credit to Accounts Payable are made. During the month (daily usually), individual postings are made to the Accounts Payable subsidiary ledger.

2 Answer **a**—a sales journal would be used for credit sales. Individual postings of each sale are necessary to the Accounts Receivable subsidiary ledger, but a single total of all sales for the month is posted at the end of the month instead of 325 individual credits to the Sales account.

3 Answer **c**—the purchases journal is used for purchases of *merchandise* on *credit* only. Purchases of other assets on credit are recorded in the general journal; purchase returns and allowances are recorded in the general journal also. Purchases of merchandise for cash are recorded in the cash payments journal.

4 Answer **c**—debits to the Cash account are due to receipt of cash; transactions involving the receipt of cash are recorded in the cash receipts journal. Credits to the Cash account are due to payments of cash; transactions involving payment of cash are recorded in the cash payments journal.

5 Answer **b**—the cash receipts journal is used for any and all transactions involving the receipt of cash. The cash receipts journal can accommodate any number of other accounts involved in the transaction.

Solutions to Exercises

1

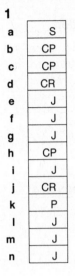

a	S
b	CP
c	CP
d	CR
e	J
f	J
g	J
h	CP
i	J
j	CR
k	P
l	J
m	J
n	J

2

	Debit	Credit
a	P, CP	J
b	J	J, CR
c	J	CP
d	J	S, CR
e	J, CP	J
f	CR	J
g	J, CP	P, J
h	S	CR, J
i	CR	CP
j	J	J

3

Sales Journal

Date		Account Debited	Invoice No.	√	Amount
July	6	Robert Baker	923	√	3,600
	15	Minden Company	924	√	8,610
	17	Pell & Warden	925	√	1,029
	26	Stonewall Corporation	926	√	17,500
	27	Robert Baker	927	√	3,000
					33,739
					(15)(40)

General Journal

Date			LP	Debit	Credit
July	18	Sales Return and Allowances	41	500	
		Accounts Receivable (Minden Company)	15/√		500
		Allowed credit to customer for return of			
		merchandise from sale of July 15.			

a

SUBSIDIARY LEDGER FOR ACCOUNTS RECEIVABLE

Robert Baker				Pell & Warden		
July	6	3,600		July 17	1,029	
July	27	3,000				

Minden Company					Stonewall Corporation		
July	15	8,610	July 18	500	July 26	17,500	

b

GENERAL LEDGER

Accounts Receivable			15		Sales Returns & Allowances		41
July		33,739	July 18	500	July 18	500	

Sales		40
	July	33,739

c

COLLINS COMPANY
Schedule of Accounts Receivable
July 31, 19__

Robert Baker	$6,600
Minden Company	8,110
Pell & Warden	1,029
Stonewall Corporation	17,500
Total (per balance of controlling account)	$33,239

APPENDIX C

APPLICATIONS OF PRESENT VALUE

HIGHLIGHTS OF THE APPENDIX

1 The *present value* of a future amount is the amount that a knowledgeable investor would pay *today* for the right to receive the future amount. The present value is always *less than* the future amount, because money on hand today can be invested to become *equivalent to a larger amount in the future*. The difference between a future amount and its present value may be regarded as interest revenue (or expense) included in the future amount

2 The present value of a future amount depends upon (a) the estimated *amount* of the future cash receipt (or payment), (b) the *length of time* until the future amount will be received (or paid), and (c) the *rate of return* required by the investor. The required rate of return is called the *discount rate* and depends upon the amount of *risk* associated with the investment opportunity and upon the return available from alternative investment opportunities.

3 Computing the present value of a future cash flow is called *discounting* the future amount. The easiest method of discounting a future amount is by the use of *present value tables*. Your textbook includes present value tables which show (a) the present value of a single, lump sum amount to be received at a future date and (b) the present value of a series of equal-sized periodic cash flows, called an *annuity*.

4 The use of present value tables can be demonstrated by finding the present value of $800 to be received annually for 10 years, discounted at an annual rate of 12%. Since this is a series of 10 *equal-sized* payments, the *annuity* table in the textbook is applicable. The present value of $1 received annually for 10 years, discounted at 12%, is *5.650*, meaning $5.65. Therefore, the present value of the $800 annuity is $800 × 5.650, or *$4,520*.

5 The interval between regular periodic cash flows is termed the *discount period*. Annual cash flows involve discount periods of one year; in these situations, the annual rate of interest is used as the *discount rate*. When the periodic cash flows occur on a more frequent basis, such as monthly, the discount rate must be expressed as a monthly interest rate. For example, an annual rate of 18% must be expressed as a monthly rate of $1\frac{1}{2}$% when the cash flows occur monthly. *The discount rate must relate to the time interval of the discount period.*

6 The concept of present value has many applications in accounting, including the valuation of certain assets and liabilities, determining the portions of certain cash flows that represent payment or receipt of interest, and evaluating investment opportunities. Many of these applications are discussed below.

7 Accountants use the term *financial instruments* to describe cash, equity investments in another business, and any contracts calling for the receipt or payment of cash. Examples include cash, accounts receivable, investments in marketable securities, and all common liabilities except for unearned revenue and deferred income taxes.

8 Whenever the present value of a financial instrument *differs* significantly from the sum of the expected future cash flows, the financial instrument initially is recorded in the accounting records at its *present value*. Differences between this recorded present

value and the actual future cash flows are accounted for as interest.

Assume, for example, a company borrows $10,000 for one year, signing a $10,000, 9% note payable. The cash outlay at the maturity date will be $10,900. But the note originally is recorded as a *$10,000* liability—an amount equal to its present value at the date of issuance. The other $900 will be treated as interest expense.

9 In the preceding illustration, the terms of the note clearly distinguish between the principal amount (a present value) and interest. In other cases, however, the present value of the obligation must be *computed*.

10 Consider, for example, *capital lease agreements* (capital leases are discussed in Chapter 11). When an asset is "sold" under a capital lease, the lessor records a receivable equal to the present value of the future lease payments, and the lessee records this present value as a liability. The present value of the future lease payments is computed by discounting these payments at a realistic interest rate.

11 Companies sometimes issue notes payable which make no mention of an interest charge. The present value of such "non-interest-bearing" notes can be determined either by present value computations or, sometimes, by appraising the consideration received in exchange. If this present value is substantially *less* than the payments to be made on the note, the note should be recorded at its *present value*. The excess of the future payments over this present value will be treated as interest expense.

12 Short-term financial instruments, such as normal accounts receivable and accounts payable, usually appear in financial statements at their face amounts. Technically, these face amounts are future values. But because these instruments mature in a matter of a few weeks, the difference between their present value and face amount usually is not material.

13 Present values increase over time toward the actual amount of the future cash flow. Also, present values may fluctuate because of changes in the market interest rate, which is used as the discount rate. The present value of a financial instrument at a particular date after its issuance is called its *current value*.

14 Some financial instruments (cash, investments in marketable securities, and postre-tirement obligations) are *adjusted to their current value* at the end of each accounting period. For other financial instruments, the current value should be *disclosed* if it differs significantly from the carrying value shown in the financial statements.

Obligations for postretirement benefits are shown at the *estimated present value* of the future benefit payments earned by employees during the current and prior accounting periods. Because these benefits will be paid many years in the future, their present value is *much less* than the expected future outlays. (Accounting for postretirement costs is discussed in Chapter 11.)

15 If postretirement benefits are *fully funded*, the employer recognizes an expense equal to the present value of the future payments, and pays this amount to the trustee of the pension plan. The trustee invests these funds so that the pension plan grows over time to an amount that will cover the future payments to employees.

16 If the postretirement benefits are *unfunded*, the employer recognizes the present value of the expected future payments both as an expense and as a liability. Over time, this liability increases to the actual amounts that will be paid. This annual growth in the unfunded liability is a form of interest expense. (However, this "interest expense" appears in financial statements as an element of the company's annual "postretirement benefits expense.)

17 The only long-term liability *not* recorded in financial statements at its present value is deferred income taxes payable. This is because there is no "contract" determining the amount or payment date of deferred taxes. However, many accountants believe that deferred tax liabilities are *overstated* because they are not discounted to their present value.

18 Present value computations often are used in *capital budgeting* decisions. In this context, comparing the estimated present values of future cash receipts and payments indicates whether or not the proposed investment will earn a rate of return at least equal to the discount rate.

TEST YOURSELF ON APPLICATIONS OF PRESENT VALUE

True or False

For each of the following statements, circle the T or the F to indicate whether the statement is true or false.

T F 1 The present value of an amount to be paid or received in the future is always less than the future amount.

T F 2 The discount rate used in computing the present value of a future cash receipt may be viewed as the investor's required rate of return.

T F 3 Using a higher discount rate results in a higher present value.

T F 4 The longer the length of time until a future amount will be received, the lower its present value.

T F 5 The concept of present value is applicable to future cash receipts, but not to future cash payments.

T F 6 All the factors in table showing the present value of $1 to be received in *n* periods are less than 1.000.

T F 7 The interest rate shown in a present value table must be interpreted as annual rates, even if the time interval of the discount period is only a month.

T F 8 Both accounts receivable and accounts payable are examples of *financial instruments*.

T F 9 Financial instruments initially are recorded in the accounting records at their present values whenever these present values differ substantially from the expected future cash receipts or outlays.

T F 10 At every balance sheet date, the carrying values of all financial instruments are adjusted to their current values.

T F 11 An actuary estimates that because of their services during the current year, employees have earned the right to receive payments totaling approximately $5 million over the period of their retirement. The pension expense for the current year amounts to $5 million, but the employer will report no liability if the pension plan is fully funded.

T F 12 When the net present value of a proposed capital expenditure is zero, the proposal provides no return on investment.

T F 13 When equipment is purchased in exchange for a "non-interest-bearing" installment note payable, the cost to be recorded is equal to the present value of the note.

T F 14 The market price of a bond may be regarded as a present value, whereas the maturity value of the bond is a future value.

T F 15 The present value of $1,000 to be received annually for five years is greater than $1,000 but less than $5,000.

Completion Statements

Fill in the necessary words or amounts to complete the following statements:

1 The process of determining the present value of a future cash receipt or payment is termed _____ the future cash flow.

2 The basic premise of the _____ _____ concept is that a dollar available today is worth (more, less) _____ than a dollar that will not be available until a future date.

3 The present value of a future cash flow depends upon three things: (a) the estimated _____ _____ of the future cash flow, (b) the _____ ____ _____ until the cash flow will occur, and (c) the _____ _____ used in computing the present value.

4 An *annuity* is a series of periodic cash flows that are _____ in dollar amount.

5 Present value tables may be used with discount periods of any length, but the _____ _____ must apply to the period of time represented by one discount period.

6 Super Store borrowed $30,000 from First Bank by issuing a six-month note payable in the face amount of $31,200. At the date the loan is made, the present value of Super Store's liability to the bank is $_____; the difference between this amount and $31,200 represents _____ included in the face amount of the note.

7 The market price of bonds may be regarded as the present value to bondholders of the future _____ and _____ payments to be received.

Multiple Choice

Choose the best answer for each of the following questions and enter the identifying letter in the space provided.

_____ **1** The present value concept is based on the premise that:

a A cash flow that will not occur until a future date is equivalent to a smaller amount of money receivable or payable today.

b The present value of a future cash flow is greater than the actual amount of the future cash flow, because money on hand today is more valuable than money due at a future date.

c Money invested today can be expected to become equivalent to a smaller amount at a future date.

d The present value of a future cash flow may be greater or smaller than the future amount, depending upon the discount rate.

_____ **2** Which of the following factors does **not** affect computation of the present value of a future cash flow?

a The discount rate.

b The period of time until the future cash flow will occur.

c Whether the future cash flow will be a cash payment or a cash receipt.

d The dollar amount of the future cash flow.

_____ **3** The present value of $121 due in two years, discounted at an annual rate of 10% is:

a $91.90.

b $96.80.

c $100.

d $110.

_____ **4** Wine Country Safari purchased a hot-air balloon on a contract requiring 24 monthly payments of $730, with no mention of interest. An appropriate annual rate of interest for financing the purchase of the balloon would be 12%. To determine the cost of the balloon and the present value of the contract payable, Wine Country Safari should discount:

a $730 for 24 periods at 12%.

b $17,520 for two periods at 12%.

c $730 for 24 periods at 1%.

d $17,520 for two periods at 6%.

_____ **5** The present value of $1,000 due in five years, discounted at an annual rate of 12%, is $567. If this $1,000 future amount had been discounted at an annual rate of 15%, the present value would have been:

a $497.

b $582.

c $621.

d $747.

_____ **6** The present value of $500 due in five years, discounted at an annual interest rate of 10% is $311. If the $500 is due in six years, rather than five, its present value would be approximately:

a $282.

b $311.

c $374.

d $500.

_____ **7** Present value techniques are **not** used to determine the financial statement valuation of:

a Long-term notes payable with interest charges included in the face amount.

b The long-term liability for deferred income taxes.

c A long-term note payable with no stated interest rate.

d The liability arising from entering into a long-term capital lease.

Exercises

1 Listed below are six technical accounting terms introduced or emphasized in this appendix:

Discount rate	_Present value table_
Annuity	_Discount period_
Present value	_Annuity table_

Each of the following statements may (or may not) describe one of these technical terms. In the space provided below each statement, indicate the accounting term described, or answer "None" if the statement does not correctly describe any of the terms.

a The interval between regular periodic cash flows.

_____

b A table that shows the present value of $1 to be received periodically for a given number of periods.

_____

c An investor's required rate of return.

_____

d The amount that a knowledgeable investor would pay today to receive a certain amount in the future.

_____

e A series of equal-sized periodic cash flows.

_____

2 Use the present value table in your textbook to determine the present value of the following cash flows:

a $10,000 to be received annually for seven years, discounted at an annual rate of 15%.

b $4,250 to be received today, assuming that money can be invested to earn an annual return of 12%.

c $400 to be paid monthly for 24 months, with an additional "balloon payment" of $10,000 at the end of the 24th month, discounted at a monthly interest rate of $1\frac{1}{2}$%.

3 On November 1, Airport Transport purchased a new van by making a cash down payment of $3,000 and issuing an installment note payable in the face amount of $12,000. The note is payable in 24 monthly installments of $500 each, beginning on December 1. The following statement appears at the bottom of the note payable: "The $12,000 face amount of this note includes interest charges computed at a rate of $1\frac{1}{2}$% per month."

In the space provided below, prepare the journal entries needed on (a) November 1 to record the purchase of the van, and (b) December 1 to record the first $500 monthly payment and to recognize interest expense for one month by the effective interest method. (Round interest expense to the nearest dollar.)

General Journal			
Nov. 1	Vehicles		
Dec. 1			

SOLUTIONS TO APPENDIX C SELF-TEST

True or False

1 **T** The amount by which the future cash receipt exceeds its present value represents the investor's profit.

2 **T** Factors affecting the investor's required rate of return are the degree of risk associated with a particular investment, the investor's cost of capital, and the returns available from other investment opportunities.

3 **F** The higher the discount rate used, the lower the present value.

4 **T** Cash of $100 to be received in three years has smaller value today than $100 to be received next week.

5 **F** The process of discounting cash flows applies to both cash receipts and cash payments.

6 **T** The present value of an amount is always less than the future amount.

7 **F** Present value tables can be used with discount periods of *any length*; the discount rate shown is the *rate per period*.

8 **T** The term *financial instruments* describes cash, equity investments in other businesses, and contracts calling for the receipt or payment of cash. This latter category includes both receivables and payables.

9 **T** The difference between this present value and the future cash flows is accounted for either as interest revenue or interest expense.

10 **F** The carrying values of *some financial instruments* (investments in marketable securities and liabilities for postretirement costs) are adjusted to their current values at each balance sheet date, but the carrying values of other financial instruments are not. For these other instruments, the current values usually are *disclosed* in notes accompanying the financial statements.

11 **F** The pension expense for the current year will be *substantially less* than $5 million. The $5 million is an estimate of cash payments that will be made many years in the future. The pension expense for the current period is equal to the *present value* of these future payments.

12 **F** When the net present value is zero, the proposed investment provides a rate of return equal to the rate used in discounting the cash flows.

13 **T** The negotiated purchase price is the present value of the note payable; part of each payment constitutes interest expense.

14 **T** The market price is the price investors are willing to pay *today* (present value) for the future *principal and interest payments.*

15 **T** The present value of *each* $1,000 receipt is less than $1,000; therefore, the present value of five such payments is less than $5,000.

Completion Statements

1 Discounting. **2** Present value, more. **3(a)** Dollar amount, **(b)** length of time (or number of periods), **(c)** discount rate. **4** Uniform (or equal). **5** Discount rate. **6** $30,000; interest. **7** Principal (or maturity value), interest.

Multiple Choice

1 Answer **a**—a present value is always *less* than the future amount. Answers **b** and **d** are incorrect, because they both state that a present value is greater than the future amount. Answer **c** is incorrect, because money invested today should earn interest and thereby become equivalent to a larger amount in the future.

2 Answer **c**—three factors involved in computing the present value of a future amount: (1) the size of the future amount, (2) the period of time until the future cash flow will occur, and (3) the discount rate. Whether the future amount is a cash receipt or a cash payment is *not* relevant.

3 Answer **c**—($121 ÷ 1.10 ÷ 1.10 = $100).

4 Answer **c**—the discount rate must relate to the discount period. As we are using *monthly* discount periods, we must state the interest rate as a monthly rate.

5 Answer **a**—$497. You need not compute this amount to answer the question. Use of a higher discount rate results in a *lower* present value. Only answer **a** is lower than the original present value of $567.

6 Answer **a**—$282. You need not compute this amount to answer the question. The longer the time until a future cash flow will occur, the *smaller* its present value. Only answer **a** is lower than the original present value of $311.

7 Answer **b**—The liability for deferred income taxes is the *only* long-term liability to which present value concepts are not applied. This obligation is not a *financial instrument*, because there is no "contract" for payment. Tax laws may change at any time. Because of the uncertainty as to future tax rates and payment dates, no effort is made to reduce the deferred tax obligation to its present value. Many accountants believe that current practices can cause this liability to be substantially *overstated*.

Solutions to Exercises

1
a Discount period
b Annuity table
c Discount rate
d Present value
e Annuity

2
a $41,600 ($10,000 × 4.160)
b $4,250 (An amount received or paid today is stated at its present value.)
c Present value of $400 per month for 24 months, discounted at 1½% per month ($400 × 20.030) ..... $ 8,012
Present value of $10,000 due in 24 months, discounted at 1½% per month ($10,000 × .700) ..... $ 7,000
Total $15,012

3

General Journal			
Nov. 1	Vehicles	13,015	
	Notes Payable		10,015
	Cash		3,000
	Purchased van paying part cash and issuing an installment note payable		
	with a present value of $10,015 ($500 monthly payment for 24 months		
	discounted at 1½% per month; $500 × 20.030 =10,015)		
Dec. 1	Notes Payable	350	
	Interest Expense	150	
	Cash		500
	To record monthly payment on installment note payable:		
	Payment $500		
	Interest ($10,015 x 1½%) 150		
	Reduction in principal $350		

INTERNATIONAL ACCOUNTING AND FOREIGN CURRENCY TRANSACTIONS

HIGHLIGHTS OF THE APPENDIX

1 Accounting for business transactions which span national borders comprises the field of international accounting. Companies that do business in more than one country are called **multinational** corporations. However, any business that engages in a business transaction with a foreign company may need to apply certain international accounting concepts in order to properly record the transaction.

2 One of the major problems of international accounting arises because different currencies are used in different countries. Assume, for example, that a British company sells merchandise to an American company. The British company will want to be paid in British **pounds**, but the American company's bank account contains only U.S. **dollars**. Thus, one currency (dollars) must be converted into another (pounds).

3 Most banks are able to convert one currency into another by purchasing the needed amount of the foreign currency at the prevailing **exchange rate**. From the viewpoint of American businesses, an exchange rate represents the "price" of units of a foreign currency, stated in terms of U.S. dollars.

4 Exchange rates fluctuate from day to day. A sample of some recent exchange rates is shown below.

Country	Currency	Exchange Rate
Britain	Pound (£)	$1.5075
France	French franc (FF)	.1700
Japan	Yen (¥)	.0092
Mexico	Peso ($)	.3221
Germany	Deutsche mark (DM)	.5772

Remember that this table is just an illustration. Today's exchange rates might be very different.

5 Exchange rates are used to determine how much of one currency is equivalent to a given amount of another currency. To **translate** an amount of foreign currency into U.S. dollars, we multiply the amount of foreign currency by the exchange rate. For example, how many U.S. dollars are needed to buy 100,000 British pounds (expressed £100,000) at the date of our table in paragraph **4**? The answer is **$150,750**, computed as £100,000 × $1.5075 per British pound.

6 Exchange rates fluctuate continuously, based upon the worldwide supply and demand for particular currencies. Many factors affect exchange rates. Two very important factors are (a) the ratio of a country's imports to its exports, and (b) the real rate of return available in the country's capital markets.

7 A currency is said to be "weak" when its exchange rate is **falling** relative to other exchange rates. A currency is considered "strong" when its exchange rate is **rising**.

8 No special accounting problems are encountered when an American company engages in a transaction with a foreign company if the transaction price is stated in U.S. dollars. However, if the transaction price is stated in terms of the foreign currency, the American company must translate this price into an equivalent number of U.S. dollars in order to record the transaction in its accounting records.

9 A second accounting problem arises when a purchase or a sale is **made on account** at prices stated in foreign currency. If the exchange rate *changes* between the date that the credit transaction is initially recorded and the date that the related receivable or payable is settled, the company dealing in the foreign currency will have a *gain* or a *loss*.

10 Companies with accounts *payable* in foreign currencies will sustain losses if the exchange rate for the foreign currency rises between the date of the transaction and the date of payment. If the exchange rate falls, on the other hand, companies with foreign accounts payable will have a gain from the rate fluctuation.

11 Companies with accounts *receivable* in foreign currencies will have gains if the exchange rate rises between the date of the transaction and the date of collection. If the exchange rate falls, however, companies with foreign accounts receivable will incur losses.

12 The entries to record the gain or loss from changes in foreign currency exchange rates generally are made when the foreign account is settled. However, adjusting entries also are made at the end of each accounting period to recognize the gains or losses relating to any foreign account payable or receivable existing at the balance sheet date.

13 Carefully review the examples in your textbook illustrating the computation of gains and losses from fluctuations in foreign exchange rates. Gains and losses from fluctuations in foreign exchange rates are reported in the income statement following the subtotal "income from operations."

14 American companies that import foreign products are likely to have liabilities payable in a foreign currency; American exporters are likely to have large receivables stated in a foreign currency. As foreign exchange rates (stated in dollars) fall, American importers will gain and exporters will lose. The importers can pay their liabilities with fewer dollars, but the exporters hold receivables stated in specific amounts of a foreign currency that is worth fewer American dollars. When foreign exchange rates rise, the reverse is true—importers will lose as it costs them more American dollars to settle the liabilities stated in the foreign currency.

15 *Hedging* is the strategy of taking offsetting positions in a foreign currency to avoid losses from fluctuations in foreign exchange rates. A company that has similar amounts of accounts receivable and accounts payable in the same foreign currency automatically has a hedged position. A company that does not have similar dollar amounts of receivables and payables in the same foreign currency may *create* a hedged position by buying or selling *future contracts*, or *futures*.

16 A future contract is in effect an account receivable in foreign currency. A company with only foreign payables may hedge its position by *purchasing* a similar dollar amount of foreign currency future contracts. A company with only foreign receivables would hedge its position by *selling* future contracts, i.e., creating an offsetting liability payable in foreign currency.

17 Fluctuations in exchange rates change the relative prices of goods produced in different countries. A strong U.S. dollar (falling or relatively low exchange rates) makes American goods more expensive to customers in foreign countries, and imported products less expensive to American consumers. On the other hand, a weak dollar (relatively high exchange rates) makes foreign imports more expensive to American consumers, and American products less expensive to customers in foreign countries. In summary, a strong U.S. dollar helps companies that sell foreign-made goods in the American market. A weak dollar gives a competitive advantage to companies that sell American products both at home and abroad.

18 Many corporations have subsidiaries organized and operating in foreign countries. These foreign subsidiaries should be included in the parent company's consolidated financial statements. Several complex technical issues are involved in preparing consolidated statements that include foreign subsidiaries. First, the accounting records of the subsidiary must be translated into U.S. dollars. Next, the accounting principles in use in the foreign country may differ from American generally accepted accounting principles.

19 Readers of the financial statements of American-based corporations need not be concerned with these technical problems. Once accountants have completed the consolidation process, the consolidated financial statements are expressed in U.S. dollars and conform to American generally accepted accounting principles.

TEST YOURSELF ON INTERNATIONAL ACCOUNTING

True or False

For each of the following statements, circle the T or the F to indicate whether the statement is true or false.

T F **1** An American company that buys from, or sells to, a foreign company may have gains and losses from fluctuations in currency exchange rates even if the American company does not have a foreign subsidiary.

T F **2** Restating an amount of foreign currency in terms of the equivalent number of units of domestic currency is termed *translating* the foreign currency.

T F **3** The *exchange rate* for a foreign currency will tend to fall if the worldwide supply of currency exceeds demand.

T F **4** If the U.S. dollar is strengthening in the world currency markets, an American company with large accounts payable due in specified amounts of foreign currencies will experience losses from exchange rate fluctuations.

T F **5** If the exchange rate for a particular foreign currency is rising, an American company with receivables in this currency will recognize gains from the exchange rate fluctuations.

T F **6** Large imports but small exports tend to weaken a country's currency.

T F **7** High interest rates relative to the rate of inflation tend to weaken a country's currency.

T F **8** The balance sheet of a multinational corporation has multiple money columns, showing the financial statement amounts in various currencies, such as dollars, yen, and pounds.

T F **9** The accounting standards and principles used in the preparation of financial statements vary from one country to another.

T F **10** A multinational corporation headquartered in the United States prepares consolidated financial statements which include its foreign subsidiaries and which are in conformity with American generally accepted accounting principles.

Completion Statements

Fill in the necessary words or amounts to complete the following statements:

1 The process of restating an amount of foreign currency in terms of the equivalent number of U.S. dollars is termed _____ the foreign currency.

2 Assume that an American company purchases merchandise on account from a Japanese company at a price of ¥500,000. At the date of this purchase, the exchange rate is $.0092. The American company should record a liability of $_____.

3 Assume that the exchange rate for the British pound is falling relative to the U.S. dollar. American companies making credit sales to British companies will experience (gains, losses) _____ and American companies making credit purchases from British companies will experience (gains, losses) _____ as a result of the fluctuation in the exchange rate.

4 Assume that an American company incurs a liability for 100,000 French francs when the exchange rate is $0.1700 per franc, and that the company pays off this liability when the exchange rate is $0.1800 per franc. The company will report a (gain, loss) _____ of $_____ from the fluctuation in the exchange rate.

5 An American exporter with substantial amounts of contracts stated in a foreign currency may avoid losses from fluctuations in foreign exchange rates by _____ future contracts. This strategy of holding offsetting positions in the foreign currency is called _____.

Multiple Choice

Choose the best answer for each of the following questions and enter the identifying letter in the space provided:

_____ **1** Fashion House, an American company, purchased merchandise on account from a French company at a price of 40,000 French francs. Payment is due in 90 days and the current exchange rate is $.1700 per French franc. On the date of this purchase, Fashion House should:

a Record a liability of 40,000 French francs.

b Record a liability of $6,800.

c Record a liability of $235,294.

d Disclose the obligation in a footnote to the financial statements, as the amount of the liability cannot be determined with certainty until the exchange rate at the payment date is known.

_____ **2** In the evening news, a newscaster made the following statement: "Today a weak U.S. dollar fell sharply against the German deutsche mark, but rose slightly against the British pound." This statement indicates that today:
a The exchange rate for the deutsche mark, stated in dollars, is falling.
b The exchange rate for the pound, stated in dollars, is rising.
c The pound was a weaker currency than the dollar.
d The pound was a stronger currency than the deutsche mark.

_____ **3** European Look purchased cashmere sweaters from England on account at a price of £10,000. On the purchase date the exchange rate was $1.51 per British pound, but when European Look paid the liability the exchange rate was $1.48 per pound. When this foreign account payable is paid, European Look should record a:
a Liability of $300.
b Loss of $300.
c Receivable of $300.
d Gain of $300.

_____ **4** Assume that the exchange rate for the British pound is rising relative to the U.S. dollar. An American company will incur _losses_ from this rising exchange rate if the company is making:
a Credit sales to British companies at prices stated in pounds.
b Credit purchases from British companies with prices stated in U.S. dollars.
c Credit sales to British companies at prices stated in U.S. dollars.
d Credit purchases from British companies at prices stated in pounds.

_____ **5** Assume that the exchange rate for the German deutsche mark is _falling_ relative to the U.S. dollar. An American company will incur _losses_ from this falling exchange rate if it is making:
a Credit sales to German companies at prices stated in deutsche marks.
b Credit purchases from German companies at prices stated in U.S. dollars.
c Credit sales to German companies at prices stated in U.S. dollars.
d Credit purchases from German companies at prices stated in deutsche marks.

Exercises

1 Listed below are eight technical accounting terms introduced or emphasized in this appendix:

Multinational company
"Weak" currency
International accounting
Exchange rate
"Strong" currency
Translating
Foreign currency
Gain on fluctuations in foreign exchange rates

Each of the following statements may (or may not) describe one of these technical terms. In the space provided below each statement, indicate the accounting term described, or answer "None" if the statement does not correctly describe any of the terms.

a A business that is organized and operating in a different country from its parent company.

b The process of restating an amount of foreign currency in terms of the domestic currency (dollars).

c Any unit of foreign currency worth more than one U.S. dollar.

d The ratio at which one currency may be converted into another.

e A condition of the domestic currency that helps companies that sell domestically produced products, either at home or abroad.

f Accounting for business activities that span national borders.

g A currency whose exchange rate is rising relative to that of most other currencies.

2 Translate the following amounts of foreign currency into an equivalent number of U.S. dollars using the exchange rates in the table in Highlight **4**.
a DM15,000

b £130,000

c ¥300,000

3 Jill Adams owns a company that imports perfume from France. In the space provided, prepare journal entries to record the following events:

Nov. 24 Purchased perfume from St. Jean, a French company, at a price of 50,000 francs, due in 60 days. The current exchange rate is $.1713 per franc. (Adams uses the perpetual inventory method.)

Dec. 31 Adams made a year-end adjusting entry relating to the account payable to St. Jean. The exchange rate at year-end was $.1700 per franc.

Jan. 23 Issued a check for $8,540 (U.S. dollars) to Global Bank in full settlement of the liability to St. Jean. The current exchange rate is $.1708 per franc.

General Journal		
19X1		
Nov. 24	Inventory		
Dec. 31			
19X2		
Jan. 23			

SOLUTIONS TO APPENDIX D SELF-TEST

True or False

1 T Whenever an American company buys or sells merchandise in a *credit* transaction with a foreign company and the contract price is stipulated in the *foreign currency*, any fluctuations in the exchange rate will cause gains and losses.

2 T Exchange rates are used to determine how much of one currency is equivalent to a given amount of another currency

3 T Exchange rates (the "price" of one currency stated in terms of another) fluctuate based upon supply and demand.

4 F A *gain* results because fewer dollars are needed to repay the debt (stipulated in a foreign currency) than when the debt arose.

5 T An increase in the exchange rate causes a creditor to incur a gain on receivables in that currency and a debtor to incur a loss on payables stipulated in that currency.

6 T With small exports, there is not a great demand by purchasers for the country's currency to pay for the goods exported. Low demand causes the exchange rate to decline relative to other countries' currencies.

7 F When a politically stable country offers high interest rates relative to inflation, foreign investors will want to invest funds in that country. To do this, they must obtain that country's currency; high demand strengthens a country's currency.

8 F A company's financial statements are presented in one currency; financial statement amounts for foreign subsidiaries are translated into that currency.

9 T Generally accepted accounting principles used in America are *not* in worldwide use.

10 T In addition to translating the accounting records of foreign subsidiaries to U.S. dollars, the parent company must adjust a foreign subsidiary's accounting records to U.S. GAAP.

Completion Statements

1 Translating. **2** $4,600. **3** Losses, gains. **4** Loss; $1,000. **5** Selling, hedging.

Multiple Choice

1 Answer **b**—(40,000FF × $.1700 per franc = $6,800). Answer **d** is incorrect; the amount of the liability *is known* as of the purchase date. Any changes in the amount of this liability will be *future* events and will be recorded if and when they occur.

2 Answer **c**—if the dollar "rose slightly" against the pound, the exchange rate for the pound (stated in dollars) has declined. Thus, the pound was a weaker currency than the dollar.

3 Answer **d**—European Look's liability to the English company originally was $15,100 (£10,000 × $1.51 per pound). However, European Look ultimately paid only $14,800 to settle this liability (£10,000 × $1.48 per pound), thus resulting in a $300 gain from the fluctuation in the exchange rate.

4 Answer **d**—as a result of the rising exchange rate, the American company will have to pay *more dollars* to settle its liability (for a fixed number of pounds) at the settlement date than was required earlier, at the date of the initial purchase. This difference is a *loss* from exchange rate fluctuations. Answer **a** is incorrect, because the seller's receivable (which is fixed in pounds) becomes equivalent to more dollars as the exchange rate for the pound rises. Answers **b** and **c** are incorrect; if the receivables or payables are fixed in dollars, the American company will experience neither a gain nor a loss from exchange rate fluctuations.

5 Answer **a**—if the exchange rate for the deutsche mark is falling, an American company with receivables of a fixed number of deutsche marks is seeing the value of this asset decline.

Solutions to Exercises

1

a None (The statement describes a foreign subsidiary; a multinational company is one that does business in more than one country.)

b Translating

c None (The terms *strong currency* and *weak currency* refer to the direction of recent changes in the exchange rate, not to the absolute level of this rate.)

d Exchange rate
e "Weak" currency
f International accounting
g "Strong" currency

2
a $8,658 (DM15,000 × $.5772 per deutsche mark)
b $195,975 (£130,000 × $1.5075 per British pound)
c $2,760 (¥300,000 × $.0092 per yen)

3

General Journal		
19X1		
Nov. 24 Inventory	8,565	
Accounts Payable—St. Jean		8,565
Purchased perfume from St. Jean for 50,000 francs; exchange rate,		
$.1713 per franc (50,000FF × $.1713 = $8,565).		
Dec. 31 Accounts Payable—St. Jean	65	
Gain on Fluctuation in Foreign Exchange Rates		65
To adjust liability to St. Jean based on year-end exchange rate:		
Original balance $8,565		
Adjusted balance (50,000FF × $.1700) 8,500		
Gain through year-end 65		
19X2		
Jan. 23 Accounts Payable—St. Jean	8,500	
Loss on Fluctuation in Foreign Exchange Rates	40	
Cash		8,540
Paid 50,000 franc liability to St. Jean; exchange rate,		
$.1708 per franc (50,000FF × $.1708 = $8,540).		

HIGHLIGHTS OF THE APPENDIX

1 Income tax returns are based upon accounting information. In many ways this information is similar to the accounting concepts we have discussed in earlier chapters. However, the measurement of taxable income includes some unique rules and computations which differ from those used in preparing financial statements. The rules for reporting income in federal income tax returns are established by the United States Congress.

2 There are four classes of taxpayers: *individuals*, *corporations*, *estates*, and *trusts*. A *partnership* does not pay income tax, but it must file an *information* return. Partners must include their share of the partnership net income in their *personal* income tax returns, regardless of the amount they withdraw from the business.

3 The earnings of corporations are subject to *double taxation*. Corporate earnings are subject to corporate income tax *when earned* by the corporation and then are subject to personal income tax *when distributed* as dividends to stockholders.

4 In terms of revenue produced (to government), the four most important taxes are *income taxes*, *sales taxes*, *property taxes*, and *excise taxes*. Income taxes exceed all others and are most important in business decisions.

5 Because taxes have become such a significant expenditure, careful *tax planning* is essential to operating a business efficiently. Tax planning refers to determining in advance the income tax effect of every proposed business action, so the burden of taxes may be considered in the business decision.

6 The current system of collecting income taxes is one of *self-assessment*—taxpayers measure their own income, compute their taxes, and file returns reporting these items. Enforcement of this "self-assessment system" is possible due to the following:

a *Third-party reports* to taxing authorities of income earned by taxpayers, such as W-2 forms and 1099 forms.

b *Audits* of income tax returns by the IRS.

c Imposition of financial *penalties*: interest on taxes owed; fines and penalties in the case of negligence or fraud, as well as possible criminal sentencing.

7 Almost all individual tax returns are prepared on the *cash basis* of measuring income. Individuals may use the accrual basis if they choose, but the cash basis is simpler, requires less record keeping, and permits tax savings by allowing the taxpayer to shift the timing of revenue and expenses from one year to another.

8 Income tax rates are *progressive*—that is, as you earn more money, the additional amounts are taxed at a higher rate. The amount of earnings taxed at a particular *tax rate* is called a *tax bracket*.

9 Tax brackets and the tax rates are subject to frequent change. The tax structure assumed throughout this text and its problem material are as follows:

Bracket	Rate
Single individuals:	
First $23,000 earned	15%
Next $31,000 earned	28%
Next $61,000 earned	31%
Next $135,000 earned	36%
Earnings above $250,000	40%

Married individuals filing a joint return:

First $37,000 earned	15%
Next $53,000 earned	28%
Next $50,000 earned	31%
Next $110,000 earned	36%
Earnings over $250,000...................................	40%

Actual tax brackets and tax rates in any given year will vary from these assumed amounts.

10 The income tax formula for individuals is as follows: Total income minus exclusions equals gross income. Gross income minus certain deductions equals adjusted gross income. Adjusted gross income minus itemized deductions (or the standard deduction) and minus personal exemptions equals taxable income. The tax on the taxable income minus any tax credits equals the tax payable to the government.

11 Gross income of individuals includes *all items of income not specifically excluded by law*. Among the items *excluded* are:
a Interest on municipal bonds.
b Gifts and inheritances received.
c Life insurance proceeds resulting from death of the insured.
d Worker's compensation benefits.
e Military bonuses, pensions to veterans, and at least half of social security benefits received.
f Compensation for personal damages.

12 Deductions *to arrive at* adjusted gross income are:
a Business expenses of a sole proprietorship.
b Expenses attributable to earning rent.
c Losses from the sale of property used in a trade or business.
d Net capital losses up to $3,000 in any one year.
e Net operating loss carry-overs from preceding years..
f Some contributions to retirement plans (IRAs and Keoghs).
g Alimony paid.
h Penalty on early withdrawals from long-term savings deposits.

13 By deducting from gross income the various items described in paragraph 11, we arrive at a very significant subtotal called *adjusted gross income*. This amount is significant because several itemized deductions, such as medical expenses, are only deductible to the extent that they *exceed a specified percentage* of adjusted gross income.

14 Taxpayers have an option with respect to deductions from adjusted gross income. They may either deduct a lump-sum amount, called the *standard deduction*, or they may *itemize* their deductible expenditures. In recent years, the standard deduction has been approximately $3,700 for a single person and $6,200 for a married couple filing a joint return. The amount of the standard deduction is adjusted annually for inflation. (For convenience, we will use the amounts of *$3,700* and *$6,200* in our problem material.) The standard deduction is increased for taxpayers who are elderly or blind.

15 Taxpayers should elect to itemize their deductions whenever these deductions exceed the amount of the standard deduction. Expenditures that taxpayers may list as itemized deductions include:
a *Mortgage interest* on a principal residence and one other home.
b *State and local income taxes and property taxes.*
c *Charitable contributions* to recognized charitable organizations. (Gifts to friends, relatives, or needy individuals are not deductible.)
d *Medical expenses*, but only to the extent that these expenses exceed $7\frac{1}{2}\%$ of adjusted gross income.
e *Casualty losses* in excess of $100 per loss, but only to the extent that these losses exceed 10% of adjusted gross income.
f *Certain miscellaneous expenses*, such as union dues and unreimbursed employee expenses, to the extent that these items exceed 2% of adjusted gross income.

16 Up to 80% of certain itemized deductions are "phased-out" for high-income taxpayers. Thus, these taxpayers do not receive as much "tax benefit" from itemized deductions as one might think.

17 A *personal exemption* may be deducted for the taxpayer, spouse, and each dependent. Each personal exemption was $2,000 in 1989. After 1989, the amount is adjusted for inflation. (For convenience, we will use *$2,400* in problem material.)

Under current rules, the personal exemption gradually is "phased out" for high-income taxpayers. This process makes the tax structure more "progressive" than is indicated by the tax rates alone.

18 The preceding steps lead us to the *taxable income* of an individual (or a couple filing a

joint return). The appropriate tax rates are then applied to determine the tax liability.

19 Assets not used in a trade or business are classified as **capital assets** under the tax laws. Thus, capital assets include assets held for investment and personal assets. **Gains** from sales of capital assets are taxable as are other types of income. However, restrictions apply to the deductibility of many losses stemming from sales of capital assets. First, **no deduction is available for a loss from the sale of a personal asset**, such as your home or your car. Next, deductible capital losses may be offset against capital gains, but if the taxpayer has **net** capital losses, the deduction is **limited to $3,000 in any one year**. A net capital loss in excess of $3,000 may be carried forward to future tax years.

20 The treatment of capital gains has varied over the years. Sometimes they receive preferential tax treatment. Today, capital gains are taxed as ordinary income. However, **long-term** capital gains are subject to a **maximum tax bracket of 28%**. Thus, high-income taxpayers need not apply the 31%, 36% and 40% bracket to long-term capital gains. This "preferential treatment" is intended to encourage investment.

21 Many people believe that investors benefit from losing money because of "tax losses." This is simply not true. Except for the allowable $3,000 deduction for capital losses, capital losses are deductible only against capital gains. Thus, an investor who loses $50,000 and has no capital gains may take only a $3,000 tax deduction in the current year. Assuming this investor is in the highest tax bracket of approximately 40%, a $3,000 deduction saves only $1,200 in taxes. Although the excess may be carried forward to future years, the investor will **never** come out ahead for having lost money.

22 After determining the amount of taxable income in paragraph **18**, we can compute the **gross tax liability** by using the tax rate schedule. The gross amount of tax owed is then reduced by subtracting any **tax credits** and **tax prepayments**.

23 **Tax credits** differ from deductions. A deduction, such as a charitable contribution, reduces the **income subject to tax**, but a tax credit is subtracted **directly from the tax owed**. Tax credits are available for a percentage of certain child-care expenses, and for the "earned income" of low-income taxpayers.

24 The federal income tax law stresses a pay-as-you-go system for all taxpayers. If the income is in the form of salaries, an amount of tax is **withheld** from each paycheck.

25 Quarterly payments of estimated tax are required for self-employed persons and for others having income not subject to withholding. Both estimated tax payments and the amounts of income tax withheld, above, are treated as tax prepayments to be deducted at year-end in determining the taxpayer's remaining tax liability or amount of tax refund.

26 Individuals who compute their income on the calendar-year basis must file an income tax return by April 15 of each year. Corporations must file a return $2\frac{1}{2}$ months after the end of their fiscal year.

27 One objective of the Tax Reform Act of 1986 was to assure that every person with a large income paid a significant amount of income tax. Thus, high-income taxpayers with large deductions may be subject to an Alternative Minimum Tax. The **Alternative Minimum Tax** is computed by adding back to taxable income certain deductions and tax preferences, such as accelerated depreciation. A tax rate of **26%** is then applied to this adjusted figure. (A 28% rate is applied to taxable income above a certain level.) The taxpayer must pay the **greater of** (a) the tax liability computed by the regular method or (b) the tax liability computed by the Alternative Minimum Tax calculation.

28 **Partnerships** are not taxable entities. The income of a partnership flows through to the partners and is taxed at their individual income tax rates. Although a partnership pays no tax, it must file an **information return** showing the computation of net income or loss and the share of net income or loss allocable to each partner.

29 A **corporation** is a separate taxable entity. Income tax expense therefore appears in the income statement of a corporation and income taxes payable appears as a current liability in the balance sheet.

30 Tax rates on corporations are shown below:

	Rate
First $50,000 of taxable income	15%
Next $25,000 of taxable income	25%
Next $25,000 of taxable income	34%
On amount over $100,000 up to $335,000	39%
On amount over $333,000 up to $10 million	34%
Amount over $10 million	35%

31 In large part, determining the taxable income of a corporation involves the same concepts as preparation of an income statement. We start with total revenue, and then deduct ordinary and necessary business expenses. However, tax laws do differ from GAAP. Some special factors to be considered in corporate tax returns are:

a *Dividends received*   A corporation must include dividends received from other corporations in gross income. However, 70% of this amount then may be deducted. The result is that only 30% of a corporation's dividend revenue is included in taxable income

The deduction from dividend revenue increases to 80% if the investing corporation own 20% or more of the other corporation. If the investing corporation owns 80% or more of the other corporation's stock, the deduction is 100%. (In our problem material, we use only the 70% deduction.)

b *Capital gains and losses*   Capital gains are taxable as ordinary income. However, capital losses may only be offset against capital gains. A corporation cannot deduct any net capital loss.

c *Other variations from taxation of individuals*   The concept of adjusted gross income does not apply to corporations. Also, there is no standard deduction and no personal exemption.

d Corporations are subject to an *Alternative Minimum Tax*, similar to that calculated for high-income individuals.

32 *Accounting income* before taxes often differs from *taxable income* because each is computed with different purposes in mind. Furthermore, taxable income is computed by reference to specific laws, and laws generally do not govern the computation of accounting income.

33 The items causing differences between accounting income and taxable income may be classified into two broad categories:

a *Permanent differences*   Most permanent differences result from special *tax law* provisions granting special tax treatment of revenue and expenses. (For example, municipal bond interest and 70% of dividend revenue are excluded from taxable income, whereas political contributions and amortization of goodwill are not deductible in a corporation's income tax return.)

b *Timing differences*   Timing differences arise when the *same* dollar amount of revenue or expense is recognized for accounting purposes and in the income tax return, but the *timing* of that recognition in the income tax return differs from that under accounting principles. Timing differences are often caused by choosing alternative accounting methods for tax purposes and financial reporting (for such items as inventories, depreciation, and installment sales). Business executives generally select an accounting method for tax purposes that will minimize their *current* tax liabilities.

34 When significant differences between accounting income and taxable income arise due to *timing differences*, *interperiod income tax allocation* should be used to avoid the distortion of net income computed for financial reporting purposes. The objective of interperiod tax allocation is to *accrue income taxes expense in relation to accounting income* whenever differences between accounting and taxable income are caused by differences in timing of revenue and expenses (including those differences resulting from the use of alternative accounting methods).

35 Assume Bernardo Corporation reports pretax *accounting* income of $800,000, but *taxable* income of $700,000 (due to the use of accelerated depreciation in the income tax return). The application of interperiod tax allocation requires recognition of *income tax expense* of $272,000 ($800,000 accounting income times 34%), and a *current income tax liability* of only $238,000 ($700,000 times 34%). The difference of $34,000 is the portion of the current year expense that is deferred to a future year—a *deferred income tax liability*. Deferred income tax liabilities are classified as long-term liabilities in the balance sheet. Deferred income tax liabilities arise when pretax accounting income is *greater* than taxable income, and are reduced when the reverse occurs.

36 Income tax considerations may be of great importance in making certain business decisions. Some of these decisions are:

a Choice of the form of business organization.

b Choice of accounting methods for inventories, depreciation of plant and equipment, long-term construction contracts, etc.

c Timing and manner in which property is sold.

d Allocation of values to assets when a business is acquired or sold.

e Types of securities to be issued in raising capital to finance a business.

37 **Tax shelters** are investments which produce a loss for tax purposes in the near term but hopefully will prove profitable in the long run. For example, investments in real estate may show a short-term loss because of deductions for interest, property taxes, and depreciation but may prove profitable in the long run because of rising market values. May tax shelters lose money, however, and the tax savings **never offset the full amount of the loss**.

TEST YOURSELF ON INCOME TAXES

True or False

For each of the following statements, circle the T or the F to indicate whether the statement is true or false.

T F 1 Income tax rules are established by the Financial Accounting Standards Board.

T F 2 There are four major classes of taxpayers: individuals, partnerships, corporations and trusts.

T F 3 Tax planning is illegal.

T F 4 Tax evasion is illegal.

T F 5 One feature of the Tax Reform Act of 1986 is to allow many high-income individuals to pay no income taxes at all.

T F 6 A prize won on a television game show is included in taxable income.

T F 7 Interest on municipal bonds is included in taxable income.

T F 8 An individual who incurs net capital losses of $5,000 may deduct this amount in arriving at the adjusted gross income for the year.

T F 9 An individual who incurs net capital gains of $5,000 must include this amount in adjusted gross income for the year.

T F 10 As a result of the Tax Reform Act of 1986, long-term capital gains are now taxed more like other types of income.

T F 11 A taxpayer should deduct from adjusted gross income the greater of (a) itemized deductions or (b) the standard deduction.

T F 12 In computing taxable income, state income taxes qualify as a deduction, but state sales taxes do not.

T F 13 Tax laws encourage home ownership.

T F 14 Personal exemptions may only be deducted by those taxpayers who elect to itemize their deductions.

T F 15 A taxpayer in the 31% tax bracket saves more money as a result of a $5,000 deduction than does a taxpayer in the 15% tax bracket.

T F 16 If you allow the government to withhold more than necessary from your paycheck, the government will pay interest on the excess when you file for your tax refund.

T F 17 Low-income individuals have a choice between computing their income taxes by the regular method or paying the Alternative Minimum Tax.

T F 18 It is usually advantageous for individuals to use the cash basis of accounting in preparing their income tax returns.

T F 19 Corporations must use the same accounting methods in their income tax return as they use in their financial statements.

T F 20 Corporations may not deduct net capital losses in computing their taxable income.

T F 21 The highest tax bracket for corporations is higher than the highest tax bracket for individuals.

T F 22 The need for interperiod tax allocation procedures stems from the fact that revenue and expenses may be recognized in different periods for tax purposes and for financial reporting purposes.

T F 23 In the short run, a tax shelter is expected to produce a loss, thus reducing the income taxes due.

Completion Statements

Fill in the necessary words and percentages to complete the following statements:

1 The four classes of taxpayers are _____, _____, _____, and _____.

2 The four types of taxes which raise the most revenue for government are _____ taxes, _____ taxes, _____ taxes, _____ taxes.

3 Itemized deductions may include:
   (a) _____ _____ on a principal residence and one other home.
   (b) State and local _____ taxes and _____ taxes.
   (c) _____ _____ in excess of $7\frac{1}{2}$% of adjusted gross income.
   (d) _____ in excess of 10% of adjusted gross income and $100 per event.
   (e) Certain miscellaneous expenses to the extent that they exceed ____% of adjusted gross income.
   (f) All _____ _____.

4 The _____ _____ _____ is a provision of the Tax Reform Act of 1986 designed to ensure that every person or corporation with a large income pays a significant amount of income tax.

5 A partnership does not pay any tax but must file an _____ return.

6 A procedure designed to accrue income tax expense in relation to pretax accounting income is called ____ ____ ____ ____. This procedure is used when differences in accounting income and _____ income are caused by differences in the _____ of revenue or expenses.

Multiple Choice

Choose the best answer for each of the following questions and enter the identifying letter in the space provided.

_____ 1 Which of the following is an example of **tax evasion**, rather than **tax planning**, for a cash basis taxpayer?
a Omitting from gross income money received as a gift.
b Paying bills in December, even though the bills are not due until January of the following year.
c Selecting an accounting method that minimizes the amount of taxable income reported in the current year.
d Omitting from gross income capital gains from the sale of personal property.

_____ 2 Use by an individual taxpayer of the cash basis provides all of the following advantages **except**:
a The taxpayer has some control over the year in which a deduction is taken when bills for deductible expenses are received near year-end.
b The government allows a cash discount to taxpayers who pay their income taxes in cash.
c If the taxpayer bills customers for services rendered by the taxpayer, the taxpayer may shift revenue earned shortly before year-end into the following tax year.
d It is relatively simple and requires less record keeping than does measuring taxable income by the accrual basis.

_____ 3 Which of the following **cannot** be deducted by a taxpayer who itemized deductions from adjusted gross income?
a The standard deduction.
b State income taxes.
c Charitable contributions.
d Mortgage interest payments.

_____ 4 Which of the following saves a taxpayer the most money?
a A $100 exclusion.
b A $100 deduction to arrive at adjusted gross income.
c A $100 deduction from adjusted gross income.
d A $100 tax credit.

_____ 5 Susan had salary of $30,000, net long-term capital gains of $6,000, and net short-term capital losses of $10,000. Susan should report adjusted gross income of:
a $26,000.
b $27,000.
c $30,000.
d $36,000.

_____ 6 John and Judy Lee have an adjusted gross income of $50,000 on their joint tax return. They paid mortgage interest of $6,000, state property taxes of $2,000, medical expenses of $2,500, and made charitable contributions of $1,000. The standard deduction is $6,200 and each personal exemption is $2,400. The Lees have two small children. The Lees' taxable income is:
a $36,200.
b $31,400.
c $28,900.

d Some other amount.

_____ **7** Under current law (1994), long-term capital gains:

a Are not taxable to individuals.

b Are given preferential tax treatment; only 40% of the gain is subject to income taxes.

c Are taxed as any other type of taxable income.

d Are taxed as ordinary income, but the maximum tax rate applied to capital gains is limited to 28%.

_____ **8** The number of *personal exemptions* that may be claimed by a corporation is:

a Zero.

b One.

c Equal to the number of directors.

d Equal to the number of stockholders.

_____ **9** Taxation of individuals and corporations are alike with respect to:

a Dividends received.

b Net capital losses.

c Tax rates and brackets.

d None of the above.

_____ **10** Which of the following does *not* cause a difference between the accounting income and the taxable income of a corporation?

a Paying salaries to employees who report their earnings on the cash basis.

b Computing depreciation by different methods in tax returns and in financial statements.

c Valuing inventory by different methods in tax returns and in financial statements.

d Earning interest from an investment in municipal bonds.

_____ **11** In deciding whether a corporation should raise needed capital by borrowing or by issuing capital stock, an important income tax planning consideration is that:

a Interest payments are deductible to a corporation.

b Dividends received from a corporation are not taxable to an individual.

c Interest received from a corporation is not taxable to an individual.

d Dividend payments are deductible to a corporation.

Exercises

1 Listed below are eight technical accounting terms introduced or emphasized in this appendix:

Standard deduction	*Capital loss*
Personal exemption	*Tax credit*
Itemized deduction	*Exclusion*
Taxable income	*Tax shelter*

Each of the following statements may (or may not) describe one of these technical terms. In the space provided below each statement, indicate the accounting term described, or answer "None" if the statement does not correctly describe any of the terms.

a For a portion of certain expenditures (such as medical expense) to be deductible, total expenditures within the year must exceed a specified percentage of this subtotal within the tax return.

_____

b Gross income, less certain exclusions, deductions, and exemptions specified in the tax law.

_____

c An amount which may be subtracted from adjusted gross income for the taxpayer, the taxpayer's spouse, and each dependent.

_____

d An amount subtracted directly from the amount of taxes owed.

_____

e An expense incurred by the taxpayer that may be subtracted from adjusted gross income as a step toward determining taxable income.

_____

f A type of deduction that can reduce other types of taxable income by only $3,000 in any given year.

_____

g Amount due to the taxpayer because amount withheld during the year exceeded the final tax liability.

_____

2 Robert and Betty Hill have six dependent children. In preparing their income tax return you obtain the following information:

Gross income:

Salaries (before deductions)

Robert Hill	32,000
Betty Hill	32,000
Dividends from domestic corporations	580
Proceeds on life insurance policy upon death of father	25,000
Interest on City of Medford bonds	2,100
Interest on savings account	1,320
Gain on stock held over one year	8,200
Loss on stock held two months	(13,200)
Inheritance from father's estate	62,500
Christmas gift from family friends	150

Personal expenses:

Living expenses: food, clothes, etc.	15,800
Sales taxes	700
State income taxes paid	4,800
Contribution to church and other allowable organizations	800
Property taxes on residence	1,650
Federal excise taxes	150
Interest on home mortgage	11,700
Medical expenses	1,695
Federal income tax withheld by employer	8,810
Social security taxes withheld by employer	4,800

Instructions Assuming that the standard deduction is $6,200 and the personal exemption is $2,400, compute the taxable income that Robert and Betty Hill should report in a joint return.

ROBERT AND BETTY HILL
Computation of Taxable Income for 19__

Gross income:		
Salaries	$64,000	
	____	$____
Deductions to arrive at adjusted gross income:		
		____
Adjusted gross income		$____
Deductions from adjusted gross income (itemized):		
	$____	
	____	
Total itemized deductions	$____	
Personal exemptions	____	____
Taxable income		$____

3 The income statement of Miller Corporation shows income before taxes of $100,000 which includes, among other items, the following:

Dividends from other corporations	$20,000
Net capital loss	8,000
Interest received on municipal bonds	4,500

Compute the income that would be taxable to the Miller Corporation.

Income before taxes		$100,000
Add:		
Subtotal		$____
Less:		
	$____	
Taxable income		$____

SOLUTIONS TO APPENDIX E SELF-TEST

True or False

1 **F** The United States Congress establishes income tax rules.

2 **F** The four classes of taxpayers are individuals, corporations estates, and trusts.

3 **F** Tax planning is smart as well as legal; tax planning means arranging business and financial affairs in a manner that will minimize tax liability.

4 **T** Tax evasion is illegally reducing taxes by purposeful understatement of taxable income.

5 **F** The purpose of the Alternative Minimum Tax (AMT) has been to assure that every person with substantial income pays a significant amount of tax.

6 **T** All income items not excluded by law are included in taxable income; there is no exclusion for game show prizes.

7 **F** Interest earned on state and municipal bonds is specifically excluded from gross income.

8 **F** Individual taxpayers may deduct a maximum of $3,000 in net capital losses per year.

9 **T** Capital gains in excess of capital losses are included in gross income, without any limit.

10 **T** The Tax Reform Act of 1986 eliminated most of the preferential treatment capital gains used to receive.

11 **T** Individual taxpayers have a choice of either the standard deduction or their total itemized deductions; it would be wise to deduct the greater of these two amounts so as to minimize taxable income.

12 **T** The sales tax deduction was eliminated by the Tax Reform Act of 1986.

13 **T** Individuals are allowed to deduct home mortgage interest on two homes as well as property taxes; no deduction is allowed for rent paid.

14 **F** Regardless of whether an individual itemizes deductions or takes the standard deduction, a personal exemption is allowed for the individual and each dependent.

15 **T** The higher the taxpayer's tax bracket, the more money a deduction saves the taxpayer.

16 **F** The federal government pays no interest on excess withholding.

17 **F** The Alternative Minimum Tax is designed to impose some minimum tax on **higher**-income taxpayers who were avoiding taxes through loopholes and tax preference items.

18 **T** The cash basis is easy to use and allows taxpayers to save taxes by shifting the timing of revenue and expense transactions.

19 **F** Financial statements are prepared in accordance with generally accepted accounting principles, which differ from tax rules in many respects.

20 **T** Corporations may only offset capital losses against capital gains; **net** capital losses may be deducted up to a $3,000 maximum by **individuals**.

21 **F** The top rate for individuals is approximately 40%; the top rate for corporations is 39%.

22 **T** Interperiod tax allocation is required when financial statement income differs from taxable income due to differences in the timing of revenue or expenses

23 **T** A tax shelter is intended to reduce (shelter the taxpayer from) taxes in the near future. Thus, the tax shelter must produce a loss for income tax purposes which can be offset against some or all of the taxpayer's taxable income from other sources.

Completion Statements

1 Individuals, corporations, estates, trusts. **2** Income, sales, property, excise. **3(a)** Mortgage interest, **(b)** Income, property, **(c)** Medical expenses, **(d)** Casualty losses, **(e)** 2%, **(f)** Charitable contributions. **4** Alternative Minimum Tax. **5** Information. **6** Interperiod income tax allocation, taxable, timing.

Multiple Choice

1 Answer **d**—omitting capital gains from gross income is illegal, and therefore, an act of tax evasion. The other actions all are permissible under current tax law.

2 Answer **b**—taxes must be paid in cash; no "discount" is given for cash payment. The cash basis does give taxpayers some control over the timing of revenue and expenses for tax purposes and does require less record keeping than does the accrual basis.

3 Answer **a**—the standard deduction is an **alternative** to itemizing deductions. Therefore, it is not available to a taxpayer who has elected to itemize deductions.

4 Answer **d**—answers **a**, **b**, and **c** reduce taxable income, thus saving the taxpayer the amount of the reduction multiplied by the taxpayer's marginal tax rate. A tax credit, however, reduces the amount of tax owed by the full amount of the credit, thus saving the taxpayer 100% of the amount of the credit.

5 Answer **b**—Susan has net capital losses of $4,000 ($6,000 – $10,000). However, in any given tax year, the deduction for net capital losses is limited to $3,000. Thus Susan's adjusted gross income is $27,000 ($30,000 salary – $3,000 maximum net capital loss deduction).

6 Answer **b**—$31,400 [$50,000 – $6,000 – $2,000 – $1,000 – (4 × $2,400)]. The medical expenses were not deductible because they did not exceed 7½% of adjusted gross income; the standard deduction is not available to taxpayers who itemize deductions.

7 Answer **d**—the treatment of long-term capital gains has varied over the years. As of 1994, however, long-term capital gains were taxed as ordinary income, except that they are not subject to tax rates above 28%.

8 Answer **a**—zero, the tax concept of personal exemptions applies only to individuals, not to corporations.

9 Answer **d**—taxation of individuals and corporations differ with respect to answers **a**, **b**, and **c**. Individuals are taxed on all dividend revenue, but corporations may exclude 70% of dividends received from domestic corporations. Individuals may deduct net capital losses of $3,000, but corporations may only use capital losses to offset capital gains. Different rates and brackets exist for individuals and corporations.

10 Answer **a**—a corporation using the accrual basis of accounting will report the same amount of salaries expense in its financial statements and its income tax return.

11 Answer **a**—interest payments are deductible to a corporation. Individuals must pay taxes on both dividend and interest received from a corporation. Dividend payments are ***not*** deductible to a corporation.

Solutions to Exercises

1

a None (The statement describes adjusted gross income.)
b Taxable income
c Personal exemption
d Tax credit
e Itemized deduction
f Capital loss
g None (The statement simply describes a tax refund.)

2

ROBERT AND BETTY HILL
Computation of Taxable Income for 19__

Gross income:		
Salaries	$64,000	
Dividends	580	
Interest on savings account	1,320	$65,900
Deductions to arrive at adjusted gross income:		
Net capital loss (limited to $3,000)		3,000
Adjusted gross income		$62,900
Deductions from adjusted gross income (itemized):		
State income taxes paid	$ 4,800	
Contributions to charities	800	
Property taxes on personal residence	1,650	
Interest on home mortgage	11,700	
Total itemized deductions	$18,950	
Personal exemptions ($2,400 × 8)	19,200	38,150
Taxable income		$24,750

3

Income before taxes		$100,000
Add: Net capital loss (not deductible)		8,000
Subtotal		$108,000
Less: 70% of dividends from other corporations	$14,000	
Interest received on municipal bonds	4,500	18,500
Taxable income		$ 89,500

ANALYSIS AND INTERPRETATION OF FINANCIAL STATEMENTS: A SECOND LOOK

HIGHLIGHTS OF THE APPENDIX

1 *Financial statements* represent a report on a company's performance. Financial statements are of interest to many groups, each with a different set of needs. In order to interpret the information contained in financial statements, the user should understand the workings of the accounting system.

2 The published financial statements of corporations have been audited by CPA firms and reviewed in detail by governmental agencies such as the Securities and Exchange Commission. Consequently, users of these financial statements may have confidence that the information in the statements is reasonably reliable and is presented in accordance with generally accepted accounting principles.

3 Critics of business often blame "excessive" corporate profits for rising prices and other economic problems. In evaluating the reasonableness of corporate profit, we must relate the dollar amount of net income to the volume of sales and the value of the economic resources necessary to produce that profit. Also, we must consider the need for profits as a means of financing expansion, creating jobs, and increasing the supply of goods and services.

4 Some sources of financial data available to users of financial statements include:

a Annual reports of corporations.

b Data filed with the Securities and Exchange Commission.

c Investment advisory services and stock brokerage firms.

d Organizations such as Moody's Investors Service, Standard & Poor's Corporation, and Dun & Bradstreet, Inc.

5 A given figure contained in financial statements is seldom significant to the reader; the *relationships* among figures, or the *changes* over time, generally are much more useful.

6 Four techniques commonly used in the analysis of financial statements are:

a Dollar and percentage changes.

b Trend percentages.

c Component percentages.

d Ratios.

7 *Dollar and percentage changes* relate a financial statement item to the same item in last year's statements. This analysis indicates whether things are getting better or worse in the short-term.

8 *Trend percentages* show the tendency of a financial statement item to change over a series of years. This type of analysis gives clues to long-run growth patterns and other important trends.

9 A *component percentage* is the percentage relationship between a financial statement item and a total (such as total assets or net sales) which includes that item. The analysis indicates the relative importance of the item.

10 A *ratio* measures the relationship of one item to another. Ratios may be used to identify unusual relationships, such as a high rate of return. By computing ratios for several years, we also can see whether key financial indicators, such as the current ratio, are improving or deteriorating.

11 In interpreting the significance of percentage changes, component percentages, and ratios, some *standards of comparison* should be used. Two widely used *standards* are:

a The past performance of the company.

b The performance of other companies in the same industry or the performance of the industry as a whole.

12 Comparison of data over time (*horizontal* analysis) gives some idea of the company's performance compared with its past record and may be helpful in forecasting future performance.

13 Comparison of a company's performance with that of other companies similarly situated or with the aggregate results for an industry offers valuable clues relating to a company's ability to compete and perhaps to surpass the industry's performance.

14 The key objectives of financial analysis are to determine a company's *future earnings performance* and the *soundness of its financial position*. To evaluate earnings performance and financial soundness, we are interested not only in the *amount* of earnings and assets, but also in the *quality of earnings*, the *quality of assets*, and the *amount of debt*.

15 The quality of earnings depends upon the *source* and *stability* of those earnings. The quality of earnings helps us to evaluate how likely it is that earnings will continue to grow or whether future earnings are likely to fluctuate widely. An analysis of the accounting principles and methods used by a company is helpful in evaluating the quality of earnings reported by the company.

16 A company may become insolvent even though it is profitable. The health and even the survival of the company may therefore be dependent not only on earnings, but also on the *quality of assets* and the *amount of liabilities* outstanding. A firm with an inadequate cash position, slow-moving inventories, past-due receivables, and large amounts of short-term liabilities may be facing serious financial difficulties.

17 It is also important to remember that during periods of inflation financial statements based upon historical cost tend to overstate the profitability of a business by failing to recognize the current value of the resources consumed in the production of revenue. The FASB *recommends* that companies include in their annual reports supplementary schedules showing the effects of inflation upon their financial statements. Inclusion of these supplementary disclosures is voluntary, *not* mandatory.

18 *Stockholders and potential investors* in the common stock of a company are primarily interested in the following:

a Earnings per share.

b Price-earnings ratio.

c Dividends paid and the yield based on the market value of the stock.

d Revenue and expense analysis (the increase or decrease in specific revenue and expense items).

e The rate of return on assets used in the business.

f The rate of return on common stockholders' equity.

g Debt ratio (the proportion of total assets financed by borrowing).

19 The concept of return on investment (called *ROI*) is a measure of management's efficiency in using the resources under its control. The ROI concept is used in many situations such as evaluating the performance of a company, product line, or particular investment. ROI is computed several different ways, depending upon the circumstances; two common measures of ROI are *return on assets* and *return on stockholders' equity*. A summary of these and other ratios is contained at the end of the appendix in your textbook.

a *Return on assets* "Return" is defined as *operating income*, since interest expense and income taxes are determined by factors other than the manner in which assets are used.

$$\text{Return on assets} = \frac{\text{Operating income}}{\text{Average total assets}}$$

b *Return on equity* "Return" to stockholders is the net income of the business. Therefore:

$$\text{Return on equity} = \frac{\text{Net income}}{\text{Average total stockholders' equity}}$$

20 Financing a business with fixed-return securities (bonds and notes payable and preferred stock) is known as using *leverage* or *trading on the equity*. If the rate earned on total assets is *greater* than the rate paid on the fixed-return securities (the cost of borrowing), the common stockholders will gain from the use of leverage. Common stockholders will gain because the capital provided by the fixed-return securities is being invested to earn more than the amount which must be paid to the providers of that capital. The excess of the earnings generated by that capital over the fixed return paid out belongs to the common stockholders.

21 If the return earned on total assets is *less* than the cost of borrowing the common stockholder will *lose* by using leverage.

22 The *debt ratio* (total liabilities ÷ total assets) measures the degree to which a company is traded on the equity. A *high* debt ratio means that a high percentage of the total assets is financed by creditors and that the company is making use of leverage. A high debt ratio may be profitable to common stockholders in periods of prosperity (when return on assets is greater than cost of borrowing) but can lead to serious trouble in a period of low earnings if return on asset falls *below* the cost of borrowing.

23 *Long-term creditors* are primarily interested in the following measurements:

a The rate of return on investment, known as the *yield* on bonds.

b The firm's ability to meet periodic interest requirements.

c The firm's ability to repay the principal of the debt at maturity.

24 The *yield* on bonds is the *effective interest rate* that an investor will earn by buying the bonds at their current market price and holding them to maturity. The yield varies *inversely* with changes in the market price of a bond. The safety of an investment in bonds depends on the ability of a firm to meet the interest and principal payments. An indication of the ability to pay *interest* is the *number of times* that the interest requirement was earned. This *interest coverage ratio* is computed by dividing the income from operations by the annual interest expense. The safety of *principal* is, to some extent, measured by the *debt ratio*. The lower the debt ratio, the safer the position of creditors.

26 *Short-term creditors* are primarily concerned with the relationship of *liquid assets* to current liabilities and the *turnover* of accounts receivable and inventories. These are usually analyzed by computing the following:

a Working capital: the excess of current assets over current liabilities.

b Current ratio: current assets divided by current liabilities.

c Quick ratio: quick assets (cash, marketable securities, and receivables) divided by current liabilities.

d Inventory turnover: cost of goods sold for the year divided by the average inventory during the year.

e Turnover of accounts receivable: credit sales for the year divided by the average receivables for the year.

27 Short-term creditors consider the quality of working capital as well as the dollar amount. Factors affecting the quality of working capital include (a) the nature of the assets comprising the working capital and (b) the length of time required to convert these assets into cash. Turnover ratios give an indication of how rapidly inventory and receivables can be converted into cash.

28 The inventory turnover and accounts receivable turnover may be expressed in *days* by dividing 365 (days in a year) by the number of times the average inventory or receivables have turned over in one year. The result is the number of days necessary to turn inventory into receivables and receivables into cash.

29 Adding the days required to turn over (sell) inventory to the days required to turn over (collect) receivables gives the days necessary to convert inventory into cash. This is the *operating cycle* for a merchandising business (for firms that manufacture their inventory, this would be only part of the operating cycle). An operating cycle which lengthens from one period to the next may indicate that the firm is having trouble selling its inventory or collecting its accounts receivable.

30 No analysis of financial position is complete without cash flow analysis. A company's ability to generate sufficient cash flow from *operating activities* is of importance to both stockholders and creditors. The specific items comprising cash flow from operations, as well as the dollar amount and trend of this statistic, can be determined by examining the statement of cash flows for successive years.

31 An integral part of a corporation's financial statements are the *notes*, which contain information essential to proper interpretation of those statements. Summary of accounting methods, material loss contingencies, current market value of financial instruments, unused lines of credit and post balance sheet events are but a few of the items disclosed in the *notes to the financial statements*.

TEST YOURSELF ON ANALYSIS OF FINANCIAL STATEMENTS

True or False

For each of the following statements, circle the T or the F to indicate whether the statement is true or false.

T F 1 The dollar amount of a change during a period in a certain item appearing in financial statements is probably less significant than the change measured as a percentage.

T F 2 Percentage changes are usually computed by using the latest figure as a base.

T F 3 It is possible that a decrease in gross profit rate may be more than offset by a decrease in expenses, thus resulting in an increase in net income.

T F 4 In a common size income statement each item is expressed as a percentage of net sales.

T F 5 Industry standards tend to place the performance of a company in a more meaningful perspective.

T F 6 Two earnings per share figures frequently appear in an income statement: earnings per share before taxes and earnings per share after taxes.

T F 7 Dividing the market price of a share of common stock by the dividends per share gives the price-earnings ratio.

T F 8 If some expenses are fixed (do not fluctuate in proportion to change in sales volume), net income should increase by a greater percentage than the increase in sales volume.

T F 9 Dividing net sales by average inventory gives the inventory turnover rate, which is a measure of how quickly inventory is selling.

T F 10 If the rate of return on assets is substantially higher than the cost of borrowing, the common stockholder should want the company to have a low debt ratio.

T F 11 The common stockholder will lose from the use of leverage when the cost of borrowing exceeds the return on assets.

T F 12 A high current ratio may indicate that capital is not productively used and that inventories and receivables may be excessive.

T F 13 It is possible to improve many balance sheet ratios by completing certain transactions just before the close of the fiscal period.

T F 14 Certain account balances at the end of the accounting period may not be representative for the entire year, and as a result the ratios (or turnover figures) may be misleading.

Completion Statements

Fill in the necessary words or amounts to complete the following statements:

1 The four most widely used analytical techniques are _____ and _____ changes, _____ _____; _____ _____ and _____.

2 The four groups that supply capital to a corporation are _____-____ _____, ____-____ _____; _____ _____, and _____ _____.

3 The market price of common stock divided by earnings per share is known as the _____- _____ _____.

4 The current ratio is 3 to 1; working capital amounts to $100,000, and the quick ratio is 1.5 to 1. Compute the following: (a) current assets, $_____; (b) current liabilities, $_____; (c) total investment in inventories and short-term prepayments, $_____.

5 The interest coverage ratio is primarily important to _____-_____, _____., and may be found by dividing _____ _____ _____ by the annual _____ _____.

6 When the _____ ____ _____ is less than the cost of borrowing, common stockholders should prefer a _____ debt ratio.

7 Cost of goods sold during a year divided by the average cost of _____ gives the _____ _____ _____ for the year.

8 The _____ turnover plus the _____ _____ turnover, expressed in *days*, measures the length of the _____ _____ of a merchandising business.

Multiple Choice

Choose the best answer for each of the following questions and enter the identifying letter in the space provided.

_____ **1** An investor wants to evaluate the relative profitability of several companies of different size. In order to put the earnings into perspective, the investor would be *least* likely to compare the net income of each company with that company's:

a Stockholders' equity.   **c** Working capital.
b Total assets.   **d** Net sales.

_____ **2** Which of the following sources of financial information is *not* generally available to an individual considering investing in a large publicly held corporation?

a Data published by Standard and Poor's Corporation and other investors' services.
b The company's accounting records.
c Audited financial statements for the current and prior years.
d Financial information that has been filed with the Securities and Exchange Commission (SEC).

_____ **3** An income statement showing only component percentages is known as a:

a Common dollar statement.
b Condensed income statement.
c Common size income statement.
d Comparative income statement.

_____ **4** Which of the following is *not* a valuable standard of comparison in analyzing financial statements of a company engaged in the manufacture of mobile homes?

a Past performance of the company.
b Performance of another company engaged in the manufacture of mobile homes.
c Performance of all companies engaged in manufacture of mobile homes.
d Performance of companies engaged in construction of apartment buildings.

_____ **5** Maxwell Corporation and Nardo, Inc., each report net income of $500,000 for 1994. If the companies are of similar size and other aspects of their operations are equal, which of the following *independent* additional pieces of information would indicate that Maxwell's earnings are of *higher "quality"* than Nardo's?

a Maxwell uses the FIFO method of inventory valuation; Nardo uses LIFO (assume rising prices).
b Maxwell depreciates vehicles over a useful life of seven years; Nardo depreciates vehicles over a three-year life.

c Maxwell has had a history of increasing earnings; Nardo's earnings have been erratic over the past several years.
d Maxwell's financial statements are audited by a large prestigious CPA firm; Nardo's are audited by a smaller CPA firm.

_____ **6** *Common stockholders* would be *least concerned* with which of the following?

a Earnings per share of stock.
b Revenue and expense analysis.
c Book value per share.
d Number of times interest earned (interest coverage ratio).

_____ **7** A company has a current ratio of 2 to 1 at the end of the current year. Which one of the following transactions will *increase* this ratio?

a Sale of bonds payable at a discount.
b Declaration of a 50% stock dividend.
c Collection of a large account receivable.
d Borrowed cash from bank, issuing a six-month note.

_____ **8** *Bondholders* would be *most* interested in which of the following?

a Quick ratio.
b Inventory turnover.
c Times interest earned (interest coverage ratio).
d Operating cycle.

_____ **9** If we added the average number of days required to turn the inventory over and the average age of receivables (in number of days), we would have an estimate of:

a The company's fiscal period.
b The sales volume of the business.
c The company's operating cycle.
d Nothing meaningful.

_____ **10** In projecting the future profitability of a merchandising company, *investors* will be *least* concerned with changes in:

a The gross profit rate.
b The rate earned on total assets.
c The quick ratio.
d Sales volume.

_____ **11** If sales increase by 10% from 1994 to 1995 and cost of goods sold increases only 6%, the gross profit on sales will increase by:

a 4%.   **c** 6%.
b 10%.   **d** Some other percentage.

_____ **12** Carlisle Corp. has both common and preferred stock outstanding. In computing return on common stockholders' equity for Carlisle Corp. the "return" that is divided by average common stockholder's equity consists of:

a Net income.
b Net income minus preferred dividends.

c Operating income.

d Net income minus the call price of all preferred shares outstanding.

_____ **13** A positive net cash flow from *operating activities* of $100,000:

a Represents cash flow remaining *after* payment of interest and dividends.

b Is generally viewed as sufficient by stockholders and creditors.

c Means that the company is both profitable and solvent.

d May be viewed as unsatisfactory if dividends annually are $300,000.

Exercises

1 Listed below are eight technical accounting terms introduced or emphasized in this appendix:

Current ratio   *Component percentage*
ROI   *Horizontal analysis*
Debt ratio   *Price-earnings ratio*
Leverage   *Operating cycle*

Each of the following statements may (or may not) describe one of these technical terms. In the space provided below each statement, indicate the accounting term described, or answer "None" if the statement does not correctly describe any of the terms.

a An indication of the relative size and importance of each item in a total.

b Comparison of the change in a financial statement item during two or more accounting periods.

c A measurement of management's efficiency in using available resources.

d Current assets divided by current liabilities.

e A measurement of the proportion of total assets financed by creditors.

f A measurement of the cash return earned by stockholders, based on current price for a share of stock.

g Buying assets with money raised by borrowing.

2 There are 10 transactions or events listed below. Opposite each item is listed a particular ratio used in financial analysis. Indicate the effect of each transaction or event on the ratio listed opposite it. Use the following symbols: Increase = *I*, Decrease = *D*; No Effect = *NE*. (Assume that the current ratio and the quick ratio are higher than 1 to 1.)

	Transaction or Event	Ratio	Effect
a	Purchased inventory on open account.	Quick ratio	
b	A larger physical volume of goods was sold at reduced prices.	Gross profit percentage	
c	Declared a cash dividend of $1 per share.	Current ratio	
d	An uncollectible account receivable was written off against the allowance account.	Current ratio	
e	Issued additional shares of common stock and used proceeds to retire long-term debt.	Rate earned on total assets (before interest and income taxes)	
f	Distributed a 20% stock dividend on common stock.	Earnings per share of common stock.	
g	Operating income increased 25%; interest expense increased 10%.	Interest coverage ratio	
h	During period of rising prices, company changed from FIFO to LIFO method of inventory pricing.	Inventory turnover	
i	Paid previously declared cash dividend.	Debt ratio	
j	Issued shares of common stock in exchange for plant assets.	Debt ratio	

3 From the following comparative balance sheet for the Gulfstream Company, compute the dollar and percentage changes from 1995 to 1996:

GULFSTREAM COMPANY
Comparative Balance Sheet
1995 and 1996

Assets	1996	1995	Increase (or Decrease) Amount	Percentage
Current assets	$150,000	$120,000	$	
Investments	160,000	80,000		
Plant and equipment (net)	360,000	300,000		
Intangibles	80,000	100,000		
Total assets	$750,000	$600,000	$	

Liabilities & Stockholders' Equity				
Current liabilities	$ 76,000	$ 80,000	$	
Long-term debt	116,000	100,000		
Capital stock, $5 par	250,000	200,000		
Retained earnings	308,000	220,000		
Total liabilities & stockholder's equity	$750,000	$600,000	$	

4 The balance sheets of the Olympia Corporation at the beginning and end of 1996 and the income statement for 1996 are presented below:

OLYMPIA CORPORATION
Comparative Balance Sheet

Assets	Dec. 31 1996	Jan. 1 1996
Cash	$ 60,000	$ 45,000
Marketable securities	30,000	40,000
Accounts receivable (net)	50,000	70,000
Inventory	140,000	130,000
Plant and equipment (net of accumulated depreciation)	420,000	330,000
Total assets	$700,000	$615,000

Liabilities & Stockholders' Equity		
Accounts payable	$ 95,000	$ 30,000
Accrued liabilities	10,000	15,000
7% bonds payable, due in 2005	80,000	100,000
Capital stock, $5 par	300,000	300,000
Retained earnings*	215,000	170,000
Total liabilities & stockholders' equity	$700,000	$615,000

---

*Dividends paid amounted to $0.65 per share.

OLYMPIA CORPORATION
Income Statement
For Year Ended December 31, 1996

Net sales (all on credit)	$800,000
Cost of goods sold...	490,000
Gross profit on sales...	$310,000
Operating expenses (includes depreciation of $25,000)............................	160,000
Income from operations.....................................	$150,000
Other expense: bond interest expense	7,000
Income before income taxes	$143,000
Income taxes...	59,000
Net income..	$ 84,000
Earnings per share	$ 1.40

On the basis of the information in the Olympia Corporation financial statements, fill in the blanks below with the appropriate amounts (do not compute the ratios):

a   The *current ratio* at the end of 1996 would be computed by dividing $_____ by $_____.

b   The *acid test* (or *quick ratio*) at the end of 1996 would be computed by dividing $_____ by $_____.

c   The *average turnover of receivables* during the year would be computed by dividing $_____ by $_____.

d   The *average turnover of inventories* during the year would be computed by dividing $_____ by $_____.

e   The *interest coverage ratio* during 1996 (before income taxes) would be determined by dividing $_____ by $_____.

f   The *rate earned on average investment in assets* would be determined by dividing $_____ by $_____.

g   The *debt ratio* at the end of 1996 would be determined by dividing $_____ by $_____.

h   The *rate of return on the average stockholders' equity* would be determined by dividing $_____ by $_____.

i   The *earnings per share* of capital stock would be determined by dividing $_____ by _____ shares outstanding.

j   If the capital stock had a market value at the end of the year of $42 per share, the *price-earnings ratio* would be determined by dividing $_____ by $_____.

k   The *yield* on the stock, assuming a market value of $42, is computed by dividing $_____ by $_____.

l   The *gross profit percentage* would be computed by dividing $_____ by $_____.

SOLUTIONS TO APPENDIX F SELF-TEST

True or False

1 **T** The percentage change allows better comparison between years and shows the growth or decline of the company.

2 **F** Percentage changes are computed by dividing the dollar amount of change between the comparison year and a base year by the amount for the base year. The base year is usually the prior year.

3 **T** Net income is computed as gross profit minus expenses; a large decrease in expenses can more than offset a decrease in gross profit, resulting in higher net income.

4 **T** By definition, a common size income statement is one in which all items are expressed as a percentage of net sales.

5 **T** Industry standards provide one method of comparing operating results of one company with those of its competitors.

6 **F** Earnings per share is determined from net income (after income taxes have been subtracted). When convertible preferred stock exists, both primary and fully diluted EPS amounts are shown.

7 **F** The price-earnings ratio is computed by dividing the market price of common stock by the earnings per share.

8 **T** If sales volume increases, causing net sales to increase, while certain expenses remain unchanged, net income should increase by a greater percentage than the increase in sales volume.

9 **F** The inventory turnover ratio, which tells the number of times the inventory is sold each year, is computed by dividing the *cost of goods sold* by the average inventory.

10 **F** If borrowed capital can be used to generate a greater return than the cost of borrowing, the common stockholders would want the company to have a high debt ratio.

11 **T** When the cost of borrowing exceeds the return on assets, there is a reduction in net income and a decrease in the return on common stockholders' equity.

12 **T** A high current ratio could indicate excessive amounts of inventory, poor collection of accounts receivable, or excessive current assets that could be invested for a greater return.

13 **T** Many balance sheet ratios are determined using figures in existence at balance sheet date; thus, it is possible to manipulate these amounts by strategic timing of certain transactions.

14 **T** In determining turnover ratios, it would be best to have a running average balance for accounts throughout the period.

Completion Statements

1 Dollar, percentage, trend analysis, component percentages, ratios. **2** Short-term creditors, long-term creditors, preferred stockholders, common stockholders. **3** Price-earnings ratio. **4(a)** $150,000; **(b)** $50,000; **(c)** $75,000 **5** Long-term creditors, income from operations, interest expense. **6** Return on assets, low. **7** Inventory, inventory turnover rate. **8** Inventory, accounts receivable, operating cycle.

Multiple Choice

1 Answer **c**—to compare relative profitability of several companies, each company's earnings can be compared with its total assets and with its invested capital, as well as with sales. Total assets and invested capital are the resources utilized by management to generate earnings. Sales are the source of income generated, and the amount of profit *per dollar of sales* is a more useful indicator of profitability than the absolute dollar amount of net income. Working capital measures short-run debt-paying ability and bears no direct relationship to net income.

2 Answer **b**—answers **a**, **c**, and **d** are all available to stockholders, potential investors and creditors, and the general public. A company's internal accounting records are not made public.

3 Answer **c**—a common size income statement is an application of component percentages where all items on the income statement are expressed as a percentage of net sales. Comparative income statements would have two or more years of data (in dollars) side by side in adjacent columns. Condensed and common dollar income statements would show dollar amounts, not percentages.

4 Answer **d**—in order for a ratio or a comparison to be useful, the two amounts being compared must be logically related. Answers **a**, **b**, and **c** are all logically related in some way to the current year financial statements of a company engaged in the manufacture of mobile homes. Answer **d** refers to an unrelated industry.

5 Answer **c**—in assessing the quality of earnings, we look at the accounting principles selected by management as well as at the source and stability of earnings. Answers **a** and **b** describe situations in which **Nardo** is using the more conservative accounting policies (hence **Nardo's** earnings would be judged of higher quality). The size and prestige of the CPA firm performing the audit does not, in and of itself, indicate which company's earnings are of higher quality.

6 Answer **d**—number of times interest earned is a statistic of interest primarily to bondholders and other long-term creditors.

7 Answer **a**—the current ratio is computed as current assets divided by current liabilities. Sale of bonds, even at a discount, will increase current assets and have no effect on current liabilities—hence the ratio will increase. Answer **c** simply alters the composition of current assets, but has no effect on total current assets or current liabilities. Answer **b** has no impact on either current assets or current liabilities. Answer **d** increases both current assets and current liabilities by the same amount. Since the current ratio is 2 to 1 already, this transaction will cause the current ratio to decrease.

8 Answer **c**—answers **a**, **b**, and **d** are all statistics of interest primarily to **short-term** creditors.

9 Answer **c**—the operating cycle is defined as the average time period between the purchases of merchandise and the conversion of this merchandise back into cash. This period is the total time required to sell the inventory (turnover) **and** collect the accounts receivable (average age of receivables).

10 Answer **c**—the quick ratio is a measure of the **short-term liquidity** of the firm. Changes in the statistics in answers **a**, **b**, and **d** are of more significance in projecting the future profitability of a company.

11 Answer **d**—as sales are increasing faster than the cost of goods sold, gross profit will increase even faster than sales.

12 Answer **b**—return on common stockholders' equity is computed by dividing net income minus the **preferred dividend requirement** by the average common stockholders' equity.

13 Answer **d**—although positive, the $100,000 cash flow from operations is insufficient to cover current year dividends. Interest payments have already been deducted in arriving at the $100,000 figure, but dividends have not; therefore answer **a** is not correct. The $100,000 net cash flow from operations must be evaluated in comparison to interest payments, net income, prior years' cash flows, dividend requirements, etc., in order to determine whether it is "sufficient." A company may operate at a loss and yet have a positive cash flow from operations. In addition, a company may generate cash flow from operations and have such substantial liabilities that it is insolvent.

Solutions to Exercises

1
a Component percentage
b Horizontal analysis
c ROI
d Current ratio
e Debt ratio
f None (The statement describes dividend yield.)
g Leverage

2 a D
  b D
  c D
  d NE
  e NE
  f D
  g I
  h I
  i D
  j D

3

GULFSTREAM COMPANY
Comparative Balance Sheet
1995 and 1996

Assets	1996	1995	Increase (or Decrease) Amount	Percentage
Current assets	$150,000	$120,000	$ 30,000	25%
Investments	160,000	80,000	80,000	100%
Plant and equipment (net)	360,000	300,000	60,000	20%
Intangibles	80,000	100,000	(20,000)	(20)%
Total assets	$750,000	$600,000	$150,000	25%
Liabilities & Stockholders' Equity				
Current liabilities	$ 76,000	$ 80,000	$(4,000)	(5)%
Long-term debt	116,000	100,000	16,000	16%
Capital stock, $5 par	250,000	200,000	50,000	25%
Retained earnings	308,000	220,000	88,000	40%
Total liabilities & stockholder's equity	$750,000	$600,000	$150,000	25%

4 **a** $280,000 by $105,000
  b $140,000 by $105,000
  c $800,000 by $60,000 [($50,000 + $70,000) ÷ 2]
  d $490,000 by $135,000 [($140,000 + $130,000) ÷ 2]
  e $150,000 by $7,000
  f $150,000 by $657,500 [($700,000 + $615,000) ÷ 2]
  g $185,000 by $700,000
  h $84,000 by $492,500 [($515,000 + $470,000) ÷ 2]
  i $84,000 by 60,000 shares
  j $42 by $1.40
  k $0.65 by $42
  l $310,000 by $800,000

ISBN 0-07-043350-X

90000>

EAN

9 780070 433502